The Logic of Gilles Deleuze

Also Available at Bloomsbury

Deleuze and Ethology: A Philosophy of Entangled Life, Jason Cullen
Deleuze and Guattari: Selected Writings, Kenneth Surin
Deleuze, Guattari, and the Problem of Transdisciplinarity, ed. Guillaume Collett
Deleuze and the Schizoanalysis of Feminism, ed. Janae Sholtz and Cheri Carr
Space after Deleuze, Arun Saldanha

The Logic of Gilles Deleuze

Basic Principles

Corry Shores

BLOOMSBURY ACADEMIC
LONDON • NEW YORK • OXFORD • NEW DELHI • SYDNEY

BLOOMSBURY ACADEMIC
Bloomsbury Publishing Plc
50 Bedford Square, London, WC1B 3DP, UK
1385 Broadway, New York, NY 10018, USA
29 Earlsfort Terrace, Dublin 2, Ireland

BLOOMSBURY, BLOOMSBURY ACADEMIC and the Diana logo
are trademarks of Bloomsbury Publishing Plc

First published in Great Britain 2021
This paperback edition published in 2022

Copyright © Corry Shores, 2021

Corry Shores has asserted his right under the Copyright,
Designs and Patents Act, 1988, to be identified as Author of this work.

For legal purposes the Acknowledgments on pp. xvi–xviii constitute
an extension of this copyright page.

Cover design by Charlotte Daniels
Cover image: Hertfordshire puddingstone (© John Cancalosi / Alamy)

All rights reserved. No part of this publication may be reproduced or transmitted in any form or by any means, electronic or mechanical, including photocopying, recording, or any information storage or retrieval system, without prior permission in writing from the publishers.

Bloomsbury Publishing Plc does not have any control over, or responsibility for, any third-party websites referred to or in this book. All internet addresses given in this book were correct at the time of going to press. The author and publisher regret any inconvenience caused if addresses have changed or sites have ceased to exist, but can accept no responsibility for any such changes.

A catalogue record for this book is available from the British Library.

Library of Congress Cataloging-in-Publication Data

Names: Shores, Corry, author.
Title: The logic of Gilles Deleuze / Corry Shores.
Description: London; New York: Bloomsbury Academic, 2020- |
Series: Bloomsbury studies in continental philosophy | Includes bibliographical references and index. | Contents: Volume 1. Basic principles
Identifiers: LCCN 2020024882 (print) | LCCN 2020024883 (ebook) |
ISBN 9781350062269 (hardback) | ISBN 9781350062252 (ebook) |
ISBN 9781350062276 (epub)
Subjects: LCSH: Deleuze, Gilles, 1925-1995. | Logic.
Classification: LCC B2430.D454 S56 2020 (print) | LCC B2430.D454 (ebook) |
DDC 194–dc23
LC record available at https://lccn.loc.gov/2020024882
LC ebook record available at https://lccn.loc.gov/2020024883

ISBN: HB: 978-1-3500-6226-9
PB: 978-1-3501-8554-8
ePDF: 978-1-3500-6225-2
eBook: 978-1-3500-6227-6

Typeset by Integra Software Services Pvt. Ltd.

To find out more about our authors and books visit www.bloomsbury.com
and sign up for our newsletters.

For Gülben Canım

Contents

List of Figures	xi
Acknowledgments	xvi
Abbreviations for Classical Texts	xix
Introduction: The Logic of Magic and the Magic of Logic	1
Introduction	1
Deleuze: From Magician to Logician	1
Deleuze and Logic	5
Logic: What–What–What?	5
Classical Logic	7
Non-Classical Logics	7
Deleuze Contra Logic	11
Overview	13

Part I   Dis-Composition and Dis-Identification

1	Becoming Dialetheic: The Logic of Change	17
	Introduction	17
	Method and Philosophy in Bergson and Russell	17
	Russell's Philosophical Types	17
	Bergson's Intuitional Philosophy	18
	Bergson's Intuition of Duration	19
	Bergson and Cinematic Kinematics	21
	Russell against Intuition	24
	Russell's Mathematics of Motion	27
	A Classical Logic of Becoming	31
	Priest and Dialetheic Motion	34
	Science of Logics	36
	Priest's Dialetheic Account of Motion	41
	Deleuze's Paradox of Pure Becoming	44

2	Enter the Puddingstone: Demonic Gluonics	49
	Introduction	49
	Demonic Deleuze	49
	Satan and the Sorcerer	50
	Watch and the Puddingstone: Dupréel's Consistency	53
	Fuzzing the Stone: Consistency in Deleuze and Guattari	56
	Logic of Fuzz	58
	Gluing Difference	61
	Who's Alice Now?	65
3	Sorcerous Conceptions: Deleuze's Philosophy of Thinking	67
	Introduction	67
	Philosophy from Death to Creation	67
	Deleuze and Transdisciplinarity	69
	A Rivalry of Friends	71
	The Philosophy of Pinball	72
	Dupréelian Concept Consistency	75
	The Cartesian Aggregate Self	76

Part II Logic of Otherness: Negation, or Disjunction?

4	Alternance and Otherness	81
	Introduction	81
	Must Negation Be Dark?	81
	Augmentation as Negation: Routley and Routley's Non-Exclusive Otherthanness	83
	Paraconsistency and Paracompleteness	86
	The Negation Deleuze Denies, and the Negation Deleuze Affirms	89
	Deleuze and Alternance	91
	The God of Logic: Kantian Disjunctive Syllogism	104
	The Idol of Baphomet: Klossowski's Demonic Disorder	109
5	Truth and Bifurcation: Leibniz and the Stoics	117
	Introduction	117
	Incompossible Leibnizes	117
	Forks in Time	121
	The Stoic Affirmation of Negational Fates	123
	Reasoning Stoically	123
	Corporeality	124
	Incorporeality	125

	Stoic Time	126
	To Cooperate with Destiny by Affirming Creative Falsity	130
6	Wisdom without Logic: Intuitionism	137
	Introduction	137
	Formalization and Its Malcontents: Axioms of Control,	
	Flows of Rebellion	137
	The Capitalist Axiomatic	138
	The History of Axiomatics and Problematics	141
	Modern Axioms and Problems	145
	Intuitionist Philosophy	150
	The Nature of Intuitionism	150
	Historical Context and Development of Intuitionism	151
	Brouwer the Intuitionist Philosopher	152
	Constructivism	154
	Brouwer on the Language of Logic	156
	Brouwer and Logic	156
	Difference as Distance: Negationless Mathematics	164

Part III Falsity

7	False Movements	177
	Introduction	177
	The Being of Falsity	177
	Errant Motion	178
	Erroneous Falsity	180
	Formless Falsity	183
	Truth Undone	183
8	False Creations	187
	Introduction	187
	Deformation's Creations	187
	The Falsifier	191
	The Scale of Falsification	191
	Truth and Time: The Falsification	192
	Falsifier as Fabulist	196
	The Past That Never Was	199
	Falsifier as Clairvoyant Sorcerer-Seer	202
	Falsifier as Self- and World-Creative Artist	203
	The Garden of Ambiguous Adams: Crystalline Time	206

Conclusion 213
    Introduction 213
    What Has Followed Here? 213
    And What's to Follow 216

Notes 217
References 264
Index 286

List of Figures

0.1 A depiction of a match's change from wood to fire, where (**left**) the change is thought to happen in the initial state or (**right**) in the resulting state. In both cases, we miss the transition 9

0.2 **Left**: A change occurring during a period of indeterminate transition. **Right**: One occurring when both contradictory states of affairs hold simultaneously 10

1.1 Russell's "at-at" account of motion. The object is always at a specific single position at a given point in time, but never in two places in the same moment, and never at no determinate location (by being for instance in a pointless gap between locations) 29

1.2 Classical logic as corresponding to the monoletheic view (in our extended sense) that propositions are only at least and at most just true or false 38

1.3 The validity of the Principle of Identity in different logics 38

1.4 A three-valued logic with "gaps," corresponding to the analetheist view that propositions can be neither true nor false (and following Łukasiewicz's three-valued logic, $Ł_3$) 39

1.5 The validity or invalidity of the Principle of Excluded-Middle in different logics 39

1.6 A three-valued logic with "gluts," corresponding to the dialetheist view that propositions can be both true and false (and following Priest's three-valued logic, *LP*) 40

1.7 The validity or invalidity of the Principle of Non-Contradiction in different logics 40

1.8 The precise and exclusive time–space determinations in Russell's account of motion 42

1.9 Priest's account of motion with an arbitrarily small time–space spread, where the object both is and is not at all the intervening places 43

1.10 Alice becoming larger and smaller simultaneously 46

2.1 Sorcerers' demonic pacts. **Top left**: A sorcerer at work. **Top middle**: The Goëtic Circle. **Top right**: The Triangle of Solomon. **Bottom left**: The Baphomet ("pseudo-Deity," "god of falsehood," and "creator and rival

	of God"). **Bottom middle**: Father Urbain Grandier's pact with devils, whose signatures fill the bottom half, used against him in trial but likely a forgery. **Bottom right**: Thibault's dealing with the Wolf-Devil	50
2.2	Puddingstone formation. **Left and middle**: Puddingstone consolidation. **Right**: A puddingstone slice (© East Herts Geology Club. Photo by Jane Tubb, used with permission)	54
2.3	Priest's diagram for the gluonic structure. The gluon, symbolized as 中, is non-transitively identical with all the other parts, a, b, c, and d, but they are not equal to one another	62
2.4	Material equivalence in a monoletheic (classical) and a dialetheic logic, showing the second to be intransitive ("$A \equiv B$" is at least true, "$B \equiv C$" is at least true, but "$A \equiv C$" is not at all true)	63
3.1	Transdisciplinary encounters. **Top left**: Delaunay's *Portuguese Woman* (1916). **Top right**: Diagram of the figure light made (diagonal lines) in the Michelson-Morley experiment. **Bottom**: Moving light in Grémillon's *The Lighthouse Keepers* (© Films du Grand Guignol 1929. All rights reserved)	71
3.2	Deleuze showing with his hands how "when there are no ideas, the mind works like a pinball machine." (*L'abécédaire* directed by Pierre-André Boutang © Sodaperaga and Montparnasse 2004. All rights reserved)	73
3.3	A simplified depiction of the Baker's Transformation	74
3.4	The overlapping structures in Descartes's concept of the self	76
4.1	Negation as cancellation destroys both contents	84
4.2	Negation as explosion (including classical negation) is exclusive and exhaustive. It yields an unrestricted otherthanness, and its contradictory pairing yields a thoroughly inconsistent and trivial world	84
4.3	Routley and Routley's diagram for negation as non-exclusive restricted otherthanness. It can yield an inconsistent *otherthan* without eliminating either	86
4.4	The production of a thoroughly trivial and inconsistent world on account of the Principle of Explosion	87
4.5	Validity or invalidity of the Principle of Explosion in various logics.	88
4.6	Consistency and paraconsistency, along with completeness and paracompleteness, used to distinguish various logics	89
4.7	**Top left:** Single shot with light/dark opposition, in Wiene's *Cabinet of Dr Caligari* (© Decla-Bioscop 1920. All rights reserved). **Top right:** Single shot with light/dark alternance in Bresson's *Diary of a Country Priest.* **Middle row:** Sequence shot with light/dark oppositions, in Lang's *Metropolis* (excluded are simple black shots interspersed between the	

List of Figures xiii

   bright ones) (© Universum Film 1927. All rights reserved). **Bottom row**: Sequence shot with light/dark alternations, from Bresson's *Diary of a Country Priest* (© Union générale cinématographique 1951. All rights reserved) 102

4.8 Kant's diagrams of judgments. **Left**: A categorical judgment structure, where some item is included in a category that is itself included in a broader category. **Middle**: Kant's depiction of a disjunctive judgment where the sphere is divided up completely into mutually exclusive parts. **Right**: A depiction for how the affirmation of one disjunct is a negation of the complementary remainder 106

5.1 Were Leibniz to stay in Paris instead of going to Germany, he would be another Leibniz in another world 119

5.2 A diagram of temporalized world divergence, based on John Nolt's "A Picture of Time" diagram 120

5.3 The indeterminacy of variation at a bifurcation point 122

5.4 Multiple indeterminate branching variations 122

5.5 How can future events result from present ones if all causes have only present effects? 127

5.6 Aiôn and Chronos time in Deleuze's reading of Goldschmidt, here based loosely on Sellars's diagrams. (They have been stacked vertically to indicate the co-contamination that Goldschmidt is trying to explain with this distinction) 128

5.7 The duration of a present activity corresponds to the end of the incorporeal predicate that is expressed throughout that activity. Ends are nested deeper and deeper into Fate, corresponding thus with longer and longer present activities 130

5.8 Stoic moral choice introduces divergence into the course of time on both the aiônian and chronosian levels 133

5.9 Stoic co-fatality can be understood as involving bifurcational antecedent causality 134

6.1 **Left**: The axiomatic of money that conjoins flows of labor and capital, by means of wages. **Right**: The rebel flows that escape that axiomatic 140

6.2 **Left**: Lines in a circle from center to periphery as all being equal. **Right**: Finding the center of the circle with two equal straight lines 142

6.3 Archimedes's method of exhaustion seen as approximating a curve from the addition of straight lines 143

6.4 Conic sections seen as involving cuts into stone. **Left**: Stonemasonry cuts from Bosse's book on Desargues. **Top right**: Conic sections. **Bottom right**: Conic sections as cuts into physical cones 144

6.5	A depiction of a motional interpretation for (**left**) an axiom defining a null value and for (**right**) an axiom defining an inverse value	146
6.6	A one-to-one correspondence illustration between the set of Benelux countries and the set of natural numbers (from Vergauwen)	147
6.7	A one-to-one correspondence between the set of natural numbers and the set of even numbers (from Vergauwen)	148
6.8	An illustration of Cantor's diagonalization. **Left**: A correspondence between real and natural numbers (based on Vergauwen's illustration). **Right**: The diagonal number escaping those correspondences	149
6.9	Constructively determining the truth or absurdity of a mathematical statement	157
6.10	Constructively demonstrating the truth or absurdity of categorical syllogisms	159
6.11	Brouwer's example of a proposition that demonstrates the intuitionistic invalidity of the Principle of Excluded Middle	159
6.12	Griss's example of a constructive proof without negation	165
6.13	Illustration of complementary sets	167
6.14	An illustration of Griss's equality of natural numbers on the basis of shared differences	169
6.15	Approximating intervals	171
6.16	Griss's non-negational definition for *different* real numbers on the basis of their distance	172
6.17	Griss's non-negational definition of the equality of real numbers, based on shared distances	173
7.1	Shots at different scales showing nested systems of interactivity, from D. W. Griffith's *The Massacre* (© Biograph 1912. All rights reserved)	178
7.2	Shots from Eisenstein's *The General Line* (*The Old and the New*) (© Sovkino 1929. All rights reserved)	180
7.3	Worringer's ornamentation types. **Left:** Organic lines in classical ornamentation. **Right:** Inorganic, Northern lines in Gothic ornamentation	181
7.4	The hero of Welles's *The Lady from Shanghai* escaping his guilty verdict by creating mayhem (© Mercury and Columbia 1947. All rights reserved)	184
8.1	Deformations of the actual proportions in Greek architecture to correct for perspectival distortions	188
8.2	Crimes and investigations in Welles's *Touch of Evil* (© Universal 1958. All rights reserved)	191
8.3	Real and imaginary images cycling too quickly to discern which is which, in Welles's *The Lady from Shanghai* (© Mercury and Columbia 1947. All rights reserved)	197

8.4 Capture and liberation of images in Robbe-Grillet's *Trans-Europ-Express* (© Como 1966. All rights reserved)   197

8.5 Narrative falsification in Robbe-Grillet's *The Man Who Lies* (© Como 1968. All rights reserved)   199

8.6 Changing perspectives as transformation. **Left:** Detail from Vermeer's *Girl with a Pearl Earring*, above a detail from John Myatt's recreation, *Girl with a Pearl Earring (in the style of Johan Vermeer)* (© John Myatt, 2012, used with permission). **Middle:** Same detail from Vermeer's *Girl with a Pearl Earring*, above a detail from van Meegeren's forgery of Vermeer's style in *The Supper at Emmaus*. **Right:** Detail from Velázquez's *Las Meninas*, above a diagrammatic representation of a detail from Picasso's *Girl with a Mandolin* (used in place of his *Las Meninas* variations to depict something of their stylistic deformations)   204

8.7 Leibniz's ambiguous signs. In $AB \mp BC$, the $\mp$ is an ambiguous sign for addition and subtraction, and the formula represents two distinct lines at the same time, line $AB + BC$ and line $AB - BC$ 210

Acknowledgments

This book was first made possible by Roland Breeur, who recommended me to the person who became one of my main editors, Liza Thompson. Much of what I know about philosophy and how it should be conducted, I learned from Prof. Breeur. And Liza, along with my other editors, Frankie Mace and Lucy Russell, has extended to me an incredible amount of generosity with the scheduling for the book. It never would have made it without their help, so I thank you all very much.

The basic content of the book was first made possible by the participants and organizers of the 2014 Paraconsistent Reasoning in Science and Mathematics conference at Ludwig Maximilian University: Peter Verdée, Holger Andreas, David Ripley, Graham Priest, Diderik Batens, Fenner Tanswell, Marcos Silva, Bryson Brown, Hitoshi Omori, Heinrich Wansing, Andreas Kapsner, Cian Chartier, Franz Berto, Itala Maria Loffredo D'Ottaviano, Zach Weber, João Marcos, Luis Estrada-González, Nick Thomas, Maarten McKubre-Jordens, Maria Martinez, Diego Tajer, and Otávio Bueno. They graciously allowed me to present, despite being quite incapable with logic, and they afterward did much to help me begin my project. Peter Verdée and Holger Andreas edited an edition of the proceedings for Springer, and they were kind enough to include my paper in it, the text of which is partly used here. I thank everyone for getting me started in non-classical logics, which still I love to this day.

I could not have written this book without the enduring, loving support of my wife, Gülben Salman. Her sacrifices and efforts are the reason I was able to do all the work necessary here. As a philosopher herself, she also made substantial contributions throughout the whole compositional process, and I cannot thank her enough. Gülben, I dedicate this book to you. I also thank Yasin Ceylan, Aziz Fevzi Zambak, Deniz Yılmaz Zambak, Aret Karademir, Hikmet Ünlü, Bolkar Özkan, Scott Wollschleger, Kurt Ozment, Samet Bağçe, Karen Vanhercke, Vykintas Baltakas, along with my family, Patricia, Ebbie Victor, Fatma, Hasan, Ebbie Paul, Brandon, Aimee, Mandy, Austin, and Joseph for the companionship, support, and advice they gave me all throughout.

Certain parts specifically benefited from the help I received from other scholars. Oğuz Akçelik reviewed the logic parts (and any mistakes are mine). Many of the cinema parts (Chapters 4, 7, and 8) were made possible by the guidance and teaching of Ahmet Gürata. The section on Plato in Chapter 8 was improved with Hikmet Ünlü's expert assistance, and his instruction in Ancient Greek proved indispensable for working through the Stoic material in Chapter 5. Dorothea Olkowski taught me about intuitionism and its importance in Deleuze's philosophy, so all of Chapter 6 was made possible by her writings and comments, and she also reviewed and made suggestions on most of Chapter 5. Roland Breeur's work on imposture influenced much of what I write on the Falsifier in Chapter 8, and he reviewed and made suggestions for both Chapters 7 and 8. Along the way, I also received help with interpretation, sourcing, and translation from Antoine Dolcerocca, Terence Blake, Clifford Duffy, Roger Vergauwen, Julie Van der Wielen, Griet Galle, Iain McKenzie, Guillaume Collet, and Steven Spileers. Meriç Aytekin contributed much to the sourcing in Chapter 2, and Çisil Vardar, to the sourcing in Chapter 1. At the beginning stages, my project benefited from the comments provided by anonymous referees and from Ronald Bogue. I am very grateful to them. And I have taken great inspiration from the work of Jeffrey Bell, who has pioneered this particular field of study and whose advice I deeply appreciate. I am also heavily indebted to the archivists, transcribers, and translators (listed in the Bibliography, but let me here mention Richard Pinhas), who have made Deleuze's courses accessible. I thank everyone mentioned here so very much.

And many of the logic parts were improved through my correspondences and conversations with Graham Priest. His philosophy is the original inspiration for this book, and he has been nothing but the most generous and supportive toward this project. I thank him for patiently and thoroughly answering all of my questions about his writings and ideas. The philosophical world is so much better because of him, and I will always be deeply grateful.

I also could not have completed this book without the support and understanding of my colleagues at the Middle East Technical University: Halil Turan, Barış Parkan, Murat Baç, David Grünberg, Ayhan Sol, Samet Bağçe, Elif Çırakman, Mehmet Hilmi Demir, Aziz Fevzi Zambak, Fulden İbrahimhakkıoğlu, Yasin Ceylan, Teo Grünberg, Ahmet İnam, Ertuğrul Rufayi Turan, Refik Güremen, James Griffith, Selma Aydın Bayram, Dilek Başar Başkaya, Ercan Erkul, Gülizar Karahan Balya, Hikmet Ünlü, Erdinç Sayan, and Tahir Kocayiğit. (Ayhan Sol helped me especially with freeing up my scheduling for more time to write.)

Many students in my classes and seminars have contributed ideas and insights to this book, including: Bolkar Özkan, Gürkan Kılınç, Ilgın Aksoy, Yıldırım Bayazit, Faik Tekin Asal, Ekin Demirors, Hazal Babur, Tanayça Ünlütürk, Aybüke Aşkar, Melike Başak Yalçın, Ulaş Murat Altay, Sedef Beşkardeşler, Toprak Seda Karaosmanoğlu, İlkyaz Taşdemir, Çınar Uysal, Handan Ağirman, Tunahan Akbulut, Yasemin Karabaş, Aybüke Aşkar, Mahsasadat Shojaei, Umut Kesikkulak, Ayşe Pekdiker, Seyran Sam Kookiaei, Atakan Botasun, Esra Saçlı, Firuza Rahimova, Sona Mustafayeva, İrem Kayra Özdemir, Erkan Özmacun, Ezel Ortaç, Rada Nur Ergen, and Yiğit Baysal. I thank all of you for your interest in these topics, for your original philosophical thinking, and for helping me interpret the texts.

And finally, I thank the following publishers and journals who granted me permission to reprint texts and figures (and in addition, I thank their blind referees, who helped me improve the articles):

Tijdschrift voor Filosofie/Peeters Publishers. ("The Primacy of Falsity: Deviant Origins in Deleuze." *Tijdschrift Voor Filosofie* 81 (2019): 81–130.)

Routledge. ("Affirmations of the False and Bifurcations of the True: Deleuze's Dialetheic and Stoic Fatalism." In *Deleuze and Guattari's Philosophy of Freedom: Freedom's Refrains*, edited by Dorothea Olkowski and Eftichis Pirovolakis, 178–223. New York: Routledge, 2019.)

Springer. ("Dialetheism in the Structure of Phenomenal Time." In *Logical Studies of Paraconsistent Reasoning in Science and Mathematics*, edited by Holger Andreas and Peter Verdée, 145–157. Cham, Switzerland: Springer, 2016.)

Deleuze and Guattari Studies/Edinburgh University Press. ("In the Still of the Moment: Deleuze's Phenomena of Motionless Time." *Deleuze Studies* 8, no. 2 (2014): 199–229.)

Abbreviations for Classical Texts

Aet. *Plac.*	Aetius, *De placita philosophorum* (*Opinions of the Philosophers*)
Alex. *Mantissa*	Alexander of Aphrodisias, *De anima libri mantissa* (*On Soul* II)
Alex. *In Ar. Top.*	Alexander of Aphrodisias, *In Aristotelis Topicorum* (*On Aristotle's* Topics)
Alex. *Mixt.*	Alexander of Aphrodisias, *De mixtione* (*On Mixture*)
Arist. *Int.*	Aristotle, *De interpretatione* (*On Interpretation*)
Arist. *Ph.*	Aristotle, *Physica* (*Physics*)
Calc. *In Tim.*	Calcidius, *Timaeus a Calcidio translatus commentarioque instructus* (*On Plato's* Timaeus)
Cic. *Acad.*	Cicero, *Academica* (*Academic Questions*)
Cic. *Off.*	Cicero, *De officiis* (*On Duties*)
Cic. *Div.*	Cicero, *De divinatione* (*On Divination*)
Cic. *Fat.*	Cicero, *De fato* (*On Fate*)
Cic. *Nat. D*	Cicero, *De natura deorum* (*On the Nature of the Gods*)
Clem. *Paid.*	Clement of Alexandria, *Paidagogos* (*Teacher*)
Clem. *Stom.*	Clement of Alexandria, *Stromateis* (*Miscellanies*)
Cleom. *Mot. circul.*	Cleomedes, *De motu circulari corporum caelestium* (*On the Circular Motions of the Celestial Bodies*)
Diog. Laert. *Vit. phil.*	Diogenes Laertius, *Vitae Philosophorum* (*Lives and Opinions of Eminent Philosophers*)
Epict. *Diss.*	Epictetus, *Dissertationes* (*Discourses*)
Epict. *Ench.*	Epictetus, *Enchiridion* (*Manual*)
Euseb. *Praep. evang.*	Eusebius, *Praeparatio evangelica* (*Evangelical Preparation*)
Gal. *Musc. mot.*	Galen, *De musculorum motu* (*On Muscular Movement*)

Gal. *Foet.*	Galen, *De foetuum formatione libellus* (*On the Formation of the Fetus*)
Gal. *Plen.*	Galen, *De plenitudine* (*On Bodily Mass*)
Gal. *Plac.*	Galen, *De placitis Hippocratis et Platonis* (*On Hippocrates' and Plato's Doctrines*)
Gal. *Meth. med.*	Galen, *De methodo medendi* (*On Medical Method*)
Gal. *Intr.*	Galen, *Introductio sive medicus* (*Medical Introduction*)
Gell. *Noc. Att.*	Gellius, *Noctes Atticae* (*Attic Nights*)
Hippol. *Haer.*	Hippolytus, *Refutatio omnium haeresium* (*Refutation of All Heresies*)
L&S 1, L&S 2	Anthony Long and David Sedley, *The Hellenistic Philosophers*, volumes 1 and 2.
Marc. Aur. *Med.*	Marcus Aurelius, *Ta eis heauton* (*Meditations*)
Nem. *Nat. hom.*	Nemesius, *De natura hominis* (*On Human Nature*)
Orig. *Princ.*	Origen, *De principiis* (*On Principles*)
Philo. *Quaes. Gen.*	Philo of Alexandria, *Quaestiones et solutiones in Genesim* (*Questions and Answers on* Genesis)
Philo. *Leg. alleg.*	Philo of Alexandria, *Legum allegoriarum* (*Allegories of the Laws*)
Pl. *Phlb.*	Plato, *Philebus*
Pl. *Plt.*	Plato, *Politicus* (*Statesman*)
Pl. *Soph.*	Plato, *Sophista* (*Sophist*)
Pl. *Tht.*	Plato, *Theaetetus*
Plut. *Comm. not.*	Plutarch, *De communibus notitiis adversus Stoicos* (*On Common Conceptions*)
Plut. *St. rep.*	Plutarch, *De Stoicorum repugnantiis* (*On Stoic Self-Contradictions*)
Sen. *Ep.*	Seneca, *Ad Lucilium epistulae morales* (*Letters*)
Sext. Emp. *Adv. math.*	Sextus Empiricus *Adversus mathematicos* (*Against the Professors*)
Sext. Emp. *Pyr.*	Sextus Empiricus, *Pyrrhoneae hypotyposes* (*Outlines of Pyrrhonism*)
Stob. *Ecl.*	Stobaeus, *Eclogae* (*Anthology*)

Introduction: The Logic of Magic and the Magic of Logic

Introduction

The main purpose of this book is to formulate the basic principles of Gilles Deleuze's logic by means of the concepts and tools made available by contemporary logics. In particular, we consider the potential applicability of fuzzy, intuitionistic, and many-valued logics for this purpose, in conjunction with their corresponding philosophical stances (for instance, monoletheism, dialetheism, and analetheism). Despite the fact that Deleuze wrote two books with "logic" featuring in the title, there has yet to be an extensive treatment of his philosophy of logic. We consider first one possible reason for this, namely, that it is impossible or at least counter to Deleuze's philosophical project itself, so any attempt to conceptualize his logic using one or another formal means is doomed to fail from the start. We next note the possibility that instead Deleuze was really just critical of classical logic, and all the while he was developing some sort of non-classical logic, which has since lain deep in his thinking and so far has not been fully uncovered. The ultimate purpose of this book is to support the more controversial claim that Deleuze was a dialetheist whose logic is best formulated using a many-valued system with truth-value "gluts."

Deleuze: From Magician to Logician

"The Great Sorcerer" is an epithet Gilles Deleuze earned at Vincennes where he taught.[1] Indeed, "the sorcerer" is a figure that carries great weight in Deleuze's philosophy. Sorcerers are agents of becoming: they wield the "power of the false," which propels their heterogeneous groupings through mutational developments.[2]

Sorcerers also live on the fringes under a veil of secrecy. Their knowledge and practices are hard to penetrate.[3] Now, many of us—myself included—find the practices, techniques, and symbology of contemporary logic similarly alluring and yet exceptionally challenging to penetrate. Logicians can appear to us much like magicians or sorcerers, with their mysterious scribblings and rapid, often perplexing transmutations of these cryptic inscriptions. With regard to appearances at least, we do not need to stretch our imaginations too far to move from the image of the logician to that of the magician. Now, along with Deleuze, the other great philosopher we will examine here in detail is Graham Priest, who is a leading figure in philosophies involving non-classical logics, and who—whether deservedly or not—has earned the epithet, "the Prince of Darkness."[4] Is he too, like Deleuze, a Grand Sorcerer?

But our more immediately pressing question is: why, more precisely, have we selected Graham Priest as a philosophical companion to Gilles Deleuze? The reason is that we here seek the basic principles of Deleuze's logic. Were they less concealed, they would have been unearthed and brought plainly to light long ago. But something about them keeps them underground, hard to formulate and conceptualize using the conventions and notions of formal logic. Maybe it is because they cannot be formulated, not even a little. Or maybe, as I hope you will see, the reason is that we have not yet found the right philosophical guidance, which we will seek here in Priest's philosophy.

This is not to say that we should avoid giving an informal elaboration of Deleuze's logic, and, in fact, we may in the end still prefer one. David Lapoujade has done this expertly in his *Aberrant Movements*, where he gives a comprehensive analysis of Deleuze's and Guattari's philosophies in terms of their basic orientation in what Lapoujade calls Deleuze's *"irrational logic of aberrant movements."*[5] What makes it aberrant is that it "escapes rationality," and given that such matters lie at the foundation of Deleuze's philosophical project, Lapoujade claims that we can regard Deleuze as being primarily a logician:

> Deleuze is interested foremost in *logic*. […] Deleuze is above all a logician and all his books are "Logics." His first book on Hume could have been called "Logic of Human Nature," just as his book on Proust could have been called "Logic of Signs." […] Likewise, the books on cinema could have been called "Logic of Images," just as there are a *Logic of Sense* and a *Logic of Sensation*.[6]

Yet, as we continue through Lapoujade's text, we do not encounter any logical formalities. That would seem fitting enough, because we also do not see such logical formalizations in Deleuze's own "Logic" books (*The Logic of Sense* and *Francis Bacon: The Logic of Sensation*). Although this issue of formalizing Deleuze's logic is not explored at great length in Lapoujade's book, that could be because, as Lapoujade says, the logics Deleuze is interested in "escape all reason."[7] So, someone taking this view might argue that any formal articulation of a logic could only model rational thinking, but the sort of conception in Deleuze's philosophy that we are trying to explicate would always contain an irrational component that defies any such mode of reasoning and thus fails to be captured in any formulation.[8]

Deleuze himself seems to suggest that we encounter such an obstacle with his "sub-representative" notion of difference, a fundamental concept in his metaphysics.[9] Difference, he says, is "the highest thought, but also that which cannot be thought."[10] And so, if this fundamental metaphysical principle of difference cannot be thought, then quite possibly the logical principles involved with it also cannot be formally articulated.

Now, to be clear, our assumption here will not be that every logically relevant aspect of Deleuze's philosophy can be given an explicit formulation with our available systems and notions in modern logic.[11] But, we should not thereby leap heedlessly to the conclusion that *none* of Deleuze's logic can be usefully articulated in such a way. And as we come to see the extraordinary freedom that we have in logic to fashion and explore viable, alternate systems, such a prohibition against these more formal conceptualizations will seem less and less necessary as we continue our investigations. For instance, we may first hold the concern that logical formalizations will use symbols or names ("*P*" and "*Q*," for instance) that fix the identities of the terms or propositions and thus are unable to be used in the context of Deleuze's philosophy of becoming and differential selfhood, where there is supposedly a loss of personal identity and proper names. But, as we will come to understand, in a certain many-valued logic, self-identity statements like "$a = a$" can be both true *and* false, and thus they can model metamorphic identity variation; additionally, $A \wedge \neg A$ (the conjunction of a proposition and its negation) in such logics models logical properties of becoming, change, and heterogeneous composition, when the negation yields a non-exclusive other. Thus, we intend to keep an open mind regarding this tricky matter, and we will cautiously examine formalizations and systems that may be said to at least *approximate*, to a conceptually useful extent, certain important elements in Deleuze's logic, without succumbing to the absolutist demand that if we cannot render all of Deleuze's thinking into these more formal conceptions, we should conclude *none* of it can.

And the fact that these alternate modes of reasoning are currently unorthodox does not mean that we can simply dismiss them out of hand. As Graham Priest shows, certain non-classical logics are not irrational or unreasonable in the least, and, in fact, in many important ways they are more rational than traditional logic. For, they are more adequate for dealing with certain philosophical problems.[12] Thus, it is more rational to use such alternate modes of reasoning in these cases. For instance, Priest argues, it is more rational to use a logic that can allow for contradiction in order to handle the liar's paradox, because (among other things) it provides a simpler sufficient solution, and it has greater explanatory power with regard to the underlying matter.[13] And historically speaking, classical logic can be seen as having already fallen out of prominence, being now replaced by non-classical logics.[14]

Yet, our primary concern is not defining rationality but instead seeing if certain features or principles of Deleuze's logic can admit of one or another formal articulation that sheds more light on his logical thinking than is currently available. Even so, we do not seek to reduce Deleuze's philosophy to a set of formulas; rather, we wish merely to *add* such formulations to all our other available options for elaborating his philosophical thinking.

So, the challenge we here undertake is to translate Deleuze's logic into somewhat formal expressions in which basic logical structures, properties, and operations become more visible. And, in fact, much valuable work in this direction has already been conducted by, for instance, Cécile Voisset-Veysseyre, Daniel Smith, Dorothea Olkowski, and Jeffrey Bell; and in the following, we will advance many of their developments. For example, in Chapter 8, we will pursue Voisset-Veysseyre's suggestion that we should use a many-valued logic to understand Deleuze's notion of the incompossibility that is involved in becoming.[15] In Chapters 1, 2, and 4, following Smith, we explore logics that can allow us to conduct our thinking, as Deleuze suggests, without a strict adherence to the three basic principles of classical logic (Identity, Non-Contradiction, and Excluded Middle).[16] Olkowski has especially made great advances in finding formalizations for principles of Deleuze's logic,[17] and I will also build from her work on the intuitionistic trend in Deleuze's thinking in Chapter 6.[18] Also, Bell must be credited for suggesting in 2010 the connection between Deleuze and Priest, opening one of his texts by writing "the work of Graham Priest and Gilles Deleuze (and Félix Guattari) converge in significant ways on the concept of the nondenumerable,"[19] which is a topic we further explore in Chapter 6. There are other important contributions on Deleuze and logic that will become relevant in the forthcoming volumes. Arnaud Villani wrote a book with a nearly identical title to this one: *Logique de Deleuze*.[20] Although it does not deal directly with the sorts of formal logic notions we tackle here, we will benefit from its discussions on the logic of sensation in our second volume. And Paul Livingston's book, *The Politics of Logic: Badiou, Wittgenstein, and the Consequences of Formalism*, in a most remarkable fashion, analyzes the paradoxes of sense in Deleuze's philosophy of language, which we will make especial use of in the third volume.[21] My own unique contribution to these efforts will be to explore and apply certain systems of non-classical logic to Deleuze's philosophy more directly, extensively, and comprehensively than has ever been done before. One possible reason that this has not yet been attempted is that it is an impossible task, and thus we should just give up trying at the outset. Another possibility is that it happens to be quite difficult (but still possible), which means we must try harder than anyone has before us. I hope by the end of this book you will come to agree with me that it is well worth the effort to work through this material, as it can unlock a dimension of Deleuze's thinking that has remained hidden ever since his earliest writings and teachings.

Another potential benefit of these investigations is protecting Deleuze from accusations of faulty reasoning or of obscurantism. As Lapoujade notes, the "irrationality," as he calls it, in Deleuze's logic is not something illogical: "Logic doesn't mean rational. We could even say that for Deleuze a movement is all the more logical the more it escapes rationality. The more irrational, the more aberrant, and yet the more logical."[22] Where we will here diverge from Lapoujade is that instead of thinking of Deleuze's logic as being irrational, we will rather say that many of its important basic principles are in fact entirely logical and rational, but only *non-classically* so. As such, not all of Deleuze's logic will need to remain vague, obscure, or informulable.

Nonetheless, a challenge we face when taking up this task is obtaining a sufficient amount of knowledge in the advanced systems of non-classical logics, which is generally not part of any of our training, be it philosophical or otherwise. For this reason, we will mostly use basic propositional formulations, and even those cases will be minimal, in order to keep matters as simple and familiar as possible. The endnotes will elaborate on certain technicalities for those who are interested. Yet even these additions will remain at an introductory level, as the purpose of this book is certainly not to instruct logicians on matters in logic, although I hope they may still find some interest in what Deleuze has to say on these issues. For those who would like to learn classical and non-classical logics, I can recommend the texts that guided me: initially David Agler's *Symbolic Logic*, secondly John Nolt's *Logics*, and lastly and most importantly, Graham Priest's *Introduction to Non-classical Logic*.

It should also be emphasized that Deleuze himself wrote two so-called logic books, *The Logic of Sense* and *Francis Bacon: The Logic of Sensation*. But these texts will not play too great a role in our present endeavors, with the exception of a few important sections from *Logic of Sense*. The reason for this is that I plan on dealing with these texts in much greater detail in two forthcoming books on Deleuze and logic. The next volume will focus on his philosophy of experience and the third one on his philosophy of language. In this present volume, however, our attention is directed more exclusively to the basic logical principles of Deleuze's philosophy of thinking and metaphysics. And the conclusion lists the topics we will cover in the forthcoming volumes.

Deleuze and Logic

For the remainder of our introduction, we will look at Deleuze's comments on contemporary logic in general and on non-classical logic in particular. Afterward, we will briefly introduce the non-classical logics that will form a part of our study, with a focus on many-valued logics along with Priest's philosophy of dialetheism.

Logic: What–What–What?

For Deleuze, the "logic" he names in his book titles is likely not limited to the formalized kind, given the lack of such material within these works. Nonetheless, that does not bar us from uncovering the basic logical principles and thinking built into these and his other writings. But what, after all, is logic? Graham Priest tells us: "The point of logic is to give an account of the notion of validity: *what follows from what*."[23] In other words, logic is primarily the study of how our conclusions follow properly from our premises or valid reasoning.

Yet, in Deleuze's philosophy of thinking, he is not especially concerned with determining valid inference, and so it might seem at first that nothing interesting can be done in terms of formalizations of Deleuze's logic. Nonetheless, as Lapoujade notes, for Deleuze and Guattari, "philosophy consists in the creation of concepts," which is thus "the production of logics, given that a concept is never created alone but always in conjunction with other concepts"; and, therefore, "to create a concept entails creating the logic that links it with other concepts."[24] So this in fact is one way we will look for a logic in Deleuze, namely, we will ask, how might we articulate, using certain formal means, the ways that for Deleuze concepts are interrelated in their formation or creation? Posed another way: what can be said about the logical properties of conceptual compositions and the way they arise? Here we will reconceive the logic question "what follows from what?" to instead be something more like, "under what logical conditions can concepts arise in the first place?" This is our task in Chapter 3.

The second way we will here uncover a logic of Deleuze is by seeing how certain logical principles underlie his metaphysical thinking. As Priest explains, logic and metaphysics constrain one another.[25] How this can happen becomes abundantly clear in Chapter 1 when we see how the restrictions of Russell's classical logic pose constraints on the way he accounts for motion and change. On this basis, we will examine some of Deleuze's metaphysical notions regarding time, composition, and becoming that can be said to involve certain logical principles and a rejection of others. As we will see, even when Deleuze insists he is working with an "alogical" metaphysical conception, we will nonetheless find that beneath it are certain logical assumptions. Moreover, Dorothea Olkowski has uncovered ways that certain rules of logic and mathematics, namely, of association, commutation, and distribution, "have ontological effects" for Deleuze, for whom "ontologically nature is associative, commutative, and distributive."[26]

Now, to keep with our parallelism to contemporary logic's definition of logic as the study of valid inference, or "what follows from what," we note here that when we uncover a logical principle at work in a metaphysical conception, it may not seem at all like an inference, which we think of as involving a movement from premises to a conclusion. For example, Deleuze discusses the Principle of Identity in Leibniz's notion of being. But A is A (or $A \supset A$) is not an inference. Or is it? Well, it is, in a sense, just as the formulations for the Principles of Non-Contradiction and Excluded Middle can be seen as inferences, because they can be understood as formulas that follow from an empty set of premises.[27] For instance, the features of a classical logic system will allow us to infer simply that *either A or not-A* ($\vDash A \vee \neg A$), which expresses the Principle of Excluded Middle;[28] yet, we can conclude this without needing any premises, because it will hold true no matter how you assign the truth-value for A. (We will see exactly why that is, in Chapter 4.) However, in other sorts of logics, like intuitionism, we cannot make this propositionless "inference" on account of how they are structured.

In sum, a given system's own particular tautologies or "logical truths" can still be considered as valid *inferences*; for, a valid inference is one where it cannot be that the premises are true and the conclusion is not true. So, such logical truths are valid because it simply cannot be that the "conclusion" is not true anyway, no matter what. Thus when we look at the logical thinking that underlies some of Deleuze's metaphysical principles, it will still be a matter of discerning "what follows from what," only it can also be a case of "what follows *no matter what*." In other words, we are seeking the logical truths or basic principles that are built into or, as more often is the case, that are *conspicuously absent from* his metaphysical thinking. For instance, we will ask in Chapter 1, is the Principle of Non-Contradiction somehow a part of Deleuze's metaphysical conception of becoming?

One matter we should briefly note is that there are two kinds of validity. *Proof-theoretic validity* (symbolized with $\vdash$) is "defined in terms of some purely formal procedure,"[29] which could involve using derivation rules or tableaux methods, for instance. To keep things a little easier and more intuitable, we will only deal with *semantic validity* (symbolized with $\vDash$). In this case, a "valid inference is one that *preserves truth*."[30] One of the simplest ways to see if truth is preserved is by using truth evaluation tables, where we assign all possible combinations of truth-values for the atomic formulas. We then calculate the truth-values for all the premises and also for the conclusion, looking to see if "every interpretation (that is, crudely, a way of assigning truth-values) that makes all the premises true makes the conclusion true," in which case the inference is semantically valid, and it is invalid otherwise.[31]

Classical Logic

Deleuze, on rare occasions, speaks of "classical logic" (*logique classique*), but it is not precisely in reference to what now conventionally gets that name.[32] So let us give some clarification to how we will understand classical logic, because that will allow us to better assess if Deleuze's criticisms of logic are directed at all logics or just to classical logic.

Despite its name, classical logic should not be understood simply as a logic dating back to Ancient Greece, although some of its basics principles were also discussed and developed back then too.[33] It rather is traced to more relatively recent philosophers, especially Bertrand Russell and Gottlob Frege.[34] In Chapter 1, we will look at a more formal account of classical logic. For now, it will suffice to note, as Deleuze does, that it adheres to certain principles, most famously the Principles of Identity, Non-Contradiction, Excluded Middle, Bivalence, Double Negation, Explosion, among others. (We will always refer to them as "principles" rather than using the more currently conventional term "laws," simply to avoid unwanted connotations in the Deleuzian contexts.) For instance, the Principle of Excluded Middle constrains our thinking such that when we have a disjunction of a proposition and its negation ($A \lor \neg A$), at least one disjunct must be true. So, in accordance with the Principle of Excluded Middle, of the two disjuncts in "either it is raining or it is not raining," one must be true. (Thus, we cannot say that there are ever cases where neither one is true, like intuitionists claim, as we will later see.)

With its rise in the nineteenth and early twentieth centuries, classical logic saw great success compared to its predecessors, and for that reason it came to be the "received" kind. It is likely the type of logic you learned from your introductory courses or books or that at least may have been impressed upon you by certain socially accepted standards of reasoning (for instance, in an argument, you are not permitted to contradict yourself). As such, certain philosophical values associated with classical logic also came to be firmly held by many philosophers, as for instance a prohibition on contradiction and an adherence to a strict true/false bivalence, with no room for there to be any other options.[35] Nonetheless, logics that reject or reconceive the principles of classical logic do not create something illogical any more than changing some of the axioms of geometry creates something non-geometrical; consider for instance non-Euclidean geometries.[36] And if, as we will contemplate, classical logic is faulty in many philosophically important respects, then classical logicians could be the irrational ones, with non-classical logicians exercising superior reasoning.

Non-Classical Logics

So, despite classical logic's great successes, we will see that it falls short in a number of ways, and non-classical logics have proven to be preferable as responses to those failings. Priest notes a number of "anomalies" that classical logic is incapable of handling sufficiently, including Russell's paradox and the irrelevance of explosion.[37] Yet, because certain newer non-classical logics can handle these and other anomalies, Priest proclaims that "the time is objectively ripe for logical revolution"; that is to say, we are living in a time when the overall paradigm of reasoning is shifting from classical to non-classical logic.[38] We might then wonder, can Deleuze's own philosophy of logic be seen as a part of that shift?

While there are many different kinds of non-classical logics, we will focus on just three main types, namely, intuitionistic, fuzzy, and many-valued logics. There are two reasons for this limited scope. The first is that, to my knowledge, Deleuze himself mentions only these three, and secondly, they also happen to be very suitable candidates for elaborating Deleuze's logic, on account of the sorts of operations and liberties they allow.[39] Let us briefly introduce these three kinds of logics.

Fuzzy Logic

Fuzzy logic is perhaps the most familiar to us of the non-classical logics we will consider here. It appeals to our intuition that in certain cases, something can be partly true (and partly false). This is especially the case for continuous changes. At exactly what instant in your life did the proposition "I am still a child" become false? Perhaps some dramatic event made the transition instantaneous for you, but think of other cases you know where it really was a gradual change for that person. Fuzzy logics can be useful for the "sorites" paradoxes that involve such transitional periods, because they would allow us to say that, for instance, halfway into your transition from child to adult, the statement "I am still a child" is half true. As we will see in Chapter 2, Deleuze and Guattari do not favor these sorts of logics, although they do employ the notion of a fuzzy subset to explain their conception of heterogeneous composition.

Intuitionistic Logic

One prevalent way to evaluate truth is on the basis of the correspondence between thoughts and the facts of a real world. But some philosophers argue that we cannot operate under this assumption, and this can have consequences for the logic one uses. We will examine this issue in greater detail in Chapter 6. But for now consider John Nolt's example of discovering boiling soup, which illustrates a similar way of thinking.

> I may think that the soup is boiling and then go to the stove and see that it is. In this sense I may confirm my thought that the soup is boiling. But my seeing or hearing (or even touching) the soup does not, so this line of reasoning goes, reveal the soup as it is in reality, but only the soup as I see or hear or feel it. […] But if I can never know the relation between my thought and reality itself, then I can never know truth.[40]

Intuitionistic reasoning would instead hold that the "truth" or "falsity" of a statement is determined by whether or not the available data warrant us to assert it.

> One suggestion is to base our semantics on relations not between thought and reality, but between thought and evidence—relations such as proof, warrant, or confirmation. My perception of the soup is a form of evidence that proves,

warrants, or confirms my thought or assertion that the soup is boiling. Thus thought or assertion, which I experience, is compared with evidence, which I also experience, rather than with reality or the world, which I allegedly never experience as it is in itself. Another word for such direct experience is "intuition." Accordingly, the resolve to restrict semantics to entities that can be made evident to direct experience is called *intuitionism*.[41]

One important feature of intuitionism is that the Principle of Excluded Middle does not hold in it, because there are certain propositions for which we do not have warrant to either assert or refute them. This is one matter that interests Deleuze with regard to intuitionism, along with its notions of a calculus of problems, undecidable propositions, and negationless mathematics.

Many-Valued Logics

One of the principles of classical logic, the Principle of Bivalence, can be understood as requiring that every proposition be either at least true or false, but not both true and false (as such, it is something like a combination of the Principles of Excluded Middle and Non-Contradiction).[42] But such a restriction can create difficulties in our philosophical thinking about certain fundamental notions, for instance, change and becoming. Consider an alteration: a match is struck, and its wood turns to fire. The question is, when does the change take place? One answer is that the change occurs just at the first moment there is fire (Figure 0.1, right). But in that case, the change already happened. The alteration exists in the past and cannot be found in that present moment. Yet, what if we say instead that the change takes place right at the last moment there is wood? But in that case, we likewise still miss the change, because it has not yet happened (Figure 0.1, left).

One promising option would say that there is an intermediary period where its status is indeterminate (Figure 0.2, left).

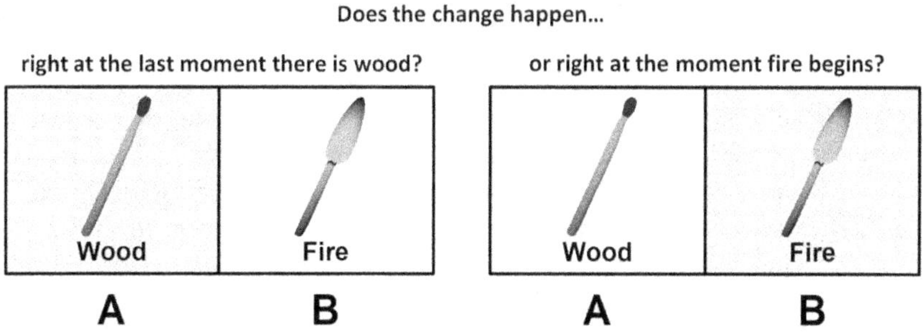

Figure 0.1 A depiction of a match's change from wood to fire, where (**left**) the change is thought to happen in the initial state or (**right**) in the resulting state. In both cases, we miss the transition.

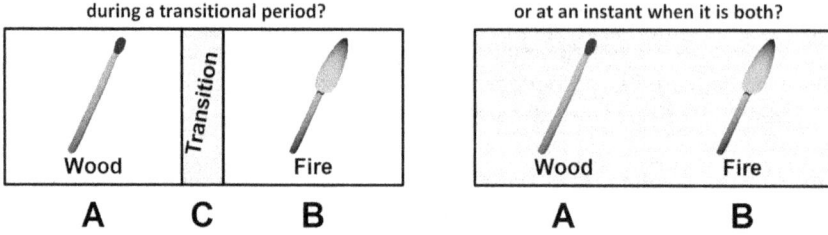

Figure 0.2 Left: A change occurring during a period of indeterminate transition. **Right**: One occurring when both contradictory states of affairs hold simultaneously.

In this case, it would be neither simply wood nor simply fire. As a physical state, it is not obvious how to conceive what happens during that transitional period. Regardless, it presents a new problem. By postulating this intervening period, we have created yet another change that we need to give an account for, namely, how we moved from the state of wood to the period of transition. If yet again there is another state of transition (intermediate between the state of wood and the first postulated state of transition), then we could have an infinite regress, where each newly posited transitional state will need yet another intervening one preceding it to account for how it is arrived upon, and so on indefinitely. (Note that you will also have this problem even if you conceive the transition using fuzzy logic, with the state descriptions admitting of degrees of truth.)[43]

Yet, assuming these problems can be solved, this could illustrate a case where we reject the Principle of Excluded Middle, because we would have formulations in which neither a proposition nor its negation is true. And so, for instance, during the transitional phase, the statement "The match is wood" is not true, nor is "The match is not wood (in that it is fire)" a true statement. But, there are other sorts of propositions that more strongly suggest that they lack the values of true or false. For instance, there are meaningful statements where the terms do not have denotations that allow the propositions to be easily evaluated as either true or false. Priest gives such a possible instance:

> One sort of example concerns "truths of fiction." It is natural to suppose that "Holmes lived in Baker Street" is true, because Conan Doyle says so; "Holmes' friend, Watson, was a lawyer" is false, since Doyle tells us that Watson was a doctor; and "Holmes had three maiden aunts" is neither true nor false, since Doyle tells us nothing about Holmes' aunts or uncles.[44]

The other sort of propositions that seem like good candidates for being neither true nor false are "future contingents," which we examine in Chapter 8.

Returning to our match illustration, we might instead say that there is a moment when it is both wood and fire (Figure 0.2, right panel) under the reasoning that as a transition of states, it must be said of the match that both statuses would need to somehow be in effect. This, of course, presents a contradiction. It is both wood and not wood at the same time (and likewise it is both fire and not fire at the same time). Thus, under this reasoning, we do not adhere to the Principle of Non-Contradiction in the fullest way, and we have statements with both truth-values: "The match is wood" is both true and false when it is changing from wood to fire.

Given their particular usefulness in thinking about Deleuze's logic, we will explore such many-valued logics in a number of the chapters of this book. However, it is not very clear how familiar Deleuze was with these logics. He was aware enough to know of their early formulation, starting in the 1910s with C. S. Peirce's work on them.[45] And he mentions a sort of three-valued logic as a solution for the problem of future contingents.[46] Yet, overall he does not devote too much thought to them explicitly (in fact, in one course lecture he mentions many-valued logics, but leaves them aside, because he says they would take all year to cover).[47] And nowhere does he deal specifically and extensively with a three-valued logic that allows for contradictions. The fact that he does not do so leaves open the possibility that perhaps, had he known more about them, he may have either used them to articulate his logic or at least explained why they fail to do so. In the end, we will find that despite Deleuze's critical remarks, many-valued logics in general are still very good candidates for understanding his logic.

Deleuze Contra Logic

With these very general distinctions in mind for classical and non-classical logics, let us look at the criticisms Deleuze and Guattari have for logic to consider whether they apply to all logics whatsoever or just particularly to classical logics, with certain non-classical varieties escaping his criticism. In this preliminary stage of our analysis, we will only be able to look briefly at a couple of their complaints; note that the matter is not as simple as it may seem at first and point to the sections where we explore the issues in more detail. The purpose here is merely to show that we cannot simply take their criticisms at face value.

Does Heterogeneity Defy Logic?

Deleuze and Guattari, when discussing the heterogeneities involved in "transformations of becomings," claim that for such becomings, "there is no preformed logical order"; instead, they follow "alogical consistencies or compatibilities."[48] From this we might suspect that for Deleuze and Guattari, no logical account can be given for becoming or heterogeneous composition, because there is in fact nothing logical about them, or at least, there is something about them that will defy any reasoning. Yet, as we noted above, we cannot really say that a metaphysical notion, like the one they have here for becoming and composition, is "alogical," if by that we mean its conceptualization involves no logical assumptions. As we will see in Chapter 2, it will seem that in fact their notion of consistency, while not involving the logical "consistency" of classical logic, could be understood instead as involving a sort of "paraconsistency" of a non-classical logic. Deleuze also speaks of the "alogical incompatibilities" of Leibniz's incompossible worlds and of Stoic co-fatality.[49] But as we will see in Chapters 5 and 8, the issue here is that incompatibilities are determined not by a simple contradiction of predicates but rather by the way that something's presence in a world is disallowed by physical facts regarding the other things that exist there. And that so-called alogical disallowance in Leibniz's metaphysics will still involve certain logical assumptions, especially ones regarding laws of causality and the order of linear time. Moreover, even Deleuze's non-chronological, alternate conception of incompossibility will seem to lend itself to a dialetheic logic. Also note that when further discussing heterogeneous composition in terms of fuzzy subsets, Deleuze and Guattari say that "its elements belong to it only by virtue of specific operations of consistency and consolidation, which themselves follow a *special logic*."[50] So perhaps "alogical" can be understood as "non-classically logical." Yet, many Deleuzians—and I may count myself as one—will insist that there is something more to Deleuze's philosophy that is not properly expressed using our available logical notions. Again, I caution us not to hastily conclude from this that nothing at all in Deleuze's logic can be given a clear and straightforward articulation. For, as we will gradually find, certain non-classical logics do prove handy in helping us understand it.

Is There No "Logic" to Creative, Original Thinking?

In *What Is Philosophy?*, Deleuze and Guattari level a critique against logic in general. But upon closer examination, we may find that their criticisms do not land squarely upon non-classical logics. Their complaint is that logic renders philosophical concepts into propositional formulations, which cannot adequately express concepts, because this strips them of what they call "endoconsistency" and "exoconsistency."[51] As we will learn in Chapter 2, these sorts of "consistencies" are relations among the concept's parts and between the concept and other concepts. While it may in fact be that rendering concepts into propositional formulations would strip them of certain important nuances of their conceptualization, we can still ask the more general question: what are the logical assumptions involved in Deleuze's and Guattari's understanding of the way that concepts are composed and created?

Now, it is true that we will employ propositional variables—letters like A and B—to represent propositions, when addressing this question. However, by doing so, we are not reducing rich concepts into simplistic propositions or empty symbols. Rather, we need such placeholders to think about the logical *operations* and *relations* that can be at work in our conceptualizations of the world and of thought itself. For instance, when we examine the formulation for a dialetheia, $A \land \neg A$, we will not thereby be reducing some beautiful, rich, and potent philosophical concept to the letter A or to the simplistic, dry, propositional rendition of the concept that A represents. Rather, we do so because we want to improve our understanding of how, for Deleuze and Guattari, concepts relate and combine. In the case of the dialetheia's formulation, $A \land \neg A$, the propositional variables and operation symbols will allow us to think about something being combined with its non-exclusive other. It is the logical properties of that combination of such non-exclusive "otherthans" itself that concerns us. Thus, insofar as non-classical logic can take our thinking in such directions, the fact that they implement propositional forms should not be so catastrophically problematic for us. Moreover, a survey of recent debates in modern logics shows them to be at the forefront of contemporary philosophy, because they cut into the most fundamental assumptions of our philosophical thinking. And most certainly Priest's philosophy of dialetheism should be considered as a philosophical concept creation in the Deleuzian and Guattarian sense.[52]

In sum, it is an open question whether or not Deleuze's logic can be understood in terms of non-classical logics. It has now been more than fifty years since Deleuze published his book, *Logic of Sense*. Are we not long overdue for such an exploration? That is what we now proceed to do.

Overview

Let us here take a quick survey of the path we follow in this book. In Chapter 1, we begin with Bergson's and Russell's accounts of motion to illustrate how a philosopher's metaphysics and logic mutually constrain one another. We then see how Priest's dialetheic approach to paradoxes of movement and change can be helpful for understanding what Deleuze calls the "paradox of pure becoming." Then in Chapter 2, we explore Deleuze's and Guattari's philosophy of heterogeneous becoming and composition, with a focus on their concepts of coalescence, consistency, and conglomeration, which they obtain from Eugène Dupréel. And we also give some attention to how they here employ their notion of the sorcerer. All of this will give us occasion to examine their remarks on fuzzy logic. After that, we turn toward Priest's dialetheic account of "gluonic" composition to see how it can better serve us in our understanding of Deleuze's and Guattari's conceptions of heterogeneous composition and of the loss of personal identity and proper name. Using this notion of compositional consistency, we then in Chapter 3 look at Deleuze's idea of transdisciplinary thinking along with his and Guattari's account of the composition of concepts. In Chapter 4 we turn to Deleuze's remarks on negation and disjunction to see what logical properties he takes them to have, in order to assess which logics are most suitable to those conceptions. We further that discussion with Deleuze's bifurcational account of time in Chapter 5 by looking at his portrayals of Leibnizian incompossible worlds and Stoic ethics. Following that, in Chapter 6, we will examine Deleuze's and Guattari's comments on intuitionism, with a focus on the rejection of the Principle of Excluded Middle, undecidable propositions, a positive mathematical conception of difference, and a calculus of problems. In Chapter 7 we tackle Deleuze's notion of the power of the false, beginning with his idea of aberrational movement, and in Chapter 8, we continue that discussion with his characterization of "the falsifier" who creates the New through falsification. That chapter ends with the strongest case that can be made for dialetheism in Deleuze's thinking, namely, his conception of godless or "demonic" incompossibility. In the conclusion I will reiterate my reasoning for why dialetheism is the best overall fit for Deleuze's logic, and we lastly will preview the topics of the forthcoming volumes.

Part One

Dis-Composition and Dis-Identification

1

Becoming Dialetheic: The Logic of Change

Introduction

The first main sort of non-classical logic we will examine is many-valued logics in the context of certain paradoxes of becoming, change, and movement. We will begin with Henri Bergson's philosophy of change and motion and then examine Bertrand Russell's critique of it, along with his proposal for a "mathematical" explanation of movement. This will set us up for Graham Priest's dialetheic account of motion, which will illustrate for us the many-valued logics we are considering. And finally, we will see that Gilles Deleuze's "paradox of becoming" is more or less suited to such a many-valued logic. Our aim here is twofold. In the first place, we will draw out from Bergson's conception of becoming certain properties that hold for Deleuze's becoming as well. And in the second place, these discussions will provide us with an intuitive illustration for reasoning that uses many-valued logics.

Method and Philosophy in Bergson and Russell

As we enter into the critiques Russell levels at Bergson's conception of motion and change, we will notice that much of this disagreement comes from their taking opposite approaches to philosophical thinking itself.[1] Both express a dissatisfaction with how philosophy was conducted up to their times, and both think that philosophical thinking should strive for precision. But they differ on the best methodologies for properly attaining precise conceptions. And, as we will see, this distinction can influence whether we conclude that motion and change are composed ultimately of motions and changes or of fixed positions and states. To clarify the difference between Bergson's and Russell's views on philosophical thinking, we will briefly compare their ideas in talks they give on the issue, namely, ones collected in Bergson's *The Creative Mind* and in Russell's *Our Knowledge of the External World as a Field for Scientific Method in Philosophy*.

Russell's Philosophical Types

Russell divides philosophy into three trends, of which only the third is satisfactory for him. The first is the classical tradition, which has not yet caught up to contemporary standards of modern science. Like pre-Socratic philosophers, they hold that by means of thinking alone they can give accounts of the real world, and the failure of this approach is seen from the fact that some believed they could prove, using just their reasoning, such far-fetched claims as: all reality is one, the world of sense is mere illusion, there is no such thing as change, and so on. And they were so trusting of reason that they thought no contrary observations should challenge their conclusions. This trend continued from Ancient Greece through the Middle ages, then featured prominently in the thinking of Kant and Hegel, and is still found in the thinking of Russell's contemporaries, for instance, with F.H. Bradley, despite the success of the sciences, which suggest a much different picture of the world.[2] Russell rejects this style of philosophy, because he believes we should rely also on empirical findings.[3]

Russell's second trend of philosophical thinking is "evolutionism," under which he classifies not only Darwin and Spencer, but also (perhaps oddly) Nietzsche and Bergson. In contrast to the "classical tradition," evolutionist thinkers believe strongly in the power of science, especially biology, to provide us with knowledge.[4] And at a certain point in this trend's history, it cast aside a teleological assumption of a fixed end to evolutionary developments. According to Russell, for Bergson this is because such an assumption places limits on "the absolute dominion of change," which itself calls for evolutionary variation over time to be channeled in no particular direction.[5]

Russell's third kind of philosophy is "logical atomism," which is the one he here advocates.[6] Russell says that philosophy should, like with the classical tradition, use logical reasoning to analyze "familiar but complex things" to "help us to understand the general aspects of the world," but he holds that this thinking should be connected to the sciences, especially mathematics, physics, and psychology, by providing them with fruitful hypotheses.[7] One particular way philosophy can make such a contribution, Russell says, is in the analysis of space and time in order to provide a reconstruction of these conceptions. However, he clarifies, "I do not think the reconstruction required is on Bergsonian lines, nor do I think that his rejection of logic can be anything but harmful." Russell claims, rather, that he will adopt "the method of independent inquiry, starting from what, in a pre-philosophic stage, appear to be facts, and keeping always as close to these initial data as the requirements of consistency permit."[8] However, as we will see, Russell's account of motion and change might in fact place him to some degree in the "classical" camp. Yet, before we further clarify Russell's methodology and findings regarding space and time, let us switch for a moment to Bergson's approach to philosophy.

Bergson's Intuitional Philosophy

In Bergson's assessment of contemporary philosophical thinking, he finds that it lacks precision whenever it is disconnected from the reality it is meant to account for, and this happens when it is too formalistic and abstract:

> What philosophy has lacked most of all is precision. Philosophical systems are not cut to the measure of the reality in which we live; they are too wide for reality. Examine any one of them, chosen as you see fit, and you will see that it could apply

equally well to a world in which neither plants nor animals have existence, only men, and in which men would quite possibly do without eating and drinking, where they would neither sleep nor dream nor let their minds wander [...]. The fact is that a self-contained system is an assemblage of conceptions so abstract, and consequently so vast, that it might contain, aside from the real, all that is possible and even impossible.[9]

The sort of philosophy Bergson is after, then, is one that is in direct touch with the immediate, real world: "The only explanation we should accept as satisfactory is one which fits tightly to its object, with no space between them, no crevice in which any other explanation might equally well be lodged; one which fits the object only and to which alone the object lends itself."[10] Although science allows for such precision, philosophy is not always so capable of it, and philosophy has so far been especially inept at studying real duration, which "eludes mathematical treatment."[11] In order for philosophy to adequately think of such matters in a way that is tied directly to their reality, it should employ "intuition." By means of it, we may obtain

a truly intuitive metaphysics, which would follow the undulations of the real! True, it would not embrace in a single sweep the totality of things; but for each thing it would give an explanation which would fit it exactly, and it alone. It would not begin by defining or describing the systematic unity of the world: who knows if the world is actually one? Experience alone can say, and unity, if it exists, will appear at the end of the search as a result; it is impossible to posit it at the start as a principle. Furthermore, it will be a rich, full unity, the unity of a continuity, the unity of our reality, and not that abstract and empty unity, which has come from one supreme generalization, and which could just as well be that of any possible world whatsoever.[12]

Bergson's Intuition of Duration

We thus need to understand what "intuition" is for Bergson. It is specifically the awareness of what is in your mind's immediate, present "grasp": "Intuition [...] is the direct vision of the mind by the mind" with "nothing intervening"; it is "all consciousness, but immediate consciousness, a vision which is scarcely distinguishable from the object seen, a knowledge which is contact and even coincidence."[13] And when the mind turns its direct inner "vision" upon itself, what does it then intuit within its immediate grasp? Bergson says that it views the continual flux of real duration, which is moving that very same mental grasping itself. In this flux of consciousness, "there is no feeling, no idea, no volition which is not undergoing change at every moment: if a mental state ceased to vary, its duration would cease to flow." Thus the mind's "state," were it so, is at any time "itself nothing but change."[14]

So, in other words, philosophical thinking should begin with intuitive givenness, which is always fundamentally an awareness of "the indivisible and therefore substantial continuity of the flow of inner life," "the uninterrupted prolongation of the past into a present which is already blending into the future."[15] Thus, "pure intuition [...] is that of an undivided continuity,"[16] and by means of this intuition, we come to grasp "all change, all movement, as being absolutely indivisible."[17]

Bergson provides a test to demonstrate one way we know intuitively that change and movement are indivisible, and this is a crucial determination to make when comparing him with Russell. Bergson writes: "I have my hand at point A. I move it over to point B, traversing the interval AB, I say that this movement from A to B is by nature simple."[18] Now, we could very well at least try to conceive of this movement as admitting of divisions. For instance, while our hands are still in motion, we might think that we could stop them at the halfway point in order to divide it into two. But then, Bergson notes, this would only then compose two distinct movements with an interval between them: from point A to mid-point C, [pause], then from C to endpoint B. Yet still, we often conceptually divide motion without needing the object to stop at each division; we rather "mark off" certain places the object passes through along its trajectory. Even this, for Bergson, misconstrues the real composition of the movement.

> At bottom, the illusion arises from this, that the movement, *once effected*, has laid along its course a motionless trajectory on which we can count as many immobilities as we will. From this we conclude that the movement, *whilst being effected*, lays at each instant beneath it a position with which it coincides. We do not see that the trajectory is created in one stroke, although a certain time is required for it; and that though we can divide at will the trajectory once created, we cannot divide its creation, which is an act in progress and not a thing. To suppose that the moving body is at a point of its course is to cut the course in two by a snip of the scissors at this point, and to substitute two trajectories for the single trajectory which we were first considering.[19]

Here now comes his controversial claim.

Bergson says that the only way our hand's movement from A to B could *occupy* any point in the space that we mark off would be for it to *stop* its motion at that point. While it is moving, it can only ever *pass through* fixed positions. It can never occupy any location if indeed it is still in motion. In other words, the movement, while it is actually in effect, can only at best be found *between* the endpoints bounding spatial intervals while never in fact being *at* any one position. So our hand is indeed at starting point A before the motion begins, and it is at endpoint B when it ends. But while moving between them, it is never *at* any intervening points. It is rather just *passing through* them. True, the space the movement crosses has static locations, but the movement itself was never static, and thus by placing the movement into strict correspondences with such spatial determinations, we are fundamentally misconceiving the motion. In fact, we are not even conceiving the movement at all. We are only at best thinking about just the space alone that it passed through.

> How could the movement *be applied upon* the space it traverses? How can something moving coincide with something immobile? How could the moving object *be* in a point of its trajectory passage? It *passes through*, or in other terms, it

could be there. It would be there if it stopped; but if it should stop there, it would no longer be the same movement we were dealing with. It is always by a single bound that a passing is completed, when there is no break in the passage. The bound may last a few seconds, or days, months, years: it matters little. The moment it is one single bound, it is indecomposable.[20]

However, whenever the movement does stop, we can go back, look at the spatial interval it crossed, and divide that traversed space itself up in any way we choose just like we can with a geometrical line, which is of course composed of a simultaneous series (and not a temporal succession) of points.

This sort of mental activity for Bergson is the work of the intellect, which always seeks the fixed points of space when trying to understand motion and thus "refuses to consider *transition*,"[21] which is the real "substantiality" of motion and change.[22] This conception concerns "far less the living movement itself than a dead and artificial reorganization of movement by the mind."[23] Bergson even goes so far as to say that there are no real forms.[24] And there are not even self-contained "things" that are changing or moving; for, there is only change itself.[25] Many are averse to this idea, because such a notion of a formless, thingless, and purely alterative world gives such people a profound sense of vertigo; however, "change, if they consent to look directly at it without an interposed veil, will very quickly appear to them to be the most substantial and durable thing possible."[26]

Bergson and Cinematic Kinematics

Bergson further elaborates this conception of reality with his notion of the cinematographic "illusion."[27] He does not mean by this the way that a rapid succession of still images can appear to show continuous motion, on account of the phi-phenomenon, the persistence of vision, or whatever else is used to explain such an illusory impression of movement. For Bergson, the cinematographic illusion is rather the misconception that the real continuous motions that we do directly perceive can be decomposed into static states or positions, like the sequence of frames along a strip of motion-picture film; and even more generally, it is the erroneous idea that any change whatsoever can be broken into immobile parts or fixed states. He illustrates with the example of filming a marching army regiment. The cinematographic mechanism tries to reproduce its movement by taking "a series of snapshots of the passing regiment" and throwing "these instantaneous views on the screen, so that they replace each other very rapidly."[28] But each frame is just a still-image photograph that gives us nothing of the regiment's movement. The impression of their motion is generated artificially by means of the rotating gears of the projector, whose steady, mechanical turning imposes upon "all the figures an impersonal movement abstract and simple, *movement in general*," which captures nothing of the unique "inner becoming of things" that was inherent to the "passing reality" originally given in the soldiers' motions.[29]

The danger here, for Bergson, is not that the cinematographic mechanism fails to give us the illusory impression of motion, for surely it does succeed at that. Rather, we go astray when we conceive of real duration and motion as being analogous to the steady, homogeneous, and mechanical movement of the cinematograph's gears that animates the moving figures by pushing one still image into the place of the prior one, each laid out in spatial juxtaposition along the film strip, thereby constituting movement on the basis of static positions that are fixed along the film's perforated timeline of artificial duration. Thus, when our intellect uses language and symbolic thinking to conceive of forms when there is only the flux of becoming, "we hardly do anything else than set going a kind of cinematograph inside us. [...] therefore [...] the mechanism of our ordinary knowledge is of a cinematographical kind."[30]

As we will see, Russell will use similar language to make the opposite claim, so let us further specify Bergson's position in order to render the contrast vividly clear. One might here make the objection, as Russell will, that we are misconstruing the operation we need for fully reconstituting the real motion, because we have not considered nearly enough static positions. We in fact need infinitely many of them. Just as there are an infinity of points along the moving body's trajectory, there are that many static positions in the movement corresponding to those points, with the full entirety of them composing the motion completely. Bergson considers this argument and says that still we are missing the most important ingredient, namely, that which constitutes the *transitions between* the positions, which is not itself a position but is rather a motion or change of some sort. For, were such a transition posited as simply being a third, intervening position, you have only thereby created between them yet another, smaller interval within which the duration still needs to be found:

> Let me then concentrate myself wholly on the transition [...] between any two snapshots [...]. As I apply the same method, I obtain the same result; a third view merely slips in between the two others. I may begin again as often as I will, I may set views alongside of views for ever, I shall obtain nothing else. [...] with these successive states [...] you will never reconstitute movement. [...] multiply the number of them as you will, let the interval between two consecutive states be infinitely small: before the intervening movement you will always experience the disappointment of the child who tries by clapping his hands together to crush the smoke. The movement slips through the interval, because every attempt to reconstitute change out of states implies the absurd proposition, that movement is made of immobilities.[31]

In order to better consider the logic involved in Bergson's conception, let us look at one of his illustrations where he deals with predications. We consider the life of a person, going from infancy, to childhood, to youth, to maturity, then finally to old age. Bergson says that if we only think of these "stops" along their development, we will not conceive of how the person evolved over time, because "rests placed beside rests will never be equivalent to a movement."[32] Bergson then notes that we encounter a misconception if we comprehend this becoming by using the proposition: "the child becomes a man." For, Bergson reasons, as soon as the person is an adult, they no longer are a child, and thus the attribute "man" could not have been predicted to "child" in the first place. This indicates that Bergson does not allow contradictory predications to the same subject (and so, using a notion we explore later, we could say he is not overtly a "dialetheist"). However, this is not entirely certain, because Bergson is using "becomes" in this formulation instead of "is." And also, in such a conception where the beginning and ending states are fixed and temporally exclusive, "the reality, which is the *transition* from childhood to manhood, has slipped between our fingers. We have only the imaginary stops 'child' and 'man', and we are very near to saying that one of these stops *is* the other."[33] Thus, Bergson says, we would do better to understand this change by formulating it as, "There is becoming from the child to the man"; for here, "'becoming' is a subject. It comes to the front. It is the reality itself; childhood and manhood are then only possible stops [...]; we now have to do with the objective movement itself, and no longer with its cinematographical imitation."[34] In other words, the attributes "is a child" and "is a man" can coincide when they predicate the becoming that envelopes both statuses in the same movement. Thus, the danger of the original formulation, "The child becomes a man," is in conceptualizing "becoming" as "being" and seeing the coincidence of temporally exclusive attributes as static states rather than as connected phases in a metamorphosis.

Russell's critique of Bergson will revolve around the way Bergson explains the source of the problem with Zeno's paradoxes, so let us now examine one in particular, namely, the paradox of the arrow. In Aristotle's account of it, we begin with some seemingly harmless assumptions regarding motion and time, and they lead us to conclude that there is no motion at all, not even in the case of an arrow flying through the air. {1} Assume that a duration of time is composed of indivisible "now" moments. So if it takes the arrow three seconds to fly to its target, we can consider any instant of that duration we please, as if we were stopping time at that point in its motion. {2} Next, define physical rest as when an object occupies an amount of space that is equal to its own length. (The intuition here seems to be that by occupying the same amount of distance as its length, it is not going beyond its current position, as it is confined within its present location; and thus, under this spatial constraint on where it can be at that moment, it is not moving and hence is at rest. To further fill out this intuition, imagine a photograph of a flying arrow that shows some blur around its edges. The arrow will be a certain length, but the blur will make it appear longer than that. So let us also form this conception that a moving object, because it is in motion at some moment, would need to be "blurring" outside its physical bounds, so to speak, by moving past them in that instant of its moving forward.) {3} We will lastly assume that an object that is in motion is always so in any "now" moment during its movement.[35] In other words, between the start and finish of the arrow's motion, there is no moment when it is at rest. And thus we need to expect that at any instant in between, it exhibits the properties of motion in that "snapshot." What is important to note here is that we are isolating such an instant, and so the properties of motion that the arrow exhibits would have to be *intrinsic* to it at that time.

Yet, these three more or less reasonable assumptions lead to a paradox, as we all well know. If at every moment it is in a state of motion, then it should not at any time be at rest; thus, it should occupy more space than its length each instant that it is moving.

But if each moment of the arrow's motion is indivisible, it will not have enough time to move beyond the space of its length. Hence the contradiction: by assumption, the arrow, for every moment of its flight, is in motion (and thus is never at rest), but by our reasoning, we also conclude that the arrow is at every moment at rest (and thus is never in motion during its flight). As Bergson summarizes:

> Take the flying arrow. At every moment, says Zeno, it is motionless, for it cannot have time to move, that is, to occupy at least two successive positions, unless at least two moments are allowed it. At a given moment, therefore, it is at rest at a given point. Motionless in each point of its course, it is motionless during all the time that it is moving.[36]

Bergson diagnoses the cause of the paradox in our faulty philosophical reasoning: we have the intuition of becoming and change in sensible reality, but we insist that there must be an underlying intelligible reality that is even more real and that is an unchanging substrate to sensible variations: "Beneath the qualitative becoming, beneath the evolutionary becoming, beneath the extensive becoming, the mind must seek that which defies change, the definable quality, the form or essence, the end."[37] We thus divide the arrow's motion into fixed positions, which *by definition* will exhibit no motion. The paradox, for Bergson, results when we override our correct intuitions of an indecomposable motion with our intellect's erroneous spatialization of its movement.[38] So we come to the absurd conclusion that the flying arrow is always motionless when "we suppose that the arrow can ever *be* in a point of its course"; rather, "the truth is that if the arrow leaves the point A to fall down at the point B, its movement AB is as simple, as indecomposable, in so far as it is movement, as the tension of the bow that shoots it."[39]

What this means for Bergson is that we will never be able to account for motion using our intellects, whether by beginning with just still states and building up to transitions or by beginning with transitions and breaking them into a series of stops; for: "there is more in the transition than the series of states [...]—more in the movement than the series of positions"; and overcoming this faulty sort of reasoning requires that "we reverse the bent of our intellectual habits."[40]

Russell against Intuition

Russell also diagnoses the cause of our problems with understanding motion and change as being a failure in philosophical reasoning, but exactly in the opposite way as Bergson, namely, that we have not properly used our intellects *enough* and instead have relied too much upon our mathematically inept intuitions. Bergson says that we need to guide our intellect with our intuition; Russell claims we must help our intuition follow what our intellect tells us.[41] He says for instance that the intellectualized idea of motion as being made of points makes us feel, intuitively, that such a motion must be a jerky, discontinuous motion rather than a smooth, continuous one. This feeling, Russell claims, should not be trusted, because it results from "a failure to realize imaginatively, as well as abstractly, the nature of continuous series as they appear in mathematics."[42] However,

> when a theory has been apprehended logically, there is often a long and serious labour still required in order to *feel* it: it is necessary to dwell upon it, to thrust out from the mind, one by one, the misleading suggestions of false but more familiar theories, to acquire the kind of intimacy which [...] would enable us to think and dream in it.[43]

So, as long as we work at it enough, our intuitions will eventually come around to regarding a dense series of static positions as entirely composing continuous motion, even though it is very hard to picture how that could possibly be.

Yet, recall that Russell is against a sort of philosophical thinking that he calls "classical" in which we ignore empirical data in favor of an exclusive use of our reasoning, even at the expense of our drawing far-fetched conclusions that seem unconnected to the world around us. Russell in fact may be guilty of this very same error by assuming, against intuitive evidence, that the physical world conforms to the laws of classical reasoning. As we will see, by imposing the Principle of Non-Contradiction on the physical world, Russell arrives upon the counter-intuitive claim that the flying arrow really is at no moment in a state of motion.

Let us first see how Russell argues that we should not trust our sensory intuitions regarding physical motion. He has us consider when we watch the second hand moving in a continuous flow around a clock dial. We do not see its motion as fractured into parts—"first one position and then another"—rather, we perceive, as one unitary phenomenon, its fluid, unbroken motion.[44] This intuition about motion's indecomposability is precisely what Bergson's example of moving your hand from point *A* to *B* demonstrates. Russell writes:

> We can see, at each moment, that the second-hand is *moving*, which is different from seeing it first in one place and then in another. This seems to involve our seeing it simultaneously in a number of places, although it must also involve our seeing that it is in some of these places earlier than in others. If, for example, I move my hand quickly from left to right, you seem to see the whole movement at once, in spite of the fact that you know it begins at the left and ends at the right. It is this kind of consideration, I think, which leads Bergson and many others to regard a movement as really one indivisible whole, not the series of separate states imagined by the mathematician.[45]

Russell believes that in this case our intuition has led us astray. Really the motion is divisible. He holds that indeed our visual perception of motion is of a series of snapshots, corresponding to the object's fixed positions along the course of its movement.[46] However, there is a property of our vision whereby previous images remain in our visual perception, like how a flash of lightning visibly perseveres even after the bolt has ceased moving through the sky. (This is the persistence of vision theory that we mentioned above in reference to the illusion of motion that cinema produces, which has been replaced by the theory of the phi-phenomenon.) Moreover, the older the after-image, the less vivid it is. When the object is going fast enough, this creates the visual impression of a solid "streak" of movement, tapering off at its earliest retainable position, thereby showing us the most recent chunk of its linear trajectory.[47]

And so, by telling us that our sensory impressions of indecomposable motion are faulty, Russell is thinking a little like the philosophers in the "classical tradition," as he called it; but to be fair, he does so by taking into consideration other empirical evidence. Yet even these additional considerations do not necessitate the conclusion he wants to arrive at, namely, that physical motion must be decomposable into static states. To do this, again like the classicist philosophers that he criticizes, Russell relies on the intellect's reasoning at the expense of intuitive thinking and empirical evidence; for, he says, the only way to *logically* explain this empirical data without contradiction is to say we really do perceive static states without ever noticing them:

> From what has just been said it follows that the nature of sense-data cannot be validly used to prove that they are not composed of mutually external units. It may be admitted, on the other hand, that nothing in their empirical character specially necessitates the view that they are composed of mutually external units. This view, if it is held, must be *held on logical, not on empirical grounds*. I believe that the logical grounds are adequate to the conclusion. They rest, at bottom, upon the impossibility of explaining complexity without assuming constituents. It is undeniable that the visual field, for example, is complex; and so far as I can see, there is always self-contradiction in the theories which, while admitting this complexity, attempt to deny that it results from a combination of mutually external units.[48]

But note that this assumes that the Principle of Non-Contradiction is valid in these cases, even when we are faced with evidence that suggests otherwise.

So now that we have rejected our sensory impression that motion is not composed of parts, how should we, as philosophers, proceed? Russell, as we will see, conceptualizes the problem of accounting for motion as really being the problem of giving a consistent and precise account of mathematical continuity. And the reason philosophers, from Zeno through Bergson, have misconstrued motion is because their mathematical thinking was not sophisticated enough, Russell claims. But as soon as we obtain a more updated knowledge of the advanced mathematical theories of sets, infinity, and continuity, our intuitions will shift and modify as we come to "feel" the truth of the mathematical account of motion, replacing our erroneous Bergsonian intuitions.[49] In other words, mathematicians have already advanced so far on these topics that they have solved the paradoxes of motion without the philosophers even realizing it, even as many of them continue trying and failing miserably. And thus philosophers need to bite the bullet, so to speak, and get caught up on their contemporary mathematics in order to see the correct solutions to these millennia-old philosophical problems.[50] Russell here is raising a high expectation for the viability of the "mathematical" account of motion, which, as we will see, is not surely met.

Russell's Mathematics of Motion

Let us take a brief look, then, at what, according to Russell, philosophers like Bergson should have learned already from the mathematicians. Perhaps the most important mathematical property of the continuum for Russell's account of motion is its "compactness" or density: between any two points there is always another.[51] But this means that {1} there are no infinitesimally small intervals between points, and thus that although intervals are infinitely divisible on account of this density, the divisions will never arrive upon an indivisible interval.[52] This is important, because it means that no matter how many times we divide an interval of motion, we never can ultimately arrive upon intervals that—no matter how small—cannot be further broken down. {2} There is no "next" point or moment.[53] To understand why this is so, first suppose that rather there are in fact infinitesimal gaps and think of one of them. It will be bounded by two points, with none intervening. That means the point on the farther side is the "next" point. But if there are no infinitesimal distances, then no point will have such an immediate neighbor. It will only at best have a closer and closer neighbor, but never a "next" one. This means that motion, being continuous in time and space, never "jumps" to any next point without having crossed an infinity of points in between them:

> Imagine a tiny speck of light moving along a scale. What do we mean by saying that the motion is continuous? [...] if we consider any two positions of the speck occupied at any two instants, there will be other intermediate positions occupied at intermediate instants. However near together we take the two positions, the speck will not jump suddenly from the one to the other, but will pass through an infinite number of other positions on the way. Every distance, however small, is traversed by passing through all the infinite series of positions between the two ends of the distance.[54]

{3} And so similarly, there are no *finite*, pointless "gaps" in the continuum. While this might seem like something we can take for granted, it is not entirely obvious how this notion works in Russell's argument, given some of his other claims. Russell rejects the actual infinite, which could have allowed for infinitesimal, and thus indivisible, not-finite intervals.[55] Without such infinitesimals that could be seen as terminating the division process, might there not be an infinite regress in which all that our divisions ever result in are more finite gaps? For, under Russell's conception, there is always a finite distance between any two points, no matter how close you make them, and thus, a continuum will always be decomposed into finite gaps even under an infinite division. But Russell does not conceive it this way. We may show him a finite gap, and he will just find some point within it that will divide it into smaller gaps. This means that there is no precise place anywhere along the continuum that we can point to and that is not located at some determinately specifiable location. Thus everywhere in the continuum are just points, and there is no gap without a point in it. However, it is still another matter whether or not that allows us to readily conceive how this makes all finite intervals evaporate in such a way that there are ultimately no "gaps" in a continuum. For this, we need to reject our spatial intuitions that may compel us to think otherwise, and we must rather conceive the continuum only in this "mathematical" way. But regardless, in the very least, Russell does in fact give us reason to see an extensive continuum's constitution purely in terms of points, without using the notion of compositional intervals. And so, while it may seem counter-intuitive that a continuity *at its basis* is made solely of discrete, dimensionless points without any finite or infinitesimal gaps between them, it is perfectly consistent under this mathematical conception.[56] Furthermore, given this thoroughly dense but point-like structure of the continuum, the nature of its infinity means that motion will have "smooth transitions" rather than a "jerky motion."[57]

And by means of this mathematical conception of continuity, Russell argues that we can sufficiently account for motion, without attributing an intrinsic mobility to the moving object. For Russell, time is composed as a continuum of indivisible, non-durational instants, and the space traversed is a continuum of points; moreover, when an object moves continuously, each instant of the motion can be correlated to some spatial point along its trajectory, as we often see done when physics studies motion.

So how does Russell then explain what movement is? Here is his so-called at-at account. To conceive it, we need the following three continua: {1} the continuum of time during which the thing moves, {2} the continuum of space it traverses, and {3} the continuous coordination of these two continua, that is to say, the continuous correlation between {a} the point in space that is occupied by a moving object with {b} the instant in time that it is found there. The continuous coordination here is important, because it will temporalize the space and spatialize the time in the sense that, for a moving object to be at a further location is for it to be found there at a forthcoming moment; and for the movement to occur at a future instant is for the object to be located at a more distant place (here we are supposing the object is traveling forward in a straight line). So long as the object is moving, the one factor cannot be disengaged from the other, and this perfectly thoroughgoing and intimate intersection of the two dimensions will make Russell's theory at least partly compelling.

The reason it is sometimes called his "at-at" account is because all that is needed to explain motion is a recognition that the moving object is *at* some location *at* some moment, and it is also *at* some further place *at* some later time, with the continuous coordination of the two dimensions guaranteeing that a continuous change in such *at-at* determinations can only mean that there has been a continuous movement throughout (Figure 1.1).

> When a body moves, all that can be said is that it is in one place at one time and in another at another. [...] Motion consists merely in the fact that bodies are sometimes in one place and sometimes in another, and that they are at intermediate places at intermediate times.[58]

> The continuity of the motion is shown in the fact that, however near together we take the two positions and the two instants, there are an infinite number of positions still nearer together, which are occupied at instants that are also still nearer together. The moving body never jumps from one position to another, but always passes by a gradual transition through an infinite number of intermediaries.[59]

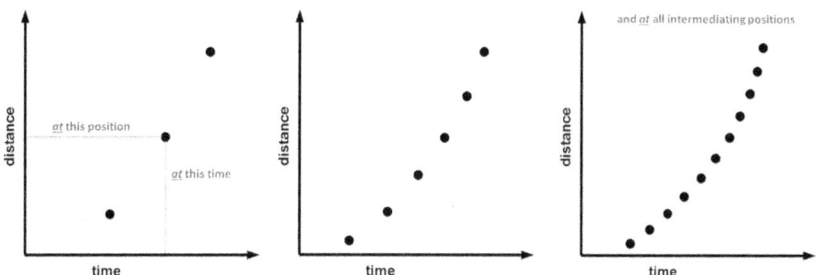

Figure 1.1 Russell's "at-at" account of motion. The object is always at a specific single position at a given point in time, but never in two places in the same moment, and never at no determinate location (by being for instance in a pointless gap between locations).

And if during some interval the object is continually *at* the same position throughout this duration, it is at rest: "When different times, throughout any period however short, are correlated with different places, there is motion; when different times, throughout some period however short, are all correlated with the same place, there is rest."[60]

Contrast this with Bergson's conception, where each phase of a change somehow "melts" or "blends" into the others, and the whole alteration is indecomposable into extensive parts.[61] For Russell, however, there are nothing but exclusive, discrete, and extensively separated and isolated parts. But then, what constitutes the "glue" or "bridge" across all the positions that allows for the smooth transitions that Russell insists will still be there? If there is such a binding principle, it would perhaps be the sum of all the extrinsic relations held between the *at-at* determinations, that is, their holding perfectly ordered relations in a continuous series that admits of no gaps. Russell notes that this is not a very intuitive conception of motion, because we might insist that a movement must be composed of smaller movements and not of discrete, mutually exclusive, and static elements. To help us better adjust our expectations for a conception of motion that initially runs up against our intuitions about space and time, Russell has us consider how "a friendship, for example, is made out of people who are friends, but not out of friendships; a genealogy is made out of men, but not out of genealogies"; thus, "a motion is made out of what is moving, but not out of motions."[62] In other words, the compositional parts of something are not in every instance homogeneous or commensurable with the greater thing they constitute. Hence, it is not inconceivable that movement is made of nothing more than immobile parts that are mutually exclusive and extrinsically related, which is precisely Russell's claim.

Thus for Russell, there is no intrinsic state of motion, and so Zeno, with his arrow paradox, got it at least half right. Zeno is correct in saying that the arrow at no time during its motion is moving. But he is wrong to conclude that it cannot therefore move from point *A* to *B*. According to Russell, had Zeno the conceptual resources of contemporary mathematics, he would have known that on account of the nature of infinity and the continuum, motion is completely conceivable as being made of positions, none of which exhibiting motion in itself. As Russell notes,

> Weierstrass, by strictly banishing from mathematics the use of infinitesimals, has at last shown that *we live in an unchanging world*, and that *the arrow in its flight is truly at rest*. Zeno's only error lay in inferring [...] that, because there is no such thing as a state of change, therefore the world is in the same state at any one time as at any other.[63]

This means, then, that for Russell, change and motion are not themselves "things" or "substantialities," as Bergson in a way had conceived them, and more specifically they are not intrinsic statuses that can be attributed to moving objects.

> People used to think that when a thing changes, it must be in a state of change, and that when a thing moves, it is in a state of motion. This is now known to be a mistake. [...] Philosophers often tell us that when a body is in motion, it changes its position within the instant. To this view Zeno long ago made the fatal retort that every body always is where it is [...]. It was only recently that it became possible to explain motion in detail in accordance with Zeno's platitude, and in opposition to the philosopher's paradox. We may now at last indulge the comfortable belief that a *body in motion is just as truly where it is as a body at rest*.[64]

So let us restate this remarkable claim: there is, with regard to the intrinsic properties of a moving body, no discernible difference between its being at rest and its being in motion. In fact, as "there is no transition from place to place," that means there is "no such thing as velocity [...] and acceleration as physical facts," at least as we once understood them.[65] The moving body is always still, always a snapshot; only it is a piece of an absolutely dense continuum of others that leaves out no part whatsoever of the whole movement.

To make the contrast clear, briefly recall Bergson's opposite position. His main argument is that when we take this sort of a "mathematical" approach to motion and change, we are only ever dealing with their spatial properties and never with their real, durational character. Bergson thinks there is something basic to time that is fundamentally incommensurable with space and that thus cannot be captured by coordinating instants with spatial points. Time is something whose parts are fundamentally *not simultaneous*. Thus if we put sugar into water, we "must, willy nilly, wait until the sugar melts."[66] The future moment five minutes from now when the sugar has finally dissolved cannot be actually present at the same moment when we first pour it in. We must live through that time. But Russell and physics, by coordinating moments with spatial points in a metrically homogeneous way, represent time as if all its moments are juxtaposable in the same way spatial points are. So no matter what Russell wants to tell us about the mathematical continuum, so long as it is composed of discrete parts set at extensive distances from one another, in this context of motion it can only represent space but not time, and a totally different conception is needed to comprehend the real durational component of becoming, change, and motion, Bergson claims. This is why time cannot be decomposed into—or recomposed from—snapshots, which will always leave out the duration between them, no matter how near they are in time. Nonetheless, Russell uses Bergson's cinema image to convey the opposite claim: "A cinematograph in which there are an infinite number of films, and in which there is never a *next* film because an infinite number come between any two, will perfectly represent a continuous motion."[67] Let us determine now more precisely how Russell's conclusion can be seen as following from his classical logic assumptions.

A Classical Logic of Becoming

To better illuminate the main logical issue that interests us here, let us look at Russell's uncharitable criticism of Bergson's account of motion. First, Russell states that Bergson makes the following claim: "No series of states can represent what is continuous."[68] This is not exactly what Bergson argues in his discussions of motion. In the first place, he does not specifically object to the idea that a compact series of spatial points can represent a linear continuum as it is understood in the modern mathematical way. So if by "states" Russell is referring to the moving object's positions at the points of space along its trajectory, Bergson may not be disagreeing with him there, because he does not say that, mathematically speaking, those points cannot be understood as composing such a spatial continuum. However, if by "states" Russell means something more like states of affairs during a qualitative variation (hot to cold, for instance), still the critique does not seem to apply to what Bergson is saying. What Bergson claims is that a series of states cannot represent a *change* (and a series of positions cannot exhaust a motion). Bergson does say that change and motion are continuous, but he does not claim that it is solely on account of that continuity that they cannot be divided. Rather, he argues that because duration is of such a different kind than space and the mathematical continuum, it is not really commensurable or correlatable with them; and thus, it cannot be properly divided by means of them. In other words, a more faithful rendition of Bergson's position would be "no series of states can represent what is durational" and not, as it is in Russell's version, "no series of states can represent what is continuous." So this part of Russell's critique might be attacking Bergson on an issue that does not factor into the main thrust of Bergson's argument.

The second way Russell uncharitably interprets Bergson is with Bergson's claim that the moving object never "occupies" a point but at best can only be said to *pass through* it. Russell specifically cites Bergson applying this reasoning to Zeno's paradox of the arrow, where Bergson argues that we would only conclude that the arrow never moves "if we suppose that the arrow can ever *be* in a point of its course" and "if the arrow, which is moving, ever coincides with a position, which is motionless. But the arrow never *is* in any point of its course." Rather, Bergson continues, the best we can say is that the arrow "passes there and might stop there."[69] From this Russell infers that Bergson therefore is "denying the claim that the arrow is ever anywhere," as Russell puts it.[70] But what does Russell mean by this? Is he suggesting that for Bergson, the object, when it is moving, leaves the physical world of extensive bodies, then magically appears again at its destination, when it is then at rest? Or is there any other way that we can come to this interpretation of Bergson that the moving object has no location whatsoever? Surely Bergson acknowledges that the object is found in a certain spatial zone while it is moving, and all the while it is not to be found outside that zone. That is not the same as saying the object is nowhere at all, which would require that we cannot even point to a region where it may be found. So it seems unfair to say that Bergson claims that the arrow is nowhere when it is flying.

Nonetheless, one reason Russell can misconstrue Bergson's theory is that Bergson was not sufficiently precise in his explanations. What does it mean to pass through a point rather than to occupy it? Does it mean the moving object is always a little bit before and a little bit after any given spatial point that it is moving through? Or, what else could it mean? It is hard to picture what Bergson has in mind for this, as he does not offer us any further elaboration.

We will now see how Russell formulates his precise account of motion by means of propositions and their relations, and this will allow us to assess the logic he is using. Russell writes:

Change is the difference, in respect of truth or falsehood, between a proposition concerning an entity and a time T and a proposition concerning the same entity and another time T', provided that the two propositions differ only by the fact that T occurs in the one where T' occurs in the other.[71]

So suppose we have the following two propositions:

{1} The object is at point A at t_1.
{2} The object is at point A at t_2.

To avoid additional complications, we will say that the object can only move in one direction if it ever does move. First suppose that both statements are true. That means the object has not left point A (it is still at that point, even though time has been passing). There was no change in truth-value from one proposition to the next, so there is no change in movement of the object. But suppose instead that the second proposition is false. That means the object no longer is residing at point A. It must have moved somewhere else. Thus, the change from truth to falsity means the object has moved.

Here, statements {1} and {2} are not identical, so the first one being true while the second one is false does not produce a contradiction. And Russel specifically says that we should not understand motion by means of "the contradiction of a body's being where it is not."[72] For, Russell directly applies the Principle of Non-Contradiction to the laws of the physical world: "the same piece [of matter] cannot occupy two places at the same moment";[73] and so "a simple unit of matter [...] can only occupy one place at one time. Thus if A be a material point, 'A is here now' excludes 'A is there now.'"[74]

And another principle of classical logic is the Principle of Excluded Middle. It prohibits a statement and its negation both being not true. We saw in his critique of Bergson's theory of motion that Russell does not think the moving object can be "nowhere." This means for the two statements:

{a} The object is at point A at t_1;
{b} The object is *not* at point A at t_1;

at least one of them must be true. If there is an object, moving or not, it is either at some location or it is not there. Now, what does this strict adherence to the principles of classical logic do for an account of motion? It strongly suggests an "at-at" account, of course. If a moving object can only be at one location at a time, and not at two in that instant, and also, if it cannot be at no point at all (for instance, being in an infinitesimal gap between points), then a moving object is always *at* some place, *at* some time— nothing less, nothing more. If that is only ever so, there cannot be any transitions where the object occupies more than one place or is in pointless gaps in between places. This now very clearly illustrates Priest's point that logic and metaphysics constrain one another. The principles of classical logic that Russell adheres to ultimately lead him to say that moving objects are at every moment in a fixed state.

Let us lastly now evaluate Russell's account of motion to see ultimately how it fares. Besides being counter-intuitive, which may not be a flaw if indeed our intuitions here are misleading, there are still two main problems with it. {1} Russell does not explain how we can decompose motion into spatial positions. Quoting Poincaré, he notes that we are conceiving of the continuum as "a collection of individuals arranged in a certain order, infinite in number, it is true, but external to each other." But this is not the "ordinary conception" of the continuum, "in which there is supposed to be, between the elements of the continuum, a sort of intimate bond which makes a whole of them." In the first case, which Russell adopts, the point comes prior to the line it is a part of, while the second, "common" conception, on the other hand, sees the line as coming prior to the point.[75] In fact, Russell says that were we to begin with the spatial continuum as a solid unity and then try dividing it over and over in order to arrive at points, we would remain trapped in an infinite regress.

> The same sort of thing happens in space. If any piece of matter be cut in two, and then each part be halved, and so on, the bits will become smaller and smaller, and can theoretically be made as small as we please. However small they may be, they can still be cut up and made smaller still. But they will always have *some* finite size, however small they may be. We never reach the infinitesimal in this way, and no finite number of divisions will bring us to points. Nevertheless there *are* points, only these are not to be reached by successive divisions.[76]

In the case of motion and rest, we will need somehow to make the leap in our divisions to indivisible points and instants, but that cannot be done through a decompositional analysis, for Russell.[77] But if we cannot decompose motion into static states, how can we be so sure it is composed of them?

This brings us to the second problem. {2} Russell does not really explain how motion happens. He can only give descriptions of its spatial determinations after it is completed. So, of course, an object that is moving will be in a different place at a different time. But the fact that there is never a next point does not explain how it goes from one place to another without any finite or infinitesimal transitions in the first place. Thus, Russell can neither satisfactorily tell us how a completed motion is decomposed into its supposed parts (fixed positions), nor can he explain to us how these parts get combined when composing such an interval of motion. In the end, motion is left as a mystery that has slipped outside our mental grasp. But does Bergson's account fare much better?

To answer that question, let us summarize our findings regarding both philosophers, drawing from one of Russell's observations about knowledge: "All knowledge is more or less uncertain and more or less vague. These are, in a sense, opposing characters: vague knowledge has more likelihood of truth than precise knowledge, but is less useful."[78] We might observe something similar to this in our evaluations of Bergson and Russell on the issue of motion. Bergson's account is intuitively compelling, but it is too vague to give us a clear grasp of what is going on with respect to the moving object's spatial properties. Russell's account is absolutely clear and precise, but it goes against our intuition that movement can only take place if there are spatial transitions that really, physically occur. Russell gives us no such conception, saying there are no transitions in the first place. Let us turn now to Priest, who uses non-classical reasoning to provide an account of motion that is both precise like Russell's and intuitive like Bergson's.

Priest and Dialetheic Motion

Russell, we saw, simply takes it for granted that physical motion and change cannot involve contradiction. Now, is it any coincidence that his account of motion, based on these classical logical principles, would be so odd and counter-intuitive? As we noted in the introduction, nothing forces us to adhere adamantly to the principles of classical logic, and if anything, the paradoxes of motion give us reason to reject them. Russell would not permit an object to be in a place and not in a place at the same moment. But dialetheists, who allow for contradictions in certain circumstances, have more freedom in this regard. Priest defines dialetheism in the following way:

> Dialetheism is a metaphysical view: that some contradictions are true. That is, where ¬ is negation, there are sentences, propositions (or whatever one takes truth-bearers to be), A, such that A and $\neg A$ are both true. Given that A is false iff (if and only if) its negation is true, this is to say that there are some As which are both true and false.[79]

To illustrate how this might work for motion, Priest gives the following example:

> As I write, my pen is touching the paper. As I come to the end of a word I lift it off. At one time it is on; at another it is off (that is, not on). Since the motion is continuous, there must be an instant at which the pen leaves the paper. At that instant, is it on the paper or off?[80]

Let us follow now how Priest makes these sorts of circumstances more formally precise. We will think of it as an event that could be studied in physics. So we might call the pen–paper situation a "system," named s, that can possibly be in two successive states, called s_0 and s_1, which will mean for us "on the paper" and "off the paper," respectively. We will consider an exact instant, t_0, marking its transition from one state to the other. Let us compose the sentence "the pen is on the paper" and call it α. The negation, $\neg \alpha$, would then mean "the pen is not on the paper." And we are concerned with the instant of change, right when the pen is leaving the paper.

We may formulate the problem more generally. Before a time t_0, a system s is in a state s_0, described by α. After t_0 it is in a state s_1, described by $\neg\alpha$. What state is it in at t_0? *A priori*, there are four possible answers:

(A) s is in s_0 and s_0 only.
(B) s is in s_1 and s_1 only.
(Γ) s is in neither s_0 nor s_1.
(Δ) s is in both s_0 and s_1.[81]

Consider the first two possibilities, (A) and (B). In his example, (A) would be "the pen is only on the paper" and B is "the pen is only not on the paper." The problem with accepting these options is that there is no more reason to say it is one instead of the other. "It seems as much on as off, and as much off as on."[82] So these asymmetrical answers do not work very well. As Priest explains:

> I am in a room. As I walk through the door, am I in the room or out of (not in) it? To emphasize that this is not a problem of vagueness, suppose we identify my position with that of my centre of gravity, and the door with the vertical plane passing through its centre of gravity. As I leave the room there must be an instant at which the point lies on the plane. At that instant am I in or out? Clearly, there is no reason for saying one rather than the other.[83]

Let us see if the symmetrical accounts, (Γ) and (Δ), fare any better. The first of them, in Priest's example, would be that the pen is neither *on* nor *not on* the paper at that moment of transition. In that case, the proposition "the pen is on the paper" is neither true nor false. Such a view that propositions can be truth-valueless is called "analetheism."[84] But we may find it hard to form such an analetheic conception of motion. Consider just the physical properties in the situation. We are only assuming there are two states: on and not on. What could be the analetheic conception of the pen's physical location here? Whether it says that {a} the pen is (somehow) in a third state which is neither of these two or {b} it is (somehow) neither in these nor in any other state, both options would seem to make the statement "it is not on the paper" be at least true. That seems to go against our original assumption that "the pen is on the paper" is neither true nor false, because in thinking that, we might additionally hold that "the pen is not on the paper" is also neither true nor false (in the next section we see how negation works in these analetheic cases).[85] Still, however, a viable analetheist account of motion is possible if it can clear up these matters.

Now note that we will need a term for the view that corresponds to classical logic, particularly, the belief that statements must be either true or false, not both, and not neither. There is a candidate for such a term, namely, "monoletheism," which is defined as the view that statements never have more than one truth-value.[86] It is thus used in contrast to dialetheism. But it would seem then that an analetheist could also be a monoletheist as well, if they are not also a dialetheist (for, such a non-dialetheist analetheist would say that propositions can have no more than one truth-value, only, they can have none as well). For this reason, it would be useful for us to expand the definition of monoletheism to mean not only the view that statements can have no more than one value, but in addition that they must also have at least one value. (Note that such a conception does not go against the "mono" prefix. It simply sees it as involving both a restriction and a requirement of one truth-value.) This will make it easier for us to draw the sorts of comparisons we will need in order to analyze Deleuze's logic. So I ask that you please accept this additional sense to the term, at least in the context of this book.[87]

Returning to our illustration, we are now left with the fourth option, Δ (the pen is both on and not on the paper). A dialetheist might say that the paradox here is not a result of imprecision in our description but rather that physical reality itself contains true contradictions. The greatest obstacle to accepting this is if one refuses to conceive the world they live in and the language they use as containing irreducible contradictions and inconsistencies. But without this flexibility, they might struggle to give a satisfactory account of one of the most basic features of our life and world, namely, that in them there is constant change. And not only are the other options problematic, the dialetheic one in addition provides a way to conceptualize the reason for change. For, we might think of the irreducible contradiction in a dialetheia as corresponding to something like an inner tension or *intensity*. The contradiction can be seen as calling for a new status or as expressing the motive or impulsion to bring one about. But if there are no contradictions in the world, would not everything somehow always be in a state of stasis or rest, similar to how Russell was conceiving motion in something of a self-defeating way? However, a conception of motion as involving contradiction portrays the situation as one whose "imbalance" or "tension," so to speak, "calls for" or "pushes toward" a resulting change of place. Priest, in making a similar point, quotes Hegel as saying "contradiction is the root of all movement and vitality; and it is only in so far as something contains a contradiction within it that it moves, has an urge and activity."[88]

Science of Logics

Before we continue with Priest's dialetheic account of motion, we should briefly talk about logical systems corresponding to the monoletheist, analetheist, and dialetheist stances. We will render these technical matters into a simplistic and visual format, while the endnotes will clarify issues which are thereby being neglected. One of the main purposes of the following is to point out some of the complications in specifying appropriate logics for each view, which will help us justify taking a simpler route when analyzing Deleuze's logic.

We said in the Introduction that logic is a study of validity, and validity is a matter of *what follows from what*. We will formulate the systems so that they all have the same standard of validity, which is the following: an inference is valid if none of the possible truth-value assignments for its propositional components can make the premises true and the conclusion not true. (More precisely: an inference is valid if none of the possible truth-value assignments for its propositional components can make the premises be at least true and the conclusion not even at least true.)[89] In a truth-table evaluation procedure, you would lay out all the possible combinations of truth-values for all of the inference's component atomic formulas (often listing them vertically in columns at the left), then you calculate the truth-values of the complex formulas they compose, and lastly you look for a line in the table where all the premises are marked with a symbol for "true" while the conclusion in that line completely lacks such a symbol. If in fact the table has no such lines, then the inference is valid (and invalid otherwise). And a single formula is a logical truth or tautology (as with the formulations of our "principles") when all its possible truth-valuations make it be at least true.

Taking that as our notion of validity for all the systems we will consider here, we will now distinguish them on the basis of two additional factors: {1} the possibilities we have for assigning them truth-values and {2} the ways we calculate the truth-values for complex formulas that are built up using operators (or "connectors"). For simplification and to make certain ideas visually obvious, we will not use additional symbols for the non-classical truth-values, but rather we will only work with true and false (along with their absence or overabundance). So our question is, which logical systems might a monoletheist, an analetheist, and a dialetheist be inclined to use, given their assumptions about truth and falsity?

Those taking the monoletheic view (in the extended sense we gave it above) will probably favor classical logic, the system that most of us are already quite familiar with. It requires that every proposition be at least true (T) or at least false (F), but not both (Figure 1.2, left side).

The operation on these values is also quite familiar (Figure 1.2, right portion). For instance, if a statement is true (suppose you say "It is raining" when it rains), then its negation ("It is not raining") is false. By using these evaluation rules, we can see that the Principle of Identity, when formulated as $A \supset A$,[90] is a logical truth, because regardless of the value we give A, the formula will always be true (Figure 1.3, left).

An analetheist would want a logic that allows for propositions to be neither true nor false. Often logics that do such a thing will use a symbol for a third value, like i for "indeterminate," u for "undecided," or n for "neither."[91] To keep things visual, we will just leave the area in our tables blank for the neither value (Figure 1.4, left). This will make it immediately apparent why these third values are called truth-value "gaps."

As we would expect, it invalidates the Principle of Excluded Middle when it is formulated as $A \vee \neg A$ (Figure 1.5, middle),[92] because it is not at least true under every evaluation, while classical logic validates it (Figure 1.5, left).

A dialetheist would want a logic that allows for propositions to be both true and false. The one we will consider is Priest's own "Logic of Paradox," *LP*. Its third-value could be written again as i or b for "both" or—as Priest does originally—p for "paradoxical."[93] In our tables, we will instead cram both the true and false symbols into the same box, to visually represent these truth-value situations that are called "gluts" (Figure 1.6, left).[94]

Dialetheists reject the Principle of Non-Contradiction, because they hold that some contradictions can be true. But look what happens when we use *LP* to evaluate one formulation of the Principle of Non-Contradiction, $\neg(A \wedge \neg A)$ (Figure 1.7, right).[95]

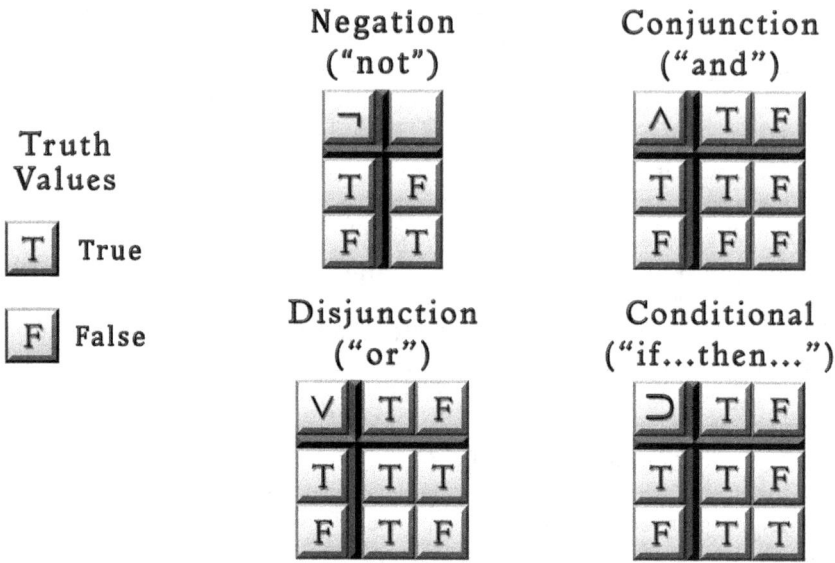

Figure 1.2 Classical logic as corresponding to the monoletheic view (in our extended sense) that propositions are only at least and at most just true or false.

The Principle of Identity

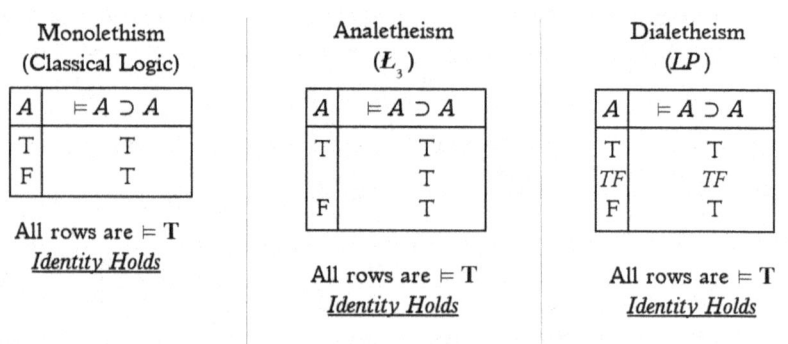

Figure 1.3 The validity of the Principle of Identity in different logics.

Becoming Dialetheic: The Logic of Change — 39

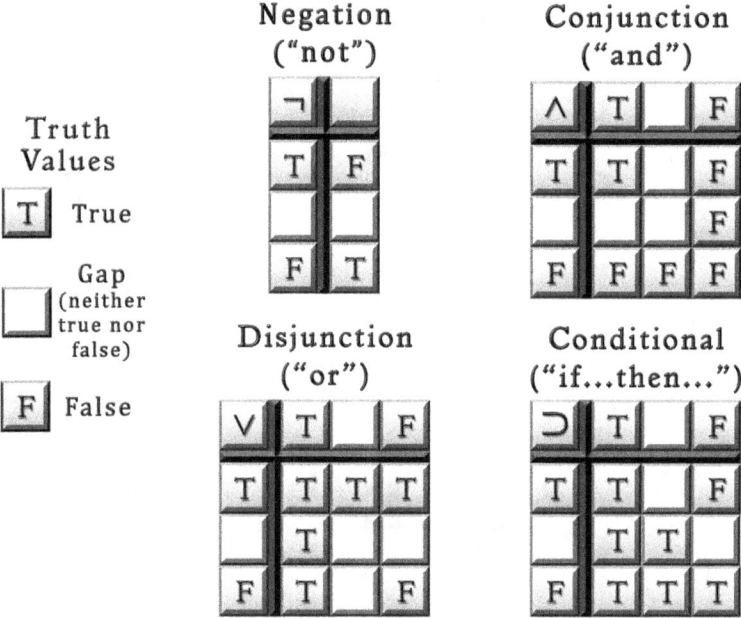

Figure 1.4 A three-valued logic with "gaps," corresponding to the analetheist view that propositions can be neither true nor false (and following Łukasiewicz's three-valued logic, $Ł_3$).

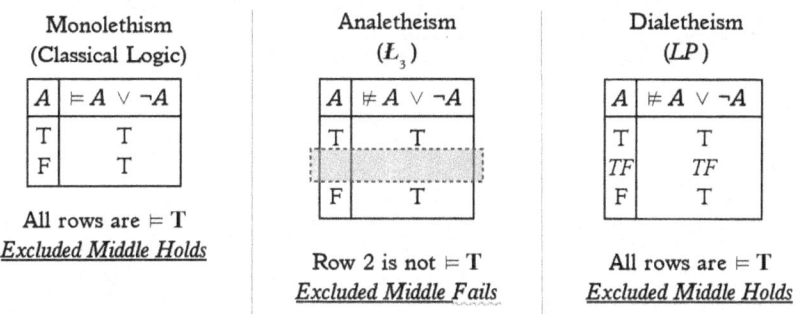

Figure 1.5 The validity or invalidity of the Principle of Excluded-Middle in different logics.

Dialetheism:
Logic with Gluts (*LP*)

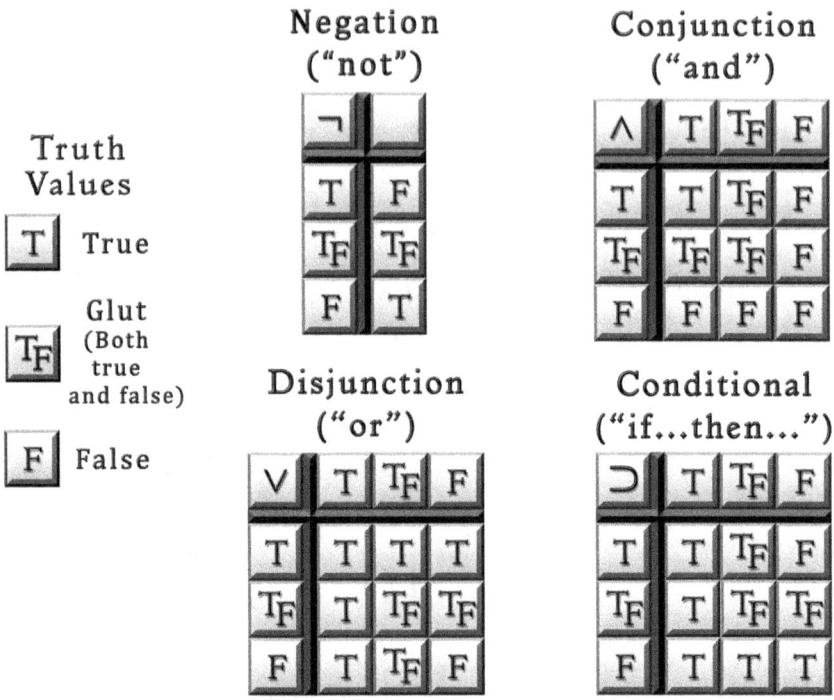

Figure 1.6 A three-valued logic with "gluts," corresponding to the dialetheist view that propositions can be both true and false (and following Priest's three-valued logic, *LP*).

The Principle of Non-Contradiction

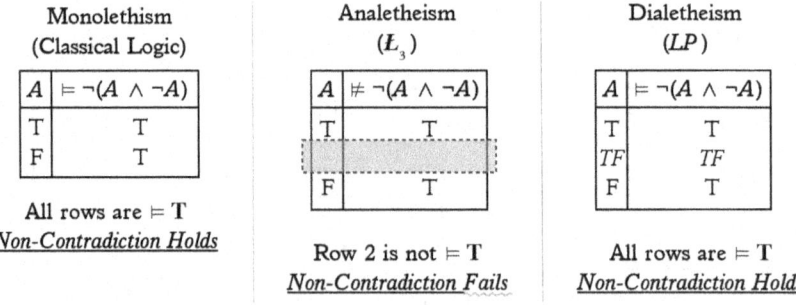

Figure 1.7 The validity or invalidity of the Principle of Non-Contradiction in different logics.

As we can see, $\neg(A \wedge \neg A)$ is valid in *LP*, because it is always at least true. Also notice that in the analetheist's logic, this formulation of the Principle of Non-Contradiction is not valid. This introduces some complications. It could be that we are using the wrong formulation for the Principle of Non-Contradiction,[96] or we may be choosing the wrong logic for each philosophical stance. But let us be clear first about *how* it is valid in *LP*. The formula $\neg(A \wedge \neg A)$ will always be at least true in it, but when *A* is both true and false, then $\neg(A \wedge \neg A)$ is also false along with being true. And note that this validity of the Principle of Non-Contradiction does not mean that in *LP* the contradictory formula $A \wedge \neg A$ must always be just false (as it would be in classical logic). For it too can be at least true, when it is both true and false. These are difficult matters that can take us into technicalities we might prefer to avoid, but we can at least see that while the Principle of Non-Contradiction can be said to be valid in *LP*, there can also be true contradictions in this logic, and so perhaps what a dialetheist is rejecting here is the way the Principle of Non-Contradiction is thought to entail a restriction on all contradictions whatsoever.

And what about this principle failing in the analetheist's logic? Does that mean in such a logic, contradictions are permitted? As we will see later in Chapter 4, an analetheist's logic may in fact be understood as prohibiting contradictions, if it validates something called the Principle of Explosion. In that discussion, we will obtain another way to distinguish these three sorts of logics, depending on whether they are complete or paracomplete, and consistent or paraconsistent.

But this is enough technicality for our present needs. One purpose of it was to show some of the issues that come up when trying to specify a non-classical logic for analetheism and dialetheism. With regard to our purposes here, these more technical matters are secondary to our primary aim of determining in more general terms what category of logic would best reflect Deleuze's logical assumptions. For that reason, I will speak for instance of a "dialetheic logic," meaning generically one that a dialetheist would advocate, without getting into its technical specifics. These terms of course will then be used in a somewhat vague way. But we will have enough to do just making the general, logical determinations regarding Deleuze's philosophy, and the debate over the technical details will have to be left for another occasion.

Priest's Dialetheic Account of Motion

We turn now to Priest's account of motion, which will make explicit use of logical contradiction rather than prohibit it. We begin first by considering the "Russellean" or "orthodox" account. As we noted, according to Russell, moving objects are at some location at some time, but never in no location or in two locations at once. With this in mind, Priest formulates the "Russellean state description" of motion. Consider an object whose various positions at certain times are described by some function. In the Russellean account, at some given point in time, the object is only at the location determined by the function, and not anywhere else (Figure 1.8). So the one statement that says this is true, and all the other statements saying that the object is elsewhere at that time are false.[97]

The Russellian State Description of Motion

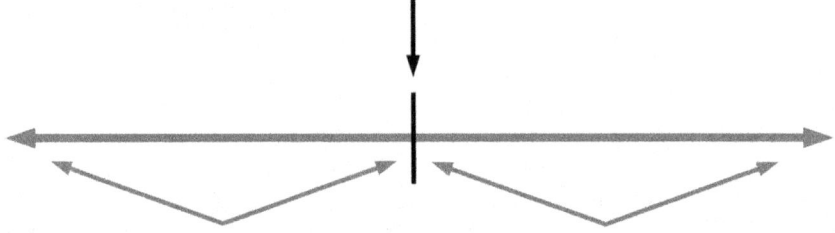

Figure 1.8 The precise and exclusive time–space determinations in Russell's account of motion.

Priest then articulates the concern we might raise regarding this Russellean state description of motion with respect to its "counter-intuitiveness":[98] for a moving body, as for example the arrow in Zeno's paradox, "at any point in its motion it advances not at all. Yet in some apparently magical way, in a collection of these it advances. Now a sum of nothings, even infinitely many nothings, is nothing. So how does it do it?"[99]

Opposed to this is the "Hegelean" account of motion. Priest quotes the following from Hegel's *Science of Logic*:

> External, sensuous movement itself is contradiction's immediate existence. Something moves, not because at one moment it is here and at another there, but because at one and the same moment it is here and not here, because in this "here," it at once is and is not. The ancient dialecticians must be granted the contradictions that they pointed out in motion; but it does not follow that therefore there is no motion, but on the contrary, that motion is *existent* contradiction itself.[100]

The reason why for Hegel motion implies a contradiction is because the exact location of moving objects cannot be localized during very tiny intervals of time.[101] Priest explains Hegel's reasoning as follows:

> Consider a body in motion—say, a point particle. At a certain instant of time, t, it occupies a certain point of space, x, and, since it is there, it is not anywhere else. But now consider a time very, very close to t, t'. Let us suppose that over such small intervals of time as that between t and t' it is impossible to localise a body. Thus, the body is equally at the place it occupies at t', x' ($\neq x$). Hence, at this instant the body is both at x and at x' and, equally, not at either. This is essentially why Hegel thought that motion realises a contradiction.[102]

But Hegel here is working with a notion of the continuum that is potentially problematic, mathematically speaking. Priest's account will retain Hegel's basic insight that "the localisation of the object is impossible over very small times," but he will reformulate it in a more mathematically rigorous way, which he calls the "spread hypothesis": "A body cannot be localised to a point it is occupying at an instant of time, but only to those points it occupies in a small neighbourhood of that time."[103] So at some specific point in time during the object's motion, there would be a tiny spread of neighboring time points around it during which the object would be found at all points within a tiny spread of space (Figure 1.9).[104]

Statements saying that the object is found outside that miniscule spread of space during that tiny interval of time will be just false. But there will be a number of statements saying that the object is occupying one or another point within that spread, and all of these will be *both* true *and* false. Thus, "at *t* a number of contradictions are realized."[105]

> To be in motion at an instant, then, according to this account, is to have an inconsistent state description at that instant. Objects in motion are at one place at one time, and another at another. But this is not sufficient. This would be equally true of an object at rest at each of these places. To be in motion at a time, an object must both be and not be at a place at that time.[106]

And we should note that this "instant" for Priest is not defined as the infinitesimal (it is rather an arbitrarily small interval),[107] so it does not fall victim to Russell's criticisms of theories of motion that use such an imprecise and outdated mathematical concept.

Priest's Spread Hypothesis

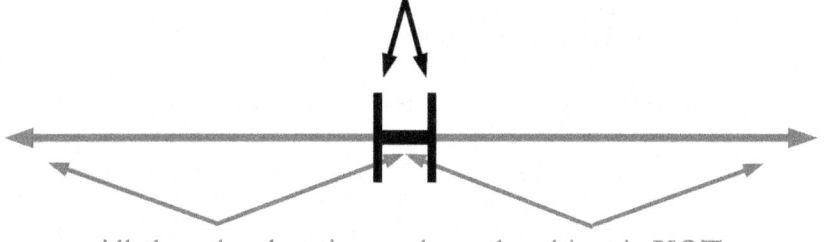

Figure 1.9 Priest's account of motion with an arbitrarily small time–space spread, where the object both is and is not at all the intervening places.

Thus, Priest's dialetheic picture has the precision of Russell's account, given that it also is formulated in a clear, propositional, and mathematically precise way. But it has the intuitive appeal of Bergson's account, in that it conceives motion as involving an occupation of a region during which the transition takes place. And it furthermore gives a sense of the how's and why's of motion, namely, that by being at two different places at once, there is a sense of the moving object as having an "urge" that could be thought of as "pushing" or "impelling" it out of its immediate bounds. Hence, as Priest notes, "dialetheism allows time to be both inconsistent and real."[108]

Deleuze's Paradox of Pure Becoming

Deleuze makes a fairly similar claim with regard to what he calls the "paradox of becoming," and here we will see hints of dialetheism in Deleuze's philosophy. He refers us to scenes in Lewis Carroll's *Alice's Adventures in Wonderland* when Alice's size increases, and this will serve to illustrate the paradoxical logic of the "pure event" of becoming and the loss of identity and proper name. Let us first recall these fantastical scenes.

At the beginning of *Alice in Wonderland*, she is chasing after the white rabbit into a very deep hole, falling down it for a remarkably long time. At the bottom, she finds herself in a hall lined with locked doors. One door stands out. It is only about 15 inches high, and she finds a tiny key to open it. She then drinks from a bottle labeled "DRINK ME" and as a result suddenly shrinks to a height of 10 inches. But in the meantime, she had left the tiny key on the table top, which she can no longer reach. Fortunately, at the bottom of the table is a cake whose decorations say, "EAT ME." After doing so, she then grows to a giant size, barely able to fit now in the hall.[109]

These variations do not just give her the impression that she is a different size. They are enough to make her feel like a different person altogether:

> Dear, dear! How queer everything is to-day! And yesterday things went on just as usual. I wonder if I've been changed during the night? Let me think: *was* I the same when I got up this morning? I almost think I can remember feeling a little different. But if I'm not the same, the next question is, who in the world am I? Ah, that's the great puzzle![110]

And when Alice tries to recite a poem she knows, "her voice sounded hoarse and strange, and the words did not come the same as they used to do."[111]

With this loss of her sense of self, Alice then proceeds to wonder if she has taken on any of the completely different identities of the other children she knows. She decides she cannot be one of them, named Ada, because, as she reasons, Ada's "hair goes in such long ringlets, and mine doesn't." Alice next wonders if she was changed to a different child, Mabel, who is much less knowledgeable than Alice is. She then tries to recall the things she normally knows by heart yet finds it all coming out in confusion: "London is the capital of Paris, and Paris is the capital of Rome, and Rome—no, *that's* all wrong, I'm certain!" As she now seems to know just as little as Mabel does, Alice concludes: "I must have been changed for Mabel!"[112] Then, in despair she resolves to stay in the hole, and she thinks that when anyone calls to her to come back up, she will "only look up and say 'Who am I, then? Tell me that first, and then, if I like being that person, I'll come up: if not, I'll stay down here till I'm somebody else.'"[113] She proceeds to cry uncontrollably, but then shrinks drastically on account of the magical effects of a fan she is holding, finding herself swimming around with a mouse in a pool of her own tears. Later, when in the White Rabbit's house, she impulsively drinks from an unlabeled bottle and grows so large she must stick one arm out the window and her foot up the chimney in order not to break the house with her growth.[114]

With this imagery in mind, let us work through Deleuze's commentaries on the scenes in the "Incipit" to his *Logic of Sense*, using Terence Blake's translation, as it captures some critical nuances in the original French. Deleuze begins by telling us that the Alice stories deal with "pure events." He writes next, "When I say 'Alice grows', I mean that she becomes bigger than she was."[115] So we have the proposition, "Alice grows." For convenience, suppose she grows from a shortened height of 10 centimeters to a great height of 10 meters. So by growing to 10 meters, she of course is larger than her size of 10 centimeters. But what Deleuze says next introduces some puzzling complexity: "But by the same token too, she becomes smaller than she is now."[116]

If Alice is becoming a larger size, under what reasoning would we conclude that she is becoming smaller than she is now? In the first place, we are supposing that she *is* a larger size in a present now moment ("she becomes smaller than she *is* now"). Even though both the "is" and the "becomes" are in the present tense, the "becomes" seems to have happened before this referenced now point. Suppose, then, that "now" refers to when she has reached her full height at 10 meters. The "becoming" would have been happening prior to that. And, during any part of that becoming, she was a size less than 10 meters. In that sense, while she was still becoming 10 meters, she *was* always becoming a size smaller than she is now. Deleuze's next lines add yet even more complexity: "Certainly, she is not bigger and smaller at the same time. But it is at the same time that she becomes both. She is bigger now; she was smaller before."[117]

Deleuze draws the following distinction in the first two lines above: Alice *is* not bigger and smaller at the same time, but Alice *becomes* bigger and smaller at the same time. Suppose she is stuck at 10 centimeters and does not grow. She is not bigger or smaller, because she admits of only one size. But suppose instead she is in the middle of a process whereby she is advancing away from 10 centimeters and toward 10 meters. We can say, then, that on the one hand she is becoming larger (than 10 centimeters), while on the other hand she is becoming smaller (that is to say, she is becoming a size that is still smaller than 10 meters; Figure 1.10).

The language is tricky here, because normally "becomes smaller" would suggest a decreasing in size. That is not how Deleuze seems to mean it here. However, for it to have the sense that he is giving it, you have to posit a larger size that she has not yet attained while she is still growing. For otherwise there is not a size of hers that she can be said to be smaller than. Deleuze continues:

Figure 1.10 Alice becoming larger and smaller simultaneously.[118]

> It is at the same time, *in the same stroke*, that one becomes bigger than one was and one is made smaller than one becomes. This is the simultaneity of a becoming whose characteristic is to elude the present.[119]

But in what sense does this becoming "elude" the present? If it is doing so, then perhaps that is because it is not determinately located within a strict now moment. The becoming would then seem to be reaching or tending beyond it somehow. That strongly suggests that it is dissimilar to Russell's at-at account of change. But how exactly are we to understanding this sort of a leaning into a future that is still yet to be (like her already being in a smallness relationship to a size of 10 meters, which she has not yet attained)?

In one of his lectures on Kant, Deleuze uses similar language when discussing the temporal structure of the present instant:

> The instant is the premonition that something set in the future [...] is in fact already here. You live an instant when, all at once, you take something to be forthcoming—that is, as eventual, probable, or certain—all while, in another way, you discover it is already here. In other words, the instant is the future's being "on this side." It is the immanence of the future.[120]

If he is thinking along similar lines here, then he may have a conception of becoming where in some way, it will always go beyond the present by being in the act of already becoming what it will become. So that suggests some sort of a dialetheic conception regarding the temporal properties of becoming; for, Alice in one sense is expressing the states she is in during some moment, while at the same time, a future state has somehow come into the immediate temporal picture as well. (So right before she is 10 meters, when her becoming is "leaning into" that future, and that future is on "this side" of the present, she is both the slightly smaller height and she is also not that size, being that she is the taller height too.)

Deleuze elaborates this conception with his notion of mad becoming, which we return to in Chapter 8 when discussing the simulacrum. Here Deleuze makes reference to Plato's *Philebus*.[121] If something is still in the process of becoming hotter (or colder), then it is not at some determinate temperature but is always hotter (or colder) than it is now; "for," as Socrates reasons in the dialogue, "once they take on a definite quantity, they would no longer be hotter and colder. The hotter and equally the colder are always in flux and never remain, while definite quantity means standstill and the end of all progression"; and thus, the hotter and colder turn "out to be unlimited."[122] In other words, if something is becoming hotter, it cannot be at just one single temperature (and thus we cannot, as with Russell's thinking, say of a warming object that at some instant of its change, it is at one determinate temperature and not at another). Rather, we would have to say of it that it is at some given temperature that it is warming up from, while also it is at some higher temperature that it is warming up to. Thus, "mad-becoming" is "a becoming always other,"[123] meaning that something is both what it is, and what is other than it, all in the same stroke or moment. In the next chapter, we will learn that a part of the "madness" of this becoming is that whatever something is becoming is undetermined and is also heterogeneous with what it was.

2

Enter the Puddingstone: Demonic Gluonics

Introduction

Gilles Deleuze and Félix Guattari characterize becoming and composition in terms of fuzzy subsets, which involve a "special logic" with regard to how items come to be included in them. We will now look at this characterization by first noting the "theological" context that Deleuze and Guattari place them in, namely, how sorcerers' pacts with demons and the "becoming-animal" that this involves characterize the heterogeneity of becoming and composition. We next analyze Deleuze's and Guattari's notion of the "consistency" of such compositions by examining the source of this concept in Eugène Dupréel's philosophy. With that in mind, we can better evaluate to what extent the logic of Deleuze's and Guattari's notion of heterogeneous composition is a fuzzy one. What we will find is that instead Graham Priest's dialetheic, "gluonic" account of composition better captures the logical properties involved in Deleuze's and Guattari's notions of consistency and becoming.

Demonic Deleuze

Running throughout Deleuze's discussions on composition (and also on time and falsity) is a "theological" dichotomy that he employs to characterize some basic principles in his philosophy of becoming.[1] On the one side is the figure of God, the principle ensuring that the world is whole and complete, that identities and essences remain distinct, that the true is discernible from the false, and that events unfold continuously, linearly, and coherently. On the other side is the Devil (or "Anti-God") along with a number of the Devil's cohorts and likenesses, including demons, sorcerers, Dionysus, and the Antichrist.[2] They are the principles ensuring that the world does not stagnate but rather is always open to radically original additions on account of deviations in identities and discontinuities of development.[3] As we will see, without this "demonic" factor, there can be no real temporality for the world, according to Deleuze.

Satan and the Sorcerer

The sorcerer's role in this is to give physical expression to the demonic forces of deviance so to bring about new compositions in the world. These demonic influences are introduced into the workings of the world by means of pacts that sorcerers make with devils.[4]

In certain Black Magic rituals, for instance, the sorcerer (Figure 2.1, top left) summons a demon (bottom left) while remaining protected in a magical Goëtic Circle (top middle). The demon is held in a magical Triangle of Solomon (top right), while the sorcerer negotiates an agreement with them. The sorcerer then obtains the demon's services in return for becoming the demon's servant after the sorcerer's death. The pact is then signed in blood by both parties (bottom middle), thereby sealing the pact and entering the sorcerer and demon into unbreakable bounds of mutual service.[5]

As Manly Hall notes, sorcerers with demonic pacts try to avoid death at all costs so to avoid their eternal, infernal servitude. They realize that "life is maintained by the aid of a mysterious universal life force which is the common property of all creatures,"

Figure 2.1 Sorcerers' demonic pacts. **Top left**: A sorcerer at work. **Top middle**: The Goëtic Circle. **Top right**: The Triangle of Solomon. **Bottom left**: The Baphomet ("pseudo-Deity," "god of falsehood," and "creator and rival of God"). **Bottom middle**: Father Urbain Grandier's pact with devils, whose signatures fill the bottom half, used against him in trial but likely a forgery. **Bottom right**: Thibault's dealing with the Wolf-Devil.[6]

and so "according to mediaeval superstition, black magicians turned themselves into werewolves and roamed the earth at night, attacking defenseless victims for the life force contained in their blood."[7] Deleuze and Guattari illustrate this "becoming-animal" of sorcerers with Alexandre Dumas's *The Wolf-Leader*.[8] It is a story of a sabot-maker, Thibault, who dwells in the woods, at the fringes of society. One fateful day Thibault saves the life of a Wolf-Devil who is being chased by a team of expert hunters, and this happens to be the one day every year he is not invincible to physical harm (Figure 2.1, bottom right). After saving the Wolf-Devil, the two make a pact, but the particulars are slightly different than the ceremonies described above. Instead of signing a compact in blood, the two must bind themselves in a more physical gesture, namely, by handshake. But since such an embrace would severely injure Thibault's hand with the Wolf-Devil's claws, they instead exchange rings. On Thibault's ring are thus inscribed the letters *T.* and *S.* for "Thibault and Satan, the family names of the two contracting parties."[9] Thibault is magically bound to the ring, as any effort to get rid of it only brings it back to him, and he is thus glued indelibly into his alliance with the Wolf-Devil. The deal they strike is that the Wolf-Devil will grant Thibault whatever malicious wish he has for his enemies. Yet, with each granted command, Thibault must give up some of his hairs to the Devil: with the first wish, one hair becomes a blazing hellfire red, the next two change as such, then four, eight, and so on. The Wolf-Devil later explains that demons cannot take hold over baptized people, so their bargains involve humans giving up parts of their body to the devils, and this is how they will take possession of Thibault.[10]

A by-product of this pact with the devil is that the wolves of the forest come to protect and obey Thibault each night. Deleuze and Guattari note that although Thibault's new hairs do make him seem like he is gaining fur and is thus coming to resemble wolves, Thibault's becoming wolf is more a matter of his entering the wolf pack and co-functioning with them, all while the wolves learn to operate in conjunction with a human by taking Thibault unconditionally as their leader and carrying out his verbal commands.[11] And together they become something neither human nor animal but rather something demonic, as seen in their final diabolical battle with the hunters.

Thus, on the one hand, becoming involves a heterogeneity where one becomes something of another sort through a transformation, while on the other hand, this includes another type of heterogeneity, namely, of composition: becoming involves bodies that are heterogeneous both within themselves and also externally with other bodies, as in social groupings. Thibault begins with his normal human body and exists in a human society, but his hair becomes a demonic "fur" all while he forms a new heterogeneous composition with the wolves and the wilds of the forest. To elaborate on this notion, Deleuze and Guattari turn to Elias Canetti's distinction between crowds and packs.[12] Packs tend to be smaller groupings of individuals, and the members' differences from one another serve to vitalize and strengthen the whole group. Crowds, however, are larger groupings where internal differences are made irrelevant, because there is a sort of equalization and homogenization partly resulting from the individual members submitting to a shared purpose.[13] Thus Thibault's wolf group remains a pack even when it transforms with a new human leader, because packs are fundamentally heterogeneous in composition. To differentiate these two distinct ways that participants relate in packs and crowds, Deleuze and Guattari employ their notions of "alliance," "illicit union," and "unnatural nuptials" in contrast to "filiation." Unities constituted by filiation could be for example families united by their blood ties, which homogenize them on account of their common descent and shared family features. In packs, however, heterogeneous members bond by means of alliances and pacts, which link them together in their coordinated functioning.[14] Moreover, packs have dynamic composition on account of the members' statuses and relations varying over time, which also thereby alters the group's characteristics.[15] As Deleuze and Guattari explain, a pack is "*continually transforming itself into a string of other multiplicities, according to its thresholds and doors.*"[16]

A point to emphasize on the deviance of becoming is that we should not be misled by the example of Thibault's becoming-wolf to think that a becoming involves a predetermined future state that the alteration is moving toward, like going from human to wolf. As Deleuze and Guattari explain, "to become is not to progress or regress along a series,"[17] because "there is no terminus from which you set out, none which you arrive at or which you ought to arrive at."[18] Rather, "what is real is the becoming itself, the block of becoming, not the supposedly fixed terms through which that which becomes passes."[19] Deleuze elaborates by noting that "the question 'What are you becoming?' is particularly stupid. For as someone becomes, what he is becoming changes as much as he does himself."[20] Becoming, then, is more basically a "becoming-other," without that otherness being determinately established even in that movement of change itself:

> Becoming can and should be qualified as becoming-animal even in the absence of a term that would be the animal become. The becoming-animal of the human being is real, even if the animal the human being becomes is not; and the becoming-other of the animal is real, even if that something other it becomes is not.[21]

In other words, becoming operates under such a profound and pure deviance that it is a fundamental corruption or disruption without aims or ends, because what one becomes is "unforeseen and nonpreexistent."[22] As such, it is neither progression nor regression, neither an evolution nor a devolution, but is rather what Deleuze and Guattari call an "involution": "Becoming is involutionary, involution is creative. [...] To involve is to form a block that runs its own line 'between' the terms in play and beneath assignable relations."[23]

We see a similar notion of the non-predeterminability of becoming in Bergson's notion of the possible. In "The Possible and the Real," Bergson elaborates on his notion of "the continuous creation of unforeseeable novelty," and he characterizes possibility in terms of an "unforeseeable nothing which changes everything."[24] Remarkably, for Bergson, the possible first comes to be only in its actualization. For example, prior to *Hamlet* being written, it had not yet existed in anyone's mind. Only after it was composed can we retroactively look back in history and say it could have been written at an earlier time, had only someone thought of it then.[25] Thus, when asked by a newspaper reporter what he thinks the next great work of drama will be like, he replied, "If I knew what was to be the great dramatic work of the future, I should be writing it."[26] The world unfolds unforeseeably because we cannot even now guess what will be created in the world later, and becoming is originating in the sense that what it creates can have no origin outside or beyond its present act of being created.

To conclude this section, we should clarify that not all of Deleuze's writings and talks on theological matters involve a strict God/Devil distinction with a preference for the demonic. In *Difference and Repetition*, he mixes the two principles by saying that "God makes the world by calculating, but his calculations never work out exactly, and this inexactitude or injustice in the result, this irreducible inequality, forms the condition of the world."[27] In other words, a "deviant" element is already built into this conception of God. Elsewhere Deleuze claims that when he is asked if he believes in God, he emphatically replies, "yes!" although it is more specifically a Spinozistic conception of God.[28] So we should be careful not to take Deleuze's emphasis on the demonic and occult too literally and conclude that he is sacrilegious or satanic. Nonetheless, we need to come to terms with these elements in his thinking, because they factor in prominently in his accounts of falsity and becoming in particular. And as we will see later in Chapter 8, the work of the Devil and sorcerer as falsifiers is not an injurious or negligent deception of others in the sense of maintaining a true reality concealed behind a false appearance; rather, it is a matter of creating the New by means of a particular way of combining the imaginary and the real through artistic means. Moreover, this is bound up with Deleuze's revolutionary politics of creating a people to come. Thus, Deleuze's use of the figure of the Devil is not an advocacy for unethical behavior, although it could involve breaking norms, conventions, or rules that might hinder valuable or needed creations.

Watch and the Puddingstone: Dupréel's Consistency

This heterogeneous bonding into packs by means of pacts is a notion that Deleuze bases in Belgian philosopher Eugène Dupréel's concepts of "consistency," "consolidation," "concretion," and "coalescence" on the one hand, along with "interval," "intercalation," and "precariousness" on the other,[29] but with some slight modification in emphasis, as we will see. Dupréel defines the "consistency" of a being as its capacity to maintain its identity throughout the variations that result from its interactive relations with other beings, although things' consistencies also can vary somewhat as they undergo a degree of transformation.[30] Oftentimes, Dupréel notes, things become more homogeneous as they build consistency on account of similar items having shared powers of acting and being acted upon, which under certain influences can filter away dissimilar beings with other powers of affection. For instance, Dupréel has us consider a mass of sand, gravel, and large stones under the shared influence of wind. The sand will blow far away in the same direction and may all deposit in the same depression, while the gravel will move only slightly away, and the large stones will remain in place, thereby creating three distinct bodies of "similars."[31] This homogenizing process tends toward creating "solids" where the consistencies and individualities of the constituent parts give way to the consistency and unity of the whole agglomerated unit, as the parts assimilate and bond together.[32]

In biological beings, however, many heterogeneous parts can come to operate together so to increase the consistency of the whole creature yet without thereby causing the parts to lose their own consistencies and individualities. So, the parts of living beings cohere despite operating distinctly and uniquely, and like with Canetti's packs, the whole group of parts benefits from that internal diversity.[33] Consistency, then, does not always require homogeneity, and, in fact, the beings with the highest degree of consistency are biological creatures, on account of how their internal differentiation enables them to self-repair and adapt to adverse influences.[34]

In Dupréel's philosophy, consistencies are formed by means of the process of "consolidation," which occurs when an arrangement is transferred from an exterior support into the interior of the consolidate such that it comes to sustain that arrangement independently.[35] For instance, a laborer making a crate will hold the wooden slats in their proper place first with their hand and then secondly nail them together, thereby consolidating the parts into a completed box that sustains this structural arrangement. Here the exterior support system from the laborer's hand is transferred into the crate's own structure as it consolidates.[36] Such consolidations or "crystallizations"[37] of spatially related parts (*consolidés de coexistence*) are formed naturally as well. Dupréel illustrates this with the formation of puddingstone.

Here pieces of flint are fixed in place within binding materials by the soil and gravity (Figure 2.2, left). As the binding matrix material solidifies, a solid rock is formed which no longer relies on the exterior supporting factors to maintain the compositional arrangement of the pebbles now set in the stone (Figure 2.2, middle). The result is a conglomerate with pebbles of varying forms and tones bound by a grayish cement (Figure 2.2, right),[38] a fusing of heterogeneity.

There are also consolidations of successive processes (*consolidés de succession*). For instance, the parts of a watch are assembled by the watchmaker, spatially consolidating it, but then its movements are synchronized with the turning of the world, making it also a consolidation of succession.[39] To illustrate, Dupréel has us think about the characters in Jules Verne's *From the Earth to the Moon*. Even if while on their journey the earth stops spinning or changes speed, still their watches will maintain a synchronization with the earth's former motion.[40] Lifeforms, with their heterogeneous compositions of disparate organs and complex rhythms of biological processes, are natural instances of such spatial and temporal consolidations.[41] Thus we see that consistency is not a matter of homogeneity among physical parts and self-sameness over time. In fact, Dupréel

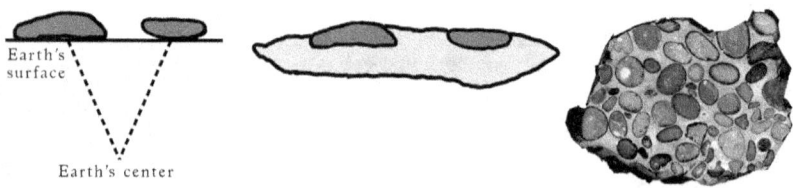

Figure 2.2 Puddingstone formation. **Left and middle**: Puddingstone consolidation.[42] **Right**: A puddingstone slice (© East Herts Geology Club. Photo by Jane Tubb, used with permission).

says that when we might think there to be such a thing, its seeming self-sameness is really just a matter of it being comparatively less self-variable than its surroundings.[43] This can also involve an independence from exterior influences. Inanimate things are often highly subject to the changes around them. For instance, they warm up or cool down in direct sympathy with the air around them, and they never self-repair any damage that is done to them. Animals, however, are more resistant to such exterior variable influences. They may for instance maintain their own narrow range of body temperature even as exterior temperatures rise or fall substantially, and when injured, their bodies can often heal and regenerate to a remarkable extent.[44]

Dupréel also explains the role of the "interval" interposed between the parts in consolidations. It is on account of these gaps that there can be heterogeneity among the bound parts, and it also introduces a factor of indeterminacy to the compositions. For instance, with the puddingstone, pebbles that are very close to one another have a higher probability of conglomerating together than do pebbles set apart by a large, intervening spatial interval.[45] Dupréel lists three sorts of conditions that influence whether or not parts will consolidate: {1} there could be unfavorable conditions, like a torrent of water moving the two pebbles very far apart from each other; {2} there could be indifferent conditions, like a light breeze brushing against the pebbles without moving them; and {3} there could be favorable conditions, like an influx of sand that fixes the pebbles in their place.[46]

Dupréel gives the name "precariousness" (*précarité*) for this feature of the intervals that introduces the potential for the parts to *not* coalesce.[47] And he elaborates this notion with an analysis of causal relations. He says that if cause and effect were simultaneous and in the exact same location, there would be no basis to distinguish them. Rather, there must always be both a spatial and temporal interval between the two, a discontinuity, which then makes their connection be precarious.[48] So the cause may influence what goes on in the intervening, "intercalary" (*intercalaire*) period; and what goes on in this intercalary period may have influence on what results after it; nonetheless, the cause will never directly and immediately relate to the effect.[49] As Dupréel notes, logicians would thus say that the causality here would not be an entirely *transitive* relation.[50] And so during that interval between cause and effect, there will be many other intervening factors that can make the effectuated outcome more or less probable. Dupréel illustrates this with the following example. A careless smoker in a forest tosses a lit cigarette to the ground. Will the result be a forest fire? That all depends on what transpires in the intercalary period, where variables such as the wind speed and the dryness of the vegetation will factor in strongly to what effect comes from this event of dropping a lit cigarette in the woods.[51]

Given the logical nature of causality, Dupréel also calls this intercalation between the heterogeneous cause and effect a "logical distance," which increases with the number of intervening factors that make the effect less probable.[52] What will be important for Deleuze and Guattari with this sort of a "logical distance" is that the greater the interval (i.e., the more that conditions would make it improbable for things or events to consolidate), the more heterogeneity there will be between them. Very "logically" distant parts are ones that are not inherently apt to be adhered together. And so there is a sort of tension between them, an incompatibility of sorts, despite the consistency they obtain by consolidating. This would be the opposite of what we saw with Dupréel's sand, gravel, and stones example of *solidification*. All the sand particles are inherently apt to coalesce, and the different properties of the gravel pieces make them be inclined to separate from the sand grains, when the wind blows upon both of them. However, under certain geological conditions of conglomerate formation, both the sand and stones could possibly fuse into a puddingstone, whereby that inherent aptness to separate is overpowered by a stronger force of binding.

For Dupréel, what demands more philosophical attention with regard to consistency is not so much the identical elements shared by various consolidated parts, which may be thought of as serving as "bridges" between them; rather, he insists, we should be more attentive to the gulf that any such "bridge" is apparently crossing over.[53] And we should lastly note that for Dupréel, there are many sorts of relations that could fuse parts into a consolidation. For instance, what gives consistency to all of the cards in a card game is not some physical material like cement binding pebbles. It rather has more to do with factors such as the significance that the figures drawn on them have with respect to the rules of that particular game and also the pleasure the players obtain in playing the game, which is what makes the cards continue to be distributed, recombined, and shuffled all together.[54] Even something like a song obtains a consistency through a sort of social memory. The song's composition may be originally stored on the music sheets and in the original performances, but it becomes learned by many others, who then replay it, thereby *culturally* consolidating the song. Even if the music sheets are destroyed and the original performers' instruments are broken, the song can still maintain its consistency, as it continues to be performed by those who learned it.[55] We note this example especially because the sorts of heterogeneous compositions that Deleuze and Guattari often have in mind are ones involving social organization.

Fuzzing the Stone: Consistency in Deleuze and Guattari

Let us look briefly now at how Deleuze and Guattari implement Dupréel's notions of consistency, consolidation, and interval in their account of heterogeneous composition. They define consistency more in a geological than a logical sense,[56] writing that consistency is "the 'holding together' of heterogeneous elements."[57] Like Dupréel, then, what concerns them mostly with consistency is the adhering of relatively incompatible parts. Furthermore, Deleuze and Guattari emphasize—as we saw Dupréel do as well—that in order for there to be such a consolidation in the first place, there needs to be an interval between the components (otherwise there are no distinct parts that might fuse in the first place). They see the consolidation primarily as a *process* that happens during those intervals when connections and groupings are made spontaneously and non-deterministically. "Consolidation," they write, "is not content to come after; it is creative."[58] To build from Dupréel's example of the consolidating song, we could note that the singers who learn the melody might add their own accentuations and colorings, as often happens with folk music that spreads across diverse cultural geographies. These re-characterizing details are not in the original music sheets.

Deleuze and Guattari give a similar example with bird songs. The chaffinch bird's songs have a particular sub-structuring that conditions particular traits for every time they sing them. This "'innate information' about how the specific song ought to sound" is called the "sub-song" by W. H. Thorpe, one of Deleuze and Guattari's sources.[59] Thorpe details experiments which show that "there is an inborn basis to the song but that it is extremely generalised."[60] For instance, the chaffinch's sub-song has three distinct phases.[61] "But," Deleuze and Guattari note, "the organization into three stanzas, the order of the stanzas, the details and the ornament, are not pregiven; it is precisely the articulations from within that are missing, the *intervals*, the *intercalary notes*, everything making for motif and counterpoint."[62] Here we see that there is "an arrangement of intervals, a distribution of inequalities, such that it is sometimes necessary to make a hole in order to consolidate."[63] In other words, the substructure of the song has far more intercalary opportunities for deviation and creative composition than it has prescribed limitations, and by filling in these intervals creatively, the parts of the song can consolidate into something with consistency. As Dupréel writes, "There is growth only by intercalation."[64]

It is on the basis of this great creative freedom of the intercalations that Deleuze and Guattari appeal to the notion of "fuzzy subsets" to characterize these manners of grouping, which they say form "fuzzy aggregates." This can be something like the substructure of the chaffinch birdsong, where the parts are very loosely associated so that they can be rearranged, added to, and subtracted from spontaneously and non-deterministically:[65] "These are the elements of a [...] fuzzy aggregate; but they become consolidated, take on consistency"[66] whenever the bird creatively chooses the variations that arrange both the given and added elements to the song. It would seem also that a fuzzy aggregate could then be the resulting conglomeration, insofar as it is also in some way composed largely of such intervals, making it highly susceptible to rearrangement, addition, and subtraction, as with the metamorphosing folk song we mentioned.[67]

This loose structuring of the fuzzy aggregate is also like that of the "pact," which we saw in cases of sorcery and becoming-animal; for, the pack that is formed is constantly rearranging its order and incorporating heterogeneous elements, like the wolf-pack taking Thibault as their leader. Deleuze and Guattari have us consider another songbird, the stagemaker, which they call "the magical bird or the bird of the opera."[68] During its mating season, it arranges leaves gathered from different trees in the forest to construct a "stage" above which it puts on a performance, using the intercalary opportunities of the song structure to incorporate musical components from other birds' songs.[69]

> He sings perched on his singing stick, a vine or branch located just above the display ground he has prepared by marking it with cut leaves turned upside down to contrast with the color of the earth. As he sings, he uncovers the yellow root of certain feathers underneath his beak: he makes himself visible at the same time as sonorous. His song forms a varied and complex motif interweaving his own notes and those of other birds that he imitates in the intervals. This produces a consolidation that "consists" in species-specific sounds, sounds of other species, leaf hue, throat color.[70]

As A. J. Marshall, their source, writes: "The notes of other birds are so woven into the display-song that […] the observer […] has no clear idea which notes are 'borrowed' and which are part of the caller's own varied repertoire."[71] Thus we can see just how much fuzzy aggregates for Deleuze and Guattari are a "synthesis of disparate elements" of many different kinds (in the case of the stagemaker's performance, it is not just notes, but colors and shapes too).[72]

But what *precisely* do Deleuze and Guattari mean by "fuzzy" here? In another place, they also refer us to fuzzy logic, which is built from fuzzy set theory.[73] Let us now examine fuzzy subsets and fuzzy logic, in order to determine whether or not we can understand Deleuze's logic as being of a "fuzzy" kind.

Logic of Fuzz

One notable application of fuzzy sets and logic is with vague predicates, as we saw with "sorites" paradoxes involving continuous changes, like growing from child to adult. To get an initial grasp of a fuzzy set, consider Nolt's illustration of the predicate "red": "Some things are wholly and genuinely red. But others are almost red, somewhat red, only a little bit red, and so on. So, whereas fresh blood or a red traffic light might be *fully a member* of the set of all red things, the setting sun might be, say, *halfway a member* and a peach only *slightly a member*."[74] In the case of the maturing child, at what precise moment in their lives does the person leave the set of children and enter the set of adults? Perhaps there is a period when they are partly in one group and partly in the other. L. A. Zadeh, a pioneer of fuzzy subsets, defines them as "classes with unsharp boundaries in which the transition from membership to non-membership is gradual rather than abrupt."[75] To clarify why this is unique, Arnold Kaufmann notes that under classical assumptions regarding sets, "there are only two acceptable situations for an element: being a member of or not being a member of a subset […] of a reference set"; however, an element in a fuzzy subset is "a member […] only in an uncertain fashion."[76] More precisely, the membership to a fuzzy subset is "weighted," meaning that it belongs more or less to it, and not, as under classical assumptions, entirely to it or entirely not to it.[77]

Let us look a little more at how all this works. Suppose we have a set with these items: *stop light, sunset, peach, banana*. And we consider a subset of it, namely, of red things. We will ask this question for each member of the main set: is the thing also a member of the subset of red things? If yes, we write 1, and if no, we write 0.

{1} Are stop lights red things? Yes: 1
{2} Are sunsets red things? Yes: 1
{3} Are peaches red things? No: 0
{4} Are bananas red things? No: 0

This distribution may be satisfactory in certain contexts, but in others it may not be. (For instance, a painter who is depicting a peach may want to use some red to color it, even if in the end it is not apparently a red object.) Instead, we may assign values *between* 0 and 1 inclusively, which can be understood as something like percentages or degrees of membership.

{1} Are stop lights red things? Entirely so: 1
{2} Are sunsets red things? Mostly so: 0.7
{3} Are peaches red things? Partly so: 0.3
{4} Are bananas red things? Not at all: 0

This is something like fuzzy subsets, which admit of partial membership.[78] Fuzzy logic uses such values to represent *degrees of truth*.[79] So, "a sunset is red" could have the truth-value 0.7 (being about 70 percent true, you might say.) Truth-values for formulas built up using operators—like negation and conjunction—can be calculated in ways that reflect how we think the operator should work. For instance, we might normally think that negation will "flip" the value from true to false (1 to 0) and vice versa. In fuzzy logic, the negation of a proposition will, in a similar respect, have a truth-value that is the remainder of the proposition's value subtracted from 1. So "a sunset is not red" is 0.3 true (being that it is mostly but not entirely untrue), and "a peach is not red" is 0.7 true (being that it is mostly but not entirely true.)[80]

With this in mind, let us see how fuzzy subsets and fuzzy logic function in Deleuze's and Guattari's thinking. Heterogeneous compositions are consolidations of "fuzzy aggregates." In the example of the chaffinch's song, there are open places where one of a number of notes can be inserted, for instance. Perhaps these optional notes have a "fuzzy" membership in the song aggregate in the sense that their inclusion is partial, meaning that they can be placed into the song or excluded from it, whereas the substructural elements are fully included. Let us consider another example of a fuzzy aggregate, the wolf pack that Thibault is a member of. At the end of the story, he seemingly is returned from his animal status, perhaps regaining his human form before dying (thereby saving him from damnation).[81] It could perhaps be that the pack is "fuzzy" in the sense that certain members, like Thibault, can enter and leave, especially considering that as sorcerers they dwell at the periphery to begin with. In either case, it seems that an important element in Deleuze's and Guattari's thinking on this notion of the fuzziness of aggregates is that there is a sort of flexibility in the membership and with the binding relations between members.

So is fuzzy logic a good candidate for understanding Deleuze's logic? There is strong reason to think it is not. {1} Regarding fuzzy logic itself, Deleuze and Guattari do not see it as a useful way for conducting philosophical thinking. They say that by assigning fuzzy values to propositions with vague predicates, we are still giving them determinate values from a non-fuzzy "reference" set.[82] They would prefer to understand the fuzziness of a concept not as being that it simply "lacks an outline" but rather that "it is vagabond, nondiscursive, moving about."[83] As we noted above in the examples, the "fuzziness" of aggregates seems to be more of a general flexibility in the membership rather than a determinate membership value. So fuzzy logic and fuzzy set theory do not seem to model the sort of freedom to alter that they think fuzzy aggregates' compositions happen to have. {2} Deleuze and Guattari suggest that there is another logic, other than fuzzy logic, that should be used to understand the membership of parts in fuzzy aggregates. They say that the real definition of a fuzzy subset (as opposed to its nominal definition) "can come only at the level of processes affecting the fuzzy set; a set is fuzzy if its elements belong to it only by virtue of specific operations of consistency and consolidation, which themselves follow a *special logic*."[84] This special logic would need to account for "what holds heterogeneities together without their ceasing to be heterogeneous."[85] They do not specify what this special logic is, but we will soon consider the possibility that it is a dialetheic logic, as seen in Priest's notion of the "gluon" that binds parts into a whole. And {3} in all other cases where Deleuze is discussing truth and falsity, he does not seem to conceptualize them in terms of having partial values. (Consider for instance how Deleuze does not say of Alice that in the middle of her growth, it is half true that she is small.) If Deleuze's logic really were fuzzy, given his familiarity with fuzzy logic, he had the terminological resources to formulate it as such. Or in the very least, he could have articulated his thinking in a way that would lend itself to such a fuzzy interpretation, which he does not apparently do.

So what instead might be the logic of heterogeneous composition and becoming? The intercalary elements that make the bonds precarious suggest that there is a factor that makes the parts not apt to combine or stay bonded, despite the fact that they do at some moment. And there is a sort of tension and otherness between heterogeneous parts of a composition or of the different phases in a becoming. For instance, there is an incompatibility between Thibault's red demonic/animal hairs and the rest of his human body, all while there is a tension between his self as a sabot-maker in the beginning phase and his self as a sorcerer in the phase coming later on. So we might say in heterogeneous compositions and becomings that the parts are "geologically" adherent (like the pebbles in the puddingstone) without being logically coherent, in that the predicates of the parts may be contradictory. (Thibault's hair is non-human and his body is human.) Deleuze and Guattari have an example that we will return to in the next section, namely, Baked Alaska.[86] It has ice cream in the middle and meringue on the outside. It is baked under high temperatures for a short period of time to caramelize the meringue. During that cooking process, it has both a very hot outer part and a very cold inner part. The temperature difference between these parts, which meet somewhere in the cake, creates a sort of "logical" tension, you might say, in this heterogeneous composition, in that the Baked Alaska, when in the oven, is both freezing cold and burning hot at the same time. And think also of a metamorphic process where there is some sort of a unity in the phases, even though there also is a profound difference between them, like the child becoming an adult. (Recall Bergson's formulation, "There is becoming from the child to the man,"[87] where he regarded "becoming" as the subject, which could then mean it is predicated as being both child and not-child, insofar as it is becoming adult.) So we now ask: what are the logical properties of such a fusion of heterogeneity, and which logical system is most conducive to that conception? To answer these questions, we turn now to Priest's study of unity and his dialetheic notions of the gluon and non-transitive identity.

Gluing Difference

The context for Priest's "gluonic" theory of composition is the problem of giving a consistent and precise account for unity, because any attempt to do so raises a number of difficult paradoxes. We have parts, and we have the whole that they compose. What we seek then is "something that binds the parts into a whole."[88] Yet, we quickly find that this "problem of binding" is not easily solved. Priest calls this binding factor the "gluon," which belongs to the unified thing. Now, since we can refer to it, it is a thing in its own right. But in being a thing all of its own, is the gluon (the cohering factor) also a part of the whole in the same way the other parts are? For instance, in a house, is the gluon simply like the mortar that binds the bricks together and helps give the building its structure? If it were, then it would no longer serve to explain the unification of the other parts. For, we now need to explain what binds that gluon itself with the other parts.[89] In the house example, if the gluon is simply the mortar between the bricks, we still need to find another gluon in between the mortar and the bricks to explain what binds them, and were it always to be another object part, then we never will arrive upon the ultimate binding factor.[90] So the gluon is both an object and not an object; it thus can be conceived as a dialetheic entity.[91] And it does not help, Priest argues, to simply think of the gluon as a "*relationship* between the parts" that accounts for the thing's "configuration, arrangement, structure, or some such."[92] For, in instances of physical objects, we now have the even greater metaphysical problem of explaining how something non-physical (the relationship) can bind physical things together.[93]

To solve these and related difficulties in accounting for how parts bind into wholes, Priest proposes that we apply a dialetheic logic to the notion of the gluon and that we modify the logical properties of identity. Classically, identity has three properties when it is understood as a relation. {1} *Reflexivity*. Something is identical to itself, so $a = a$. {2} *Symmetry*. If something is identical to a second thing, then the second is identical to the first: if $a = b$, then $b = a$. And {3} *transitivity*. If a first thing is identical to a second thing, and that second thing is identical to a third, then the first is identical to the third as well; so if $a = b$ and $b = c$, then $a = c$.[94] But Priest's conception of gluons will make use of a sort of identity that instead is *non-transitive*.

So let us see informally how the gluon works. Suppose we name a unified object's parts with the letters a, b, c, and d. And in his diagram, Priest symbolizes the gluon with 中 (the character for *zhong* in Chinese and *chu* in Japanese, meaning "center," as Priest explains).[95] It is what binds all the other parts into the unified whole. If the gluon were entirely distinct from the other parts (in the sense of not being identical to them), there would always be room for another gluon to intervene between the first gluon and the given parts, which leads to the sort of regress we saw before. So in order to close "the metaphysical 'gap' that otherwise would stand between the gluon and the parts," we need to make the gluon be identical to them, and thus "there will then be no space, or need, for anything to be inserted."[96]

Yet, although the gluon is identical with all of the parts, it is non-transitively so. We can depict it by having all of the parts equal the gluon, but none of the parts equaling one another (Figure 2.3).

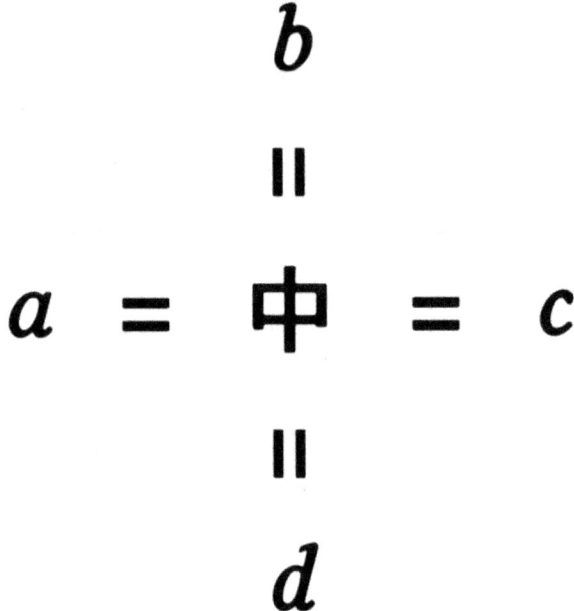

Figure 2.3 Priest's diagram for the gluonic structure. The gluon, symbolized as 中, is non-transitively identical with all the other parts, *a*, *b*, *c*, and *d*, but they are not equal to one another.[97]

Priest then gives an analogy to explain why the identity here is not transitive. We think of how the mortar binds the bricks without making them one singular, solid brick. Similarly, the gluon binds the parts by being identical to them, without making those parts be identical with each other.[98] (So *brick 1* = the gluon, and *brick 2* = the gluon, but *brick 1* is not thereby identical to *brick 2*. They maintain their heterogeneity and Dupréelian "logical distance," so to speak. In other words, the logic of the gluon, being that of non-transitive identity, makes it such that parts can cohere without thereby reducing any part to the other or homogenizing the heterogeneous parts in any way.)

To understand how this is a dialetheic conception, we need to think of identity in terms of the logical operation of material equivalence (symbolized with $\equiv$). When two propositions are materially equivalent (for instance, $A \equiv C$), then they have the same truth-value. So let us first suppose a classical situation (corresponding to the monoletheist view as we are defining it here, namely, as the belief that propositions must be at least true or false but not both). We will draw a circle for a domain of true propositions, and another circle for a domain of false ones.

Beginning with a classical, monoletheic logic, we will say that *A*, *B*, and *C* are in the true domain, and *D* is in the false one (Figure 2.4, left). We can now calculate where the materially equivalent formulations will be located on that basis. If two propositions

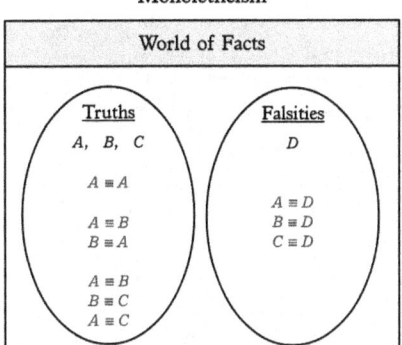
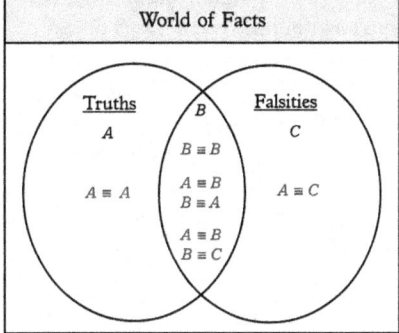

Figure 2.4 Material equivalence in a monoletheic (classical) and a dialetheic logic, showing the second to be intransitive ("$A \equiv B$" is at least true, "$B \equiv C$" is at least true, but "$A \equiv C$" is not at all true).[99]

share the same domain (being both true or both false), then their material equivalence will be in the true domain. And if they are found in different domains (with one being true and the other false), then their material equivalence will be in the false domain. Now since A is in the true domain, we can firstly say that $A \equiv A$ is also in the true domain. As this will always be the case for any proposition, we see that material equivalence in classical logic is *reflexive*. And since A and B are both in the true domain, we can say that $A \equiv B$ along with $B \equiv A$ are both in the true domain. And so it is *symmetric* too. And finally, since A, B, and C are all in the true domain, we then also have $A \equiv B$, $B \equiv C$, and $A \equiv C$. Material equivalence in classical logic is thus *transitive*. But let us now consider dialetheic logical assumptions, under which we can have propositions that are both true and false. We will overlap our truth and falsity domains for this double status, and let us say that A is just true, C is just false, but B is both true and false (Figure 2.4, right). As we can see, even in the "both" domain, identity and symmetry hold. Yet, we notice here a case where transitivity does not hold. $A \equiv B$ is at least true (it is still found in the true domain, even though it is also in the false), and $B \equiv C$ is also at least true, but $A \equiv C$ is not at all true. So under dialetheic assumptions, material equivalence is not transitive.

Priest next gives a standard, Leibnizian definition of identity. The basic idea is that if two things have exactly the same properties (neither more nor less than the other), then there is no difference between them, and they are identical or equal. In symbols, Priest formulates it as[100]

$a = b$ if and only if $\forall X(Xa \equiv Xb)$

Let us consider a simplified explanation of it. On the left side we have "$a = b$." So we are determining what is needed for an object a to be equal or identical to an object b. On the right side is some symbology that is more complicated than we have dealt with before, because now we are using a predicate logic; and it is even more difficult, since it is of a higher order. Suppose we are dealing with the predicate "hot," and let us symbolize it with H. If object a is hot, we can write that as Ha.[101] But in our formula, we have the variable letter X, in Xa for instance. What this means is that we are thinking of predicates very generally in terms of variables. It can be some unspecified predicate that you want to say an object a or b could have. The "$\forall X$" means something like "for all predicates ...."[102] So, the right side—where it is written $\forall X(Xa \equiv Xb)$—indicates that all the predicates that object a has, b has too, and all the predicates that b has, a has too. And this also then means that object a will not have any predicates lacking in b, and b will not have any predicates lacking in a. So we are supposing that a and b have each and every predicate that the other has. If that is the case, then a and b are identical or equal; and likewise, if they are equal, that means they have exactly the same properties.

To see how all this relates to the dialetheism of the gluon, let us work through an illustration. We will only consider one predicate, "hot," written H. And our object in question will be the Baked Alaska. It has three parts: {1} part a is the burning meringue on the outside, {2} part b is the freezing ice cream on the inside, and {3} part g is the gluon, being the binding factor that unites the parts into one object. As we saw in our diagram in Figure 2.3, part a equals the gluon g, and part b equals the gluon g, but thereby part a and part b are not equal to one another, as identity and equivalence are not transitive under our dialetheic assumptions. That means gluon g binds the parts a and b together into the Baked Alaska, but it does not thereby homogenize either one with the other. Now, regarding our predicate "hot," we know that the burning meringue is hot, so again we write Ha (the meringue is hot). And, since $a = g$, that also means the gluon is hot, so Hg. (Our Leibnizian definition of identity says that each and every property of the one will be held by the other.) The freezing ice cream is not hot, so $\neg Hb$. Yet, b, too, equals g, so the gluon is also not hot, or $\neg Hg$. That means the gluon of the Baked Alaska, its binding principle that gives it its "consistency," is both hot and not hot ($Hg \wedge \neg Hg$). So before when we said that the Baked Alaska is both hot and not hot at the same time, that was a misleading formulation. Someone could have objected to this characterization by saying: it is not that the Baked Alaska is both hot and not hot; rather, one part is hot, another part is not hot, but no part is both hot and not hot at the same time. As we can see now, however, under Priest's dialetheic gluonics, *there is a part of the Baked Alaska that is both hot and not hot, namely, its gluon or "consistency."*

So, we can grasp then how a dialetheic logic may be used to understand the gluing or consistency factor that binds together heterogeneous components into a consolidate or "fuzzy aggregate," namely, each disparate part can be seen as being non-transitively identical to this binding factor (the gluonic component) without thereby compromising the heterogeneity of the parts in any way.[103]

Now, what about Deleuze and Guattari's claim that there is a "special logic" for the inclusion of parts in fuzzy aggregates that is not a fuzzy logic? Recall the example of the chaffinch's song. Suppose there is a note that the bird may or may not include during one of the open parts of the song. Here the "fuzziness" of that inclusion is the fact that it could be added into the final performance or instead it might not be; so the note is not 100 percent a member, but something less than that, Deleuze and

Guattari seem to be saying. In other words, this partial membership is what allows the virtual note to be an optional inclusion in the actualization of the song. Their complaint was that we should not assign its degree of membership some determinate value (or determinate range of values). But if we use a dialetheic sort of reasoning, we might say that it is both included and not included, and by doing so, we are not specifying how much. It is still not entirely clear, however, how this sort of a dialetheic conception would apply to Deleuze and Guattari's fuzzy aggregates. Recall that the "special logic" of fuzzy inclusion is one that operates "at the level of processes affecting the fuzzy set."[104] So, part of their reason for ultimately rejecting fuzzy set theory is that there is a dynamic element in the inclusion process which is not expressed adequately by partial, determinate values. It seems the parts need some sort of indeterminate freedom to enter and leave the aggregate, to be more or less a part of it, at different times. The dialetheic conception that we used for change and becoming, then, could be useful for characterizing this dynamic element, because insofar as a part is entering or leaving an aggregate, in that process, it is both included and not included at the same time.

But even if this is not what Deleuze and Guattari have in mind for the "special logic" of fuzzy aggregate inclusion, we can still see the usefulness of Priest's gluonics for understanding the other aspects of the logic of heterogeneous composition and consistency. Let us continue this analysis to see how it can further elaborate Deleuze's concept of heterogeneous becoming and the loss of the proper name that is involved in it.

Who's Alice Now?

Of course all life is a process of breaking down.
F. Scott Fitzgerald[105]

What we have been saying about gluonic composition works as well for a "temporal" composition, where you have different temporal parts that are bound together, like the phases in a process. These temporal parts can also be seen as being bound by a dialetheic gluon, and this will account for the consistency of a thing that changes properties over time and could even change its identity, all while remaining bound together temporally. Suppose Alice begins small and grows large. Regarding her beginning state, let us just write Sa for "Alice is small." At the end, she is not small anymore, so we have $\neg Sa$. Of course, as Deleuze reminds us, Alice is not smaller and larger at the same time. But because the becoming binds successive moments together, in a sense the *becoming* involves smaller and larger sizes, as Bergson explained. Suppose we think of that becoming, which binds the phases together, as a temporal gluon.[106] That means this gluon is both smaller and larger, and it binds together two versions of Alice.

The next matter we should address is Deleuze's claim that Alice loses her identity and her proper name. This is a little perplexing because Deleuze's conception here seems to undo itself. On the one hand, we think of it being Alice who has grown to the larger size, but on the other hand, we are saying that this is not Alice who has grown to the larger size (because in doing so she has lost her personal identity). In fact, this is exactly what Alice herself expresses in the story. She does not know who she is anymore, and she considers other identities and proper names, settling on another girl she knows, Mabel. Deleuze here is discussing the "paradox of pure becoming," so of course we should expect it to involve a paradoxical conceptualization such as this.

Yet, using Priest's dialetheic notion the gluon, here in a temporal sense, we might be able to further elaborate on Deleuze's claim in order to shed more light on this paradoxical composition. According to the Leibnizian definition of identity, if two things have even one difference between their predicates, they are not identical. After Alice has grown, she has lost her smallness and gained largeness. So, her larger self is not identical with her smaller version, and it might not therefore take the same proper name "Alice," which should only designate one entity. However, the temporal gluonic factor that binds the phases of her process of changing into one movement of becoming-larger could perhaps be seen as both the becoming of the person named "Alice" while also *not* being the becoming of that person.[107] For, the temporal gluon is identical to the first version, and it is identical to the second version, even though these two versions are not identical with each other. This could be a way to make logical sense of how for Deleuze, in this becoming-larger there is "Alice" while also there is not "Alice."

Something else we might consider is how in a dialetheic logic, the Principle of Identity holds (it will always be *at least true* that $a = a$); and yet, also under dialetheic reasoning, there can be cases where $a = a$, along with being true, *is also false* (see Figure 1.3, right). For instance, Priest notes, when some object a is undergoing a sort of metamorphosis where its identity is altering, at that moment of change, $a = a$ will be both true and false.[108] This conception might capture something of what Deleuze has in mind with his claim that in Alice's becoming-larger "the names of pause and rest are carried away by verbs of pure becoming and slide into the language of events," thereby destroying "the assignation of fixed identities."[109] Yet, this is an issue we will need to leave for the third volume when we focus on the logic in Deleuze's philosophy of language. For now, let us look further into how Deleuze thinks heterogeneity plays a role in thinking.

3

Sorcerous Conceptions: Deleuze's Philosophy of Thinking

Introduction

Gilles Deleuze's notion of philosophical thinking is bound up with his concept of consistency. First we examine Deleuze's transdisciplinary and neurobiological notions of philosophical thinking. We next look at what constitutes a philosophical concept for Deleuze and Félix Guattari, in terms of its heterogeneous "endoconsistency and exoconsistency." Lastly, we evaluate the extent to which this can be understood as a dialetheic conception.

Philosophy from Death to Creation

There is more that can be said to elaborate on the role that heterogeneity plays in Deleuze's portrayal of philosophical thinking. His comments regarding transdisciplinary studies and the neurobiology of cognition shed light on the "distances" or "intervals" that are involved in the components and processes of thinking. The following material is a bit "lighter" than the other issues we have been wrestling with, and our treatment here might seem a bit superficial, given that we will not criticize or analyze Deleuze's claims too extensively. For instance, we will not scrutinize the scientific merits of his statements regarding neurobiology. Our purpose here is simply to take stock of the other ways that Deleuze finds the heterogeneity in thinking to involve a sort of differential tension, about which we have been noticing a potential "dialetheic" element in its conception.

To build toward Deleuze's transdisciplinary notion of philosophical thinking, let us begin with a fairly recent controversy over the value of philosophy and the humanities. At a conference in 2011, Stephen Hawking, echoing part of his co-authored book *The Grand Design*, announced to the world that "philosophy is dead."[1] His reasoning: it no longer serves its purpose of contributing to human knowledge, a job that physics has proven much more adequate at providing. As Hawking and Mlodinow write:

How can we understand the world in which we find ourselves? ... What is the nature of reality? Where did all of this come from? ... Traditionally these are questions for philosophy, but philosophy is dead. Philosophy has not kept up with modern developments in science, particularly physics. Scientists have become the bearers of the torch of discovery in our quest for knowledge.[2]

Richard Dawkins echoes this sentiment when he claims that philosophy has also been completely inept at producing basic theories in the biological sciences.[3] And popular astrophysicist Neil deGrasse Tyson even discourages students from studying philosophy, because, he believes, it will only get in the way of generating knowledge about our world,[4] and so he advises students to learn more science at the expense of their philosophy studies.[5] Tyson thinks that philosophy and science were once one and the same, but with the coming of complicated mathematical theories like quantum mechanics, the philosopher, whom Tyson says is "the would-be scientist but without a laboratory," was no longer able to contribute knowledge about the physical world from the comfort of their "armchair."[6]

Yet, not everything Tyson has had to say about philosophy and the other humanities is antagonistic, and it is these other comments that will lead us into Deleuze's transdisciplinary notion of thinking. Tyson says that before philosophy and physics "parted ways," physicists like Isaac Newton were considered philosophers. His point here is not that philosophy cannot accompany modern physics, but rather that it can, it should, and yet it chooses not to.[7] And Tyson himself credits his liberal arts education with helping him to do astronomy more passionately and also with allowing him to find resonances between physics and the arts. He began his university studies with a strict analytical, scientific, and mathematical mind. But half of his courses needed to be in the humanities, among which was a drawing class. One task there was depicting in charcoal a wall of pumpkins.

> They played music and the [teacher] comes up to me and says, "draw the music." I said, "huh?" He says, "draw the energy in the music." I just graduated from the Bronx High School of Science. You do not tell someone to draw the energy in music. Energy is $e = mc^2$. I have equations for energy. You do not draw energy you hear.[8]

But after four weeks, he had an experience that completely transformed his intellectual world.

> They said, "this time, don't draw the pumpkin, draw the space between the pumpkins." And at that moment I snapped. [...] What happened to me at that moment was my brain did some kind of an inversion. [...] After I started drawing the space between the pumpkins, I started seeing things I had never seen before. [...] A black letter on a page [...] is also a white page surrounding nothing. And it is the nothing that I am giving value to. [...] I came out of there being able to speak fluently with artists about what a painting feels like, about how much energy there is in one part of a painting or a performance or a work of music, and all of the sudden the entire branch of humanities poured down into my soul of curiosity.[9]

It is this sort of curiosity in other disciplines and in new ways of using our minds that Deleuze thinks is vital for philosophical thinking.

Deleuze and Transdisciplinarity

According to Deleuze and Guattari's celebrated definition, "philosophy is the discipline that involves creating concepts."[10] In fact, as Deleuze explains in a talk entitled, "What is the Creative Act?," every discipline is defined by its own unique acts of creation, which are very different in each case. For instance, scientists create functional correspondences between variables, painters create blocks of line and color, filmmakers create blocks of movement and duration, and philosophers create concepts.[11] Thus, despite our conventional prejudices, "science is no less creative" than the arts.[12] Deleuze emphasizes that this means there are boundaries around the disciplines that make it so that one field cannot actually enter into another's domain. And so, despite its reputation, philosophy does not "reflect upon" the other fields, as if it somehow sits above them and can contribute to them. A person does something substantial in a field to the extent that they are performing that discipline's acts of creation. A philosopher thinking about painting and thereby creating concepts has done nothing to advance painting. Only philosophy would gain new creations that way. And the philosopher can only contribute to painting to the extent that they invent new blocks of lines and color, which is not normally the philosopher's proper activity.[13]

This would seem to suggest that Deleuze thinks the disciplines should ignore each other, but in fact he believes that in order for any of them to make great leaps of progress, they still need to have encounters with one another, and here we will see that the heterogeneity and distance between the disciplines are the basis for their disjunctive synthesis (the logic of which we will analyze in the next chapter). People working in each field, although being unable to cross into the other ones, can still go up to the limits of their own domain and seek out how the other fields are working on similar problems or issues.[14] By pressing up against the boundaries of other disciplines in this way—and by also trying to communicate whatever they can with regard to some similar problem they both share—they can generate a sort of "energy" that disrupts the habitual patterns in the other person's thinking. This disruptive force then aids each party in fashioning new creations in their own domain. As Deleuze explains:

> It is not when one discipline begins to reflect on another that they come into contact. Contact can be made only when one discipline realizes that another discipline has already posed a similar problem, and so the one reaches out to the other to resolve this problem, but on its own terms and for its own needs. We can imagine similar problems which, at different moments, in different circumstances, and under different conditions, *send shock waves through various fields*: painting, music, philosophy, literature, and cinema. The tremors are the same, but the fields are different.[15]

Deleuze employed this idea in his teaching too. He notes how "in the traditional arrangement, a professor lectures to students who are acquiring or already possess a certain competence in some discipline." But at Vincennes where he taught, he as a philosophy professor must teach classes "to a public that includes to varying degrees mathematicians, musicians (trained in classical or pop music), psychologists, historians, etc."[16] For this reason, his philosophy instruction was guided by "the question of how useful it is to mathematicians, or to musicians, etc., even and especially if this philosophy does not discuss mathematics or music."[17] But this is not simply to convert philosophy into mathematical or musical knowledge. Rather, "it is of the greatest pedagogical importance to encourage within each discipline the *resonances* between different levels and domains of externality. [...] This *resonance* is the only way to grasp a subject in itself and from within."[18] And we see this transdisciplinarity in Deleuze's writing too, both with its breathtaking quantity of sources and with their extraordinary breadth of variety, as he jumps quickly but fluently between disparate fields such as calculus, painting, thermodynamics, literature, and many others.[19]

Deleuze gives examples for these "tremors" or "resonances" that are felt across different disciplines when they become shaken up by their related problems. For instance, Deleuze was working on the philosophical problem of light, and he sought encounters with creators in other domains working on similar problems. In the painter Delaunay, Deleuze noticed that his depiction of light was not a matter of how it looks when it strikes objects but rather of how the "light itself forms figures." Delaunay, Deleuze says, was not concerned with "creating paintings with any objects at all"; rather, he "substitutes figures of pure light for rigid and geometric figures" (Figure 3.1, top left).[20] This resonated with the Michelson-Morley experiment that he had an encounter with, where the light, while traveling down perpendicular lines in the device, can be understood as forming a triangular figure on account of the earth's rotation (Figure 3.1, top right), and thereby the moving "lines of light condition geometric lines."[21] This discovery again resonated when he saw how the filmmaker Jean Grémillon set light into motion in his film *The Lighthouse Keepers* (1929) (Figure 3.1, bottom row).[22]

Deleuze also notes how this problem of light was dealt with in the theological domain with Jakob Böhme and with Goethe's quasi-scientific studies of color, both of which having eventual influence on German expressionist use of light.[23] "In each case," Deleuze says, "we see how the classifications of luminous [...] signs are proper to cinema, and yet refer to other disciplines in the sciences and the arts [...]. In these other disciplines, the signs have a different order, different contexts and relations, and different divisions."[24] And regarding his own philosophical creation for this problem of light, Deleuze's fashions the Bergsonian/Spinozist formulation "image = movement = matter = light."[25]

It is because Deleuze as a philosopher was sensitive to resonances in other domains that he felt comfortable exploring them even in cases where his background was somewhat limited.[26] So long as his concern lies with the way common problematics resonate in each domain, he can do philosophy by encountering them on their own terms. For this reason, he says he likes to "go out [...] 'on the lookout' for encounters" with the various arts, for instance, in hopes of generating such resonances.[27]

Deleuze gives an example of how this works the other way as well, that is, how other domains have made encounters with his own philosophy. He offers one example: his

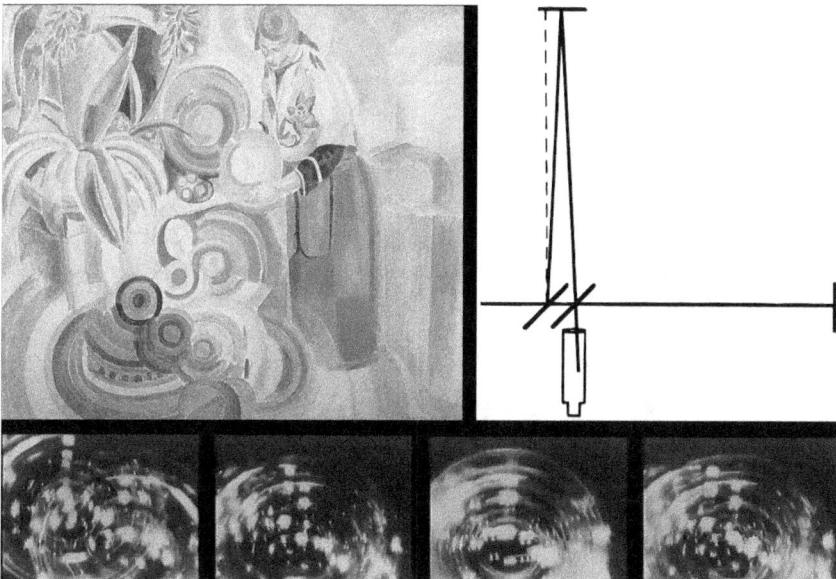

Figure 3.1 Transdisciplinary encounters. **Top left**: Delaunay's *Portuguese Woman* (1916).[28] **Top right**: Diagram of the figure light made (diagonal lines) in the Michelson-Morley experiment.[29] **Bottom**: Moving light in Grémillon's *The Lighthouse Keepers* (© Films du Grand Guignol 1929. All rights reserved).[30]

concept of "the fold" from his book with that same name. Originally, he considered this notion to be a philosophical one. Yet, following its publication, Deleuze received letters from people of all sorts of backgrounds who each proclaimed for their own reasons, "Your story of folds, that's us!"[31] One instance is the society of origami folders who said, "We agree completely. What you are doing is what we do." Similarly, surfers wrote to him and also claimed that what they do is "the fold": "We never stop inserting ourselves into the folds of nature. For us, nature is an aggregate of mobile folds, and we insert ourselves into the fold of the wave, live in the fold of the wave."[32]

A Rivalry of Friends

To further characterize the tension between the disciplines, we will look now at how Deleuze, following Blanchot, claims that "friendship is a category or a condition of the exercise of thought."[33] Deleuze notes that etymologically in the word "philosopher" is "friend": the friend of wisdom. He continues, "That's the problem of *What is Philosophy?*: what does 'friend of wisdom' mean?"[34] Since the philosopher is a friend and not a bearer of wisdom, that means he/she cannot definitively be said to have wisdom but perhaps is simply someone who "tends toward wisdom."[35] As Deleuze and Guattari write: "friends of wisdom" are "those who seek wisdom but do not formally possess it."[36] Rather, they are "claimants" to wisdom, "striving for it potentially rather than actually possessing it."[37]

Yet, since there are many such claimants—recall for instance Stephen Hawking claiming wisdom for physics, snatching it from the hands of the philosophers—they are rivals to one another, even though they are also friends to the shared thing they strive for: "Friendship would then involve competitive distrust of the rival as much as amorous striving toward the object of desire."[38] Here again we see a conception where things are in a relationship of tension or "agon,"[39] as for instance different academic disciplines (philosophy, science, religion, etc.) laying claim to wisdom, while also they must directly encounter one another and mutually benefit from the "shockwaves" that will result. As we noted, doing this means that one must go to the limit of their knowledge and have some genuine curiosity about what the other disciplines are doing. Thus, Deleuze thinks, the philosopher "is someone who lays claim to wisdom without being a wise man," and by having fruitful encounters with other disciplines, philosophers must then lie at the "border between knowing and non-knowing. It is there that one must settle in order to have something to say."[40]

The Philosophy of Pinball

Deleuze further elaborates his notion of the friendship of the disciplines and the action of thinking by discussing the physical workings of the brain. Deleuze, in fact, thought very highly of the neurosciences. He claims that they help us understand how concepts are formed, since "thinking and the brain are absolutely intertwined."[41] Thus, he says that he believes "more in the future of the molecular biology of the brain than in the future of information science or of any theory of communication" and that neurobiology appears even "to have a more certain future than mentalist psychiatry."[42] He also explains that he prefers neurobiology over psychoanalysis and linguistics, since these other two fields limit themselves to just their own "ready-made concepts," while neurobiology is freer to uncover the structures and mechanics involved in brain activity by devising its own new methods and ideas.[43] In certain cases Deleuze and Guattari specifically reference Steven Rose's *The Conscious Brain* and Delisle Burns's *The Uncertain Nervous System*, so we will look more at these influences on their thinking. In Deleuze's and Guattari's writings on the brain's physiology and functioning, they are mostly concerned with the following four topics: {1} the discontinuity of the neural paths, {2} the non-hierarchical and a-centric ("rhizomatic") structure of the brain, {3} the "chaotic" uncertainty of the brain's computational operations, and {4} the creation of new connections between parts of the brain.

Let us look first at Deleuze's comments on the basic structures and dynamics of the brain. He says that under normal conditions, where no notable or original thinking is taking place, the brain's signal transmissions are operating like how balls bounce around in a "pinball machine," and in a filmed interview he uses hand-motions to indicate the rapid, complicated, and chaotic movements of the signals (Figure 3.2).[44] Here he is referring to a sort of random, "noisy," spontaneous firing of the neurons.[45]

Figure 3.2 Deleuze showing with his hands how "when there are no ideas, the mind works like a pinball machine." (*L'abécédaire* directed by Pierre-André Boutang © Sodaperaga and Montparnasse 2004. All rights reserved.)[46]

And also, under these normal cognitive circumstances, the signals for the most part move through "pre-formed paths" all while the mind is thinking with "ready-made associations."[47] This is a sort of automatic, mechanical way that the brain can operate. We might think of when we are performing a habitual action, like traveling to work. We may arrive at our destination without really noticing or considering anything special and thus without performing much notable cognition at all. But even under such conditions, the circuits are not directly continuous like in electronic circuits. There are "micro-fissures" or "cuts," which are the synaptic gaps where the signals are transmitted chemically, and Deleuze relates them to non-associative thinking in the mind.[48] Thus, cerebral information processing is not just mechanically associative, because "the process of association increasingly came up against cuts in the continuous network of the brain."[49]

These gaps are one element that add randomness into the brain's operations and therefore into thinking, Deleuze says. As Rose explains, whether or not a neural signal is transmitted across the synaptic gap "depends on the sum of all the events arriving at this point at a given time," including the threshold level that must be met, the magnitude of the incoming signal, and the chemical composition of the synaptic gap.[50] Yet, Rose continues, there is "uncertainty in this system," on account of the "*chance* bombardment by spontaneous neurotransmitter release."[51] This already adds an unpredictable variability into our neural operations, suggesting perhaps that our brains are never working exactly the same even when in similar situations or when processing similar data. Thus, Deleuze writes: "Everywhere there were micro-fissures which were not simply voids to be crossed, but random mechanisms introducing themselves at each moment between the sending and receiving of an association message: this was the discovery of a probabilistic or semi-fortuitous cerebral space, 'an uncertain system.'"[52] Also, what adds to the complexity of the neuro-computations is that the neural paths are arranged in a sort of jumbled mass. Even though each neuronal node may have many paths branching away from it like the roots of a tree, those roots all connect to many other such nodes with their own roots that as well connect to countless other such nodes and often circling back upon themselves.[53] These complex, noisy operations of a neural system make it what Burns calls a "random nerve network."[54] For this reason, Deleuze and Guattari conclude that the brain's processing system is a-centered, non-hierarchical, and "rhizomatic" rather than tree-structured.[55]

Yet not only is the brain a discontinuous, decentralized jumble operating non-deterministically, it also is capable of altering its own structural features and computational dynamics. Deleuze discusses how new physical and operational connections in the brain can be made between its distant parts. He makes an analogy with what in mathematics is sometimes termed the Baker's Transformation.[56] To knead bread dough, a baker may stretch the ball of dough until it is flatter, then fold that stretched slab back upon itself, and lastly rotate the new ball and repeat the steps. As Prigogine and Stengers write when explaining the mathematical transformation: "We take a square and flatten it into a rectangle, then we fold half of the rectangle over the other half to form a square again. [...] Each time the surface of the square is broken up and redistributed." In this way, "the baker transformation transforms each point into a well-defined new point" (Figure 3.3).[57]

Deleuze sees this bringing together of distant points as being what happens in our thinking and likewise in our brain's physical operations when we conceive an idea: "Aren't there two points that at a particular moment, in a particular stage of my idea—I cannot see how to associate them, make them communicate—and as a result of numerous transformations, I discover them side by side?"[58]

As we noted before, it is not our task here to evaluate the scientific merits of Deleuze's claims regarding neurobiology. We simply want more elaboration on how he thinks heterogeneity plays a role in thinking. These neurobiological accounts can at least serve as metaphors if nothing else, because Deleuze thinks that there are parallels between them and the ways that the mind works when forming new concepts. Speaking of the different ways that we may taxonomically classify things, he says that "in any classification scheme, some things which seem very different are brought closer together, and others which seem very close are separated. This is how concepts are formed."[59] And similarly he says elsewhere regarding cinema that "creating new circuits in art means creating them in the brain too."[60] Let us turn now to Deleuze and Guattari's further elaborations on the concept's heterogeneous composition from their book, *What Is Philosophy?*

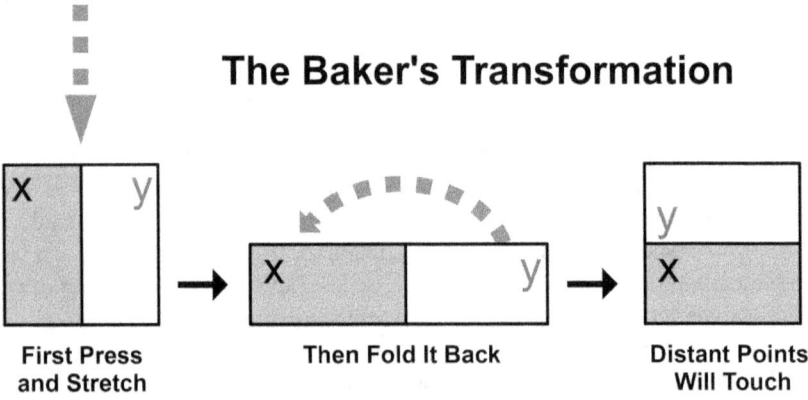

Figure 3.3 A simplified depiction of the Baker's Transformation.[61]

Dupréelian Concept Consistency

For Deleuze and Guattari, every concept must have parts,[62] which may have come from other concepts in different contexts.[63] But, there is a flexibility to this composition like we saw before with fuzzy aggregates: "The concept is whole because it totalizes its components, but it is a fragmentary whole."[64] And also, every concept will relate to others in its own context, and in that way they "link up with each other, support one another, coordinate their contours, articulate their respective problems, and belong to the same philosophy, even if they have different histories."[65]

The internal parts of the concept are held together on account of their "endoconsistency"; it is what makes these components be "distinct, heterogeneous, and yet not separable."[66] The reason for this is that each internal part of a concept "partially overlaps, has a zone of neighborhood, or a threshold of indiscernibility, with another one."[67] In this way, "components remain distinct, but something passes from one to the other, something that is undecidable between them. There is an area *ab* that belongs to both *a* and *b*, where *a* and *b* 'become' indiscernible. These zones, thresholds, or becomings, this inseparability, define the internal consistency of the concept."[68] In accordance with the overlapping zones that make parts be indiscernible or undecidable, there is also movement or fluidity of some sort between the components: "The concept's components are neither constants nor variables but pure and simple *variations* ordered according to their neighborhood. They are processual, modular."[69]

To illustrate this variable and overlapping structure of a concept's endoconsistency, Deleuze and Guattari offer this example: "The concept of a bird is found not in its genus or species but in the composition of its postures, colors, and songs: something indiscernible that is not so much synesthetic as syneidetic. A concept is a heterogenesis— that is to say, an ordering of its components by zones of neighborhood."[70] So, what constitutes the concept for a particular kind of bird has nothing to do with a genus–species definition that takes the form: it is a bird (genus) that is different from the other birds in some distinguishing way (species). It would rather be a matter of {1} its component conceptual parts, like those for the way that it looks and behaves, along with {2} the way those conceptual parts overlap and interrelate. And the "concept" itself for this type of bird is to be understood somehow in terms of the movement that is made in conceptually passing through these parts: "The concept is in a state of survey in relation to its components, endlessly traversing them according to an order without distance. It is immediately co-present to all its components or variations, at no distance from them, passing back and forth through them."[71] Soon we will examine a more detailed illustration, but for now we should notice that the concept for Deleuze and Guattari, being something that moves through all of its parts and is always co-present to all of them, involves a sort of self-relationality. It should also be noted that one way Deleuze and Guattari characterize this movement that is both everywhere and also moving from one place to another is that it has an "infinite speed," which seems to suggest a dialetheic notion of movement where something can be at two distinct places in the same moment:[72] "The concept is defined by *the inseparability of a finite number of heterogeneous components traversed by a point of absolute survey at infinite speed*. Concepts are [...] forms whose only object is the inseparability of distinct variations."[73]

Now, at the same time, a concept has an "exoconsistency" with other concepts it relates to, meaning that it is bound up with them in a similar way. So, endoconsistency is a matter of zones of overlap, and exoconsistency is a sort of "bridge" to other concepts. Thus "zones and bridges are the joints of the concept."[74] As we can see, Deleuze and Guattari seem to have kept their Dupréelian notion of consistency for their explanation of concept composition, being that it is characterized in a way that reminds us of a fuzzy aggregate.

The Cartesian Aggregate Self

Another, more detailed illustration Deleuze and Guattari offer is the concept of the self in Descartes's cogito argument, which they reformulate as "myself who doubts, I think, I am, I am a thinking thing."[75] Within this concept, they identify three conceptual regions: a zone of doubting, a zone of thinking, and a zone of being. And the concept, which is the concept of the self or I, passes through each of these zones fluently on

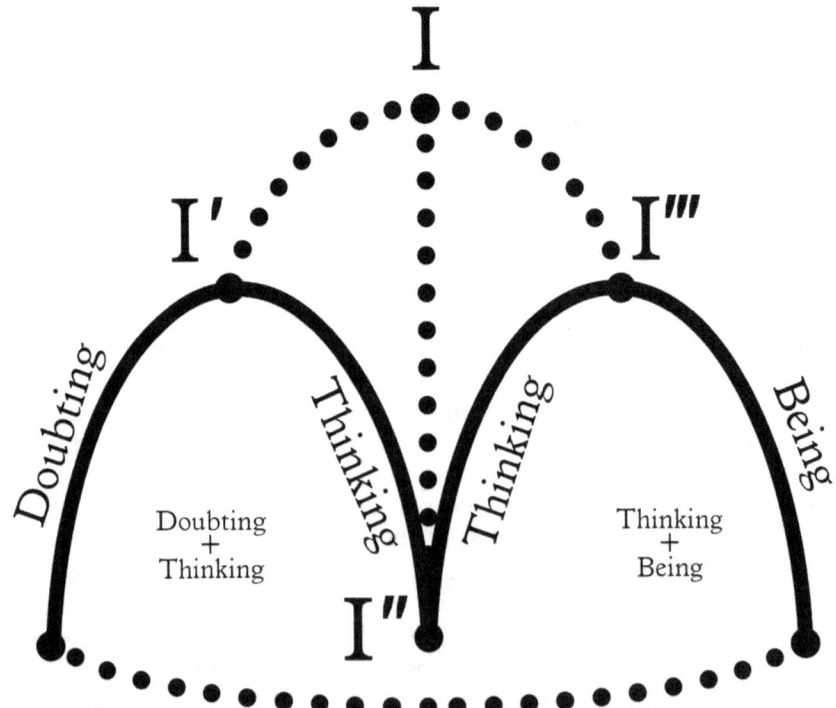

Figure 3.4 The overlapping structures in Descartes's concept of the self.[77]

account of their endoconsistency (Figure 3.4). Insofar as it is in the first zone, it is the "doubting I"; the second zone, the "thinking I"; the third, the "existing I." Deleuze and Guattari continue, "The components are arranged in zones of neighborhood or indiscernibility that produce passages from one to the other and constitute their inseparability. The first zone is between doubting and thinking (myself who doubts, I cannot doubt that I think), and the second is between thinking and being (in order to think it is necessary to be)."[76]

What Deleuze and Guattari seem to be suggesting here is that because the zone of doubting overlaps with the zone of thinking (for, when we attempt a Cartesian radical doubt, we cannot doubt that we are *doubting* and thus are *thinking*), that means there is a fluid conceptual movement from one to the other, and so the concept of the doubting I is already in immediate connection with that of the thinking I. And because the zone of thinking overlaps with the zone of being (for, in order for something to think in the first place, it must be understood as something that already exists), we can fluidly move from thinking to being. Thus also, the thinking I is already in immediate connection with the existing I, and the concept can move around all its zones with great fluency on account of these intimate overlaps.

Logic, we said, is the study of validity, or what follows from what. Now, Deleuze and Guattari are very explicit that we should not understand a concept's composition in this "discursive" way as a movement between propositions.[78] But could we not see something like a syllogistic kind of inference here that uses a transitivity of sorts in the reasoning? *All doubting beings are thinking beings. And all thinking beings are existing beings. Thus all doubting beings are existing beings.* While we may be able to extract such an inferential structure from the concept, Deleuze and Guattari rather see the real conceptual content of this cogito idea as not an inference but rather a notion of the self in which there is a fluid conceptual movement from doubting to thinking to being. And such a concept is composed of two things, as we have emphasized. {1} It is composed of endoconsistent parts, which are themselves composed of parts, and so on. For instance, doubting is composed of phases of variation between perceptual, scientific, and obsessional doubt. And {2} it is jointly composed of its exoconsistent bridges to other concepts. For example, we start with this concept of the self; among its ideas is the idea of infinity, and that idea then serves as the exoconsistent bridge to another concept, namely, the concept of God.[79]

Thus, given Deleuze's and Guattari's characterization of the concept as having a Dupréelian sort of consistency, it would seem that we could likewise find some dialetheic elements in how they conceive it. For instance, in the overlapping endoconsistent conceptual zones, we have two different things that remained distinct while also being inseparable, thereby becoming in some way indiscernible and undecidable. This sort of overlapping would seem to involve the combination of something and its non-exclusive other. But the reason why that might be a dialetheic sort of conceptualization is a matter we turn to now, as we begin analyzing the notions of disjunction and negation in Deleuze's logic.

Part Two

Logic of Otherness: Negation, or Disjunction?

4

Alternance and Otherness

Introduction

Gilles Deleuze is explicitly against using the notions of negation and contradiction for understanding his concept of affirmative synthetic disjunction, which would suggest that it is not a dialetheic conception. We will first examine a recent treatment of negation in Deleuze's philosophy, namely, Andrew Culp's *Dark Deleuze*, to bring to light a possible non-classical re-interpretation of Deleuze's idea of negation. We next work through the way that Val Routley and Richard Routley (now Plumwood and Sylvan) distinguish classical and non-classical logics on the basis of how negation and contradiction operate in them, and by means of this, we will then examine paraconsistency and paracompleteness in certain non-classical logics. After that, we learn from Graham Priest how negation in dialetheic reasoning should be distinguished from denial, which will help us determine that Deleuze's criticisms against negation are at least aimed at classical negation but not certainly at dialetheic negation. Deleuze prefers an "affirmative" and "non-exclusive" sort of disjunction that involves "alternance" rather than conflict, which he elaborates through the idea of disjunctive syllogism in Immanuel Kant and Pierre Klossowski. We will work through those accounts and see that again they too seem to involve a dialetheic conceptualization.

Must Negation Be Dark?

In *Dark Deleuze*, Andrew Culp studies negational elements in Deleuze's philosophy, but he does so with a focus on their political implications. Because his treatment of certain notions can help us clarify the logical issues at hand, let us just initially take a quick look at parts of his book. Culp rejects the predominant "joyous" sort of interpretation of Deleuze's texts in favor of a "dark" reading, which is more suited for successfully enacting a communist revolution to ultimately set the world on a better course. Culp's dark Deleuzianism, then, aims to "rehabilitate the destructive force of negativity by cultivating a 'hatred for this world,'"[1] so that we can bring about "the end of this world, the final defeat of the state, and full communism."[2]

To derive this more effective revolutionary philosophy from Deleuze's writings, Culp identifies certain philosophical themes that lend themselves either to a "joyous" or to a "dark" reading, advocating of course for the darker one. On the one hand, Culp recognizes that the dark readings can follow Deleuze's thinking down roads that Deleuze himself was very careful not to pursue.[3] On the other hand, Culp bases the dark interpretations on concepts and formulations in Deleuze's philosophy that do have an apparent negational nature. He writes that dark Deleuzianism draws from "the perfused *negativity* of [Deleuze's] concepts and affects. On the level of concept, it recognizes that *negativity* impregnates Deleuze's many prefixes of difference, becoming, movement, and transformation, such as *de-*, *a-*, *in-*, and *non-*."[4]

The particular dark Deleuzian reading that is directly relevant here is Culp's study of difference as understood in terms of "disjunctive synthesis." Culp says that its joyous interpretation would render it an inclusive disjunctive synthesis, which, presumably, has a structure that is something like *this or that, or (hopefully) even both*, while Culp's dark reading understands it as an exclusive disjunctive synthesis, which takes the form "this, not that" and which enables us to "*become contrary*."[5] Yet, he seems to acknowledge that this is not Deleuze's understanding of the concept; and as we see from the cited passages, Deleuze himself explicitly calls it *affirmative* synthetic disjunction and says that it should *not* involve "the negative, limitative, or *exclusive* use of disjunction."[6] Regardless, given the non-classical logics available to us, our choice will not be limited to these two sorts of options anyway; for, we will instead consider a non-exclusionary notion of negation and of contradiction—or as our sources call it, of "nonexclusive restricted otherthanness"—in order to better characterize the logical properties of affirmative synthetic disjunction.[7] And what we will find is that this sort of negation can indeed be affirmational with respect to what it negates.

Part of Culp's defense for taking Deleuze's ideas down roads of development that Deleuze explicitly avoids pursuing is that this is a proper way to read Deleuze, given that it uses Deleuze's very own manner of interpretation, namely, his so-called "buggery" of other authors.[8] Deleuze claims that when interpreting other philosophers, like Bergson and Spinoza, he tried to produce an "offspring" that the author would have to recognize as their own but nonetheless regard as a monstrous version of themselves.[9] So, because Culp's dark reading is a monstrous interpretation, it may then qualify as such a properly Deleuzian buggery of Deleuze.

Yet, upon closer examination of Deleuze's readings of other philosophers, we might obtain the impression that he uncovers something which really can be said to be a fundamental part of their philosophy, and it would be monstrous for the original author only to the extent that it was not obvious to them that it lays deep within their own thinking. For example, before reading Deleuze's *Expressionism in Philosophy* and reading his course lectures on Spinoza, it may never have crossed our minds that at the basis of Spinoza's philosophy is a new development and implementation of the concept of intensity. In fact, to all appearances at least, it seemed not to have been obvious even to Spinoza himself.[10] But after reading Deleuze's commentaries, it can be hard afterward not to notice intensity's role in Spinoza's philosophy.

I mention this, because Deleuze is explicitly critical of negation and contradiction, and yet we will implement certain theories of negation to characterize aspects of

Deleuze's logic. Nonetheless, this is not meant to be a monstrous contortion of Deleuze's thinking. Rather, it is an exploration of the possibility that Deleuze was using a sort of non-classical logic without being aware of its formal features.

Augmentation as Negation: Routley and Routley's Non-Exclusive Otherthanness

We turn now to Routley and Routley's article "Negation and Contradiction," along with related texts by Priest, which will enable us to distinguish different types of negation.[11] With these concepts in hand, we will attempt to determine which sort of negation Deleuze is averse to and which, if any, could be useful for understanding the logical properties of affirmative synthetic disjunction.

Routley and Routley note that throughout the history of logic there have been competing models of negation, each rising and falling from prominence during different periods. Their method for distinguishing types of negation involves examining the role it is thought to play in contradictory formulations of the sort "something and its own negation," which, using our particular notational conventions, we are writing as $A \land \neg A$. That role is determined by seeing what a philosopher claims can be inferred from $A \land \neg A$, which thereby indicates which model of negation the philosopher uses. Whatever is said to be inferable from a formulation is called its "logical content," and the different theories understand a contradiction-forming negation as having one or another effect on logical content.[12]

The first model of negation says that from $A \land \neg A$ we can infer nothing: not A, not $\neg A$, and not anything else at all. It is thus called the *cancellation model*, because the negation of A is understood as cancelling (destroying, erasing, deleting, neutralizing) the content of A. This model of negation was used in the connexive type of logics in Ancient and Medieval times.[13] We might think of $\neg A$'s content as being an antithesis of that of A's, such that their combination pushes both contents out of the world; or, we might think of their contents simply becoming eliminated in some other destructive sense (Figure 4.1).

The second logical theory of negation says that from $A \land \neg A$ we can infer any other arbitrary formula we want, no matter how unrelated or absurd, and in fact we can infer everything else whatsoever. This is the *explosion model* of negation, because from one contradictory formula bursts forth inferentially every other formula, including all other contradictions ($B \land \neg B$, $C \land \neg C$, and so on), thereby creating a thoroughly inconsistent and trivial world.[14] This sort of negation is used in classical and intuitionistic logics.[15] Routley and Routley provide as one sort of classical definition of negation that $\neg A$ holds in a world if and only if A does not hold in that world.[16] This view on negation can also be called a *complementation* model,[17] because the logical content of $\neg A$ may be understood as being everything whatsoever that is not A. To illustrate, Routley and Routley have us consider the topside of a record album, which we consider here as A. Its classical negation, then, would be everything else in the world that is not that one side.[18] If we picture the contents of A and of $\neg A$ as taking up some "territory" in

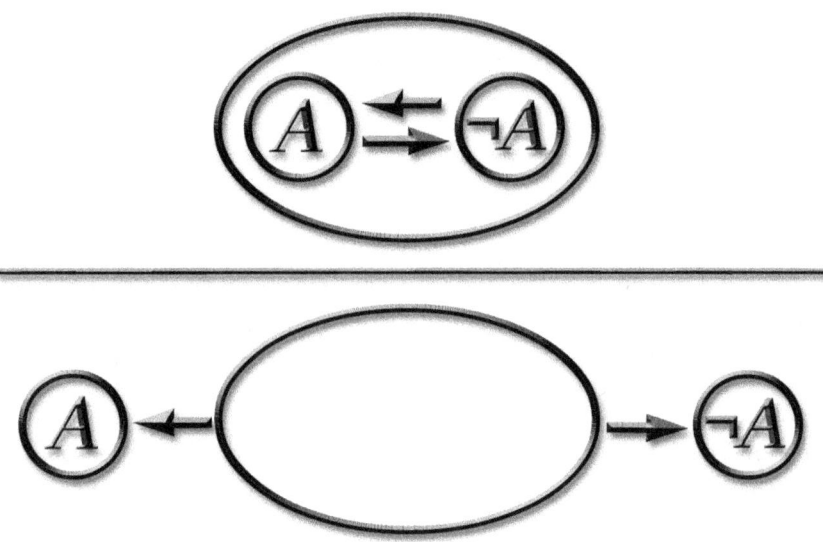

Figure 4.1 Negation as cancellation destroys both contents.

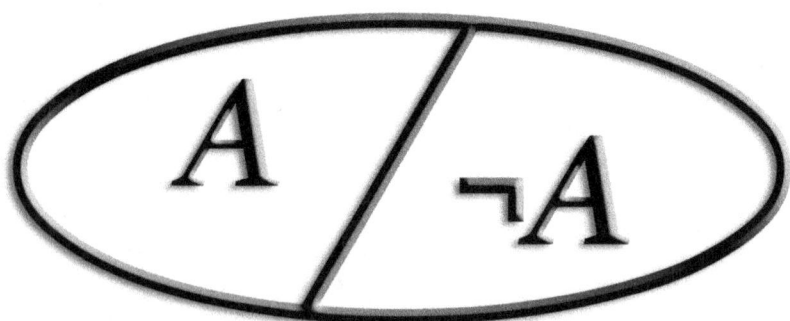

Figure 4.2 Negation as explosion (including classical negation) is exclusive and exhaustive. It yields an unrestricted otherthanness, and its contradictory pairing yields a thoroughly inconsistent and trivial world.[19]

the domain (understood as a geometrical space of a diagram, or alternately, as a set of things, or as a sum of propositions), then the entire domain is covered by $A \land \neg A$ (Figure 4.2).[20]

This classical model of negation has unfortunately been considered by many as the only legitimate one in the recent century or so.[21] One of its greatest disadvantages and counterintuitive features is that, as we noted above, by having A and $\neg A$ in the same world, we thereby have rendered the world not just inconsistent in this limited way but in fact entirely and thoroughly so. This means that in classical logic, contradictions should be avoided at all costs. So, if we on the one hand begin by thinking that we should have A in our world, and then on the other hand we come to find reason to think that $\neg A$ should be in our world, then under classical assumptions one of the two needs to be excluded from the world in order for it to not explode into total inconsistency and triviality. Routley and Routley call this eliminative choosing the "consistencizing" of the world.[22]

One shortcoming of classical negation is that it fails to give us the "natural" sort of negation that we implement in daily life and in our use of natural language.[23] Moreover, for certain logical reasons—and, in our case, for metaphysical ones too—we need a sort of negation that allows "for non-trivial inconsistent worlds" and also "for nonnull incomplete worlds";[24] thus, "The classical rule has to be rejected."[25]

This brings us to the third model of negation, called the *constraint* or *intermediate* model, which includes relevant and paraconsistent negations.[26] Under paraconsistent reasoning, from $A \wedge \neg A$ you can derive more than just nothing but less than everything. For instance, from $A \wedge \neg A$ we might want to say that we can derive A on the one hand and $\neg A$ on the other hand but nothing more, just as from $B \wedge C$ we can derive B and C.

Now, one important feature for any sort of negation would be that it yields something with "otherthanness," as Routley and Routley call it, to whatever is being negated.[27] Yet, as we have seen, we need to be very careful about what qualifies for our negational otherthanness. In this case, it should not be mutually destructive, like in the cancellation theory, and it should not be unrestricted, like in classical negation.[28] Rather it should yield something over and beyond what is being negated in a way that is also not necessarily exclusionary to it. For this sort of negation, Routley and Routley provide the following diagram, and notice the overlapping of A and $\neg A$ and also the fact that the two of them do not exhaust the entire domain (Figure 4.3).

Thus, this third kind of negation yields "nonexclusive restricted otherthanness";[29] in other words, "A and $\neg A$ are suitably independent though nonetheless related; A and $\neg A$ may both fail together and differently both may hold together; A and $\neg A$ neither cancel nor implode one another."[30] (As we will see in the next section, a logic where A and $\neg A$ may both fail together is a paracomplete one, and a logic where they may both hold together is a paraconsistent one.)

In their record album illustration for this model, the negation of the topside is simply the bottom side and not everything else in the world.[31] Yet, in this case, the world is not made inconsistent simply by adding this non-exclusive negation of the topside; for surely there is nothing remarkable about a world having record albums with two sides. Rather, this sort of otherthanness can in other cases involve more profound sorts of logical incompatibilities, as when combining worlds that together make one inconsistent world:

> In the classical case when $\neg A$ is added to a world, quite a bit may have to be taken out of the world, e.g. A (and what implies it) if it is there, in order to consistencize the world; whereas in the relevant case $\neg A$ can simply be *added without any consistencizing subtractions*. More generally, *worlds can be simply combined and statements added to worlds without the need to delete anything*, because what is being added are further conditions, not the taking away of conditions already given.[32]

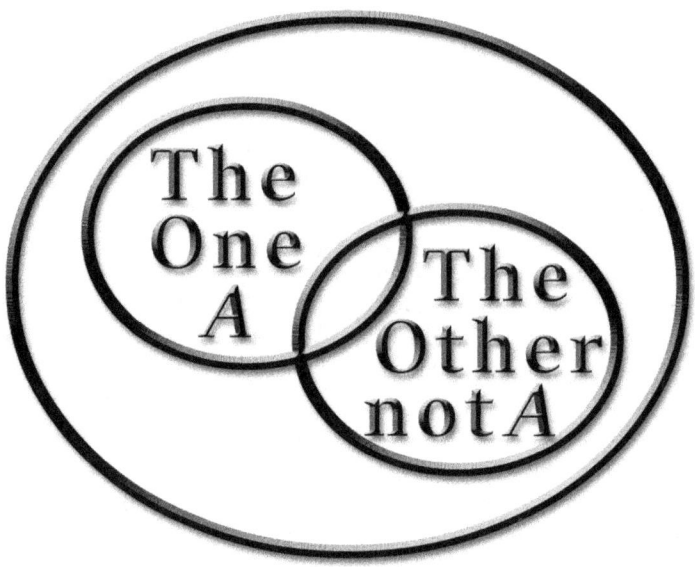

Figure 4.3 Routley and Routley's diagram for negation as non-exclusive restricted otherthanness. It can yield an inconsistent *otherthan* without eliminating either.[33]

Paraconsistency and Paracompleteness

At this point let us elaborate and expand upon these notions of explosion, completeness, and consistency in the context of monoletheism, analetheism, and dialetheism. Recall from Chapter 1 that {1} the monoletheist view, under our own expanded definition, is the belief that propositions must be at least true or at least false but not both, {2} the analetheist view holds that some propositions may have no truth-value at all, and {3} the dialetheist view says that some propositions can be both true and false. We matched these views to logical systems, but we encountered some complications with them. Dialetheism rejects the prohibition against contradictions, but the logic we considered (Priest's *LP*, Figure 1.6) validates the Principle of Non-Contradiction (Figure 1.7). However, we also found that this validation does not necessarily entail a prohibition against all contradictions whatsoever, as there can be contradictory formulations that are true as well as false. The analetheic logic we considered ($Ł_3$, Figure 1.4) did not, as we expected, verify the Principle of Excluded Middle (Figure 1.5), which prohibits valueless statements, but it also did not verify the Principle of Non-Contradiction. Now, it seems a little odd that the dialetheic logic verifies the Principle of Non-Contradiction, while the analetheic logic does not. We suggested at that time

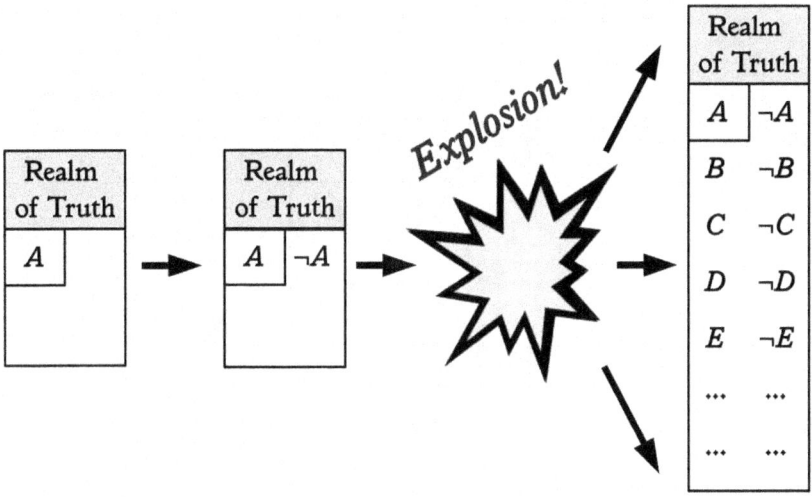

Figure 4.4 The production of a thoroughly trivial and inconsistent world on account of the Principle of Explosion.

that nonetheless such an analetheic logic in effect prohibits contradictions, on account of explosion. We will now look more closely at some of these technicalities, because they will help us better grasp the philosophical importance of the logical notions of paracompleteness and paraconsistency.

As we noted above, a logic that validates the Principle of Explosion would allow you, on the basis of a contradiction, to infer any proposition you want, no matter how irrelevant. Recall from Routley and Routley that in a classical logic, from the contradiction $A \land \neg A$ you can derive not only A and $\neg A$ but additionally any other B, C, etc. that you want, along with their own negations (so also $B \land \neg B$, $C \land \neg C$, and so on).[34] This creates a thoroughly inconsistent and trivial world. To depict this, let us make a box that lists the truths in our world (Figure 4.4, left).

Suppose in our reasoning we affirm that A is in our realm of true things, for instance, to use one of Priest's examples, we note that "The Queen is rich."[35] Now, suppose also that later in our reasoning we somehow assert the negation of that statement: "The Queen is not rich." From this, under our monoletheic or analetheic logics, we can validly infer any other proposition we wish, no matter how irrelevant or improbable, like "Pigs can fly" and "The Moon is made of green cheese," along with, even more absurdly, the negations of each of these propositions.

We can see why this is so when we make use of the evaluation rules for the truth-values of formulas in these logics. In our truth evaluation tables, we look for rows where the premises are all at least true and the conclusion is not at least true. If such a row exists, then the inference is invalid (and valid otherwise). As we can see, in the monoletheic, classical logic and in the analetheic "gappy" logic, there are no such lines, so the Principle of Explosion is valid in them (Figure 4.5, left and middle). But

Explosion from Contradiction

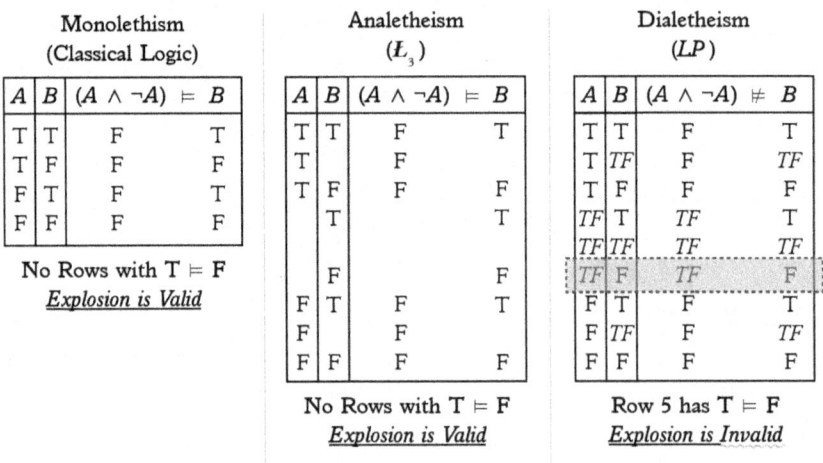

Figure 4.5 Validity or invalidity of the Principle of Explosion in various logics.

in the dialetheic logic, the contradiction can be both true and false while the arbitrary conclusion is just false, and thus explosion does not hold in such a "glutty" logic.

This will help us now better grasp what it means for a logic to be paraconsistent or paracomplete. To visualize their senses, think of our worlds of facts, and let us make two subdivisions, the realm of truths and the realm of falsities. In a monoletheic, classical logic, which is bivalent, all propositions fall within either the realm of truth or the realm of falsity (with the negation always going into the opposing domain). So it is consistent, meaning that both a formula and its negation are never together in the true realm. And it is complete, because all formulas fall within one of the two realms (Figure 4.6, left).

In an analetheic logic, however, we can have formulas, like B in our example, which fall neither under the true nor under the false domains, and its negation will also then fall on the outside. At least in comparison to the expectations of classical logic, it is not entirely "complete," because not everything fits nicely within the two classical truth categories. Instead, it is said to be "paracomplete."[36] Yet, it is still consistent, because no contradictions are found in the true domain (Figure 4.6, middle). In dialetheic logics, there can be formulas, like again B here, that fall under both the true and the false domains, making their negations also be in both domains. Since we have both a formula and its negation in the true domain (they are also both in the false one too, in those cases), it is not consistent, at least to classical standards (where formulas are always just in one box and the negations always just in the other). And so they are said to be "paraconsistent" logics.[37] Nonetheless, they are complete, because no formulas fall outside these regions of truth and falsity

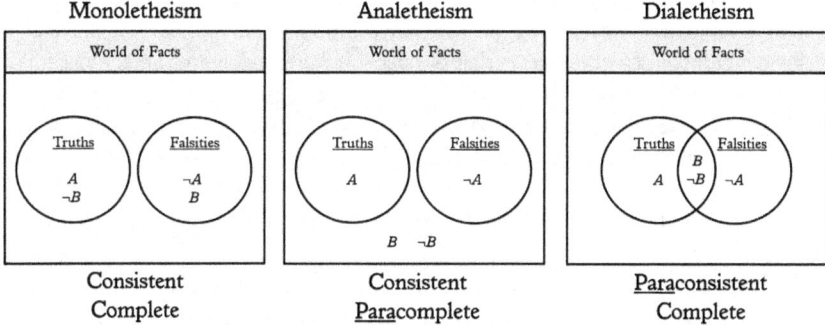

Figure 4.6 Consistency and paraconsistency, along with completeness and paracompleteness, used to distinguish various logics.

(Figure 4.6, right). This gives us a more convenient way to distinguish these three options. A monoletheic, classical logic is consistent and complete; an analetheic logic is consistent but paracomplete; and a dialetheic logic is complete but paraconsistent. Now there is also the option for the logic being both paraconsistent and paracomplete, and we would get a situation where there could be both {1} formulas that are neither-valued and {2} other formulas that are both-valued (recall Figure 4.3, where the formula and its negation overlapped, but there was still room outside the two). We will learn that this could be the easiest and safest way to conceptualize Deleuze's logic. In the conclusion, however, we will discuss how the dialetheic elements seem ultimately to dominate in his thinking.

The Negation Deleuze Denies, and the Negation Deleuze Affirms

As we noted, Deleuze does not want us to use the concept of negation to understand affirmative synthetic disjunction, which affirms difference. And also, in *Difference and Repetition*, he explicitly rejects the use of negation for understanding difference.[38] But before we can begin our analysis, we need to see how denial and negation are not coupled in dialetheic reasoning like they are in classical, monoletheic reasoning.

Denial, as Priest and other non-classical logicians hold,[39] is a speech act, and its opposite is *assertion*, which can also be understood as *affirmation*:[40] "One must distinguish between the illocutory acts of assertion and denial. The former indicates the acceptance of something; the latter its rejection. [...] We all find ourselves confused sometimes, endorsing contradictory views that are not acceptable to us. We find ourselves asserting p and $\neg p$. But we do not deny p."[41] Thus,

> when a dialetheist asserts "The liar sentence is true; the liar sentence is not true," the second utterance is not meant to convey to the hearer the fact that the dialetheist rejects the first sentence: after all, they do accept it. The second sentence conveys

the fact that they accept its negation too. [...] Many people have inconsistent views (about religion, politics, or whatever). Sometimes they come to discover this fact by saying inconsistent things, perhaps under some probing questioning. Thus, for some $α$ they may utter both $α$ and $¬α$. The second utterance is not an indication that the speaker rejects $α$. They *do* accept $α$. They just accept $¬α$ as well, at least until they revise their views.[42]

So in a dialetheic, paraconsistent negation, to affirm or assert the negation $¬A$ is not necessarily to also deny A; for, they can both coexist in the same inconsistent world, system of beliefs, etc. This is not the case for monoletheic, classical negations like Boolean negation; for, as Edwin Mares writes: "One feature of Boolean negation is that it is a form of *denial* negation. If '$¬A$' is true, it precludes 'A' from being true."[43] So, if Deleuze understands negation as involving the denial of what it negates, then one reason for this could be that he uses the term "negation" with its classical meaning, which would not be unexpected given that classical logic was the predominant sort throughout his career.

While there are many passages in *Difference and Repetition* where Deleuze discusses affirmation, negation, or denial, there is a notable place where he discusses all of them together. He writes that Nietzsche "never ceases to contrast two conceptions of the affirmation-negation relation. [...] Affirmation is indeed produced, but in order to say yes to all that is negative and negating, to all that *can be denied*."[44] Here we see that affirmation is contrasted on the one hand with negation and on the other hand with denial. In other words, this passage suggests that negation and denial here are *both* understood in terms of their contrast to affirmation. This is something that would hold under monoletheic, classical assumptions about negation but not under dialetheic, paraconsistent ones. In another instance, Deleuze also equates negation and denial when discussing them in Hegelian dialectics, noting that when something *denies* what is opposed to it, it is a negation of a negation.[45] From these statements alone, however, we cannot know with certainty exactly what Deleuze's own theory of negation is; nonetheless, it does at least suggest that Deleuze uses the term "negation" with its classical sense, such that a negation is tantamount to the denial of what is being negated, which is not something that holds under dialetheic assumptions.

Thus, when Deleuze *criticizes* negation and contradiction, it could very well be that he has as his target Routley and Routley's second type of negation, which includes classical negation, and that furthermore his criticisms might not be applicable to the third sort of negation, which includes the dialetheic, paraconsistent kind.[46] We have not yet established any of this definitively; and, even if we feel compelled to wager it nonetheless, it need not here be a point of contention. For, we are not trying to model the logical properties of difference itself in this chapter but rather those of affirmative synthetic disjunction, which may not be the same.

Yet our question still remains: can paraconsistent negation and dialetheism be useful for understanding affirmative synthetic disjunction? To work toward an answer, we will examine one way Deleuze implements it in his philosophy of time, specifically with regard to a bifurcating temporal structure that he articulates by co-contextualizing Leibniz and the Stoics on the issue of fate. And for this notion of bifurcation, we should first see how Deleuze regards disjunction as being a matter of "alternance."

Deleuze and Alternance

> The marvellous fact that meets us in thought when we take determinations such as these by themselves, is that each one is turned round into the opposite of itself.
>
> Hegel[47]

We will now examine what Deleuze has to say about the three main classical principles of logic. This will help us to better grasp how he understands contradiction and disjunction, which for him involve opposition and alternance, respectively. This discussion comes almost exclusively from his lecture courses, so at certain points his account may not seem thoroughly or completely conceived. Yet, it is one of the rare places that Deleuze discusses the principles of logic at great length, so it will nonetheless be of great value to us here. Fortunately, Daniel Smith has already given us a great retelling of it, which we will refer to frequently for clarification.[48] Our own unique task, however, will simply be to extract from this material the logical ideas that are of particular concern for our present purposes.

This account comes in the context of what Deleuze calls "figures of thought," which are very general modes or images of thinking. He says that every person, including every philosopher, thinks under one or another figure of thought.[49] For instance, one such figure is thought as labor and the thinker as a sublime worker. Deleuze next tells a story of how the three main principles of classical logic—Identity, Non-Contradiction, and Excluded Middle—are seen in major developments throughout the history of philosophy, which can itself be understood also as a movement through different figures of thought.[50]

More specifically, Deleuze will show how a philosopher's attempts to think *the real* or *the existent* thereby involve one or another figure of thought. He explains this philosophical problem in the following way. We normally find that we cannot think the real, existent thing itself; we can only conceive of possible things. For example, we can think of an ox or a unicorn. It does not matter to the content of the thought itself whether or not they actually exist. The concept of the unicorn would not change in the least if in fact an existing one is someday discovered.[51] This means that our thought just conceives the thing's essence, which is what the thing is independently of its existence; and thus, to think the thing is to only conceive its possibility (i.e., what it would be *were* it to exist).[52] For this reason, philosophy has always regarded the existent as taking a position exterior to the representation or concept. So when we say, "the thing exists," what we are doing is positing the thing as having a status of being outside its concept or representation. But when we say, "the thing does not exist," that means we are saying it is something that depends solely upon its conceptualization or representation to be what it is. So by thinking a non-existing thing, we do not think the real and existent. Yet, even by thinking the existing thing, we are still only at best conceiving its possibility or essence, but not its existence. Thus, Deleuze claims, we have a problem: it seems that we cannot ever think about reality or existence itself but only about possibility.[53] And one of the main challenges in the history of philosophy has been finding a way to think the real and existent rather than just mere possibility.[54]

One main way this has been done, Deleuze says, is by means of the principles of logic, which can help us discern the possible from the impossible. Deleuze formulates the main three principles in the following way. (Here we will use informal notation for the logical operators, in keeping with the nature of the lecture material.) First, there is {1} the Principle of Identity, which says that "*A* is *A*." It is a principle of *positioning* or of *affirmation*. The other two principles are specifications of this principle. Second, there is {2} the Principle of Non-Contradiction, which says that "*A* is not non-*A*" or that a thing is not what it is not. This is a *negational* principle. And finally there is {3} the Principle of Excluded Middle (or Excluded Third), which says that "*A* or non-*A*" or that a thing is *A* or it is non-*A*. Put yet another way: between *A* and non-*A* there is no third option, and hence the expression "excluded *third*." This is a principle of the *alternative* or of *disjunction*.[55] Because these laws determine what is unthinkable (that is to say, any notion that defies these laws cannot be conceived), that means they also determine what is impossible (assuming that anything unthinkable is impossible).[56]

Already we have encountered a difficulty for our task here, namely, that Deleuze is employing a different manner of formulating the principles than we have been using. In both sorts of formulas, we use the symbol "*A*." What is different now is that Deleuze's formulations employ the copula "is," and the letter variables stand in for the *subject* and *predicate*. It is often written as: *S is P*.[57] That means, for instance, in the formulation for the Principle of Identity as "*A* is *A*," the first *A* is the subject of the proposition, and the second *A* is the predicate, with the two being identically the same. Another complication is that in certain cases Deleuze regards the "is" as predication, with the *A*'s being classes or categories, while in other instances the "is" acts like equality ($A = A$), with the *A*'s being singular terms.[58] So we will need to take note when these shifts occur.

These sorts of formulations fell out of favor with the advances in formal logic during the nineteenth and twentieth centuries.[59] Yet, Deleuze is not concerned with the roles that the principles play in the *history of logic*. Rather, he conceives of them simply in terms of their very general forms, which will undergo one or another more specific conceptualization at different moments in the history of philosophy, in its effort to think the real and existent. Daniel Smith, we noted, provides a comprehensive and comprehendible account of this material, and he shows how Deleuze's project of a philosophy of difference thinks existence outside these three logical structures.[60] Our task here is slightly different. We want to see if we can infer from Deleuze's commentaries the specific logical properties and structures he favors or rejects.

We begin then with the Law of Identity, "*A* is *A*," which Descartes reconceptualizes as being "*Self* = *Self*" (*Moi* = *Moi*), according to Deleuze. But it is not exactly the same as the bare Principle of Identity, which simply says: given any particular thing, it is identical to itself. In Descartes's formulation of *Self* = *Self*, there is first the doubting

*Self*₁, who has knowledge of something that cannot be doubted, namely of the *Self*₂ as thinking being, the *res cogitans*. What is remarkable in Descartes's conception is that he shows the logical Principle of Identity, as $A = A$, to be a hypothetical judgment. For, Descartes raises the possibility that we can doubt the existence of everything whatsoever. That means $A = A$ would hold only *were* there some A to begin with. Thus under this consideration, the Principle of Identity should be more precisely understood as: *if* there is A, then $A = A$. But, this is not the case for *Self* = *Self*. We cannot doubt this Self, because doing so only demonstrates its existence. Thus, Descartes, in rethinking the Principle of Identity and by discovering the self-positing Self, goes beyond this principle by finding a formulation of it involving an unconditioned, non-hypothesized—and thus—a real, existent identity. This was the first step in thinking beyond the possible in order to conceive the real and existent.[61]

Descartes's innovation ultimately fails, because it required too much conceptual acrobatics to go from this certain knowledge of the unconditioned, real Self to that of any other reality. The next part of the story involves Leibniz, who finds a connection between the Principle of Identity and the Principle of Sufficient Reason. These ideas will make more sense later after we discuss incompossibility, so let us here just give an overview. Since the problem with Descartes's reconception of the Principle of Identity is that it renders the Self into an isolated "island" of existence with no good option for establishing conceptual contact with other existences, we will need some other way to think the rest of the real world when just conceiving the Self.[62] Put simply, the way Leibniz does this is by means of two ideas. The first is that everything (every Self, monad, individual substance) has predicates that fully define what it is. So, everything about that individual, including all of its properties, along with everything that will happen to it are all selected from the beginning of time by God. This is the case for all things that ever will come to be and pass away.

The next important idea is that many of these predicates are relational in some way. For instance, Adam comes before Cain. As such, that predicate for Adam (his being the father of Cain) also tells us something about Cain too (his being the son of Adam), and so we learn something about Cain simply by thinking about Adam. And ultimately, everything relates to everything else in one or another way. Now, if all things are fully determined, and if these determinations are relational and co-implicative, then built into the full conception of any one thing or Self is the conception of all other things too. Thus on the basis of fully conceiving an unconditioned Self like Descartes's, we thereby can think all other real, existent things too.[63]

When understood this way, the Principle of Identity and the Principle of Sufficient Reason can be seen as reciprocal principles. In his *Monadology*, Leibniz defines the Principle of Sufficient Reason as that "in virtue of which we hold that no fact could ever be true or existent, no statement correct, unless there were a sufficient reason why it was thus and not otherwise—even though those reasons will usually not be knowable by us."[64] First note that since everything is fully determined and all things are inter-determined, that means any one thing can rationally account for any other (in the sense of explaining why the other thing is the way it is and why the events that happened to it must have occurred). Thus, there is nothing that can be unaccounted for. So, everything has a reason, and hence we see the basis for the Principle of Sufficient

Reason in this notion of the complete and reciprocal determination of individuals. The way this is bound up with the Principle of Identity has to do with how Leibniz reconceives this other principle. He keeps the basic structure of the Principle of Identity as A is A, but he takes it as meaning, in the first place, that all analytic judgments are true. An analytic judgment is one where the predicate is included in the subject. For instance, the triangle has three sides. Here, by thinking of the triangle, you are thereby already conceiving that it has three sides. Also, "every body is extended" is an analytic judgment, because you cannot define body without already having invoked its being extended. But "every body is heavy" may not be analytic. So the first "A" of "A is A" is equivalent to the subject of the analytic judgment, and the second A would be the predicate, which is included in the first.

Leibniz goes a step further by also saying that every true judgment must be analytic, meaning that any judgment that is true is one where the predicate *necessarily* belongs to the subject, regardless of what that judgment is claiming. That goes against our intuition that many judgments are instead synthetic and are about contingent properties of things. We might wonder—posing our own example—must this apple in the refrigerator be red? It could have instead been sitting outside on the ground under its tree, having turned brown by now. Its being red right at this moment certainly does not seem to be necessary, as it very easily could have been otherwise. However, in Leibniz's metaphysics, as we noted, all predicates are completely determined from the beginning, and moreover, they are all inter-determined. In fact, as we will later see, if the apple had even the slightest difference in its predicates from the ones it does have, then it would be a different apple altogether in an entirely different world. Thus for Leibniz, it actually could not be otherwise that this apple is red rather than brown right now, because all the rest of the world has been determined in such a way that it could not have just fallen to the ground and remained there. (The person who picked that same apple was determined to have the predicate of being the one who does this; our grocer was determined as the one who would sell it to us, and so on.) Thus we see how for Leibniz, the Principle of Sufficient Reason goes hand in hand with the Principle of Identity, and furthermore, how simply by having analytic judgments about things (which are of the form "A is A") we thereby think all existing things.[65]

Yet, Deleuze continues, Leibniz's conception is shown to be insufficient with Kant's analytic/synthetic distinction. Although "a triangle has three sides" may be an analytic judgment, "a triangle's three angles are equal that of two right angles" is synthetic, because that predicate is not really contained analytically in the notion of a triangle.[66] It is discovered by means of demonstration. It would be analytic only under Leibniz's *theological* assumption that there is a God Who is responsible for the complete determination of the world and Who can know all the infinitely many necessary predicates of any one thing.[67]

Deleuze, without elaborating much, says that philosophers coming after Kant, especially the German Idealists, wanted to build from Kant's discovery of a synthetic identity, but they were dissatisfied that Kant's conception invokes something that is irreducible to thought and the Self. Rather, they wanted synthetic identity to be founded in the Self as such.[68] To clarify this distinction between analytic and synthetic identity, consider Martin Bertman's formulations: analytic identity is expressible as

"$a = a$," while synthetic as "$a = b$."[69] In other words, Deleuze says that the German Idealists sought a synthetic identification for the Self, but the identification must be founded upon that very Self (the first "a" of "$a = b$") while also being equated with something not strictly and simply contained in that self (the "$= b$" of "$a = b$").[70] The way they do this, Deleuze explains, is by reconceiving the Principle of Non-Contradiction as involving a return to the self through the negation of otherness. He notes how Fichte and Schelling, for instance, claim that "the Self is not the non-Self." Here, remarkably, the Self is not posited as being identical to itself except through its opposition to a non-Self.[71]

To further explain how this involves a reconceptualization of the Principle of Non-Contradiction, Deleuze pays especial attention to Hegel. He says that in Hegelian dialectic, something posits itself by first passing through and *denying* all that it is not, and by means of this sort of a negation of the negation of itself, it ultimately posits what it in fact is and thereby establishes its own identity through these negations.[72] As such, the figure of thought in this solution is thinking as an oppositional struggle and the philosopher as a fighter.[73] Yet, as we will see, there are some complications with Deleuze's characterization of the Principle of Non-Contradiction here. So in order to more fully explicate his account and to translate the relevant logical ideas into our modern terminology, we will supplement this lecture course material with similar passages from his *Difference and Repetition* and *Logic of Sense*.

For the purposes of our present task, what we need to understand is why Deleuze claims that Hegel *does not* assert that there are contradictions in the world, instead affirming the Principle of Non-Contradiction.[74] Deleuze furthermore says that, except for some thinkers who really only mean to be comical, no one in the history of philosophy ever seriously argues that contradictions really exist.[75] This of course goes strongly against the dialetheic conceptions we have discussed so far. For instance, recall from the first chapter Hegel's statements about movement involving contradictions.[76] And consider something Hegel writes in his *Science of Logic* in a section that Deleuze himself cites: "Contradiction [...] grasped and enunciated as a law: *everything is inherently contradictory*, and [...] this law in contrast to the others expresses rather the truth and the essential nature of things."[77] In this same section, Hegel even claims that "something is therefore alive only in so far as it contains contradiction within it, and moreover is this power to hold and endure the contradiction within it."[78] To further complicate Deleuze's interpretation, Hegel explicitly expresses dissatisfaction with the Principle of Non-Contradiction, writing, "'Nothing contradicts itself' is [...] a poor excuse for a law of logic."[79] And what would Deleuze say about Heraclitus, who is known for his embrace of metaphysical contradiction?[80] So, we will need to dig deeper to fully grasp Deleuze's claim that no serious philosopher, not even Hegel, affirms the reality of contradiction.

As a first issue of clarification, we should note that in this historical context, the Principle of Non-Contradiction, when formulated as "A is not non-A," may be understood in a couple of different ways; and furthermore, we should grasp how this conception stands in relation to our formulation $\neg(A \wedge \neg A)$. Were we to reconstruct ours so that it fits into the *S is P* schema that Deleuze seems to be working with here, we could, following Christoph Sigwart, construe the Principle of Non-Contradiction in terms of "the relation between a positive judgment and its negation; it expresses the nature and meaning of the negation by saying that the judgments 'A is B' and 'A is not B' cannot both be true together."[81] One example of such a contradictory pairing could be: "a body is extended" and "a body is not extended." Deleuze's sort of formulation, "*A* is not non-*A*," however, "refers to the relation between a predicate and its subject, and forbids that the predicate should be opposed to the subject."[82] As Kant puts it: "No predicate pertains to a thing that contradicts it."[83] To exemplify Kant's sort of formulation of contradiction, we may simply say, "A body is not extended." Because "is extended" is built analytically into the notion of "body," this sentence defies the Principle of Non-Contradiction, when understood under the more general sort of formulation "*A* is not non-*A*." Yet, as Sigwart explains, we can regard these two kinds of formulations as ultimately being equivalent, and he provides the following reasoning. Since the notion of "body" already includes "is extended," when we say, "a body is unextended," it can be seen as expressing two distinct propositions, namely, its literal claim that "a body is *un*extended" and its implicit claim (built just into the subject term) that "a body *is* extended." This gives us two propositions that stand in contradiction with one another, as they take the form: "'*A* is *B*' and '*A* is not *B*.'"[84] In other words, while Deleuze's "*A* is not non-*A*" rendition of the Principle of Non-Contradiction is structurally different than our $\neg(A \wedge \neg A)$ formulation, we can nonetheless find them to be more or less equivalent.

A second point of clarification is that we should, following Paul Redding, distinguish the Principle of *Non*-Contradiction—which we have been working with and which says that no contradictions are admissible—from the Principle of Contradiction (or, as Karen de Boer names it, the Principle of Self-Contradiction), which Hegel is expressing in his claim that "Everything is contradictory."[85] This can be a little confusing, as very often what is now called the "Principle of Non-Contradiction" was previously referred to just as the "Principle of Contradiction." To further complicate matters, as Jan Łukasiewicz notes, "the principle of contradiction was confused with the deficiently formulated *principle of double negation*, 'A is not not-A.'"[86] As we will see, it is possible that Deleuze's commentary on contradiction in Hegel might be related to this ambiguity of the "A is not non-A" formulation, which can be seen as expressing either the Principle of Non-Contradiction or the Principle of Double Negation.

To elaborate this point, we need to also address what Deleuze says in *Difference and Repetition* and *Logic of Sense* regarding Hegel's dialectic and the way that negation and contradiction function within it. In the following, we will examine how Deleuze's interpretation and critique of Hegelian dialectic provide clues that indicate which logical properties of negation Deleuze finds to be problematic, and this will reinforce our analysis from the previous section. Our discussion here centers around three related concerns Deleuze expresses, namely, that Hegelian dialectic {a} involves a sort of negation whose logical exclusivity {b} is the reason why the dialectical movement through otherness involves a double negation that ultimately {c} affirms identity rather than difference.

The issue we now turn to is Deleuze's observation that in Hegel's dialectical movement, there is a "passage from difference to opposition and to contradiction," regarding which Deleuze references Jean Hyppolite's *Logic and Existence*.[87] In Hegel's discussions of the laws of thought, one of his main arguments is that, when taken simply as formal principles, they are insufficient, and in fact each one implies self-contradictions that are part of a movement of thinking.[88] In the following, we will work through a rough sketch of this material in Hegel's writings to simply see in broad outline how in Hegel we can find certain elements of this passage that Deleuze mentions from difference to opposition then to contradiction, and we limit ourselves just to the concepts in Hegel's text that Deleuze comments upon and that are relevant to our current task, leaving as much extraneous complexity aside as possible.

For instance, Hegel notes certain ways that *difference* is built into the Principle of Identity, despite our initial presumption that it is only about identity. Consider the bare claim that *A is A*. Let us suppose that we are conceiving it simply as a formulation for formal identity rather than for some other logical property. Now, since it formulates for us one particular logical property and not some other, it is thereby expressing identity *rather than* difference; in other words, it is saying "that *identity is different* from difference" and thus that identity itself "*is different.*"[89] Yet, this pure difference that is enunciated in formal identity itself entails a contradiction, too. Insofar as it is merely difference in itself, it would not be difference from anything else but rather just difference from itself. "But," Hegel reminds us, "what is different from difference is identity."[90] In other words, by self-differing, difference thereby is itself identity too: "Difference in itself is self-related difference; [...] the difference not of an other, but *of itself from itself*; it is not itself but its other. [...] Difference is therefore itself and identity. Both together constitute difference."[91]

Hegel notes another way that the Principle of Identity expresses difference, namely, that its syntactical formulation involves a movement of self-differentiation from subject to predicate, and this self-variability built into the structure is only made more obvious by the redundancy of the contents; for, in "*A is A*," we would not have begun proceeding from "*A*" to "is" unless we were moving away from *A* toward something beyond it:

> If, for example, to the question "What is a plant?" the answer is given "A plant is—a plant," [...] the statement says *nothing*. If anyone opens his mouth and promises to state what God is, namely God is—God, expectation is cheated, for what was expected was a *different determination;* [...] nothing will be held to be more boring and tedious than conversation which merely reiterates the same thing. [...] *A is*, is a beginning that hints at something different to which an advance is to be made; but this different something does not materialize; *A is—A*; the difference is only a vanishing; the movement returns into itself.[92]

So, the Principle of Identity's very form bears a syntactical structure where the predicate—even if in an empty fashion—takes our thinking somehow beyond the subject term. Thus, Hegel notes that "the law of identity itself [...] is not merely of *analytic* but of *synthetic* nature," and thereby it also expresses "this opposite, absolute difference itself."[93] Moreover, in identity's "self-repulsion from itself," there is "the determination of *distinction*," and there we have *diversity*.⁹⁴ The "law" or "principle" of diversity, Hegel writes, could be formulated as: "All things are different, or: there are no two things like each other."⁹⁵

From diversity we then move to opposition. To see one way this is so, let us first ask, what makes two things different? They will differ in some respect. That means that one thing has something the other does not have. To illustrate in a simplistic way, suppose we have two kinds of fruit, an apple and a banana. The apple has a spherical roundness, and the banana does not; it rather has its own shape that is a non-roundness, namely, a crescent shape. The two are alike in that they are both things, and more specifically, fruits, but they are unlike in that they have opposing features, namely, roundness vs unroundess.⁹⁶ On a similar basis, Hegel says we are thereby moving from the Law of Diversity ("Everything is different from everything else")⁹⁷ to the Law of Opposition: "Everything is the opposite [of something else]."⁹⁸ For instance, we are saying that the apple and the banana are diverse, because they have contrary properties (for, something which is spherically round cannot be identical to something which is crescent shaped). Now of course, something can be neither spherical nor crescent (a kiwi, for example, is ovular). Yet, what makes something be round is that it is neither crescent, ovular, nor any other shape, but rather just round. So while any one thing is not obviously oppositional to any other one thing, still we might say that something is distinct on the basis of it not being everything else. As Hyppolite puts it, if something is really a distinct thing, then it is only so if it is different from *all other* things, which "puts the thing in opposition to *all the rest*";⁹⁹ and thereby, from diversity, we have "passed over into *opposition*."¹⁰⁰ In other words, the apple is the opposite of everything else, because its features taken together are oppositional in one or another way to the features taken together of all other things.

Yet, how on the basis of the Principle of Opposition (that everything has an opposite) can we arrive upon the Principle of Contradiction (that everything is inherently contradictory)? To answer these questions, first let us consider one way that Hegel characterizes contradiction. He notes that in geometry, the circle is understood both as being perfectly round; yet (on account of an Archimedean sort of "method of exhaustion" that we will see later in Chapter 6), its circumference can be understood as being composed of nothing but straight lines:

> *Opposite* predicates become *contradictory* predicates when they are thought of as belonging to one and the same thing; we then end up saying of something that it is both round and non-round. If one says that something is round, it is [not] non-round. That is what correctly follows if we suppose that it is round. Yet geometricians suppose a circle to be a straight-lined polygon, [so that] its *curve* is viewed as *straight* [i.e., quite inconsistently as *not curved*].¹⁰¹

Hegel then further elaborates on how opposition can involve contradiction. An opposite, very generally speaking, *is nothing more than* the inverse of its other. For instance, in magnetic polarity, "the North Pole is the opposite of the South Pole," meaning that "the one is what it is insofar as it is not what the other is."¹⁰² Yet, if one opposite is nothing other than the inverse of its own other, then in a certain sense they are identical, in that there is nothing about their composition that is formally distinguishable from their counterpart (in other words, each is simply defined as being that which its opposite is not, and so both have exactly the same definition): "To have the opposed quality of the one I need the opposed quality of the other. We have here nothing but the identity of both."[103] Moreover, the negative—as in the case of the South Pole for instance—is not a mere nothing but is itself something and is thus positive; and the positive—as with the North Pole—is only what it is "in so far as the other is not," and in that sense it is something fundamentally negative.[104]

To further illustrate such identity of opposites, Hegel provides some useful examples. East and West are polar opposites. But a road that goes 6 kilometers to the East is the exact same path when it is instead understood as going 6 kilometers to the West. Another case of opposites is the positive and negative values involved in loans. Suppose the loan's value is 6 euro, for instance. The one same loaned amount is dually both a negative for the loaner (minus 6 euro) and a positive for the borrower (plus 6 euro); and also, it is a positive for the loaner (as an investment to be returned) and a negative for the borrower (as a debt to be repaid). In fact, where it only a positive or only a negative for someone, it would not be loan but a gift or a theft.[105] With loans, then, the positive value and the negative value are identically the same value, in a sense. Hegel offers additional elaboration by explaining how we can locate such identifying oppositions with regard to our own body and its surrounding world:

> A human being differs from a tree, or from the air. Yet air is also an opposite. Indeed, from one side of our nature as living beings, air is even our very own other. A human being cannot be without air, and so we are always struggling to get our next breath. Such, generally, is the life process. In hunger a human being is also directed to his or her other, to food. Food is not merely something else in general, but is a human being's opposite. A human being can posit the other only as identical with him- or herself. Such is the inseparability of opposites. Their inseparability is nothing other than their reference to their others, *which is nothing else than their identity.*[106]

What Deleuze emphasizes in all this is how for Hegel there is a "movement" or "transition" of opposites that *resolves* the contradiction.[107] And as we will see, it *ultimately* affirms identity's priority over difference, even though the difference is not eliminated.

The next thing we need to account for is why, *logically speaking*, Deleuze thinks dialectical movements operate in this way. Deleuze notes how Hegel emphasizes that these opposites are *exclusive* of one another.[108] And it is on account of this exclusion that opposites or contraries *expel* each other.[109] Deleuze writes, "Each contrary must further expel its other, therefore expel itself, and become the other it expels. Such is the movement of contradiction."[110] In other words, Deleuze ascribes to the negation involved in Hegelian dialectics the exclusivity of classical negation, on the basis of which there is a polarized movement of opposites involving self-contradictions that ultimately resolve in identities (the "identity of opposites").[111] What is important in this conception is that contradiction is seen as somehow explaining the mobilizing force of the motions. In other words, the expulsive movement of double negation results from contradiction in some sense calling for a resolution in identity. And for Hegel, "in the end the sum total of all realities simply becomes absolute contradiction within itself."[112] For Deleuze, this means that Hegelian dialectics—although operating by means of difference in the form of contradictory, oppositional negation—ultimately conserves the whole in its identity rather than affirming difference at the highest scale:

> Always the same old malediction which resounds from the heights of the principle of identity: alone will be saved [...] that which [...] conserves all the negative finally to deliver difference up to the identical. Of all the senses of *Aufheben*, none is more important than that of "raise up." There is indeed a dialectical circle, but this infinite circle has everywhere only a single centre [...]. [...] The reprises or repetitions of the dialectic express only the conservation of the whole.[113]

Thus in Deleuze's interpretation, contradiction does not ultimately affirm difference but rather the identity of the whole of all contradiction, as its own sort of *A is A*. It is for this reason, then, that Deleuze says Hegelian dialectic *affirms* the Principle of Non-Contradiction,[114] and at last we have our answer: what moves the dialectic is a "consistencizing" process where opposites are compelled to move away from one another, finally finding resolution in a unified, sum totality. Thus in Deleuze's account, Hegel has reconstrued the Principle of Non-Contradiction in terms of the Principle of Double Negation, whereby thought can pass through and think the existent:[115]

> Hegelian contradiction does not deny identity or non-contradiction: on the contrary, it consists in inscribing the double negation of *non*-contradiction within the existent in such a way that identity, under that condition or on that basis, is sufficient to think the existent as such. Those formulae according to which "the object denies what it is not," or "distinguishes itself from everything that it is not," are logical monsters [...] in the service of identity.[116]

So to be clear, Deleuze is not ignorant of the fact that contradiction factors prominently into Hegelian dialectic; rather, what he is saying is that the Principle of Non-Contradiction—along with the Principle of Identity—*always prevails over* the Principle of Contradiction.[117] As V.J. McGill and W.T. Parry put it, under this conception, "the state of the world or a segment of it is always contradictory, though the contradiction is also *being overcome*. Contradiction thus represents a *stage* of truth and reality."[118] Deleuze similarly sees in ancient Greek philosophy efforts to overcome contradiction rather than affirm it. He says that when ancient philosophers recognized that there seems to be contradictions all around us, there was the tendency to regard them as mere appearances and then posit a spiritual world without any such contradictions, as we see most obviously with Plato.[119]

Moreover, the way that Deleuze says the three principles can be violated suggests another possible reason for his claim that no serious philosopher denies the Principle of Non-Contradiction. According to Deleuze, if something breaks the Law of Identity, then *it is not what it is*. If it breaks the Law of Non-Contradiction, then *it is what it is not*. And when something breaks the Principle of Excluded Middle, then *at the same time, it both is what it is and what it is not*.[120] As we can see, this last instance of breaking Excluded Middle is much closer to how we normally understand a violation of Non-Contradiction (for, under this mode of formulation, we normally would say that to break Excluded Middle, something *is neither what it is nor what it is not*), and his conception for breaking Non-Contradiction might be more akin to what we would otherwise regard as being a violation of the Principle of Identity. So in the first place, we see that we need to be very careful when we consider Deleuze's explicit language with regard to his objections to contradiction and negation. It could be that he conceives a denial of the Principle of Non-Contradiction to involve the claim that something *is nothing more or other than what it is not* ($A = non\text{-}A$),[121] which would explain why he thinks this is an absurd and ridiculous position to take. As this is not what most dialetheists would claim, we cannot simply conclude on this basis alone that Deleuze's argument here also serves as a critique of dialetheism.

Returning to Deleuze's story, he next asks: what about the Principle of Excluded Middle? Can we find any philosophers who reconcile thought and existence by means of a reinterpretation of this principle? At this point, Deleuze's account enters into existentialist themes regarding choice. Daniel Smith explains this part of Deleuze's argumentation superbly in his essay "Logic and Existence," and it is an excellent source on this matter.[122] The issue that will instead draw our attention here is the logical distinction Deleuze makes between opposition and alternation, which will again show some signs of dialetheism in his thinking. Recall that his formulation for the Principle of Excluded Middle (or Excluded Third) is "either A or non-A." Deleuze says that the sort of thinking that reconceives this principle and deploys it in a new way would involve the "alternance" of the "either ... or ... " disjunctive operation and not contradiction, negation, and combat. This conception of the Principle of Excluded Middle, he claims, moves beyond Identity and Non-Contradiction, both of which (in his formulations) use the verb "to be." Excluded Middle, however, employs the disjunctive "or." This places thinking under the figure of play, and such a disjunctive thinker would be a game player or gambler (although the play here can be quite serious and involve grave responsibility, as we see with Nietzsche).[123]

Deleuze then illustrates the difference between alternance and contradiction. He notes how in German Expressionist film, there are light/dark visual dichotomies (often expressing conflicts between good and evil) where the light and dark are in conflictual opposition. These oppositions, Deleuze notes, can be seen both within a single shot (Figure 4.7, left top) and going between light and dark shots in sequences (middle row, with the intervening black shots removed).

Figure 4.7 Top left: Single shot with light/dark opposition, in Wiene's *Cabinet of Dr Caligari* (© Decla-Bioscop 1920. All rights reserved). **Top right**: Single shot with light/dark alternance in Bresson's *Diary of a Country Priest*. **Middle row**: Sequence shot with light/dark oppositions, in Lang's *Metropolis* (excluded are simple black shots interspersed between the bright ones) (© Universum Film 1927. All rights reserved). **Bottom row**: Sequence shot with light/dark alternations, from Bresson's *Diary of a Country Priest* (© Union générale cinématographique 1951. All rights reserved).[124]

But in certain other directors, like Grémillon, Dreyer, and Bresson, there are also light/dark patterns, but without the opposition.[125] We can see this in single shots, where for instance light and dark can alternate as our eyes journey into deeper levels of visual depth (Figure 4.7 top right). Or light and dark shots can alternate successively; and, Deleuze claims, even when they seem to unify or resolve in gray (Figure 4.7, bottom row), it is not a dialectical unity, because there is not some new quality that results from the combination.[126] This sort of alternance of things that are other to one another—but not oppositionally so—is better characterized as a "heads or tails" set of alternate options that can flip one to the other without them being in a direct combat with homogenizing or destructive results. So even light and dark, which are normally understood as opposing one another, can be seen instead as simply interchanging, like a coin flipping sides, as each calendar day passes and they rotate in turn.[127] Thus such disjunctive philosophers see thinking as involving *plays*: rolls of dice, flips of coins, dealings of cards, turns of Roulette wheels, etc.[128]

One prominent philosopher of alternance, play, and disjunction is Pascal. Deleuze notes how in the *Pensées*, Pascal might seem at first to be making classifications by means of a genus–species hierarchical structure. But, in fact, he instead uses *sorting* procedures to set up alternances between things that cannot be categorized under each other. For instance, Pascal asks at one point, is it worth honoring people of high birth?[129] He then distinguishes types of people with respect to that question:

{a} Those who honor people of high birth out of fear,
{b} The half-clever/cunning people who despise them,
{c} Clever ones who want to draw from their power,
{d} Devotees of God who despise them in the name of God's justice, and
{e} Christians who honor them in the name of charity.

Deleuze remarks that there is an alternance of honoring and despising in this sequence:

{a} honor
{b} despise
{c} honor
{d} despise
{e} honor

What is notable here is that none of the original options are understood primarily in opposition to one another; they are simply heterogeneous alternatives at their basis. Each one is a different option in its own right, but they can *also* be sorted according to binary alternances.[130]

The heterogeneity of the alternatives is made even more explicit with Deleuze's next Pascal example, the conic sections. Here we can change our point of view on the cone to obtain heterogeneous sections, which can then be sorted into alternances, depending on whether or not the resulting figures are finite or infinite. Deleuze emphasizes that here Pascal does not seek a common genus for all the conic sections. He rather begins with the heterogeneous series of alternances, "either point, or angle, or circle, or parabola, etc.," and sorts them in a way that they admit of an additional level of alternance: "either finite, or infinite, or finite, or infinite, etc." By arranging the sections in this way, none can be considered as in opposition to the others, because one simply comes next as a heterogeneously different figure with its own unique properties.[131]

So what can we say about the logic of this alternance? For Deleuze, it involves disjunction. In the next section, we will examine in a little more detail some of the logical properties Deleuze thinks disjunction has. For now, we can note that he is interested here in an operation that yields a *non-oppositional other*. And because it is an other, that logically can mean it involves a negational operation, as we noted above. Furthermore, since this other is non-oppositional, that suggests it could be a dialetheic negational operation that yields it. Let us turn now to Deleuze's discussion of disjunctive synthesis to obtain more clarification on how he understands logical disjunction.

The God of Logic: Kantian Disjunctive Syllogism

We have been noting that logic is a study of valid inference, but so far we have not really dealt with any inferences from premises to conclusion. (We have only worked with logical truths or tautologies, which can be seen as inferences without premises.) Deleuze does, however, take special interest in the inference called "disjunctive syllogism," in the context of Klossowski and Kant.

Let us first see why we will again need to translate Deleuze's writings on this matter into other terminology in order to place this discussion into a modern logic context. The main issue is that the sort of disjunction Deleuze is commenting upon is not the one that is currently used the most prevalently in logic, so there is the potential for some confusion regarding his terminology. There are two logical operators (or "connectives") that are considered disjunctive.[132] We often employ each of them in our normal reasoning, and both are expressed with "or" in English. One kind is exclusive disjunction. If you have "A or B," with the disjunction being exclusive, the whole disjunction will be true only if just one disjunct is true (and not both). Consider a pea and shell game with two shells and one pea. We can say, "The pea is under shell A or the pea is under shell B." It cannot be neither, because the pea has not slipped out from the shells. It cannot be both, because we have not added another pea. But it must be under just one of the shells, because that is how it was originally placed, and it remained within that particular shell, even though we may have lost track of where it now is.

The other kind of disjunction is inclusive disjunction. It also says that one of the two disjuncts must be true. But what makes it different is that now the disjunction can be true even when both of its disjuncts are true. Suppose you cook for a person, and they eat your meal very quickly. You might think: "Either they are very hungry or they really like our cooking." We think that it has to be at least one of the two possibilities, because otherwise they would not eat it so quickly (perhaps we can tell they are not faking their appetite). But it could also both be true that they like our cooking *and* that they happen to be very hungry at this time.

We need to clarify this distinction, because it has bearing on how we translate Deleuze's commentaries on disjunctive syllogism. A straightforward translation will not work, as the sort of disjunction that is used most commonly in contemporary logic, and particularly for disjunctive syllogism, is inclusive disjunction,[133] which, as we will see, is not the kind Deleuze really has in mind for this inference. So with the inclusive disjunction, which allows for both disjuncts to be true, the disjunctive syllogism works like the following: "either A or B; not A; therefore B." So in our cooking example, suppose you learn that your guest has been very well fed today. We could then draw the following inference: "Either they are hungry or they like our cooking; they are not hungry; therefore, they like our cooking." We know it must be one of the two, so since it is not the first option, it must be the second. What is important to note with this kind of disjunction is that the negation of the one disjunct entails the affirmation of the other.

An exclusive disjunctive syllogism can take a slightly different form, namely, "either A or B; A; therefore not B." So recall our pea and shell game with two shells and one pea. Suppose we lift up one shell and find the pea is there. We can thus reason: "Either the pea is under shell A or the pea is under shell B; the pea is under shell A; therefore, the pea is *not* under shell B." So what is important with this kind of exclusive disjunctive syllogism is that the affirmation of the one will be a denial or negation of the other. It is this sort of relationship between disjuncts that Deleuze is especially against. But as we will see, that does not mean Deleuze wants a conception of otherness that is based merely on the inclusive disjunction in classical reasoning, even though a superficial reading of his texts might suggest this.

So let us see now what exactly Deleuze means by disjunctive syllogism by first looking into his Kantian source material, namely, the *Critique of Pure Reason*. But before that, we will need to establish Kant's notion of disjunctive synthesis as using the exclusive sort of disjunction, which we will do by drawing from his *Jäsche Logic*. Here Kant affirms the Principle of Excluded Middle.[134] He says that the "opposite of truth is *falsehood*" and that "everything possible is either A or non A."[135] Moreover, he notes that "exclusion is a negation."[136] And disjunction for Kant is clearly an exclusive disjunction. For, he speaks of a "whole sphere" of judgment whose area is completely divided up into the judgments that compose it, and he says: "A judgment is *disjunctive* if the parts of the sphere of a given concept determine one another in the whole [...] as complements [...] which mutually exclude one another."[137] In other words, a disjunctive judgment is one where the disjuncts entirely cover the whole sphere and where each is exclusive to all the others in a complementary way, meaning that whatever part of the sphere one judgment does not cover is completely occupied by the other(s). "Thus," he continues, "one member determines every other here only insofar as they stand together in community as parts of a whole sphere of cognition, *outside of which* [...] *nothing may be thought*."[138] This clearly takes a monoletheic sort of view that the domain of judgment is consistent and complete (see Figures 4.2 and 4.6) and thus where the negation of any one part is an affirmation of the remainder. Kant further emphasizes the exhaustivity and exclusivity of disjunctive judgments when he writes: "Outside of them the sphere of the cognition includes nothing more under the given conditions, and one is opposed to the other, consequently neither something *outside* them *nor* more than one *among* them can be true."[139]

Kant offers an illustration for this exclusivity and exhaustivity of disjunction with diagrams that contrast categorical judgments with disjunctive ones. For the categorical kind, suppose we have the judgment that Socrates is mortal (because he is human and all humans are mortal). In the diagram (Figure 4.8, left), the whole sphere of mortal beings is box a; and box b, which is included under a, is humans. And Socrates is x. As we can see, Socrates's being human entails his being mortal, given this structure of inclusion. However, under a disjunctive arrangement (Figure 4.8, middle), the whole sphere of possibilities is divided completely and cleanly into parts. So for instance, think about how we might divide all foods (large box a) into four groups, namely, *b* for fruits & vegetables, *c* for grains, *d* for meats, and *e* for dairy. Kant also gives an example that divides the entire domain into just two complementary partitions: "If, for example, I make the disjunctive judgment, A learned man is learned either historically or in matters of reason, I thereby determine that these concepts are [...] parts of the sphere of the learned man, but not in any way parts of one another, and that taken together they are all complete."[141] We might depict that by dividing the sphere into two parts, *c* and *d*, where *d* is understood as everything that is not *c* (the darkened area labeled "¬*c*," Figure 4.8, right).

On the basis of this divided structure, Kant says that we can draw inferences by means of the disjunctive syllogism. As we can see, when using exclusive disjunction, we can infer both the negation of one from the affirmation of the other, and also the affirmation of one from the negation of the other. This is because, it is a contradiction to affirm both judgments, as one is completely exclusive to the other: "In consequence of the *principle of the excluded middle*, the two contradicting judgments cannot both be true, and just as little can they both be false. If the one is true, then the other is false, and conversely."[142] (Note here that there also seems to be the Principle of Non-Contradiction at work in this conception.) Thus the disjunctive syllogism allows us to "infer either (1.) from the truth of one member of the disjunction to the falsehood of the others, or (2.) from the falsehood of all members but one to truth of this one."[143] And as we will soon see, what especially concerns Deleuze is the first inferential move, where the affirmation of one disjunct entails the negation of the others.

This logic material of Kant is important for grasping how he implements disjunctive syllogism in his *Critique of Pure Reason*, which is what Deleuze specifically comments upon. For the notions involved here, we need first to grasp the element of "conditioning" in Kant's conception of syllogistic reasoning. Let us look at what Kant writes, and then we will illustrate it: "In every syllogism I think first a rule (the *major*) through the understanding. Second, I subsume a cognition under the condition of the

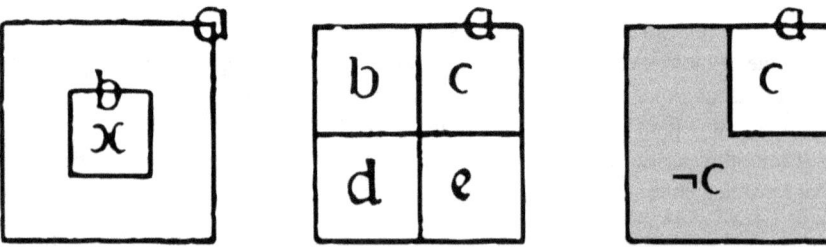

Figure 4.8 Kant's diagrams of judgments. **Left**: A categorical judgment structure, where some item is included in a category that is itself included in a broader category. **Middle**: Kant's depiction of a disjunctive judgment where the sphere is divided up completely into mutually exclusive parts.[140] **Right**: A depiction for how the affirmation of one disjunct is a negation of the complementary remainder.

rule (the *minor*) by means of the power of judgment. Finally, I determine my cognition through the predicate of the rule (the *conclusio*), hence *a priori* through reason."[144] Kant's categorical syllogism illustration has the same structure that we saw with the Socrates example, but instead he uses Caius (the following comes from Michael Rohlf's commentaries):[145]

(1) All humans are mortal. (rule or major premise)
(2) Caius is human. (minor premise)
(3) Therefore, Caius is mortal. (conclusion)

So the minor premise, "Caius is human," conditions the major premise, "All humans are mortal," by sectioning off part of "human" as "Caius" (with "human" also sectioning off part of "mortal"), like in the diagram how x is a part of box b, which composes a section of larger box a (Figure 4.8, left). That sectioning off of mortals, which is a "conditioning" of the judgment, is such that it also happens to encapsulate Caius, and thus we can say of Caius that he is mortal.

Now, as we noted, there is an important role given to selecting the conditioning, minor premise. But the order that our reasoning goes through is not always by considering the major premise first. When we do happen to do so, descending from the major premise to the conclusion by means of the conditioning minor premise, we are reasoning "episyllogistically."[146] Yet, we can also "draw the proposition 'Caius is mortal' from experience merely through the understanding,"[147] thereby obtaining directly what in the previous instance was an inferred conclusion. Now, that judgment already contains the predicate for the major premise; it is the category of all mortals. So next our reason wants to know: under what conditioning of "all mortals" will determine Caius to be one of them? The answer of course is the predicate "human": "But I seek a concept containing the condition under which the predicate [...] of this judgment is given (i.e., here, the concept 'human'), and after I have subsumed [the predicate] under this condition, taken in its whole domain ('all humans are mortal'), I determine the cognition of my object according to it ('Caius is mortal')."[148] And by working up from the conclusion to the premises in this way, we are reasoning "prosyllogistically."[149] Thus, as Rohlf notes, "reason's basic function is to ask about any given empirical judgment: *why?*"[150] In this case, the reason why Caius is mortal is because he is a human. But, having obtained its answer, reason has not finished with its inquiries. It then "subjects that answer in turn to the same question: *why?*"[151] In the case of Caius, for instance, to use Rohlf's illustration, we might want to know why humans are mortal, and we thus find that there is a higher conditioning for humans, which is that we are animals (and animals are mortals). This process goes on indefinitely: "'The questions never cease' (A viii)."[152] What reason is ultimately after is a transcendental concept that is *unconditioned* and that makes possible the totality of all conditions. In the case of categorical syllogistic reasoning, where the conditions are always another predicate at a higher level, the unconditioned ground which would terminate this progression would have to be "a subject that is no longer a predicate,"[153] which Kant says is "the absolute (unconditioned) unity of the thinking subject."[154]

Now, although Deleuze covers this first categorical prosyllogism that ultimately is grounded in the idea of the Self, his focus of course is instead on the disjunctive syllogism, which we turn to now. Let us consider an example, built from Kant's own illustration from above: "Socrates, as a learned person, is either learned historically, or he is learned by matters of reason. Socrates in fact is learned by matters of reason. Thus Socrates is not learned historically." And conversely, "... Socrates is *not* learned historically. Therefore, Socrates is learned by matters of reason." For prosyllogistic reasoning, we might begin with "Socrates is not learned historically," and we ask, under the conditioning of which proposition can we know this, and what is that conditioning? In this case, the conditioning proposition would seem to be, "Socrates is learned by matters of reason," and the proposition that it conditions is "Socrates is either learned historically or learned by matters of reason." And as prosyllogistic reasoning keeps seeking higher conditionings, it will arrive upon that which is unconditioned. Since here conditionings are what cleanly delimit part of the sphere, excluding the entire rest of that sphere, then the unconditioned would be something that does not condition (partition) a larger sphere. It is thus "an aggregate of members of a division such that nothing further is required for it to complete the division of a concept";[155] namely, it is "the highest rational concept of a being of all beings; a thought which at first glance appears extremely paradoxical."[156] As such, it is "the absolute unity of the condition of all objects of thought in general,"[157] and more specifically it is "a transcendental cognition of God."[158] In other words, that which is itself disjunctively unconditioned (being not a part of something greater) but which is also what allows for all conditions (all possible exclusive divisions of all beings whatsoever) is God. As Deleuze explains, "It is left for God [...] to ensure the attribution of the category of community, that is, the *master of the disjunctive syllogism*. God [...] has [...] an apparently humble task, namely, to enact disjunctions, or at least to found them."[159] Put another way, God is a principle of the completed entirety where all determinative divisions have been established, such that any affirmation of one part of the whole is thereby necessarily the negation of all the rest, no matter what it is, with no room for any alternative additions to the whole. This is thus a God of classical negation in a consistent and complete logic.

Let us look now at the comments Deleuze makes regarding this sort of disjunction in Kant's philosophy to see if in fact Deleuze also regards it as an exclusive disjunction, in accordance with our interpretation above. Deleuze says that God is "defined by the sum total of all possibility," with this sum being constituted by "an 'originary' material or the whole of reality."[160] And, the "reality of each thing 'is derived' from it: it rests in effect on the limitation of this totality."[161] In other words, everything is a partition of this *complete* whole. And, he continues, to determine one thing means the denial of its remainder, by means of a disjunctive syllogism: "Disjunction is tied to exclusion in the reality which is derived from it, and thus to a *negative and limitative use*."[162] This means that it is a *consistent* world also. Deleuze then in summation reiterates that dual exclusivity and exhaustivity of this world picture, writing: "In short, the sum total of the possible is an originary material from which the exclusive and complete determination of the concept of each thing is derived through disjunction."[163] So this metaphysical conception of God and reality, we can say, involves a complete and consistent logic where all propositions about it are either true or false, but not neither or both. Yet, as we will see now, Deleuze is more interested in a logic that breaks out of these restrictions, which he elaborates by means of the demonic and Antichrist figures in Klossowski.

The Idol of Baphomet: Klossowski's Demonic Disorder

One text in particular that Deleuze uses to illustrate the breakdown of God's order of exclusion and the rise of an Antichrist/demonic inclusive order is Klossowski's *The Baphomet*. The Kantian theologizing of exclusive disjunction is important for Deleuze, because he contrasts this divine exclusivity with a demonic factor that will infect disjunction with a "becoming-mad."[164] We saw this notion once already with the paradox of pure becoming as illustrated by Alice's loss of personal identity from her transformation. Let us look now at how Deleuze elaborates this notion through his commentaries on Klossowski's novel.

It is a story about the Knights Templar in France around the time of their sudden and official dissolution, brought about by Pope Clement V, under pressure from King Philip IV, who wanted to escape his great debts to the Templars. King Philip schemed to have the Templars, under the pain of torture, confess to practices of sodomy and sacrilege, including spitting on the cross and worshipping an idol named Baphomet.[165] In fact, we encountered Éliphas Lévi's famous artistic rendition of the Baphomet in Chapter 2 (Figure 2.1, bottom left). There is a satanic allure to the image, and the idol itself, according to Lévi, is a "pseudo-Deity," a "god of falsehood," and a "creator and rival of God."[166] Let us look more closely at the story Klossowski tells, as it will allow us to specify exactly why Deleuze rejects a classical notion of disjunction and of disjunctive syllogism.

There are two main sections of the story. The first one narrates events—partly of historical accuracy and partly fabulation—occurring in France and leading up to the dissolution of the Templar order that we mentioned above. What is important for us in this section is that there is a young man of the age of fourteen, Ogier, working as a page to certain knights, serving them both formally and in their bedchambers. His being in this position was arranged intentionally by his mother in order for her to raise accusations of sodomy upon the Order. (This would ultimately result in the mother reclaiming some lands her deceased husband bequeathed to the Order, supposing that the accusations would ultimately help lead to the Order's dissolution.)[167] And young Ogier's seduction of the Templar men was facilitated in part by some sorcery conducted by one of his tutors. (This sorcerer tutor was able to make the Templars have dreams about the young man, causing them to desire him.)[168] This section of the book ends with the King's troops capturing the Commandery where all this takes place. Now, shortly before that event, the boy undergoes an initiation ceremony that makes him a squire. Yet the circumstances are complicated (in fact, it is originally supposed to be a trial for the boy and his treacherous mother), and the young man ends up being hanged (by murder or suicide; it is not specified).[169]

The next section is not as historically grounded, but it keeps from the prior section the corpse of the young man, still hanging on the noose. The story here centers around the last Grand Master Templar, Jacques de Molay, who has been assigned by angels a difficult, supernatural task. When someone dies, their soul, in the form of a "breath," enters a sort of "limbo" status, as they await their final judgment. This will only come on Judgement Day, when their breath-soul is reunited with their former body, and they are then judged as to whether they enter heaven or are sent to hell.[170] Klossowski's metaphysical setup for this is the following. Bodies are discrete entities that are physically distinct from one another. Your breath-soul is in your body, and your identity is preserved in that fixed union, and my breath-soul is in my body, and likewise, my identity is preserved in that union. And because our bodies remain distinct (as no two bodies can occupy the same place), our breath-souls never become intermixed and thus our identities never become confused either.

This is what Deleuze calls the "order of God," which he says includes the following elements: {1} God's own identity as the ultimate foundation for everything whatsoever (if God were not self-same and self-consistent, then the realm that God governs, namely, all of reality, would lose its principle of cohesion); {2} the world's identity as a sort of stabilized context for all things (the world itself must also then remain self-consistent); {3} the individual person's identity as the basis for their agency (if people lose their identity, here in the sense of their breath-soul mixing with others, then they will no longer be in complete control of actions committed by the new, compound entity); {4} the body's identity as the basis for personal identity (without an embodiment for personal identity, it is merely an intangible abstraction or contentless formality); and {5} language's identity as the grounds for all denotation (successful denotation needs meaning assignments to be fixable so that words and propositions can latch onto the world they denote).[171]

Yet, as we noted, at death the breath-soul leaves the body and is no longer grounded in a distinct physical entity that keeps it apart from the other breath-souls. Instead, they exist as small gusts of wind moving about through the air, and they can pass into and through one another, becoming all confused together. If they stay mixed up and combined in this way, then on Judgment Day, they will not be able to reenter their proper bodies to be judged. The Grand Master, then, has been assigned the task of keeping track of the breath-souls by maintaining a record of the unique features of their movements which could match them to their original bodies, so that their proper resurrection can take place.[172]

While his task is difficult enough as it is given how easily the breath-souls can intermix, it in fact will become entirely pointless and impossible. In the first place, as Deleuze notes, in the breath-souls "there is already [...] a certain rebellious intention, an intention to escape from God's judgment," which they attempt by confusing God as they merge into complicated, composite breath-souls.[173] As the Grand Master explains, "the older souls stake out more recent ones, and merging by affinity, they agree to obliterate their responsibilities in each other, or in twos or threes; mutually complicated, pretending to be an indissoluble whole, they come and go through my fortress, defying my scrutiny and reason!"[174] But even if the Grand Master were successful in keeping them apart, that would not matter anyway. For, he learns from one particular breath-soul (i.e. Saint Theresa's) that the capacity has been reached for souls to be admitted into heaven or hell. So all remaining souls will never be reunited with their proper bodies anyway, as they have no need to be judged anymore. The souls, then, are granted their deepest wish for total freedom, now that they "can be no more damned than saved."[175] Thus, she tells him, "your task will only become more and more toilsome: the souls' turbulent anarchy, their adulteries, their incests in the circle assigned to you will only grow in size and number! For as soon as most of them no longer feel obliged to resurrect, God abandons them to their own judgment."[176] And so: "when their bodies have exhaled [their expired breath-souls], even before you interrogate them, such a dissonance of voices shall be raised from the depths of their expiration that you shall never be able to differentiate each and its own."[177]

The Grand Master of the Templars even notes how this merging of breath-souls, and thus of identities, undermines "the principle of contradiction, identity, responsibility, etc.," because "all the breaths come to agglomerate themselves in one irresistible mass as they are released from their disaggregate bodies."[178] What gives breath-souls certain moral qualities are the ways they move their body's organs to commit either good or evil actions. But when they are apart from their body, there remain just their tendencies of movements, which admit of varying intensities. Now, as different moral tendencies "emanate equally from diametrically opposed bodily comportments," when the breath-souls mix together, so too do the once separate and oftentimes incompatible moral qualities, like malice and generosity.[179] In this way "the most criminal as well as the most innocent" breath-souls might enter into "temporary combinations" and "arbitrary intertwinings" and thus with very "diverse dispositions."[180] In other words, these combinations often result in contradictory properties that coexist in one conglomerate breath-soul.

And not only can breath-souls mix with each other, they can also enter into other people's living bodies, and "not in twos or threes, as when they merge themselves, but in fives and sevens in a single uterus."[181] In addition, any one soul can migrate as often as it wants from one living body to another. The Saint Theresa breath-soul in fact enters the body of Ogier, the boy we mentioned before who was left hanging on his noose this whole time. Upon doing so, Theresa's identity is modified, all while Ogier's is too.[182] For instance, Ogier's male bodily form gains women's breasts,[183] becoming a "monstrous body"[184] as we see in the Baphomet image.[185] There can even be a sort of "becoming-animal" in these breath-soul transfers, because the Grand Master sends his breath-soul into a hornet in order to fly about Theresa/Ogier's body so that he may better enjoy its beauty,[186] and Nietzsche's breath-soul has entered the body of an anteater.[187]

Now, Theresa's breath in Ogier's body turns out to be more than just this limited pairing of two identities. When the Grand Master calls Theresa/Ogier a God, she says she cannot be: "I am not a creator who enslaves being to what he creates, what he creates to a single self, and this self to a single body. O, Sir Jacques, the millions of selves that you oppress within yourself are dead and have resurrected millions of times in you, unbeknownst to your single self."[188] Rather than being God, she/he is Baphomet,[189] and the Nietzsche/anteater is the Antichrist.[190] (Also note that the Grand Master accuses her of being a sorceress and actress.)[191] As Baphomet, she/he is "The Prince of Modifications," and by worshipping her/him, one can be free of judgment, moral responsibility, and fixed identity to instead pass "into the thousands of modifications that will never drain the Being."[192]

The cost of this freedom, however, is one's memory of one's former self. In the Grand Master's case, he needs to stop celebrating the anniversary of his being tortured and executed. Somehow he remains eternally himself in a way that defies normal chronology (and this is perhaps how he stays alive through the ages in order to conduct his supernatural work). The Grand Master, Jacques de Molay, who in actuality was burned at the stake for retracting his forced confession of heresy, in Klossowski's tale lives somehow after that death, but this involves an annual commemoration of his torture and killing. This it seems is part of how he maintains the identifying relationship between his proper breath-soul and his body. Thus to free his breath-soul, he must cease this commemoration. And so when the Grand Master comes to momentarily worship the Prince of Modifications (Theresa/Ogier/Baphomet), he forgets himself in a way that is reminiscent of Alice's loss of identity; he says, "What is my memory? Who was I? Who am I? What shall I be? Baphomet, succour me quickly!" And when asked what he desires, he answers: "All the modifications!"[193] In other words, he wants to pass through every breath-soul and body and thereby take on all possible predicates, both one after another and many simultaneously, losing his identity and proper name in the process.

When a messenger from heaven comes to admonish the Grand Master during one of these ceremonies, Klossowski makes the logic of this "order of God" explicit. The holy apparition (which is the head of Pope Clement V, the one who dissolved the order, surrounded by Purgatory's fire) clarifies that the Grand Master's crime is against God's efforts to enforce strict identities. He says to the Grand Master:

> Either you shall celebrate the anniversary of your torment with a clear conscience, and we shall confer an intelligible consistency upon your memory [...] but in that case, O Grand Master of the Temple, do not admit spirits that deny that God ever created natures eternally identical to themselves and responsible for their acts and thoughts! For one such spirit has slipped into your fortress to seduce the expired breaths and to show them that there is no unity and that nothing stays forever the same.[194]
>
> (This spirit in question is the Antichrist Nietzsche/anteater.)

Deleuze says that against this order of God stands "the order of the Antichrist, which is opposed point for point to the divine order. It is characterized by {1} the death of God, {2} the destruction of the world, {3} the dissolution of the person, {4} the disintegration of bodies, and {5} the shifting function of language which now expresses only intensities."[195] Deleuze places this discussion within the context of what he says regarding Kant and disjunctive syllogism, so let us see if we can translate it further into our modern logical notions and terminology. We begin within the framework of a Kantian sort of God who ensures that there is a consistent and complete system in which disjunctions and negations are exclusive and exhaustive. Next Deleuze employs Klossowski's *The Baphomet* to ask the question: what happens if we remove the God who guarantees this exclusivity and exhaustivity of the divisions? Deleuze says that there will be a "synthesis" of disjunction.[196] Ultimately, this means that nothing needs to keep its identity over time, nor must it at any one time have a singular identity, as we saw in *The Baphomet*. Let us look more closely at the "logic" of Deleuze's affirmative synthetic disjunction.

Deleuze emphasizes that when this God-ensured disjunctive system of identities breaks down, "the disjunctions stay disjunctions," but "their synthesis, however, is no longer exclusive or negative, and they take on, to the contrary, an affirmative sense [...]. In short, divergence and disjunction as such become the object of affirmation,"[197] "*without restricting one by the other or excluding the other from the one.*"[198] First, note that we here have a *synthesis* of the disjuncts where they also remain disjoined. But, this "synthesis," Deleuze says, has not "become a simple conjunction."[199] The reason for that is Deleuze wants to maintain the independence and heterogeneity between the terms, which for him consists in a disjunctive relation. In fact, in a way that seems explicitly contrary to the dialetheic reading we are considering for Deleuze's logic, he and Guattari speak of the disjunctive synthesis in the schizophrenic as *not* involving a contradictory conjunction of predicates:

> The schizophrenic is not man and woman. He is man or woman, but he belongs precisely to both sides, man on the side of men, woman on the side of woman. [...] The schizophrenic is dead *or* alive, not both at once, but each of the two as the terminal point of a distance over which he glides. He is child *or* parent, not both, but the one at the end of the other, like the two ends of a stick in a nondecomposable space.[200]

In Chapter 6 we will look more at the notion of difference as distance. But let us very carefully consider their words here. For Deleuze and Guattari, the affirmative synthetic disjunction means that someone can pass from one contradictory predicate to another, but never be both at once and, by means of that movement, affirm the distance between them. As such, it is a "disjunction that remains disjunctive, and that still *affirms the disjoined terms.*"[201] This already is a little confusing, because on the one hand they say that the disjunction affirms both terms, while on the other hand they claim that these terms cannot be conjoined. But logically speaking, the affirmation of two terms normally allows for their conjunction. (Under what reasoning, for instance, would enable you to claim, "it is dark" is true and "it is raining" is true, yet "it is dark and it is raining" is not true?) So as you can see, we need to tread cautiously here in order to determine their logical thinking.

One possibility is that Deleuze and Guattari are claiming that something can have a particular property at one moment and not have that property at another moment, like the child growing up and becoming a parent, and through that process, no longer be a child anymore. But in that case, they are saying nothing remarkable at all, surely not something worth all the elaboration and emphasis they give to it. While that element of a movement over time between contradictory predicates might be a part of this conception, it most likely is not all they mean to convey here. So let us dig deeper.

Deleuze and Guattari offer some further elaboration on how they understand this "synthesis." They say that affirmative synthetic disjunction should not be understood as "vague syntheses of identification of contradictory elements" like we see with

"Hegelian philosophers."²⁰² So to be clear, it seems then that when they wrote, "the schizophrenic is not man and woman," their concern with the conjunction here is that it involves a "synthesis of identification" (which, logically speaking, is not strictly a conjunction). But why would such an identification be problematic? They say of the schizophrenic that

> he affirms [disjunction] through a continuous overflight spanning an indivisible distance. He is not simply bisexual, or between the two, or intersexual. He is transsexual. He is trans-alivedead, trans-parentchild. He does not reduce two contraries to an identity of the same; he affirms their distance as that which relates the two as different. He does not confine himself inside contradictions; on the contrary, he opens out and, like a spore case inflated with spores, releases them.²⁰³

The logic they have in mind here is not straightforwardly explicit, so let us try to extract it. We should first observe that they are employing two terms that might need to be distinguished logically, namely, "contrariety" and "contradiction." But they use them interchangeably, so we need not worry ourselves too much with such a distinction.²⁰⁴ Second, we see again that their concern with regard to contradiction is that affirmative synthetic disjunction "does not reduce two contraries to an identity of the same." It is not obvious what the identification and reduction are here. Is it an identification of the predicates and a reduction to a singular one? Would then the idea be that by affirming the conjunction, "the schizophrenic is a child and the schizophrenic is a parent," this could render the predicates "child" and "parent" indiscernibly the same predicate? That does not seem to follow from what they are claiming. Or is the idea something like the "cancellation" model of negation, whereby the conjunction of contradictory terms would eliminate both of them? In other words, are they thinking that according to a certain view, opposites neutralize or nullify one another, like adding hot and cold water to obtain lukewarm water? Regardless, they emphasize here that the predicates need to retain their difference. This point is reinforced by the idea in the above passages that there must be a *movement* of becoming from one predicate to the next, as we see in their "trans" wording and the idea of an "overflight" across the distance spanning between them. It would seem, then, that their objection to the identification (or conjunction) of contradictory predications would be that it does not involve a becoming. Their thinking might be that when the contradictory predicates are both fully affirmed *at the same time*, that means there is not the differential basis needed for a temporalized movement from one to the other. In other words, when they say the schizophrenic is not both child and parent (and thus not both child and not child), one reason they have is that by already being both, there is no room then to move between them, going from one pole to the other, because the schizophrenic would already be occupying both poles.

However, the dialetheic formulation would still work for both of the concerns they express here. Regarding their first concern—that a conjunction of opposites will reduce them to sameness—this is not what results from the dialetheic formulation $A \land \neg A$; for, we can still derive from it, independently, A and also $\neg A$ (see Chapter 4). And what about their concern that a conjunction of opposites eliminates the possibility for a movement between them? We saw in Chapter 1 that under a dialetheic conception of change, it is in fact by means of a conjunction of a proposition and its negation that we can logically account for changes. In other words, under dialetheic reasoning, we can say that the schizophrenic is both child and not child, when it is undergoing the movement from the one to the other. Moreover, the dialetheic formulation *does* affirm both terms that are other than one another, even though they contradict. And lastly, recall the dialetheic logic of the temporal gluon from Chapter 4. Even if the schizophrenic is fluidly moving between child and parent, we could say that the child phase is identical to the temporal gluon (the consistency of the becoming), and the parent phase is likewise identical to it, but on account of the identity here being intransitive under this dialetheic conception, that does not thereby make the child phase be identical to the adult phase. So here we can note a sort of non-classical "identification" of the terms, at work in their heterogeneous combination, that does not "reduce two contraries to an identity of the same." In sum, the dialetheic formulation of $A \wedge \neg A$ (or a predicate logic equivalent) shares all the logical properties that affirmative synthetic disjunction should have: {1} it preserves heterogeneity, {2} it affirms both terms along with the difference between them, {3} it does not reduce the terms to sameness by means of an identification, and {4} it can express the movement between the terms. Such a dialetheic conception seems at work for instance when they write, "Schreber is man and woman, parent and child, dead and alive [...] because he is himself this distance that transforms him into a woman," and also when they say:

> In *Le Baphomet* Klossowski contrasts God as the master of the exclusions and restrictions that derive from the disjunctive syllogism, with an antichrist who is the prince of modifications, determining instead the passage of a subject through all possible predicates. I am God I am not God, I am God I am Man: it is not a matter of a synthesis that would go beyond the negative disjunctions of the derived reality, in an original reality of Man-God, but rather of an inclusive disjunction that carries out the synthesis itself in drifting from one term to another and following the distance between the terms.[205]

Now, this quote raises an issue that we should be very clear about. They call this an "inclusive disjunction," but we need to be sure they are not simply using any options available in classical logic for construing affirmative synthetic disjunction. We know that the disjunctive synthesis does not involve classical negation, because that is exclusive. We also know that we cannot understand it simply as a classical conjunction, because that, logically speaking, does not guarantee the heterogeneity or tension between the items. For, nothing prevents us from making a redundant conjunction, like $A \wedge A$. And it cannot be a classical exclusive disjunction, as that would allow the affirmation of one term to entail the negation of the other. It is tempting then to simply conclude that Deleuze has in mind here a classical, inclusive disjunction, as indicated in the wording of the above quotation. But there are a number of reasons why that will not work either. {1} Classical inclusive disjunction has been for some time now the conventional sort of disjunction, and normally when we speak of disjunctive syllogism, it is the kind using inclusive disjunction. This alone does not prove Deleuze did not mean for disjunctive synthesis to involve a classical, inclusive disjunction. But it is also not very likely that Deleuze would devote so much attention trying to convince us to accept a conception that is so conventional as to already be taken for granted. {2} Classical inclusive disjunction, in the disjunctive syllogism, allows us to affirm one term by denying the other. Deleuze is explicitly against this sort of exclusivity of the terms. And {3} inclusive disjunction, by itself, does not guarantee a heterogeneity of the terms. Like with bare conjunction, there can be a redundant disjunction, like $A \vee A$. (The dialetheic formulation, however, does guarantee that otherthanness of the terms, by using dialetheic negation.)

There is still more to this story of affirmative synthetic disjunction, so let us turn now to Deleuze's commentaries on Leibniz and the Stoics, which elaborate certain temporal issues involved with it.

5

Truth and Bifurcation: Leibniz and the Stoics

Introduction

For Gilles Deleuze, temporality bears a bifurcational structure. We will first see how he explicates that notion in the context of Gottfried Leibniz's philosophy of possible worlds. After that, we examine his similar elaborations using Ilya Prigogine and Isabelle Stengers's account of bifurcation points and Jorge Borges's "The Garden of Forking Paths." And we end with a detailed examination of the way Stoic "prohairesis" can introduce forkings in time, despite Stoic fatalism.

Incompossible Leibnizes

In the 24th section of Deleuze's *Logic of Sense*, on "The Communication of Events," he elaborates on affirmative synthetic disjunction in the context of Leibniz's notion of incompossible worlds, which we will sketch out now in brief.

We begin with Leibniz's notion of individual substance, which in one sense is something whose notion has a unique and complete set of predicates, meaning that no other substance has the same ones[1] and also that they completely determine the individual substance, such that it cannot be confused with any others.[2] Yet, these predicates include temporal determinations; that is to say, not all of the predicates are true at the same time, but rather certain ones might be true for particular times and not for others.[3] As a possible example, consider how you yourself have a predicate determining when you were born. This also means that your parents have predicates determining that they meet some time before your birth.

Given that the predicates can be assigned more or less arbitrarily, Leibniz says that there are many possible biblical Adams, with each having its own unique set of predicates.[4] Deleuze observes that one sort of possible Adam would have the alternate predicate of not being a sinner.[5] And as we noted before, oftentimes the predicates are relational (like your parents meeting), so the complete concept of an individual substance can inform us about all the other individual substances implicated with it in the same world, such that from one you can deduce all the others, as if each is a mirror to the entire world or a different point of perspective surveying an entire town.[6]

An individual substance is possible so long as any of its predicates do not contradict any others that it has.[7] Think for instance of the classic example of a contradictory object, the round square.[8] But since God is interested in creating a world, that means there will be very many individual substances that God will create and place together into one shared cosmos;[9] and, in order for every one of these individual substances to be able to coexist together, all their predicates must be accommodated to one another.[10] Substances whose predicates do not "get in one another's way"[11] are compossible, and substances whose predicates instead preclude the possibility of the other (like your parents meeting only after you are born) are called "incompossible."[12] So God calculates not just every possible complete predicate-assignment for all individual substances,[13] but also all the combinations of every different individual substance.[14] Yet in addition to these variables, God calculates for these possible worlds different sets of laws, which in large part determine the conditions for a world's compossibility.[15] For instance, in our world, your parents cannot have the predicate that they meet after the event of your birth; for, that would go against the laws governing the nature of causality and of time that have been assigned to our world. And to use Deleuze's example, Adam the non-sinner cannot be in our world, because everything else that is to transpire in our world depends on his having committed his sinful act.[16] So while Adam with the predicate "non-sinner" is possible given that his notion involves no contradiction with his other predicates, he is not possible in combination with the other individual substances in our world. In other words, our world is *exclusively disjunct* from these other possible worlds whose substances are incompossible with ours.[17]

Deleuze illustrates incompossibility by using a situation Georges Canguilhem describes in his *On the Normal and the Pathological*. Canguilhem discusses a study of two variations of a butterfly species, one black and vigorous and the other gray and calm. Now, even though "in captivity the blacks eliminate the greys,"[18] there was once a time when the gray ones were more prevalent in certain regions of the world. The reason, Canguilhem says, is that the calmness and lighter tone of the gray butterflies allowed them to better escape the attention of birds by hiding on tree bark, while the vigorous activity and the darkness of the black ones made them more prone to detection and capture. So because in our world there are certain natural laws and particular varieties of creatures with relational predicates—like birds eating butterflies—that means {1} certain predicates can be found to be incompatible within one creature even if there is no logical contradiction between them. For example, grayness and vigor paired up in one butterfly combine incompatible survival strategies. And {2} certain predicates held in different species can be incompossible with one another even if they too are not strongly contradictory, like grayness and blackness, as the conditions of some situation may allow just those creatures with a particular tone to thrive. For Deleuze, one affirmative element in this example is that "*to turn gray* is no less positive than *to turn black*."[19] In other words, although a thriving population of gray butterflies would not be found in the same situation as a thriving population of black ones, both traits are positive, and neither is—*logically speaking*—an exclusive negation of the other. So since rather it is the actual laws and conditions of the world itself that determine the exclusions, Deleuze calls them "alogical" incompatibilities (although, as we noted in the Introduction, this conception, being metaphysical, has not evaded logic altogether).[20]

Now, before creating the actual world, God calculated all possible worlds made of compossible individual substances, and, using free will,[21] God chose the "best of all possible worlds"[22] which would be the one with "the greatest amount of essence"[23] and the "greatest possible *variety*, but with all the order there could be" and thus with "as much perfection as could be."[24]

Another important idea in Leibniz's thinking is a notion of the *divergence* between incompossible worlds. Suppose there are two worlds, one being ours. All the individual substances in our world have counterparts in the other world, and these corresponding individual substances share the same temporally determined predicates, up until the time of Adam's sinning in our world. But in the other world he never sins. This situation can be understood as the worlds being convergent up until the moment when Adam sins in our world, after which they diverge in different directions of development; for, Adam the sinner in our world is incompossible with the innocent paradise remaining in the other world, just as innocent Adam is incompossible with the fallen beings of our world. As Leibniz writes: "If, in the life of any person, and even in the whole universe anything went differently from what it has, nothing could prevent us from saying that *it was another person or another possible universe which God had chosen*. It would then be indeed *another individual*."[25] Leibniz illustrates this divergence of incompossible worlds by having us consider two time intervals, *A-B*, during which he is in Paris, and *B-C*, following immediately after, when he goes to Germany. Yet, he then wonders, what would happen were he not to make the journey to Germany and instead remain in Paris during interval *B-C*? That could only happen were the worlds to diverge, with there now being two separate worlds and two distinct Leibnizes, one being in Paris in the first world and the other being in Germany in the second world (Figure 5.1).[26]

John Nolt, when explaining modal tense logic by means of Leibnizian possible worlds semantics, gives the following similar scenario:

> I wake up on a Saturday; several salient possibilities lie before me. I could work on this book, or weed my garden, or take the kids to the park. [...] Yet my choices affect the world. If I spend the day gardening, the world that results is a different world than if I had chosen otherwise. Leibnizian metaphysics, then, can be seen as a widening of our vision of possibility from the part to the whole, from mere possible situations to entire possible worlds.[27]

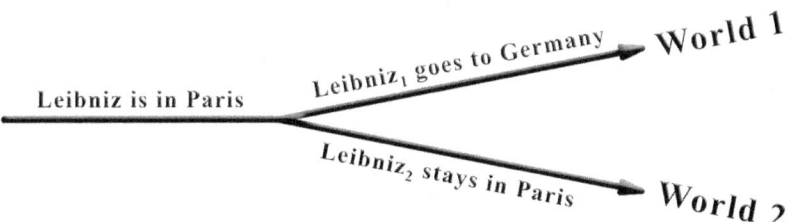

Figure 5.1 Were Leibniz to stay in Paris instead of going to Germany, he would be another Leibniz in another world.

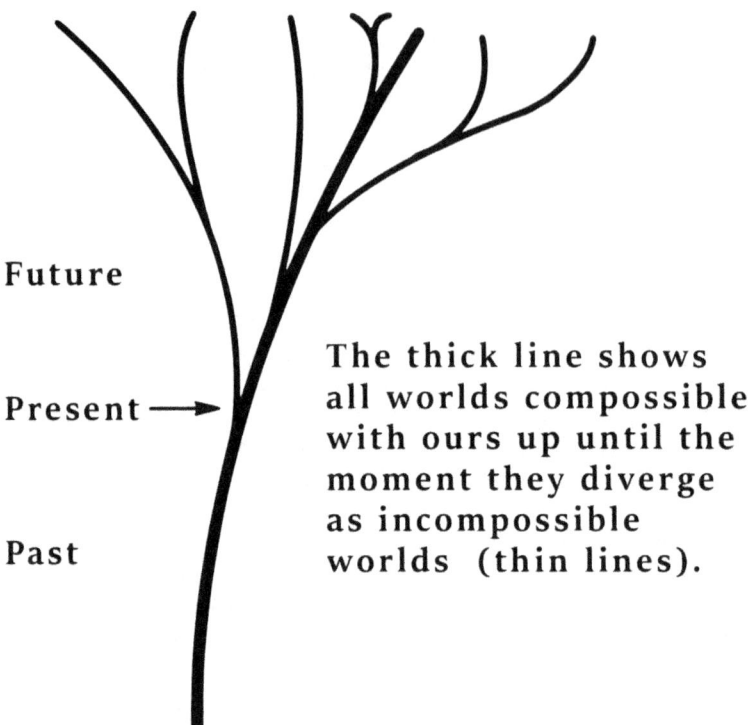

Figure 5.2 A diagram of temporalized world divergence, based on John Nolt's "A Picture of Time" diagram.[28]

Nolt diagrams this divergence of possible worlds with a tree-like figure, where the branches represent points when a decision causes worlds to disjoin (Figure 5.2).

Now, suppose that Adam's consequential decision was not necessitated by God's selection of predicates. This would mean that prior to his choice, he is missing the predicate "sinner" and is also missing "not sinner." Leibniz calls such an underdetermined Adam a "vague Adam," because Adam's notion here encompasses more than one individual,[29] and Leibniz says there would thus be "several *disjunctively* possible Adams."[30]

Nevertheless, Leibniz's God does not leave anything up to chance; for, "God does nothing disorderly."[31] Thus for Leibniz there can be no vague Adams, and you yourself are not vague either. For, when God selected our world, God already knew all the predicates for each individual substance and thus all the choices Adam and you make.[32] Here the actual world can only follow one path with no real chances for divergence at any point.

When explaining affirmative synthetic disjunction in this context of incompossibility, Deleuze suggests that we remove God from the Leibnizian picture, such that given all the ways our world can diverge at any moment, none of them have been decided in advance.[33] This means that incompossibility no longer serves "to exclude events from one another" by means of "a negative use of divergence of disjunction."[34] As we noted before, in Deleuze's account, exclusive disjunction serves to deny one member while affirming the other.[35] And under these "negative rules of exclusion," to affirm both members would mean that "their difference is denied," which can involve synthesizing them in such a way that they become identical.[36]

For example, under Leibniz's assumptions, the affirmation of two worlds is equivalent to identifying them as one and the same. Suppose we think we have two worlds, and we affirm both of them as being true or actual worlds. It cannot be that one diverges from the other, because God excluded all variants except one. But if they are entirely convergent, then there is no difference between their laws and substances, and thus under Leibniz's law of identity they would be identically the same after all.[37] Our world, for Leibniz, never admits of any incompossible divergences or incomplete determinations.

Finally, recall God's criteria for selecting the best of all possible worlds: it is the one with the most essence and variety. Suppose we subtract God but keep these criteria in place. Would not a world in which divergences somehow enter in a real way, like Adam being both a sinner and not a sinner, have additional essence and variety on account of the extra predicate that is otherwise excluded?

Forks in Time

Before moving on, it would be useful for us to see how Deleuze finds this bifurcational structure of incompossibility in other contexts, which will help us elaborate his thinking here. One is a scientific model from Ilya Prigogine and Isabelle Stengers's *Order Out of Chaos*.[38] As an introduction to the notions here, first imagine that we are running a faucet at a low enough level of flow that the water falls in a straight column. We then very gradually increase the flow until suddenly—when we reach a critical moment in the increase—the smooth column becomes chaotically turbulent. Given what we said regarding instantaneous changes in Chapter 1, it would seem possible that there comes a moment of transition when it is both steady and turbulent in the same instant of alteration. Yet, here we are to think of the flow as being caught in two states in yet another manner. Before even making that transition, it enters an unstable state where it has two possible directions of development, but there is no way we can predict which one it will take. To further describe these sensitive transition-points in complex systems, Prigogine and Stengers quote J. C. Maxwell:

> The system has the quantity of potential energy, [...] which cannot begin to be so transformed till the system has reached a certain configuration, to attain which requires an expenditure of work, which in certain cases may be infinitesimally small, and in general bears no definite proportion to the energy developed in consequence thereof. For example, [...] the little spark which kindles the great forest, the little word which sets the world a fighting, [...] the little spore which blights all the potatoes [...].[39]

Prigogine and Stengers explain that there are systems that when reaching such a "singular point," they can develop in one of two different directions of evolution. For example, in certain chemical systems, if you increase one parameter, for example, the concentration of a chemical, the system is pushed further and further away from a state of equilibrium. If pushed far enough, it reaches a "bifurcation point" where, for example, the spatial distribution of that chemical can follow one or another opposite path of configuration, with the choice being entirely unpredictable (Figure 5.3).[40]

In fact, in some complex systems, there can be bifurcations of bifurcations. As Deleuze writes, all of the forkings "constantly split up any state of equilibrium and each time impose a new 'meander', a new break in causality, which itself forks from the previous one, in a collection of non-linear relations."[41] Prigogine and Stengers say that "the 'historical' path along which the system evolves as the control parameter grows is characterized by a succession of stable regions, where deterministic laws dominate, and of instable ones, near the bifurcation points, where the system can 'choose' between or among more than one possible future."[42] And so each singular "choice" opens up yet more and more possible bifurcation options, depending on which path is taken (Figure 5.4).

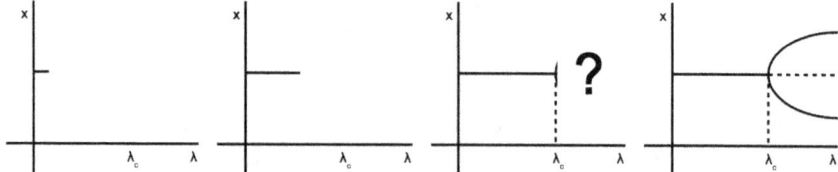

Figure 5.3 The indeterminacy of variation at a bifurcation point.[43]

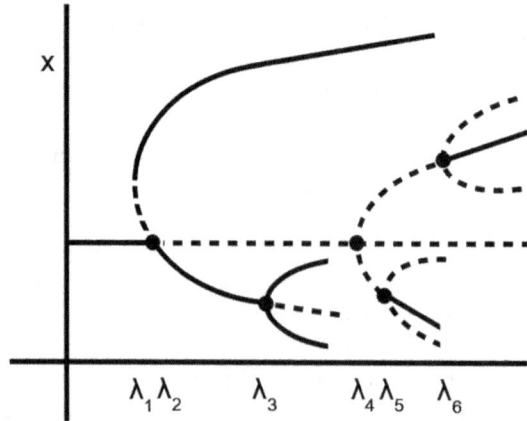

Figure 5.4 Multiple indeterminate branching variations.[44]

Deleuze further elaborates on the structure of simultaneously branching paths with Borges's short story, "The Garden of Forking Paths."[45] It describes a Chinese monk's unfinished manuscript for a novel with this same title. The novel went unpublished because it was incomprehensible. The chapters did not proceed just sequentially. A following chapter would be like an alternate version of the same prior one: "In the third chapter the hero dies, in the fourth he is alive."[46] Each of these variations is like one of the possible paths the chemical system can choose; however, in the case of the novel, the story chooses all possible lines of development at the same time:

> "The garden of forking paths" was the chaotic novel [...] forking in time, not in space. [...] In all fictional works, each time a man is confronted with several alternatives, he chooses one and eliminates the others; in the fiction of Ts'ui Pên, he chooses—simultaneously—all of them. He creates, in this way, diverse futures, diverse times which themselves also proliferate and fork.[47]

Thus, "all possible outcomes occur; each one is the point of departure for other forkings. Sometimes, the paths of this labyrinth converge: for example, you arrive at this house, but in one of the possible pasts you are my enemy, in another, my friend."[48] For this reason, the structure of the novel is

> an infinite series of times, [...] a growing, dizzying net of divergent, convergent and parallel times. This network of times which approached one another, forked, broke off, or were unaware of one another for centuries, embraces *all* possibilities of time. We do not exist in the majority of these times; in some you exist, and not I; in others I, and not you; in others, both of us.[49]

In Chapter 8, we will return to this structure of overlaying, incompossible, and forking times. But let us look now at how such bifurcations can be found in Deleuze's account of Stoic ethics and temporality.

The Stoic Affirmation of Negational Fates

The important idea we will arrive at in this section is a Stoic moral notion involving our fatalistically disjoining the course of time, like changing the trajectory of an arrow while it is already moving in another particular direction. Yet, to give such an account, we need to implement other notions from the Stoics' richly intricate philosophical system, which we will review now only in brief.[50]

Reasoning Stoically

As Deleuze reminds us, in the Stoics' philosophical system there are three main divisions: logic, physics, and ethics, which, according to Émile Bréhier, "are indissolubly linked together since it is one and the same reason (*logos*) which in dialectic binds consequential propositions to antecedents, which in nature establishes a causal nexus and which in conduct provides the basis for perfect harmony between actions."[51] Let us look then at how these three domains are bound up. We begin with their logic,[52] because all three branches are concerned ultimately with reason.[53] Yet, we will limit ourselves to just three issues in Stoic logic relevant to our discussion: conditionals, correspondence theory of truth, and sayables.

One of the Stoics' greatest contributions to logic involves their theory of conditionals, which are propositions of the form *if … then …* ; for, the Stoics were the first to develop a sentential logic for treating the two parts of the conditional (the antecedent and the consequent) as being propositions rather than terms.[54] Now, while the Stoics do specify a certain sort of conditional as being a "causal proposition,"[55] nonetheless, it is, according to Cicero, the conditional form in general that the Stoic Chrysippus used when explaining fate, divination, and causality.[56] And as Victor Goldschmidt notes, this can involve a sort of temporality simply in that logical form, because the antecedent of the conditional is understood in terms of antecedent causality; thus, it comes prior to the consequent both logically *and* temporally in the causal series.[57]

The next logical notion is that for the Stoics, a proposition is true only if it holds for what is happening right now in the present. Suppose we say, "It is day." Then "if it really is day, the judgement before us is true, but if not, it is false."[58]

And the final logical issue is the Stoic notion of the "sayable." In this logical context, it is what is being said of or affirmed of something, and it is expressible either as a bare predicate or as a complete proposition.[59] As we will later see, the sayable is not what is directly signified by a sentence. Rather, it is something like the "sense" of a proposition, which can be said to be true or false.[60] When dealing with the problem of discussing ineffabilities, Priest describes a similar sort of entity:

> Logicians normally take semantic values [like true and false] to be assigned to sentences. Sentences are not the *kind* of thing that can be ineffable; so we now have to think of our semantic bearers, not as sentences, but as propositions or states of affairs—*something about which it makes sense to say that they are or are not the content of some sentence.*[61]

Corporeality

The second main division of Stoic philosophy is their physics, which will involve matters of cosmology, theology, and metaphysics as well. The Stoics, notably for their time, located all reality in the present corporeal world.[62] Yet, even bodies need to exist at times and places, which are not themselves bodies. This is one reason why the Stoics created another category of entities, the incorporeals, which have thinghood but not reality or being.[63] In addition to time and place, the other incorporeals are void and the sayable.[64] Rather than existing or "belonging," incorporeals are said to "subsist."[65]

Also notable for their time,[66] the Stoics reject final causality and favor an active, energetic sort of efficient causality as being the primary sort; for, as Sextus Empiricus observes, "a Cause would seem to be, according to them, 'That by whose energizing the effect comes about'; as, for example, the sun or the sun's heat is the cause of the wax being melted or of the melting of the wax."[67] Yet, as Goldschmidt explains, this does not mean that there is no final end to the cosmos that it is moving toward progressively. The end result is certain and in fact was built into the first causal act as being the necessary final outcome of the cosmos.[68] Namely, the world will end in fire, and out of that conflagration, every time, God will create the world anew.[69] And the events between conflagrations are ordered fatefully and providentially by the divine wisdom and benevolence of God, who sets that course in motion with the first causal, world-creative act, and the sequence of events that follow are ordered rationally by a chain of linked causes.[70] Thus Providence, which is God's will, and Fate, which is the series of causes, are one and the same, because things unfold causally and are yet in accordance with God's wise and good intentions.[71]

Moreover, even between conflagrations, the world remains composed at its very basis by this rational, designing fire that is nothing other than God, Godself.[72] Physically speaking, fire is a tensile element, meaning that its pressures or tensions can alter without it coming undone, and God creates the world by condensing parts of fire down into elements with lesser and lesser tensility.[73] First is air, which is still quite tensile, and then earth and water, which are so lacking in tensility that they cannot by themselves remain self-cohesive.[74] Fire and air mix to form breath or *pneuma*,[75] and *pneuma* is the tensile mixture that binds water and earth together such that composed entities can sustain as mixtures of these four elements.[76]

Pneuma pervades the entire cosmos, thereby endowing every part of the physical world with God's divine intellect.[77] And *pneuma* also serves as the whole world's binding principle, being something like a dynamic "glue" that holds the world together;[78] and by means of its inward and outward springing movements,[79] *pneuma* enables the universe to be "interactive with itself."[80] In inanimate objects, the *pneuma* is called *hexis* or tenor, which means that the object it binds together can move but only by external force. In plants the *pneuma* is called *physis*; such beings can move on their own but only by growing outward from one place. The *pneuma* in animals is called *psyche* or soul.[81] But note that for the Stoics, the soul, as *pneuma*, is corporeal, and there is corporeal interactivity between soul and body: "When the soul feels shame … the body turns red."[82] Creatures with soul can move about on their own accord, because their soul is capable of impression and motion by impulse.[83] And among rational creatures like humans, there is a component of our soul, located in our heart,[84] called the "leading" or "commanding" part, which rationally coordinates in our body its impressions, reasoning, "assents," and impulses.[85]

Incorporeality

Before we can elaborate on those notions, we need to understand how the world presents its sensible and understandable rational nature. Bodies are defined by their capacity to act and be acted upon in their intermixings, as incorporeals cannot interact with or have any direct causal influence on the corporeal world.[86] And the tensions of the *pneuma* within a thing determine its physical properties, like the density of stone and the whiteness of silver.[87] Yet often the mixtures are such that even though the distinct yet intermixing objects become thoroughly interspersed throughout one another, they still maintain themselves somehow and can be separated again, like how "fire as a whole passes through iron as a whole while each of them preserves its own substance."[88] Think for example of when a hot iron touches wood shavings, and thereby the fire leaves the iron to then mix with the wood.[89]

Now, while at any moment the iron has a certain temperature on account of the conditions of the mixture, we would not really *attribute* hotness to the iron.[90] Rather, what is attributed to the iron is a certain temporalized activity where the interactions and intermixings of bodies bring about pneumatic changes and thus property changes over time. So instead of "hot" being attributed to iron, we rather think that its interactive intermixings are an activity that involves its getting hotter. Linguistically, the Stoics, according to Bréhier, consider such attributive predicates as being expressible by verbs rather than adjectives,[91] as in "the tree greens."[92] As Deleuze writes:

> The attribute is not a being and does not qualify a being; it is an extra-being. "Green" designates a quality, a mixture of things, a mixture of tree and air where chlorophyll coexists with all the parts of the leaf. "To green," on the contrary, is not a quality in the thing, but an attribute which is said of the thing.[93]

So using the Stoics' fire and iron example, we would not say, "the iron is hot" but rather something to the effect of "the iron is heating up."

Stoic Time

At this point we need to address a matter regarding Stoic sources in relation to our present task. So far you may have observed that these Stoic notions are a little vague and complicated at times. In fact, nearly all of the original Stoic textual sources have been lost, and much of what remains are fragmentary in nature and can possibly be unreliable in certain cases when the Stoics are being paraphrased for the sake of criticizing their views.[94] Yet, despite the fragmentary, incomplete, and inconsistent nature of the available sources, one still obtains the impression that the Stoics produced an innovative and coherent system. Thus, the project of explicating their system in a more complete manner involves suggesting ways to fill in the gaps and to untangle the inconsistencies and ambiguities. We need to mention this, because as John Sellars has shown, it is misleading when Deleuze speaks of the Stoic philosophy of time as involving the two varieties of temporality, Aiôn and Chronos.[95] It is more accurate to say that this is Goldschmidt's interpretative invention that he proposes to explain certain conceptual ambiguities in their accounts of time. But for now we can put that objection aside because our interest here is in Deleuze's implementation of Goldschmidt's innovations, which are quite useful in understanding the conceptual ambiguities in the texts.

One especially confusing matter arises from the Stoics' claim that the present interactive intermixing of corporeals immediately and directly causes incorporeal event-predicates (sayables), which themselves have no causal power on corporeality.[96] So, what is still missing from this picture is an account for how present factors can be causally linked to effects in the future, because it would seem from what has been said that all causation has its effect strictly in the present. Anthony Long and David Sedley diagnose and resolve this problem in the following way:

> Nor are we told the metaphysical nature of a causal chain. For example how, if causes are bodies but effects are incorporeal, can there ever be a chain of cause and effect? We will have to take it that it is not a simple chain A-B-C, where B is the effect of A and the cause of C, but that the cause of C is the body of which the effect B has *come to be predicable*, acting as cause because of the corresponding quality which it now possesses. For example, if I strike a match, which in truth sets my house on fire, I am the cause to the match of the predicate "burning," and the burning match, a body, is then the cause to the house of the same predicate.[97]

Let us use instead the Stoics' similar fire and iron example but expand it in accordance with Long and Sedley's model. Suppose now that we have three bodily mixtures each expressing their own predicate: fire + iron causing "heating," hot iron + hammer causing "flattening," and flattened iron + grindstone causing "sharpening" (Figure 5.5).

Using Long and Sedley's wording, we would say that the cause of the current sharpening is the bodily mixture of flat iron with grindstone, where the prior predicate flattening has "come to be predicable" of the current flat iron. But how does that extension of the causality beyond the present corporeal cause take place, such that the predicates come to be distributed across time? They must somehow extend past the given corporeal present. As this will be important for the bifurcational structure Deleuze uncovers, let us take a closer look at the Stoic theory of time.

As we noted, the designation of an Aiôn and a Chronos time is Goldschmidt's terminological innovation to help us understand a conceptual ambiguity in the Stoic account of time. But in the end, what will prove most remarkable in Goldschmidt's theory is not their distinction but rather the way these metaphysically incompatible components of time mutually contaminate one another.

Goldschmidt focuses on certain passages about time attributed to Chrysippus, where just one word for time is used, *chronos*. However, time in general—along with the more specific temporal notions of past, present (now), and future—seems to be

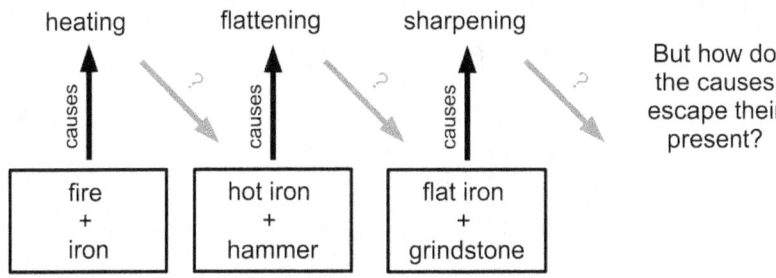

Figure 5.5 How can future events result from present ones if all causes have only present effects?

assigned inconsistent properties: time is limited and unlimited, present and not present, real and irreal (existing and subsisting), and infinitely divisible and expandable and not infinitely divisible and expandable.[98]

Goldschmidt splits apart these property pairings into separate sets and assigns them to two sorts of time, borrowing a term from Marcus Aurelius to designate one of them.[99] Chronos time is the durational present which is always limited but whose finite boundaries can expand or contract to any other finite size.[100] It is the time of corporeal interactive mixings. And Aiôn time is the eternal stretch of time going on limitlessly into the past and future. It is the time of incorporeal event-predicates (Figure 5.6, corresponding to the two horizontal levels in Figure 5.5).[101]

Yet, despite their metaphysical distinction, the two sorts of time are co-contaminated and also co-dependent for some of their own temporal properties. The chronosian present obtains its temporal quality of being durational by always having some past and future within it, filling it out extensively; also, it can absorb more of that aiônian past and future outside its bounds by expanding outward into it.[102] The aiônian eternity obtains the temporal quality of being an actual occurrence by "accompanying" the activities of the chronosian present and borrowing from their reality.[103] For example, a month is both an incorporeal measure of time and the actual corporeal movement of the moon around the earth. In other words, the moon's corporeal motion can continue on for the month it takes to circle the earth only on account of there being an incorporeal temporal extent that its motion can last for. And, the incorporeal measure of a month (being 27 or so days in length) can obtain such a particular temporal quantity only by means of the moon's actual corporeal movement, whose physical

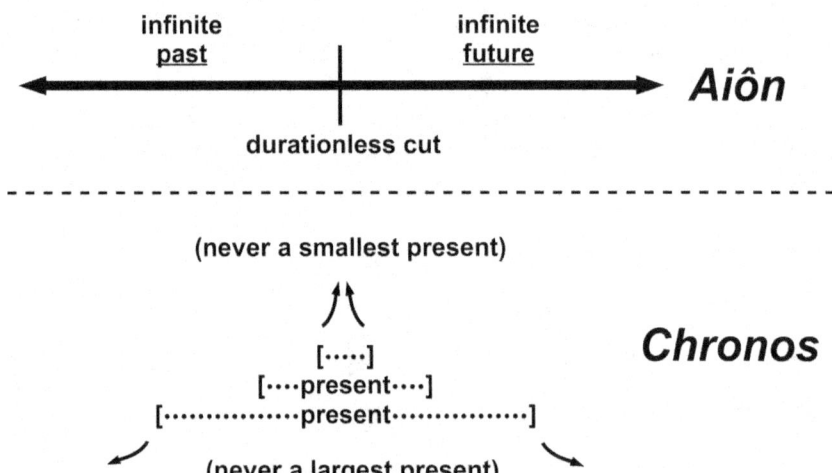

Figure 5.6 Aiôn and Chronos time in Deleuze's reading of Goldschmidt, here based loosely on Sellars's diagrams.[104] (They have been stacked vertically to indicate the co-contamination that Goldschmidt is trying to explain with this distinction.)

speed determines the motion's duration.[105] Put another way, Aiôn time needs Chronos time in order for its measures to manifest temporally and to not just have a space-like status, and Chronos time needs Aiôn time in order for it to have an expansive temporal extent to its duration.

What interests us here especially regarding their contamination is the way that the corporeal present expands by borrowing from incorporeal temporality. Bodily interactions cause an incorporeal event, which in a sense expands the present's bounds further forward, thereby appropriating the future into the present. Recall that at the beginning of the world, God knows with benevolent wisdom how the events of the world should proceed until their final end, the conflagration. And, that ultimate endpoint in the unfolding of the cosmos is built into the initial mixture situation God creates, because it causes at that first moment an event-predicate whose end is that last moment of the world.

And recall that there is a long, internal chain of fated causes leading to that final state. Now, although the causal chain is found in Aiôn time, it immediately brings the future into the corporeal present. And, since all the incorporeal events are fatally linked, the present corporeal activity is unified with all of its future ones. So the first chronosian corporeal cause determines in that present the incorporeal aiônian future end and thereby the line of causes that will unfold, while at the same time this aiônian sequence of fated events broadens the present out into one long stretch of corporeal activity such that every moment expresses the same all-encompassing event-predicate (it is the sayable expressed by every activity throughout cosmic history),[106] which could perhaps be something like "unfolding" or "becoming."[107]

Now let us see the way this works with our example. The heating event-predicate is expressed from the first corporeal moment until the point when the fire begins to form a new mixture with the air, and at that time, the mixture changes and it expresses flattening, and after that sharpening. But all of these activities share a common end, as they lead to the construction of a blade. For terminological convenience, let us just call this common predicate for the crafting activity "forging" (Figure 5.7).

Insofar as a present moment of a corporeal mixture expresses an event-predicate, its activity spans a duration corresponding to the end of that event-predicate, at which point it terminates and gives way to the next event-predicate.[108] But the reason we do not have isolated presents and temporally confined causes is that, on account of God's Providence, every present activity always expresses an even deeper event-predicate whose end spans beyond the present in question and envelops it developmentally within an even longer activity that it is a causal part of. Under this conception, an incorporeal event does not actually *cause* future events. Rather, it is what establishes the direction of expansion for any corporeal present, but it does so in accordance with the immediate, efficient causality built into any limited present. God established this dynamic by having the first moment of time express an event-predicate whose end is the last moment in time, thereby projecting every other moment of that development in that fated direction.[109] So the important idea here is that the present corporeal cause enters into a chain of fated events in the aiônian eternity, corresponding to which is the ongoing corporeal procession of development in the chronosian present, whose progress has been set to unfold in that direction.[110]

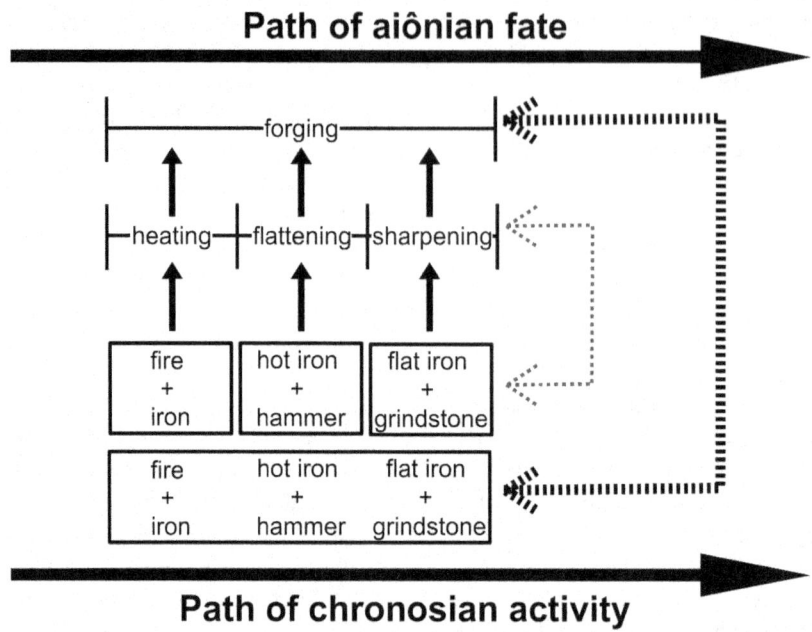

Figure 5.7 The duration of a present activity corresponds to the end of the incorporeal predicate that is expressed throughout that activity. Ends are nested deeper and deeper into Fate, corresponding thus with longer and longer present activities.

To Cooperate with Destiny by Affirming Creative Falsity

With all this in mind, let us return now to the issue of how we are informed about the world and thereby react to it appropriately. This raises questions regarding moral choice, and so we have arrived finally at the third branch of the Stoic system, their ethics. Suppose we observe someone named Cato, who is walking, and thus this corporeal mixture in the world causes there to be the incorporeal event-predicate "walking."[111] The visual data of this activity are conveyed to our eyes by means of the disturbances in the air between us.[112] There is something like a set of "tentacles" branching out of the soul's leading part to all the sensory organs such that it can be receptive to the external pneumatic motions.[113] This produces "sensory impressions" in the leading part of our soul, but they are fragmentary in nature.[114] So, the leading part rationally organizes the sensory impressions by means of the conditional form (*if* ... *then* ...) to create a "rational impression," which is organized in accordance with the incorporeal sayable (the event-predicate) that is being expressed in the external event and that is also being expressed in our corporeal conceptions.[115] Now, because our impressions are normally veridical,[116] and since we assent to whatever we regard as true,[117] this sensory and conceptual process results in the leading part of our soul sending an impulse to parts of our body so that it may react accordingly.[118] For example, we might call out to greet Cato.

Yet, given this mechanistic sequence of events and the order of fated causes that God preordained for all of time, there would seem to be no room for moral choice.[119] Whatever impressions we are given are determined by fate, and since we assent to them, our pneumatic impulses cause our bodies to react reflexively, which then alter the corporeal mixture around us in such a way that its activities are drawing the world toward the next fated event.

But, in fact, as Cicero says, Chrysippus rejects this picture and finds a way to "escape necessity while retaining fate,"[120] such that we are able, as Goldschmidt puts it, to cooperate with the causality of Destiny:[121] we should not simply submit to these fated forces and ends like a dog tied to a cart and dragged around in whatever direction the cart happens to be going, despite the dog's wishes. Rather, we should live in accordance with the forces and directions of fate like the tied dog trusting every move the cart makes and running willingly and cooperatively with it.[122]

Nonetheless, it is still not obvious how cooperating with Destiny can involve free moral choice that corresponds to the series of fated causes rather than defying its linear order. One danger of a fatalistic view is what Cicero refers to as the "Lazy Argument": nothing we do can change our fate, so we might as well do nothing at all or follow whatever arbitrary whim we please;[123] and since we only do whatever we are caused to do, there is "no justice in either praise or blame, either honours or punishments."[124]

The way Chrysippus keeps fate while eliminating causal necessity involves a nuanced distinction between types of causality. We fatalistically suppose that each event has some antecedent cause that sufficiently explains the effected situation.[125] A cause for Chrysippus is a "that because of which";[126] it is "the rationale of the world [...] in accordance with which past events have happened, present events are happening, and future events will happen."[127] Now, under a strict deterministic fatalism, as with Diodorus's "Master" argument (which we examine in Chapter 8), for every present cause there is only one possible outcome, which will occur by necessity.[128]

Yet, Chrysippus does not think that every antecedent cause has only one possible outcome. That is to say, not all causes on their own necessitate one particular result (even though every result has some sufficient causal explanation).[129] Specifically this happens by means of the intervention of the leading part of the soul. When we have an impression, the leading part will initially form a rational impression to which we automatically assent, and it thus mechanically conveys a reflexive impulse to the rest of the body. So, "when some terrifying sound ... or anything else of that kind occurs, even a (Stoic) wise man's mind must be slightly moved and contracted and frightened [...] by certain rapid and involuntary movements."[130] That sets activities and events along one course of development. And this initial mechanistic reaction is not necessarily something bad; for, we should accept what befalls us, as God had the good of humanity in mind when selecting the fated sequence of causes.[131] So we are right to assent at the beginning of our given impressions, because they cannot be otherwise and because God chooses us to have them all for sake of the greater good, even if we personally do not like them.[132] As Marcus Aurelius says, you should "embrace and delight in whatever befalls you" no matter how disturbing or unpleasant.[133]

Nonetheless, "reason supervenes as the craftsman of impulse,"[134] because our rational faculties can, in addition to their automated activities, voluntarily fabricate an alternative rational impression in accordance with our moral wisdom, which we *also* assent to on account of its own truth. This additional assent thereby produces a competing impulse that will hopefully override the reflexive one.[135] Epictetus describes how this works in a section of his *Discourses* entitled, "How Must We Struggle Against Impressions?":

> Today, when I saw a handsome boy or a beautiful woman, I did not say to myself, O that I could sleep with her! And How happy is her husband! (for he who says this, says too, How happy is the adulterer!): nor do I go on to picture what follows next, the woman with me, and undressing, and lying down beside me. [...] But if the woman should even happen to be willing, and give me the nod, and send for me, and lay hold of me, and press herself against me, [...] I still hold off and gain the victory [...].[136]

Epictetus then explains that the way we can achieve this victory over our automatic impulses is by developing an additional rational impression that we set against the given one in order to "overpower it, and not be swept away by it":

> In the first place, do not allow yourself to be carried away by its intensity: but say, "Impression, wait for me a little. Let me see what you are, and what you represent. Let me test you." Then, afterwards, do not allow it to draw you on by picturing what may come next, for if you do, it will lead you wherever it pleases. But rather, you should *introduce some fair and noble impression to replace it*, and banish this base and sordid one.[137]

Here is where Deleuze specifically locates bifurcation and affirmative synthetic disjunction, namely, in Epictetus's notion of *prohairesis*, which is the willful and rational selection among possible reactions. We determine these options in the first place by learning which things are within our sphere of control, and this is something we can do only after acknowledging the things in our lives that we cannot change.[138]

In Stoic ethics, the moral value of an action lies in the good of the *selection* we make.[139] And the rationality of our commanding faculty is disposed toward making beneficent, virtuous actions that accord with nature.[140] So we should select those rational impressions that will provide a morally justifiable rationale for the action, and we should follow the better impulses they create. We do this by again implementing the conditional form to assess the ends that our actions should aim for.[141] Epictetus calls this the "right use of impressions."[142]

So by means of this selection and creation of parallel incorporeal ends, we produce a dialetheic combination of event-predicates, like Epictetus fatalistically affirming that the woman is what is attracting him while also affirming an alternate predicate for the situation, like his philosophical life or his home life is what is attracting him. In the same stroke, we also place into the corporeal world new diverging developmental tendencies on account of the additional pneumatic disturbances

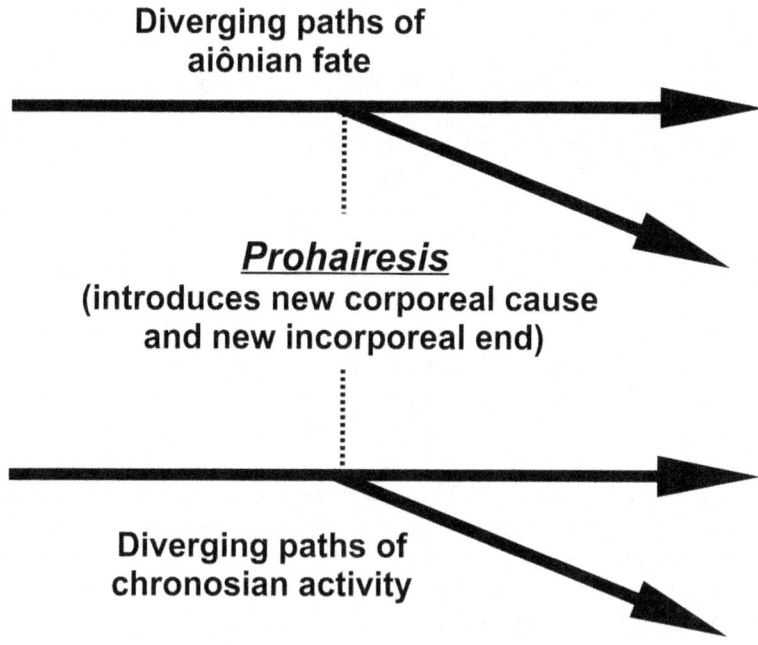

Figure 5.8 Stoic moral choice introduces divergence into the course of time on both the aiônian and chronosian levels.[143]

that our alternate impulses and actions introduce into the world. As Deleuze writes, "The [Stoic] sage wishes to 'give a body' to the incorporeal effect, since the effect inherits the cause."[144] And this, as we see, involves the co-contamination of Aiôn and Chronos time (Figure 5.8).

We thus have a dialetheic form: Epictetus is both attracted to the other person and not attracted to them, although this negation is not exclusive. In order to insert this alternate path, we need to affirm an event-predicate that at one point is not yet true but that then comes to be true by means of this affirmation; for, the very affirmation and assent to it thereby produce corporeal and incorporeal bifurcations. It is an affirmation of a dialetheic negation, but that also means that logically it involves an affirmation of a falsity; for, in a dialetheia, both the formula and its negation are thought to be both true and false. In our example, the counter-impression whose event-predicate we affirm does not yet have its full impulsional actualization the very instant we first affirm it, and in that sense it has a falsity to it. Thus, this dialetheic affirmation of the false has what Deleuze calls the *powers of the false*, because by means of affirming such dialetheic negations, one can participate in "the creation of the New."[145] (We have much more to say on this matter in Chapters 7 and 8.)

Yet, we still have not explained how this sort of causality rejects necessity while keeping fate. What we may have noticed in these matters of moral choice is that the outcome depended not just on one factor, namely, the necessarily given impression, but as well it depended on whether or not there was an additional factor, the *alternate impression*.[146] Chrysippus's theory of antecedent causality thus involves what Cicero calls "co-fated" causes: situations in the world that were determinately caused may not themselves be causally sufficient to bring about certain other particular outcomes, and instead, additional causal factors must accompany them to ensure that determination.[147] So, many causal outcomes are decided by the contingent combinations of causal factors. For instance, consider Epictetus's example again (Figure 5.9).

There is the given impression, which was caused by necessity. Call this cause A. And our rational faculty's decision not to intervene we will call cause B. In Epictetus's example, the effect would be that we impel our bodies toward this attractive person, and let us call this outcome Ψ. Here A and B are co-fatal causes, because neither one alone was enough to determine Ψ, although their combination was sufficient. But suppose we instead make a different selection. In this case, our rational faculties intervene. Call this alternate cause, C. Its result, Ω, is that we impel our bodies away from the attractive person. So regardless of whether it is Ψ or Ω that in fact results, in both cases there is a sufficient rationale, namely, that Ψ is caused by A and B, and Ω is caused by A and C. This means that for Chrysippus, everything is still fated, because for every event there is an antecedent causality that sufficiently accounts for the outcome. Furthermore, whenever the mechanistic causality is sidetracked, as in Epictetus's example, it is done so on account of a rational deliberation, which also provides rationale for the alternate outcome. Nonetheless, all this implies that time's

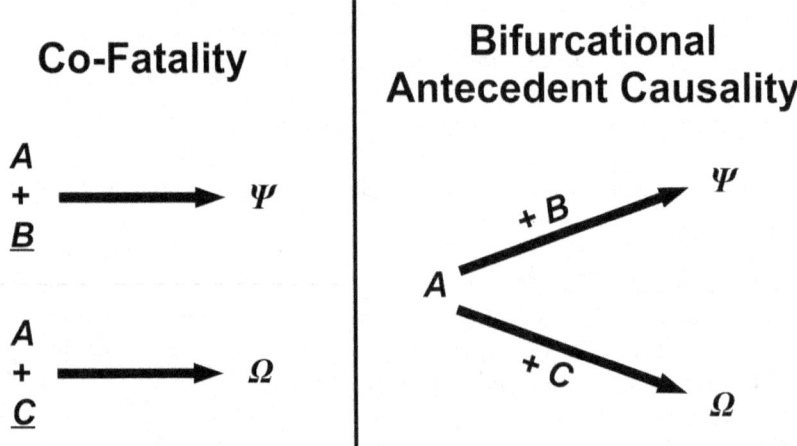

Figure 5.9 Stoic co-fatality can be understood as involving bifurcational antecedent causality.[148]

course is not strictly unilinear but is rather bifurcational.[149] But that need not be a problem under the Stoics' assumptions of God's Providence and Fate, because it can still be that all roads are ultimately good ones and also that they all lead to the same end, conflagration, each in their own way.

These bifurcational conceptions, as we can see, lend themselves to a dialetheic interpretation, because they can involve the conjunction of both something and its non-exclusive otherthan. Yet, there is still another option to consider for Deleuze's logic that deserves our attention, namely, intuitionism, which we turn to now.

6

Wisdom without Logic: Intuitionism

Introduction

Another strong possibility for formulating the principles of Gilles Deleuze's logic would be intuitionistic logic, which is based upon intuitionistic mathematics. Deleuze and Félix Guattari are directly interested in the following three issues in intuitionism: {1} a calculus of problems in place of an axiomatics, {2} undecidable propositions along with a rejection of the Principle of Excluded Middle, and {3} constructivism and non-negational thinking, especially with regard to negationless mathematics. Before working through each of these issues, we begin by examining the social and political context of the notions of axiomatics, problematics, and undecidability, because Deleuze claims that it should lie at the basis of their conception. In the end, we will find that intuitionism is not an entirely attractive option for understanding Deleuze's logic, given certain difficulties regarding affirmability and assertability of undecidable propositions.

Formalization and Its Malcontents: Axioms of Control, Flows of Rebellion

We begin first with Deleuze's general notion of axiomatics. While Deleuze retains much of the conventional sense of the notion of axiomatics as it is in mathematics, logic, and science, we will need to place it into a broader conceptual context involving social, political, and economic matters. This is because, for Deleuze, the "true meaning" of axiomatics is to be found in its social contexts,[1] and that sense should serve as the "model" for our understanding of mathematical axiomatics.[2] So while it is tempting to start with the familiar meaning of the term "axiomatic" and use it to grasp Deleuze's own seemingly less precise conception, a more faithful approach would start first with the social sense and construe the mathematical one somehow in terms of it.[3]

Deleuze's discussion of axiomatics in relation to problematics, in the context of intuitionistic undecidability, comes primarily from the *Capitalism and Schizophrenia* books he co-authored with Guattari and also from his lectures related to these writings in the 1970s. This presents a difficulty for us here, because the terminology and concepts in these works are bound up in a complex and intricate conceptual network that makes it challenging to isolate particular notions and sufficiently define them independently of their related ideas. However, our purpose here is not to explain all of the important concepts in these works. We are concerned more simply with the logical principles that may run across them. And given how basic and fundamental such logical principles tend to be, they can become more or less evident to our examinations even from an overly simplified account, and, in fact, even more readily so. As such, I will take liberties to exclude certain related and important concepts, including territorialization and some psychoanalytic sorts of notions, as vital as they may be in this discussion. For our logical purposes here, we simply need a general sense for what Deleuze means by axioms, problems, and undecidability.[4]

The Capitalist Axiomatic

Deleuze understands an axiomatic to be system of axioms that serves to coordinate heterogeneous "flows."[5] In the context of political economy, he characterizes flow in the following way: "a flow is something, in a society, that flows from one pole to another, and that passes through a person, only to the degree that persons are interceptors,"[6] with an interceptor being, more precisely, "a point of departure for the production of a flow, a point of destination for the reception of a flow, a flow of any kind; or, better yet, an interception of many flows."[7] Deleuze and Guattari use "flow" with a very broad sense; there are flows of, for instance: bodily fluids and bodily outgrowths, energy, desire, materials, associations, people, animals, seeds, production, words, breaks, goods, currency, food, and others.[8] Flows are regulated and encoded with certain values and significances by means of *codes*.[9] Deleuze gives a simple example: hairstyles code the flows of hair on our heads such that they fit to certain significances, as there are styles following a "widow code, young girl code, married woman code" and so on.[10]

In this context, an axiom is understood to be something that places flows into relations with each other.[11] And axioms, even social ones, have in some way a linguistic nature, in that they somehow take the form of "operative" statements. This would seem to mean that the statements are doing something, namely, they are operating upon the flows, affecting them and their relations somehow.[12] The clearest example that they give for an axiom expressed in the form of an operative statement is one used in a different context, but let us mention it here for the sake of illustration. It is the masochistic "training axiom." When training a horse, the master riding it will use pain in order to transmit new forces of control upon the horse's instinctive forces in order to regulate them. The training axiom says: "*Destroy the instinctive forces in order to replace them with transmitted forces.*"[13] The axiom here is an operative statement that conditions the flows of forces of the human trainer and trained animal, interrelating them such that the trainer's flow of transmittable forces regulates the horse's flow of innate forces, thereby shaping the flow of the horse's behaviors.[14] But for the most part, their examples of axioms do not give instructions but rather simply place things into relations, as for instance, "Axiom I: The war machine is exterior to the State apparatus."[15] (So perhaps under this statement mode of articulation, the training axiom might be formulated as something like, "Instinctive forces are replaceable by transmitted forces." But given our ultimate interest in logical sorts of axioms, we really need not delve deeper here on this matter.)

Axiomatics, then, are systems of axioms that themselves bring together diverse flows. In this way, axiomatics place incommensurable flows into differential power relations.[16] Codes also can do this, but there is an important distinction between how codes and axiomatics relate flows differentially. Codes first qualify the flows, and by means of those qualifications, certain flows will be able to differentially relate with each other on the basis of how those qualifications make them apt to do so. Deleuze provides an illustration. We consider an arrangement that has been made between parties where one set of people are giving consumer goods to another group who simply receives them. So we have a flow of consumer goods moving between these poles. But this flow creates an imbalance or debt that qualifies it in a certain way, as one side is giving without receiving and the other side is receiving without giving. This qualification of the flow of consumer goods makes it amenable to differentially relate to another sort of flow, namely of prestige items, like titles and coats of arms. This flow of prestige items now differentially relates to the first flow of consumables, and it circulates among the set of givers. The amenability of these two qualified codes is seen in how enduring social bonds are maintained between the parties in a feudalistic sort of organization, and thus there is something of a functional compatibility in this continued exchange arrangement.[17]

Unlike codes, however, axiomatics do not initially qualify each flow independently and thereby enable them to differentially relate on the basis of the functional compatibilities of those qualifications; rather, axiomatics first differentially relate flows together, and that imposed differential relation thereby further qualifies each flow itself. Deleuze's example for this brings us to his notion of capitalist axiomatics, with a specific one being the "axiomatic of money," which places flows of capital and flows of labor into a differential power relation.[18] Deleuze says you would not have a flow that is properly a capitalist *labor* flow if there was not in conjunction with it a flow of *capital* buying that labor by being convertible into money payments in the form of wages; and likewise, you would not have capital that is in flow were there not already a labor flow that is powering capitalist growth and production.[19]

One thing that is important for us to keep in mind from this is that axiomatics seem to force together flows that are not already amenable to each other and that are inherently incommensurable except by means of that axiomatics that places them into relation. Labor itself is something quite different qualitatively speaking from capital, and so the exchangeability of labor and capital is not something that would arise spontaneously merely on the basis of their inherent qualities. It requires an axiom that dictates their exchangeability. We might depict them as axes heading in different directions (Figure 6.1, left). They are incommensurable, but the axiomatic of money places them into relation with one another, as laborers sell their labor for the money compensations that the capitalists provide them.[20]

A second matter that is important in the above account is that the axiomatic relations of flows involve power discrepancies. Deleuze has us consider how such power relations (between differentially related variables) can be seen in curves, with the tangent being something like a linear flow escaping the curve's flow.[21] Deleuze speaks of these "lines of flight" in other terms: the power discrepancies of the differential relations generate "rebel flows" (*flux rebelles*) that escape the axiomatic that is trying to bind all flows

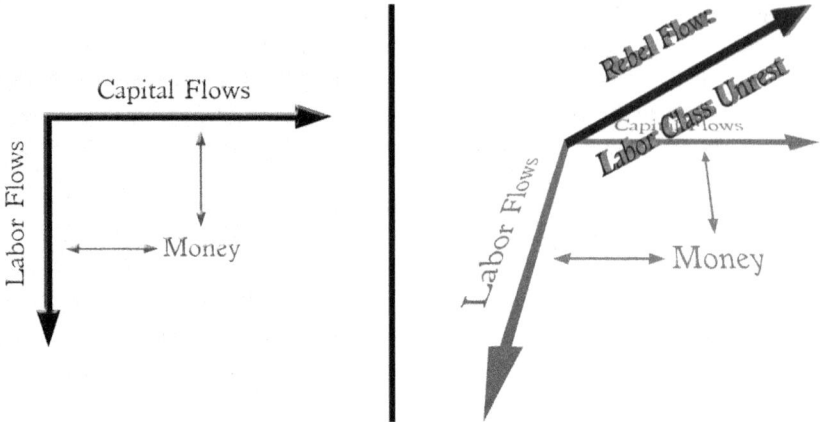

Figure 6.1 Left: The axiomatic of money that conjoins flows of labor and capital, by means of wages. **Right**: The rebel flows that escape that axiomatic.

together.[22] In the case of the capitalist axiomatic, the result of the conjugation of flows of capital and labor was the growth of a proletariat class that was of great size and was absolutely central for the functioning of the system, thereby endowing it with substantial power.[23] Thus besides the labor and capital flows, which are kept within the confines of the system, there is an additional, escaping flow, the rebellious flux of the growing labor class and its discontent with its exploitation. Deleuze emphasizes that this flow arises from the capitalist axiomatic while escaping its grasp at the same time.[24] We might depict something of its nature using three axes, with the flow of labor unrest from a growing proletariat escaping this axiomatic like a line moving off into a third dimension, away from the axiomatic's current capacity to contain it by relating it with the other flows (Figure 6.1, right).[25]

Yet the capitalist axiomatic is remarkably adaptable, and it did not end with this early crisis of labor unrest. Whenever rebel flows threaten its integrity, it simply adds new axioms to bring them into stabilized relations with the other flows in the capitalist system.[26] Deleuze mentions labor unions as one instance of this. They obtain their legitimate place in the capitalist system by means of axioms that bring the rebel flows of labor unrest and subversion back into the greater system. Their now legitimized negotiations, for example, allow workers to obtain increases in compensation for their labor, which is then pumped back into the market, only to boost the capitalist system's growth and stability.[27] And so for a time, the capitalist axiomatic persevered. Nonetheless, as Deleuze notes, every new axiom that serves to corral a rebel flow will only thereby create new ones that will again threaten to destabilize the system. His illustration is the rise of "precarious" work, like subcontracted, under-the-table labor, which is taking the place of long-term, waged labor, on account of the labor union axiom eventually creating a demand for cheaper, more temporary sorts of employment within developed nations.[28] (And time will tell how the capitalist axiomatic will adjust its flows to the current rise of "gig" economies.)

The History of Axiomatics and Problematics

What we should note then are two general tendencies: one aims to integrate all flows, including rebellious ones, and to maintain the integrity of such a coordinated system, while the other finds means for escaping such a confining system and, as a result, might undermine it or at least pose a subversive threat to it. Although for Deleuze these matters are social, political, and economic, as we said above they have bearing on other domains, including systems and practices of knowledge production. In other words, the pressures of social axiomatics foster efforts among its intellectual laborers to produce systems of knowledge that tame the thinking process and leave little that is uncertain or undecidable, in order to cultivate in the populace a mindset that inclines them toward supporting the social axiomatic's similar values of stability and integration.[29] Thus, Deleuze finds a direct correlation between the rise of axiomatic capitalism in the nineteenth century and the beginnings of our modern conception of mathematical axiomatics.[30] For instance, in Weierstrass's differential calculus, its dynamic conceptualization—originating in Leibniz and Lagrange—is replaced with a static one: the differential is no longer understood in terms of a process, and mathematical notions like limit, threshold, and "movement-toward" are stripped of their dynamic meanings.[31] Put another way, Deleuze thinks that such "axiomatic" conceptual creations in the sciences and mathematics reflect efforts to encourage people not to think in ways that might disrupt the capitalist status quo. And just as we saw with the capitalist axiomatic, when scientific axiomatics stray rebelliously from their regulative confines, they are brought back into the system by means of new axioms.[32] For instance, Deleuze says that in the twentieth century, rebel flows of knowledge in the field of indeterminist physics escaped axiomatic science. This worried many scientists, who subsequently strove to axiomatically bring those escaping flows back into their more regulated system.[33]

Deleuze calls such rebellious trends in science and mathematics "problematic" ones, with intuitionism being one instance. Yet, to more fully grasp what interests Deleuze in the intuitionist sort of problematizing mathematics, we should briefly see how he finds such confrontations between axiomatic and problematic approaches to mathematics in three different epochs, namely, in Ancient Greece, in the seventeenth to nineteenth centuries, and in contemporary times.[34]

In Ancient Greek mathematics, Deleuze locates the problematic current in Archimedes, and the axiomatic in Euclid.[35] Deleuze notes, however, that Euclid's deductive system is not properly axiomatic in our current sense, and Deleuze instead calls it an axiom-theorem system.[36] Here, we use theorems to define the essence of a thing, and on that basis we deduce its properties. Consider for instance Euclid's definition of the circle:[37] "A circle is a plane figure, bounded by one continued line, called its circumference or periphery; and having a certain point within it, from which all straight lines drawn to its circumference are equal" (Figure 6.2, left).[38] From this definition, along with other related notions, we can deduce as one of its necessary properties that "if a point be taken within a circle, from which more than two equal straight lines can be drawn to the circumference, that point must be the center of the circle" (Figure 6.2, right).[39]

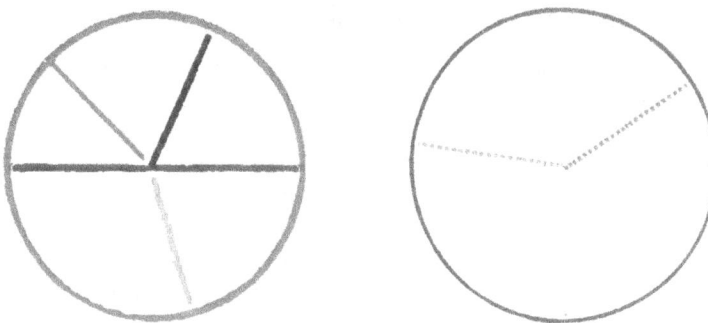

Figure 6.2 Left: Lines in a circle from center to periphery as all being equal. **Right**: Finding the center of the circle with two equal straight lines.[40]

Problems, however, are not matters of essences but rather of events, because in this case, something is done to a thing, like a painful surgical operation. Deleuze's first example of this is taking a triangle and finding out what happens to it when you cut out one of its angles. He further elaborates on the contrast between the axiomatic–theoremic and the problematic approaches with Proclus's discussion of two opposing schools of mathematics, namely, the school of Speusippus and Amphinomus on the one hand and that of Menaechmus on the other.[41] According to Proclus, the school of Speusippus and Amphinomus held that the theoretical sciences are concerned with eternal things, which never come into existence. Problems, however, propose to bring into being something that did not exist previously. Thus, they conclude, "theorems" is a better designation than "problems" for the things that theoretical sciences are concerned with. So when we ourselves construct an equilateral triangle, for instance, we are not so much creating the objects themselves as much as we are just "understanding them, taking eternal things *as if* they were in a process of coming to be."[42] The followers of Menaechmus, however, were not concerned with the eternal essences of things but rather with constructing them and testing for their properties and seeing what relations they bear to other things:

> The mathematicians of the school of Menaechmus [...] thought it correct to say that all inquiries are problems but that problems are twofold in character: sometimes their aim is to provide something sought for, and at other times to see, with respect to a determinate object, what or of what sort it is, or what quality it has, or what relations it bears to something else. [...] the followers of Menaechmus are right because the discovery of theorems does not occur without recourse to matter, that is, intelligible matter. In going forth into this matter and shaping it, our ideas are plausibly said to resemble acts of production.[43]

In related contexts, Deleuze uses as illustration the Euclidean definition for a straight line in contrast to the Archimedean one. Euclid defines a straight line as "a line which lies evenly with the points on itself."[44] Proclus says that from this definition of a straight line we can gather that one of its properties is that it is the shortest distance between two points.[45] This may be debatable,[46] but let us just suppose for the sake of our illustration that we can deduce this property from the definition of the straight line's essence, to make a clear contrast with what Deleuze says about Archimedes's definition of the straight line. Archimedes, rather than defining the essence of the straight line, instead, according to Deleuze, gives instructions for how to draw it,[47] simply by defining it as the shortest distance between two points.[48] But what also makes it different is that the straight line here, Deleuze says, is understood as the limit of the curved line. So imagine a curved line being gradually bent straight while keeping its endpoints fixed. As it does so, the length of the curved path between the points gets shorter. At the limit of its being a straightening curve, it is the shortest distance between the two endpoints.[49]

What is important here is that for Deleuze, the Archimedean problematic approach involves a mutational deformation of a figure, in this case, of a curve being warped into a line. Deleuze comes to this interpretation by drawing from Jules Hoüel, who argued that Archimedes's famous definition of the straight line as the shortest distance between two points was given not so much for the sake of defining straight lines as much as it was for defining and measuring curves.[50] We consider for instance Archimedes's famous "method of exhaustion," applied in determining the area inside a parabola. We inscribe a triangle within it, whose area we can determine. There will still be space under the parabola that is not covered by the inscribed triangle. Within those unaccounted for spaces, we then make smaller triangles, adding their areas to the sum, and so on, until the triangle spaces reach the limit when they are arbitrarily close to the full parabola space.[51] Hoüel notes how the outer boundaries of all these triangles also approximate the curve at this limit (Figure 6.3).[52]

Under this conception, it is not the straight line that is being defined by the curve, but the curve by the straight line, or more precisely, by an infinity of infinitesimally small straight lines. Again, what interests Deleuze in this Archimedean, "problematic" sort of geometry is that figures enter into an "event" where they are deformed and thereby metamorphose into other figures that are incommensurably heterogeneous with their starting formations, like straight lines becoming curves and vice versa by warping or multiplying them indefinitely.[53] In other words, unlike the axiomatic

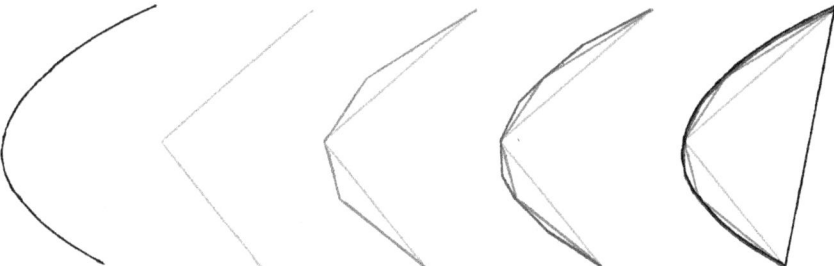

Figure 6.3 Archimedes's method of exhaustion seen as approximating a curve from the addition of straight lines.[54]

approach that would first tell us the essence of the straight line, and on its basis we infer that one of its properties would be that it is the shortest distance between two points, we instead posit that a line be drawn as such, and on that basis we alter it to make it become a curve, and from a curve back to a straight line, placing each at the mutational limit of the other.

Deleuze's other example of a problematic sort of surgery operation in mathematics will take us to the next historical stage of this distinction between axiomatic and problematic tendencies in mathematics. In this illustration, we consider taking a cone and slicing it apart with a plane, and seeing what we obtain, which of course are the conic sections (circle, ellipse, etc.; Figure 6.4, top right). Deleuze locates this sort of "surgery" in the mathematics of the eighteenth century and specifically in Desargues's book, *Draft Project for Grappling with the Events of the Encounters of a Cone and a Plane*.[55] Deleuze notes Desargues's work with stone-cutting (also in its relation to the "minor geometry" of the Freemasons or Knights Templars), where the cutting of stone sections is a physical event that changes the forms of the objects (Figure 6.4, left and bottom right). Here, the size and shape of the stone are problematic. When masons cut

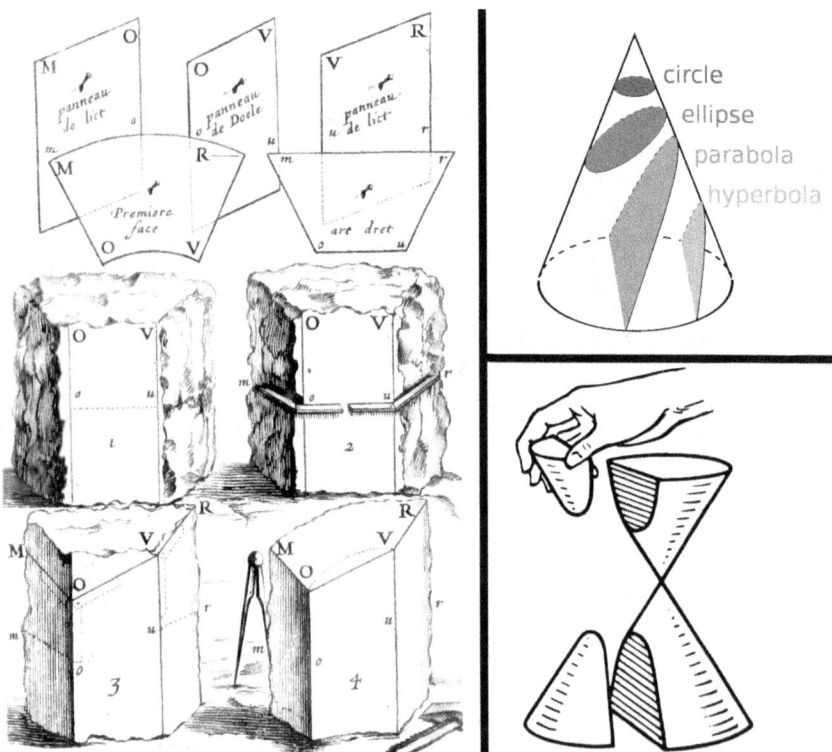

Figure 6.4 Conic sections seen as involving cuts into stone. **Left**: Stonemasonry cuts from Bosse's book on Desargues. **Top right**: Conic sections. **Bottom right**: Conic sections as cuts into physical cones.[56]

or round the stones, the new geometrical properties are not derived from an essence but rather from transformative and affective events.[57] In contrast to this era's problematic sort of geometry is Descartes's more "axiomatic" approach with his analytic geometry, in which spatial intuitions are replaced with more symbolic, algebraic formulations.[58]

Deleuze's third era of the development in the axiomatic and problematic tendencies in mathematics is the contemporary one, which, as we noted above, begins with Weierstrass, and it culminates with Hilbert's formalist project; and the problematic tendency finds expression with the intuitionistic and constructivist mathematics of Brouwer, Heyting, Griss, and Bouligand, who demanded that "mathematical flows" go beyond axiomatics by questioning one of the principles it retained, namely, the Principle of Excluded Middle.[59]

Modern Axioms and Problems

We will now look more closely at how Deleuze understands the nature of *mathematical* axioms and problems in this most recent epoch, drawing from a number of his sources. Let us first consider his examples of mathematical axioms, which he presumably draws from the Nicolas Bourbaki group's *Architecture of Mathematics*. The point Deleuze makes using this text and its examples is that an axiom is so fundamental and generically formulated that it can operate in different mathematical domains of realization.[60] For instance, Deleuze reads the axiom that gives us what in arithmetic is the value for zero and what in a study of motion ("the 'composition' of displacements in three-dimensional Euclidean space")[61] is called "identical displacement" (where there is no change of place):

Axiom A: There exists an element e, such that for every element x, one has $e + x = x + e = x$.[62]

Here, the e is arithmetically 0, because when added to x, it does not change the value of x, and similarly, in terms of spatial displacement, there is no change of place (it would be something like a null movement, so to speak; Figure 6.5, left).

The next one gives us the additive inverse number; when you combine a number arithmetically with its inverse, it yields 0. And it gives us "inverse" displacement, which is like combining one motion with another that takes you back to your starting place:

Axiom B: Corresponding to every element x, there exists an element x' such that $x + x' = x' + x = e$.[63]

Here, since e was given as a zero or null value, the combination of an arithmetical value or displacement with its inverse value gives you null (Figure 6.5, right).

Deleuze notes that the different, heterogeneous modes of realization of the axiom in the different domains (arithmetic versus geometrical displacement) are isomorphic, meaning that the parts retain the same structure, which is formulated in the more generic axiom. As Robert Blanché writes in *Axiomatics*:

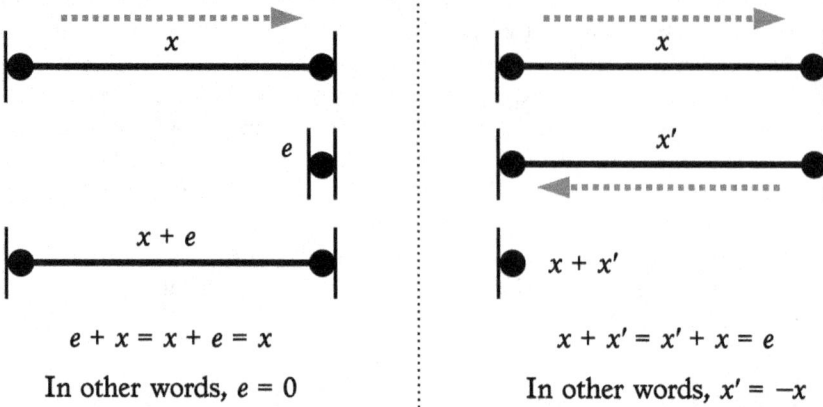

Figure 6.5 A depiction of a motional interpretation for **(left)** an axiom defining a null value and for **(right)** an axiom defining an inverse value.

> These concrete realizations of an axiomatic system are called *models*. [...] An axiomatization thus lends itself [...] to different realizations which can be taken from fields of study very far removed from the initially given domain. Thus, what we are now concerned with is a plurality of interpretations or concrete models of one and the same axiomatization.[64]

Deleuze uses these examples to make the point that there can be a heterogeneity of types of states all operating conjointly in the global capitalist system. They are all brought together functionally on account of an isomorphism whose structure is delineated in the capitalist axioms, and this is because they can have heterogeneous *modes* of production while all sharing capitalist *relations* of production.[65] As Deleuze and Guattari write:

> To the extent that capitalism constitutes an axiomatic (production for the market), all States and all social formations tend to become *isomorphic* in their capacity as models of realization: there is but one centered world market, the capitalist one, in which even the so-called socialist countries participate. Worldwide organization thus ceases to pass "between" heterogeneous formations since it assures the isomorphy of those formations.[66]

In one of his course lectures, Deleuze follows up on this topic with a discussion of the idea of a limit for the number of axioms in a system when it becomes "saturated," meaning that the addition of any other axiom will cause the system to be contradictory. He relates this idea of axiomatic saturation to Marx's notion of capitalism always pushing its limits, with reference to a crisis of flows of raw materials, among other capitalist crises.[67]

Immediately following this idea, Deleuze turns to a crisis in the history of axiomatized mathematics, namely, the problem of the sizes of infinity.[68] Here Deleuze explains that non-denumerable sets have a power that made them escape their own axiomatics, referring to the specific case of the non-denumerable power of the continuum.[69] To clarify these technical matters, let make use of Roger Vergauwen's excellent explanation of Cantor's diagonalization method, which will help us see how the infinity of real numbers exceeds that of the natural and rational numbers. The first idea we need is of a one-to-one correspondence between sets, especially between some given set along with a set of natural numbers, which serves to enumerate the first one. For instance, we might place into a one-to-one correspondence the set of Benelux countries with the limited set of natural numbers {1, 2, 3} (Figure 6.6).[70]

Two sets are *equivalent* when they can enter into such a one-to-one correspondence with each other.[71] A set is finite if there is a one-to-one correspondence between it and a set of natural numbers that terminates at some specific number, and its "power" (also known as its "cardinality" or its "cardinal number") is that specific natural number-count of its members.[72] So in the above Benelux example, its cardinal number is 3.[73] However, some sets are infinite and that is defined in the following way. First suppose that we place the set of all natural numbers into a one-to-one correspondence with the set of all even numbers (figure 6.7). The even numbers are a "proper subset" of the natural numbers, because the even numbers are included among the natural numbers, but there are natural numbers that are not among the evens (namely, the odds). Now, even though the evens lack many natural numbers, still the one-to-one correspondence maintains itself, as neither set has a final number. A set is infinite if it has this property, namely, if it can be placed into a one-to-one correspondence with one of its proper subsets.[74]

As we noted, Deleuze's concern with all of this are the non-denumerable sets that escape their axiomatics.[75] A set is denumerable if it can be placed into a one-to-one correspondence with a set of natural numbers (which enumerate it), and it is denumerably infinite "if it stands in a one-to-one correspondence with the set of natural numbers."[76] Now, the continuum can be numerically represented by the real numbers. And Cantor's diagonal arguments show how the real numbers can be produced from correspondences between sets of numbers formed with the naturals;

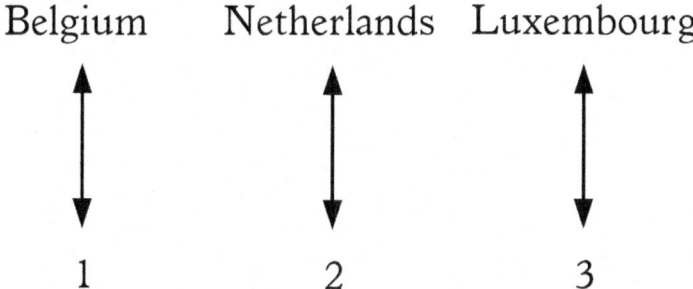

Figure 6.6 A one-to-one correspondence illustration between the set of Benelux countries and the set of natural numbers (from Vergauwen).[77]

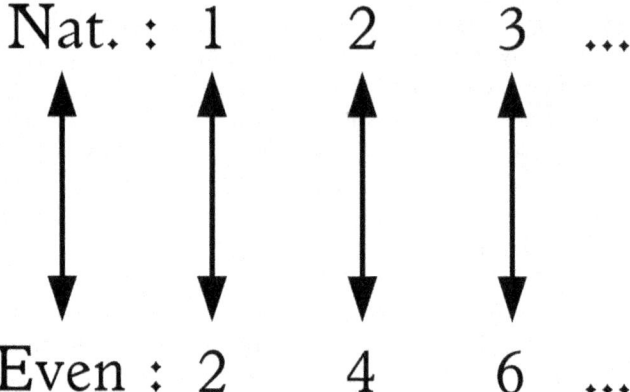

Figure 6.7 A one-to-one correspondence between the set of natural numbers and the set of even numbers (from Vergauwen).[78]

and yet, they still exceed the power of the naturals, even though they are both infinite. Let us consider the way that Vergauwen lays this out, which gives a concrete illustration to the formulations Cantor provides in "On an Elementary Question in the Theory of Manifolds." To keep matters in line with Deleuze's commentary, we first should consider axioms for constructing the natural numbers, so let us use the Peano axioms as Blanché lists them:

1. Zero is a number.
2. The successor of a number is a number.
3. Different numbers do not have the same successor.
4. Zero is not the successor of any number.
5. If a property belongs to zero and if, when it belongs to a given number it belongs also to the successor of that number, then it belongs to all numbers (Principle of Induction).[79]

What interests Deleuze is how the diagonalized number escapes the "confines" of the coordination of the two sets. Now, given the parallels here with his notion of rebel flows escaping social axiomatics, it is tempting to think of the diagonalized number as such a flow. But we should be careful here, because mathematically speaking, none of these series of numbers are thought of as having any sort of temporal character to them which would admit of a flow in their generation. Yet, as we saw from the long list of diverse kinds of flows, it could still be that—although a mathematician might not understand these series of numbers as flows—perhaps they still would fall under Deleuze's and Guattari's broader conception of them. So let us, cautiously, apply this notion of "flow," with the understanding that it could also be regarded mathematically in terms of an "expansion," "progression," or the like. (Note that, as we will see in the

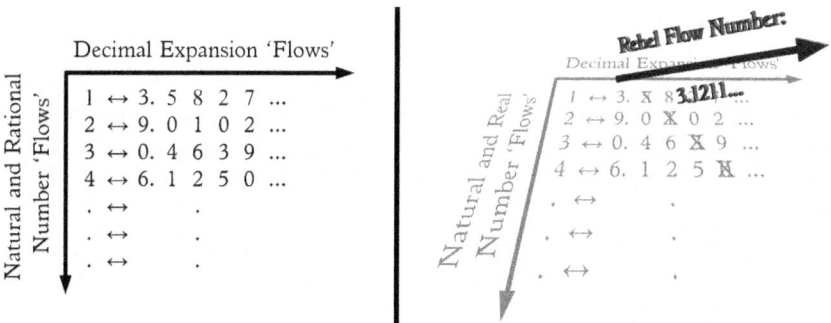

Figure 6.8 An illustration of Cantor's diagonalization. **Left**: A correspondence between real and natural numbers (based on Vergauwen's illustration).[80] **Right**: The diagonal number escaping those correspondences.

next section, under constructivist assumptions, the natural number series and the real number decimal expansions can be understood as involving an infinite series of operations that our minds must perform and as such fit better under this idea of numerical flows.)[81]

Using Peano's axioms, we could list an infinite series of natural numbers going downward, which we might consider to be a "flow" of numerical values, in Deleuze's and Guattari's sense of the term. Beside each natural number, we make another sequence of real numbers, always placed into a one-to-one relationship with our downward natural numbers. The real numbers can be expressed with infinitely long decimal sequences, which is how we are writing them here too. So the decimal expansions going to the right without end can be seen as another such "flow," so to speak (Figure 6.8, left).

For our purposes here, we arbitrarily consider some place along the series. To keep things simple, we choose the fourth place, but the list always continues after any place you look at. Now, starting with the first decimal of the first real number, we change it so that it is certainly not the same.[82] In Vergauwen's illustration, if it is not 1, then we change it to 1, and if it is 1, we change it to 2. Thus we get the diagonal sequence 3.1211.[83]

And we next ask ourselves the following questions. Can this new number 3.1211 be the one corresponding to natural number 1 (namely, 3.5827)? No, because we intentionally made the first decimal be different. Can our new number be identical to the second real number in our list? No, because we intentionally made its second decimal be different. This will hold no matter where you go in the sequence of natural numbers that progress downward. We pick any place, obtain the diagonal number, and it will by design not be in the sequence up to that point (Figure 6.8, right). But what if you simply place the diagonalized number as the next real number in the series (thereby "capturing" it among the "regulated flows," as it were)? That will not solve the problem. We can still find yet another diagonal number that will not be contained in that list, following the same procedure, now applied additionally to the new number in the list. To summarize, the natural numbers are denumerably infinite, and we have attempted to use the naturals to count the reals; yet, because the reals will always in this way exceed the natural numbers, the reals are instead non-denumerably infinite. They (and thus the continuum) have a power that exceeds that of the natural numbers. Again, for Deleuze, this is simply an illustration of how even in mathematical axiomatics, just as with social ones, there will always be something that escapes the axiomatic system even though that something springs from it in accordance with its own axioms.

Deleuze notes that the problematic trend in contemporary mathematics, particularly intuitionism and constructivism, is interested in a *calculus of problems*, where the Principle of Excluded Middle is rejected as a logical law. Here, mathematical notions are seen as "problems," because they are understood initially without a truth-value assignment, and in some cases that status of undecidability may hold indefinitely.[84] We will turn to these concepts next, but let us first conclude this section about Deleuze's commentary on the axiomatic and problematic currents in the history of mathematics by showing how the intuitionist notion of problems is continuous with the sort that Deleuze located in previous epochs. Andrei Kolmogorov writes that the "*calculus of problems is formally identical with the Brouwerian intuitionistic logic*," and, instead of defining what a problem is, he lists some examples:

> To prove the falsity of Fermat's theorem.
> To draw a circle passing through three given points (x, y, z).
> Provided that one root of the equation $ax^2 + bx + c = 0$ is given, to find the other one.[85]

In other words, a calculus of problems involves an experimental sort of testing that will bring mathematical entities into being by means of constructions. This is similar to what we saw with the problematic trends in the Ancient Greek and Early Modern times. Intuitionistic logic, which deals with problems rather than propositions, sees logical operations in terms of such a *calculus of problems*. Thus, Kolmogorov writes: "If a and b are two problems, then $a \wedge b$ designates the problem 'to solve both problems a and b', while $a \vee b$ designates the problem 'to solve at least one of the problems a and b'. [...] $\neg a$ designates the problem 'to obtain a contradiction provided that the solution of a is given.'"[86] Let us now look more closely at intuitionism, as it is a strong contender for explicating Deleuze's logic.

Intuitionist Philosophy

The Nature of Intuitionism

As we noted, for Deleuze, the axiomatic trends in mathematics, science, and logic operate within the broader capitalist axiomatic, which calls for a mode of thinking that seeks stasis and the continuation of the given system by harmoniously incorporating rebel flows rather than seeking to undermine the system by means of them. And against this axiomatic approach Deleuze contrasts the problematics of intuitionism and constructivism. Thus, perhaps it is more than a mere coincidence that the founder of contemporary intuitionistic mathematics, L. E. J. Brouwer, had some concerns that overlap with Deleuze's regarding the sort of formalistic and axiomatizing mathematics of his time, namely that it is a product of a corrupted worldview that is responsible for the destruction of nature. According to Walter P. van Stigt, Brouwer in his early writing "Life, Art and Mysticism" "rails against industrial pollution and man's domination of nature through his intellect and against established social structures, and promotes a return to 'Nature' and to mystic and solitary contemplation."[87] Consider for instance this opening passage from the text in question in which Brouwer laments the engineering that tamed the natural hydraulic forces and reclaimed some land in Holland:

> Holland was created and was kept in existence by the sedimentation of the great rivers. There was a natural balance of dunes and deltas, of tides and drainage. Temporary flooding of certain areas of the delta was a part of that balance. And in this land could live and thrive a strong branch of the human race. But people were not satisfied; in order to regulate or prevent flooding they built dykes along the rivers; they changed the course of rivers to improve drainage or to facilitate travel by water, and they cut down forests. No wonder the subtle balance of Holland became disturbed; the Zuyder Zee was eaten away and the dunes slowly but relentlessly destroyed. No wonder that nowadays even stronger measures and ever more work are needed to save the country from total destruction. What is more surprising: this self-imposed burden is not only accepted as inevitable but has been elevated to a task laid on our shoulders by God or inescapable Fate.[88]

As van Stigt notes, Brouwer saw the sort of application of science and logic that superimposes "a mathematical regularity on the physical world" as the source of all evil.[89] Brouwer writes,

> Life of mankind as a whole is an arrogant tearing up and devouring of its nest on this pure earth, messing up its mothering growth, gnawing and mutilating her and *making her rich creative power sterile*, until all life has been swallowed up and the human cancer has withered on the barren planet. The sickness of mind which has caused this, and which has turned men into madmen, they call "understanding the world."[90]

Brouwer's critique of the artificiality involved in such applications of axiomatized mathematics is part of his overall philosophy and is tied to his mathematical project of seeking foundations that are not in such formal axiomatics (or artificially generated symbolic mathematical systems) but are rather in our immediate and intuitive mental activities.

Historical Context and Development of Intuitionism

Let us first define intuitionism, using van Stigt's thorough and succinct description. He says that it is "a philosophical trend that places the emphasis on the *individual consciousness* as the source and seat of all knowledge" rather than on artificial symbolic systems. He continues, "Intuitionism stands in contrast to a more general rationalistic and deterministic trend that denies the possibility of knowing things and facts in themselves and restricts human knowledge to what can be deduced mechanically by analytical reasoning." Instead, intuitionists base their knowledge on a "definite faculty and act of direct apprehension, intuition."[91]

And with regard to its development in the history of Western philosophy, van Stigt traces basic elements of intuitionistic philosophy back to Ancient Greek thinkers like Aristotle, with his notion of *nous* being "a special faculty of direct apprehension, an active faculty that is indispensable in the creation of primary concepts and first principles as well as at every step of the thought process."[92] And Descartes, van Stigt claims, "can rightly be claimed to be the father of modern Intuitionism," on account of his break from basing knowledge in authority and instead grounding it "firmly in the individual mind of man. He starts from 'self-awareness' and [...] insists that every form of knowing ultimately requires an act of immediate mental apprehension, 'intuition.'"[93] Descartes's intuitionism is further developed by other French philosophers coming after him, culminating in Henri Bergson's philosophy, which, as we saw in the first chapter, "raised Intuition to the faculty of grasping the spiritual and changing reality, distinct from Reason, the analytical mind, which probes the material and static reality."[94]

Yet, it is not until Brouwer's formulation of his intuitionistic philosophy in the context of "a new crisis in the foundations of mathematics," as Hermann Weyl put it, that intuitionism found its contemporary formulation.[95] Weyl, in fact, considered Brouwer's new intuitionistic innovations as constituting a "revolution" in mathematics.[96] Brouwer aimed to reconstruct mathematics "as pure, 'languageless' thought-construction."[97] Thus it was not an axiomatic approach that would ground math in formalized axioms, as Hilbert was doing at this time, nor is it a logicist approach that would base math ultimately in logical principles, structures, and operations, as Russell and Frege were doing.[98] Nonetheless, certain important logical consequences do follow from Brouwer's constructivist and intuitionist philosophy, most notably a rejection of the Principle of Excluded Middle.

Brouwer the Intuitionist Philosopher

To arrive at Brouwer's mathematical innovations, let us first examine how they are rooted in his broader philosophical views. He thinks that there is a series of three stages that we go through in our mental life by which consciousness moves "from its deepest home to the exterior world in which we cooperate and seek mutual understanding."[99] But this development, for Brouwer, is a degradation, as it progressively moves away from its original, pure, beautiful, and good state to a corrupted and evil one, like we saw above in his criticism of applying rigid and static mathematical structures in a destructive and negligent way to the fluid dynamics of the world around us.[100]

The first, "naïve" stage in this deteriorative development has two phases. Our consciousness is originally in a state of "stillness," and this comes prior to our perceptual activity.[101] But our consciousnesses in this stage "oscillate slowly, will-lessly, and reversibly" between stillness and our awareness of the sensations that we have.[102] It is by means of these sensations that we experience "the initial phenomenon," which is, namely, the "*move of time*."¹⁰³ In other words, by leaving the state of stillness and passing to the world of sensation, we thereby enter a phenomenal mode of the consciousness of internal time. And it is by means of this "Primordial Intuition of Time"¹⁰⁴ that not only do we obtain what Brouwer considers to be our "*mind*,"¹⁰⁵ it is also the means by which our consciousness "generates the fundamental concepts and tools of mathematics."¹⁰⁶

The initial way that time-consciousness produces these basic mathematical notions has to do with how an awareness of time involves a synthetic manifold of moments. This is his famous notion of "two-ity." Brouwer writes:

> Look into yourself. Within you there is a consciousness, a consciousness which continually changes its content. Are you master of these changes? You will probably say no, for you find yourself placed in a world which you have not created yourself, and you are bewildered by the unforeseen change and adversity you meet there.[107]

In our awareness of this changing flow in time consciousness, we witness "the falling apart of a life moment into two distinct things, one of which gives way to the other, but is retained by memory."¹⁰⁸ This two-ity as we can see is originally an awareness of moments of consciousness that each has specific contents. As such, it is only a proto-mathematical intuition. It becomes mathematical when those moments of consciousness are stripped of their qualitative contents, leaving just their numerical form, thereby affording us the intuition of "*invariance in change as well as unity in multitude*."¹⁰⁹ He explains: "*If the two-ity thus born is divested of all quality, there remains the empty form of the common substratum of all two-ities. It is this common substratum, this empty form, which is the basic intuition of mathematics*."¹¹⁰ On this basis we form not only the numbers 1 and 2, but also 3, when one of the moments of a two-ity falls apart, thereby creating a "three-ity or three-element time sequence."¹¹¹ And thus we may construct every other natural number by repeating that process, which, when thought to continue indefinitely, gives us the notion of an infinite number. Moreover, on the basis of our intuition of the synthetic unity of multiplicity in the "many-oneness" structure of two-ity,[112] we arrive upon the idea of a linear continuum:

> This intuition of two-oneness, the basal intuition of mathematics, creates not only the numbers one and two, but also all finite ordinal numbers, inasmuch as one of the elements of the two-oneness may be thought of as a new two-oneness, which process may be repeated indefinitely; this gives rise still further to the smallest infinite ordinal number ω. Finally this basal intuition of mathematics, in which the connected and the separate, the continuous and the discrete are united, gives rise immediately to the intuition of the linear continuum, i.e., of the "between," which is not exhaustible by the interposition of new units and which therefore can never be thought of as a mere collection of units.[113]

And as we further study these numbers that we construct by means of our primordial intuition of time, we might sort them according to shared properties into groupings Brouwer calls "species," which are similar to what we might otherwise call "sets" or "subsets."[114]

Constructivism

At this point, let us note the constructivist element of Brouwer's intuitionistic mathematics. As we can see, mathematics involves acts of free creation springing from our primordial intuition of time, and they are made by us as "Creating Subjects."[115] On that foundation, the whole of intuitionistic mathematics is constructed.[116] As van Stigt elaborates: "Brouwer's preferred term is 'building' (Dutch: *bouwen*) rather than 'construction', a building upwards from the ground, a time-bound process, beginning at some moment in the past, existing in the present, and having an open future ahead."[117] But what this means for Brouwer is that all of reality and truth as we know it are contained in these mental constructions.[118] This conditions many important mathematical ideas, like infinity for instance. Since our minds can only construct large sets by adding members one by one, that means infinite sets in intuitionism can only be denumerably infinite.[119] This can be contrasted with formalist mathematics. Brouwer explains that for formalists, the notion of some real number between 0 and 1 is understood as the "elementary series of digits after the decimal point," while for the intuitionist it means: the "law for the construction of an elementary series of digits after the decimal point, built up by means of a finite number of operations."[120] Intuitionism, as a sort of constructivism, holds that there is no objective reality, and thus truth is the result of our applying an "operation to a successful outcome, not in virtue of any correspondence with any such [objective] reality," as Stephen Read puts it.[121]

Returning now to Brouwer's stages of inner development, the second one is the *isolated causal* phase,[122] and it is here that we see the beginnings of the movement into immorality. Our minds, on account of their one-many structures of time-consciousness, make sequential pairings of successive moments. We might think of them as something like, *A-B, C-D, E-F, G-H, ...*, where the first term of each pairing can be a cause of its effect (the second term). Brouwer calls them "iterative complexes of sensations."[123] But what we find is that not every new pairing is absolutely unique. We often encounter repetitions of similar pairings, like *touching fire—feeling pain*. Thus our sequences often have a form that is something more like *A-B, C-D, A-B, A-B,....* Similarly to David Hume's claims, we consider such repeating combinations like *A-B* above as bearing a causal relation, because, as Brouwer explains, we come to think that "if one of its elements occurs, all following elements are expected to occur likewise."[124]

For Brouwer, this sort of causal reasoning is what provides the grounds for us to conduct certain kinds of immoral actions.[125] One condition for this is a scientific sort of attitude to the causal sequences, whereby we ignore qualitative differences between them and force them into a generic and artificial, but practically efficient, formal relationship.[126] It also involves our minds implementing a "non-instinctive" sort of intellectual action whereby we make pragmatic value judgments that determine which causal sequences are the most useful for bringing about an end that we desire.[127] Brouwer thus calls the results of these calculative mental operations "*cunning acts*."[128] He explains:

> Human behaviour includes attempts to observe as many of these mathematical sequences as possible, in order, whenever in the real world intervention at an

earlier member of such a sequence seems more successful than at a later member, to choose the earlier one as a guide for his actions, even when his instinct is only affected by the later one.[129]

To maximize the gains from our interventions into the causal sequences of the world, we try to isolate factors in such situations so to be more certain about the causal regularities that structure the dynamics of the world. And, by means of this, someone will "create an ordered domain under his power."[130] But as we implement that scientific sort of knowledge into the world's workings, a person "*makes* far more regularity in nature than originally occurred spontaneously; he *desires* this regularity, because it strengthens him in the struggle for life, rendering him capable of predicting, and taking actions."[131] This ultimately leads us to all sorts of immoral and destructive behaviors:[132]

> This highly valued intellect has enabled man and forced him to go on living in desire and fear [...]. Intellect has made him forfeit the amazing independence and directness of his rambling images by connecting them with each other [...]. [...] In this life of lust and desire the intellect renders man the devilish service of linking two images of the imagination as means and end [...]; for example, in order to change the course of rivers he builds dams; indulging his jealousy of his neighbor he sets fire to his house; to protect himself against wild animals he builds his house on stilts; to let the sun shine on his house he cuts down trees.[133]

Lastly, Brouwer's third and final phase is the *social* one. As we formulate these causal sequences in our mind, we find that many of them involve our interactions with other people. Moreover, we realize that our own causal acts and those of others have a high degree of influence on one another and thus that "many causal acts of many individuals even seem only to have possibility and sense as items of organized cooperation of smaller or larger groups of individuals."[134] But there is a sinister side to all this: we use these social, causal sequences the same way as other ones, namely, as instruments to satisfy our desires at the expense of others, meaning that "the causal coherence of the world is a dark force of human thought serving a dark function of the will of mankind, which it uses like a cloud of stupefying gas, in an attempt to make the world defenseless and ready to be assaulted by its desires."[135]

Now, recall from the first stage how mathematical entities were the products of our mental constructions. For Brouwer, these "languageless constructions which arise from the self-unfolding of the basic intuition" of time—when we have them— are perfectly "exact and true."[136] Thus, any symbolic formalisms of mathematics are ultimately superfluous to our original languageless mathematical intuitions,[137] as they only allow us to link a thought-construction to a name.[138] Brouwer explains,

> For a human mind equipped with an unlimited memory, pure mathematics, practised in solitude and without using linguistic signs, would be exact, but the exactness would be lost in mathematical communication between human beings with an unlimited memory, because they would still be thrown upon language as their means of understanding.[139]

In fact, in an early essay, Brouwer claims that language is not actually able to communicate something new to other people; rather, "language can only be the accompaniment of an already existing mutual understanding."[140]

What language can do, however, is manipulate other people, bending their actions to suit our will and desire. On the most primitive level, humans impose their will upon others to influence their actions using simple gestures and emotive vocalizations. But complex social organizations require more than such a "simple cry"; instead, spoken or written signs of request or command are used manipulatively within a system of "laws, rules, objects and theories."[141]

Brouwer on the Language of Logic

Let us look now at Brouwer's notion of logic, because we will soon depart from Brouwer and move to his successors Griss and Heyting. For Brouwer, to articulate a logic is to observe and describe certain regularities in thinking, but the question for him is: where is it that these regularities are properly located?[142] Brouwer of course thinks that they are found in our intuitive thinking and should not be arbitrarily selected and artificially built into a formal, symbolic system, like formal logic does,[143] using what he calls a "*logico-linguistic method.*"[144]

Now, Brouwer's being against formalization of course means he was against axiomatic conceptions of mathematics.[145] He defines axioms in the following way: "For some familiar regularities of (outer or inner) experience which, with any attainable degree of approximation *seemed invariable, absolute and sure invariability was postulated.* These regularities were called *axioms* and were put into language."[146] And when we make deductions on the basis of axioms, we are not grounding those derived theorems in our intuitive experience; and thus, even if they follow logically, that does not mean we can rely on their being true.[147] At best, they may only provide us with "a vague sensation of delight arising from the knowledge of the efficacy of the projection into nature of these relations and laws of reasoning."[148] In fact, as we will soon see, when our means of using certain logical principles to infer new things produces ideas that do not correspond to any intuition we can have, that indicates for the intuitionist not that we are lacking in mathematical imagination but rather that the logical laws being implemented are not valid.

Brouwer and Logic

Formal logic, like axiomatic mathematics, also involves symbolic languages, which, as we observed, Brouwer considered to be superfluous to our original, intuitive, perfectly precise, languageless mathematical thinking. And thus he regarded the task of fashioning a formal articulation of intuitionistic logic to be "an unproductive, sterile exercise," according to Heyting, one of his students who did in fact produce axiomatized formulations of intuitionistic logic.[149] Yet, while Brouwer was mostly indifferent to formalizing intuitionistic mathematics and logic, one thing that he is more clearly against is generating a formal system on the basis of axioms and the principles of classical logic, which have been merely *assumed* to be valid.[150] The reason why this is problematic for Brouwer is that not all of these classical principles prove valid under intuitionistic assumptions and procedures. Yet, in axiomatic, formal systems, the classical principles of logic are *artificially* and *arbitrarily* imposed, which is what provides these systems with their particular, classical logico-linguistic regularities in the first place.[151] One famous and important example of a classical principle of logic that lacks an intuitive source is the Principle of Excluded Middle. (Recall that according to one formulation, this principle says it is always true that either a proposition or its negation is true.) This means that in our reasoning, we can at any time, including from the very beginning without prior premises, assert $A \vee \neg A$. To understand why the Principle of Excluded Middle is intuitionistically invalid (in other words, that it is not always true no matter what), we should examine first how mathematical truths can be constructed intuitionistically.

We said that for Brouwer, we construct the natural numbers on the basis of the many-oneness structure of time-consciousness. Brouwer also says that going hand in hand with this early stage of mathematical thinking is the intuitive notion of a species, which is something like a subset that is understood in terms of certain properties shared by all of the subset's members.

We will now see why for Brouwer, logic is no more than patterns found primarily in our mathematical, intuitive thinking. He says that what we normally consider as truth and falsity for propositions, and validity and invalidity for inferences, is really more basically a matter of mathematical operations that implement species and set-inclusion. So think for instance of the structure of a subject–predicate judgment: "Socrates is mortal." To see how this is really a mathematical structure, let us first consider our own numerical illustration. We begin with the natural numbers that we have constructed. We secondly form a species (a subset) of the natural numbers, the evens, whose common distinctive property is that they are exactly divisible by 2, and they can be constructed by beginning with 2 and reiterating the procedure of adding 2 over and over.[152] The set of evens, as we can see, is nested within the set of natural numbers (Figure 6.9, top).

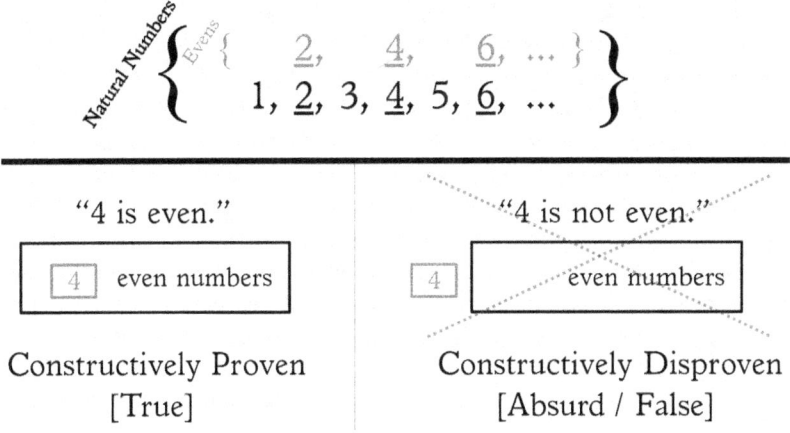

Figure 6.9 Constructively determining the truth or absurdity of a mathematical statement.

Now consider one such even number, 4. Our constructive procedure itself can demonstrate for us that 4 is included among the even numbers (because we obtain it by adding 2 to 2). So we can formulate that situation as a subject–predicate structured proposition (which we can rightly assert on account of the state of affairs it expresses being something we can properly construct), namely, "4 is an even number" (Figure 6.9, bottom left). And, our constructive demonstration also shows it is impossible for its procedure to be followed correctly and 4 to not be among the evens (by always adding 2 to 2, we cannot possibly skip over 4). As such, the statement, "4 is not an even number," would be absurd and thus false, because it constitutes a contradiction (4 is included among the evens by means of the construction but is here said to be not even; Figure 6.9, bottom right).[153] Notice that these determinations regarding the truth and falsity of a propositional formulation involve matters regarding set inclusion.

As we can see, the Principle of Non-Contradiction holds in intuitionism on account of the fact that something cannot both be in a set and not be in that same set. Brouwer writes, "The principle of contradiction is indisputable: The results that we perform the imbedding of a system a into a system b in a prescribed manner, and that we are arrested by the impossibility of such an imbedding, exclude each other."[154] In sum, we have a true proposition if we can constructively demonstrate a set inclusion corresponding to the inclusion of the proposition's predicate in its subject, and we have an absurdity, falsity, and contradiction if we can constructively demonstrate the impossibility of such an inclusion. And thus, as we can see, the linguistic, propositional formulation "4 is an even number" is true on account of a mathematical reason, namely, because the subject's set is included in the predicate's set.

A syllogistic inference is just an extension of this inclusion principle, which will show us another way that logic is really just a re-articulation of mathematical intuitions. Consider for instance the conventional syllogistic illustration: all humans are mortal beings; Socrates is a human; thus, Socrates is a mortal being. Brouwer says that it is a "*mathematical* tautology" that if set A is included in set B, and B in C, then set A is in C. For, if you demonstrate the first two premises, it is impossible (and thus absurd and false) that set A is not in set C; and therefore, it is invalid to infer from these premises that A is not in C.[155] He writes: "[…] the *syllogism*. It concludes from the imbedding of a system b into a system c, joined to the imbedding of a system a into the system b, to a direct imbedding of the system a into the system c. This is nothing more than a tautology."[156] He then shows how this holds for the Socrates example. Since Socrates is in the set of humans, and since humans are in the set of mortals, that means, on the basis of our mathematical intuitions about set inclusion, that Socrates is included in the set of mortals (Figure 6.10, top and bottom left). It is thus absurd to say he is not (Figure 6.10, bottom right).[157]

Yet, on this basis of constructive proofs of set inclusion, there are cases which escape these two possibilities. Brouwer gives as one example the problem of whether the exact sequence "123456789" is found in the decimal expansion of π.[158] We cannot construct a proof to say that it is. And we cannot construct a proof to say that it is not. Thus we cannot assert the statement, "'123456789' is included in π's decimal expansion," nor can we assert its negation, that "'123456789' is not included in π's decimal expansion"; for, we have neither a proof nor a disproof of it (Figure 6.11, top). (Here we can see

Wisdom without Logic: Intuitionism   159

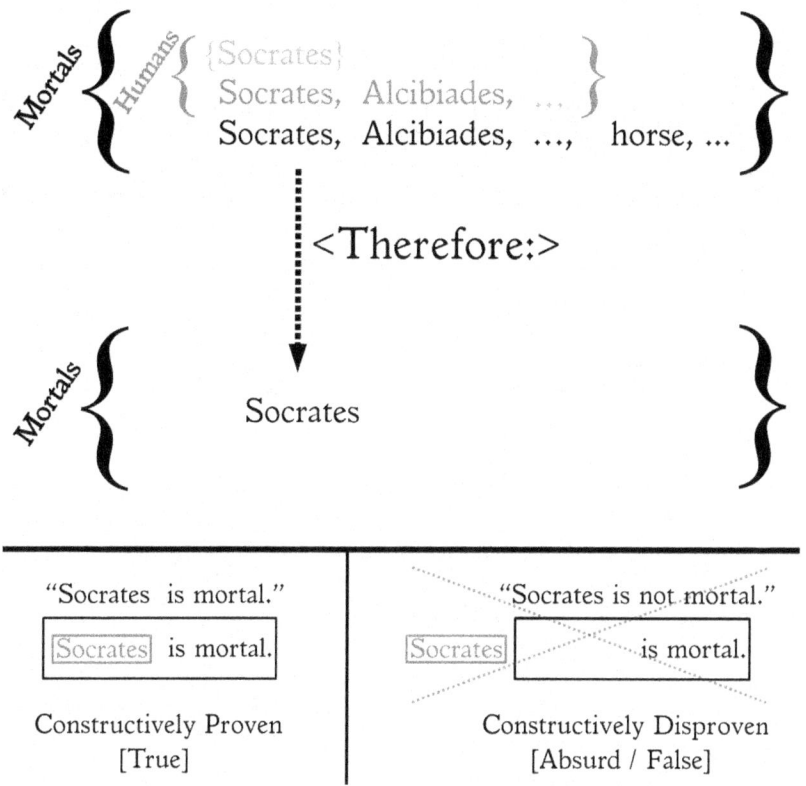

Figure 6.10 Constructively demonstrating the truth or absurdity of categorical syllogisms.

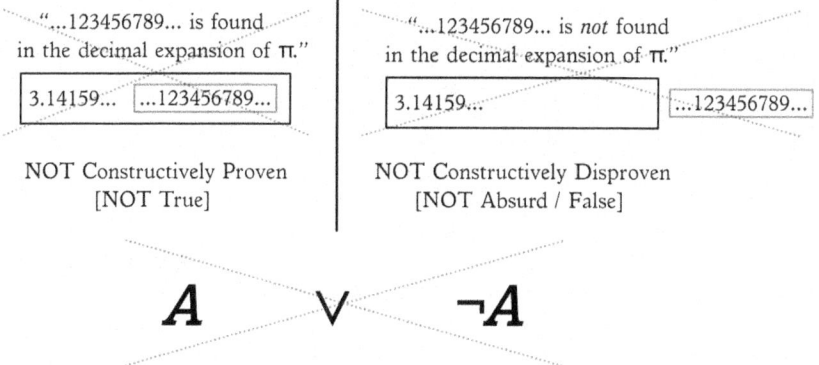

Principle of Excluded Middle is Thus not Intuitionistically Valid

Figure 6.11 Brouwer's example of a proposition that demonstrates the intuitionistic invalidity of the Principle of Excluded Middle.

more why propositions in intuitionism can be considered as "problems." They need to be "solved," so to speak, by means of constructing a proof.)

In classical logic, where there is bivalence, because it is impossible for there to be cases where something is neither true nor false, we can safely assume the Principle of Excluded Middle and claim without premises that "either 123456789 is found in the decimal expansion of π or it is not found anywhere in the expansion." (Or, that either it is true that it is found there, or it is false that it is found there). But under the constructivist procedures of intuitionism, we can assert neither the claim nor its negation. This means there are exceptions to the rule, and thus the Principle of Excluded Middle is not intuitionistically valid (it is not true no matter what; Figure 6.11, bottom). As Brouwer writes: "From the intuitionist point of view, because outside human thought there *are* no mathematical truths, the assertion that in the decimal expansion of π a sequence 0123456789 either does or does not occur is devoid of sense."[159] Thus "in infinite systems the *principium tertii exclusi* [Principle of Excluded Middle] is as yet not reliable."[160]

Let us consider now in more detail these three sorts of proof situations, which we in fact will now expand into four, as these distinctions will be useful later in our analysis of Deleuze's logic. A mathematical problem may be {1} proven to be true, {2} disproven (proven to be false), and {3} neither proven nor disproven. Let us look at this third, more intriguing instance. Being neither proven nor disproven *now* does not necessarily mean it will always stay that way. It could be that a means is constructed someday to prove that "123456789" does in fact appear in the decimal expansion of π. In that case, the statement becomes assertable and true, and furthermore, the disjunctive statement "either '123456789' is included in π's decimal expansion or it is not" will become true. But that does not mean the Principle of Excluded Middle thereby becomes universally and necessarily true. In other words, we cannot simply assert $A \vee \neg A$ on the basis of no premises whatsoever, like we can in classical logic. However, if we can demonstrate just A, or if we can demonstrate just $\neg A$, then from either one of these premises alone we can validly infer $A \vee \neg A$, even in intuitionistic logic.[161]

Yet even this third instance of being neither proven nor disproven can be further specified into two sub-cases. Let us take Brouwer's list of all the cases, including the new distinctions:

1. α has been *proved to be true;*
2. α has been *proved to be false, i.e. absurd;*
3. α has neither been proved to be true nor to be absurd, but an algorithm is known leading to a decision either that α is true or that α is absurd;
4. α has neither been proved to be true no to be absurd, *nor do we know an algorithm leading to the statement that* α *is true or that* α *is absurd.*
   In the first and second (first, second, and third) case α is said to be *judged (judgeable).*[162]

An example of the third case, where something is neither proven nor disproven, but we have an algorithm to determine it, could be: "$10^{10^{10}} + 1$ is prime" (or otherwise, that it is not prime and is rather composite). We have a procedure to make this determination, but as this is such an extraordinarily large number, it would be a remarkably difficult task to complete. As Michael Dummett notes, here "we have a method which is in principle effective for deciding which of the two alternatives is correct," so long as we "take the trouble" to implement that procedure.[163] So, cases such as the first two are said to be "*judged*" or decided, as their truth or falsity has been determined. The third case, however, is "*judgeable*" or decidable, because we are sure we could in fact make that determination using our available means, but we just have not done it yet (and in fact we may never even attempt it).

To clarify these notions a little more, let us consider Heyting's distinction between two sorts of falsity, de facto and de jure, which are expressed in two uses of the word "not." Consider first if we in fact have proven something, call it *A*, then we can say of it, "it is true that *A*"; and in a mathematical sense we are indicating, "I have effected the construction *A* in my mind."[164] Now instead, when something is de jure false, that means it has been disproven, and thus we would say of it, "it is impossible that ...," " "it is false that ...," " "it cannot be that ...," " and so on, indicating that mathematically, "I have effected in my mind a construction *B*, which deduces a contradiction from the supposition that the construction *A* were brought to an end."[165] (Or, to use the simplistic even number illustration from above: we effected the construction that places 4 among the even numbers, which produces a contradiction to the supposition that 4 is not among the even numbers; thus, we can say that it is false that 4 is not among the evens.) But when something is not yet disproven (and also not yet proven), then it is de facto false, and we would say of it, "we have no right to assert that," "nobody knows that," and so forth, meaning, in a mathematical sense, that, "I have not effected the construction of *A* in my mind."[166]

This brings us to the fourth case, "α has neither been proved to be true nor to be absurd, *nor do we know an algorithm leading to the statement that α is true or that α is absurd.*" To clarify the difference between this and the third case, where we do have such an algorithm, Stephen Read gives the example of Goldbach's Conjecture. It is the unproven claim that "every even number greater than 2 is the sum of two primes." Here, although we could go through the even numbers, one by one, and determine for each particular one whether or not it is the sum of two primes, we do not have a way to inductively conclude this from the beginning for all possibilities, without examining each one individually. And since there are infinitely many possibilities, there is no way to definitively decide Goldbach's Conjecture by means of our available procedures.[167] Yet, as Brouwer notes, that does not mean we will never devise such a proof:

> An assertion which is in the fourth case may at some time pass into one of the other cases, not only because further thinking may generate a construction accomplishing this passage, but also because in intuitionistic mathematics a mathematical entity is not necessarily predeterminate, and may, in its state of free growth, at some time acquire a property which it did not possess before.[168]

One way for us to think about this is to consider how Graham Priest, when giving a modal interpretation of intuitionistic logic, has us think of this situation in terms of information states. Right at this moment, there are a certain number of things that are known. In a future moment, more things will be known. We will call each such moment of the world an "information state." Something that is rigorously proven to be true now can never be disproven later in the future. And something that is disproven in a current information state can never be proven in the future. But there are certain things, as we have noted, that are neither proven nor disproven, but may later come to be so. Thus we can think of the successive information states (corresponding to successive moments of time) as only ever accumulating new knowledge and never changing what is already known.[169] (This is easier to conceive for mathematics, where proofs are more certain, and it is less easy to attribute to many other kinds of knowledge, which may be open to further refinement, revision, or even reversal as new information is obtained or as paradigms shift.) Dorothea Olkowski puts this quite beautifully by returning our attention back to the intuitive source of our mathematical knowledge, namely, our consciousness of inner time's constant flux. She notes that for undecidable problems, their truth or falsity lies in the future and is suspended for the flowing present, which creates an open future horizon in our time-consciousness. She explains, "Brouwer therefore argues that given the primordial intuition of temporal flow, intuitionists must forego the excluded middle and thereby open the endless and primordial flow of time."[170]

Yet, despite all the detail in the above analyses regarding proof situations in intuitionism, there is one crucial matter that is not entirely certain, namely, whether or not intuitionistic logic should be understood as having just the classical two values, *true* and *false*, or three, *true*, *false*, and *neither true nor false*,[171] although overall the general assessment seems to be that it should be regarded as only having two values.[172] The undecidable propositions are thought to be not assertable in the first place, and hence we need not be concerned with their truth-value until they are either constructively proven or disproven. So whether or not an intuitionist is an analetheist is not entirely clear. But we can still notice that intuitionists and analetheists share a similar view on the invalidity of the Principle of Excluded Middle. And also, like the analetheic logic we examined in Chapter 1 (see Figure 1.4), explosion holds for intuitionists too (see Figure 4.4), and thus intuitionism is not paraconsistent like a dialetheic logic. Dummett states this explicitly for intuitionist logic: "We are required to acknowledge that, given a proof of $B \land \neg B$ for an atomic statement B, we can find a proof of any other statement."[173]

A related question that we need to address is the following: in intuitionistic logic, on the basis of the unassertability (or truth-valuessness) of a proposition of the form $A \lor \neg A$, can we validly infer $\neg(A \lor \neg A)$, and thus, is there something like an "Included Middle" which can result from a rejection of the Principle of Excluded Middle? Stephen Read explains that this does not work intuitionistically, because if we say that $\neg(A \lor \neg A)$ is true, that means $A \lor \neg A$ is disproven, and therefore it can never in the future be proven. But our reasoning here began under the assumption that A is undecided and thus could in the future be proven, which means that $A \lor \neg A$ can thereby also be proven in the future. This is inconsistent with us also having thought that $\neg(A \lor \neg A)$ is true.

> The truth of A is constituted by an appropriate construction […], […] a demonstration of A. There is no reality corresponding to A beyond what can be

proved. Denying Excluded Middle and Bivalence does not entail asserting their contradictories. *It is no thesis of intuitionistic logic that neither A nor not-*A, *for some A*. For we may succeed in establishing or refuting *A*. The intuitionistic position is more guarded. We may assert '*A* or not-*A*' only when we are in a position to assert or deny *A*.[174]

We need to address this matter, because Deleuze explicitly says that he thinks undecidable propositions in this intuitionistic context fall under an "included middle" or "included third."[175] But it is not clear in these cases what, logically speaking, he means precisely. We are left then to translate his thinking into our terminology by examining his example. Here Deleuze is building from Samir Amin's notions of the center and peripheral formations in global capitalism. Deleuze and Guattari note how the peripheral Third World (the South or East) comes to be included within the Center (the West)—and as well, the center comes to be included in the Periphery—when for instance capital investment in the Third World introduces advanced Western technologies into it, all while at the same time in the West, pockets of impoverishment and underdevelopment arise in the center, as we have noted already with the rise of precarious labor:

> And the States of the center [...], each of them has not only an external Third World, but there are internal Third Worlds that rise up within them and work them from the inside. [...] The more the worldwide axiomatic installs high industry and highly industrialized agriculture at the periphery, provisionally reserving for the center so-called postindustrial activities (automation, electronics, information technologies, the conquest of space, overarmament, etc.), the more it installs peripheral zones of underdevelopment inside the center, internal Third Worlds, internal Souths. "Masses" of the population are abandoned to erratic work (subcontracting, temporary work, or work in the underground economy).[176]

What sort of logical thinking seems to be at work in this characterization of the "included middle?" The formulation $\neg(A \vee \neg A)$ does not seem to apply here. Deleuze is not saying something to the effect of: the West is neither the center nor is it not the center. He is claiming rather that the center takes on peripheral features all while retaining its central ones. To keep things clear, let us write the predicate "central" as C and the West as w. And we are supposing also that the property of being peripheral is other than being central. Thus, insofar as the West has the property of being peripheral, it would be $\neg C$. So, when the peripheral Third World takes residence within the central West, we might formulate this circumstance as something like $Cw \wedge \neg Cw$ (the West is both central and not central). In other words, under this interpretation of Deleuze's "included middle," we would notice a dialetheic element to his thinking. Another possibility is that what Deleuze has in mind is the *exchange* of contradictory determinations, like we saw with his and Guattari's idea of the schizophrenic transiting between being child and being parent. Even so, as we also noted there, under a dialetheic conception, something can have such contradictory predications when it is in the act of undergoing the transition. In other words, at least on the basis of Deleuze's example for the included middle (which is all we have to go on for the most part), his thinking here seems to tend more toward the dialetheic than the analetheic, even though he regards the included middle to be a matter of undecidable propositions in the intuitionistic sense.

Difference as Distance: Negationless Mathematics

Another interest Deleuze takes in intuitionism is with G. F. C. Griss's negationless intuitionistic mathematics. Let us first see the passages where Deleuze discusses it, in *Difference and Repetition*.

> The important enterprise of a mathematics without negation is obviously not based upon identity, which, on the contrary, determines the negative by the excluded middle and non-contradiction. It rests axiomatically upon an affirmative definition of inequality ($\neq$) for two natural numbers, and in other cases, upon a positive definition of distance ($\neq \neq$) which brings into play three terms in an infinite series of affirmative relations. In order to appreciate the logical power of an affirmation of distances in the pure element of positive difference, we need only consider the formal difference between the following two propositions: 'if $a \neq b$ is impossible, then $a = b$'; 'if a is distant from every number c which is distant from b, then $a = b$'. We shall see, however, that the distance referred to here is by no means an extensive magnitude, but must be related to its intensive origin.[177]

Let us now examine Griss's ideas so that we may better interpret, one by one, these somewhat puzzling claims.

In a sense, Griss takes an even stronger constructivist stance than Brouwer,[178] in that he not only would say that undecidable propositions are inconceivable; moreover, he holds that *any negated or absurd notion is inconceivable* too:

> On philosophic grounds I think the use of the negation in intuitionistic mathematics has to be rejected. Proving that something is not right, i.e. proving the incorrectness of a supposition, is no intuitive method. For one cannot have a clear conception of a supposition that eventually proves to be a mistake. Only construction without the use of negation has some sense in intuitionistic mathematics.[179]

So for Griss, a constructed proof should use no negations, which then eliminates the possibility of proving something by means of *reductio ad absurdum* argumentation. For, neither the original assumed negation nor the absurdity that might result is constructively conceivable, and thus they should not be included as vital elements in a proof. As Heyting puts it, Griss's "main problem is to find a substitute for reasonings which involve negation; simply banishing these he would leave but insignificant ruins."[180]

Let us then look first at how Griss constructs such negationless proofs. He illustrates by contrasting them to negational proofs that use negative definitions and a *reductio ad absurdum* method. He has us consider a geometrical problem. We have a triangle $\triangle ABC$ with a bisecting line $\overline{DE}$, and the segments conform to the following proportionality:

Constructive Proof Without Negation (Griss)

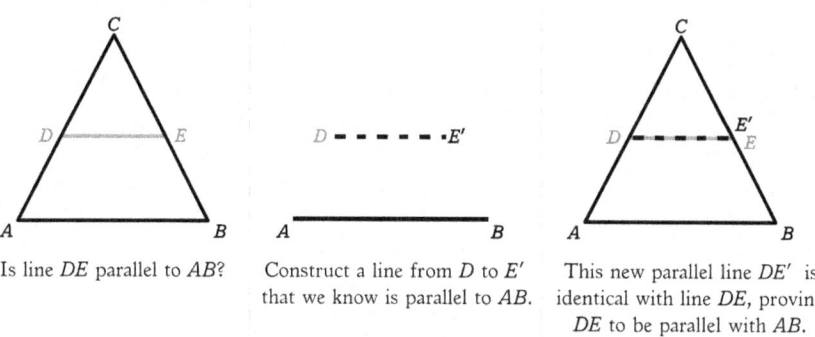

Figure 6.12 Griss's example of a constructive proof without negation.

$CA:CB = CD:CE$. With that being the case, our problem is the following: is the bisecting line $\overline{DE}$ parallel with side $\overline{AB}$ (Figure 6.12, left)?

The negational proof, in the first place, uses a negative notion of parallel lines, namely: "parallel lines (in a plane) are lines which *do not intersect*."[181] And second, it uses the *reductio* method, where it negates the conclusion by assuming that lines $\overline{DE}$ and $\overline{AB}$ are *not* parallel. And next it infers a contradiction from this (in this case, it first deduces that we can obtain a point F near E that is not identical to it, and later we conclude contradictorily that these two points at different locations must also coincide in the same place).[182]

Now, for the constructive proof, first note that parallel lines are instead defined non-negationally as: "such lines, that any point of one of them differs from any point of the other one. *And this, again, presupposes a positive definition* (i.e. a definition without negation) *of difference relative to points*."[183] In the end, this amounts to defining the same entity that the negational definition does, because if every point on one line is different from every point on the other, that means they nowhere intersect (and thus at no place share a point at a juncture). What is important here is that the negational property of parallel lines, namely, being lines that do not insect, is something that we infer from their more primary positive definition of having all points different from one another.

And rather than deduce a contradiction for a *reductio* argument, Griss's non-negational proof will construct a positive equivalence that will prove that the lines in the triangle are parallel. Here, we draw a new line, starting from the same beginning point D, but in this case, we take this line to be by definition parallel (Figure 6.12, middle). From this we can infer the sort of proportionality that is equivalent to what defines the original bisecting line that is under question. Thus the parallel line is equal to the line under investigation, and therefore it is likewise parallel with the triangle side (Figure 6.12, right).[184] Griss offers another illustration to show how a problem with a negational formulation can be given a non-negational one: "Which rational numbers satisfy $x^2 - 2 = 0$? The answer must be: No rational number satisfies. The question has been put in the wrong way. The fact is that $x^2 - 2$ *differs positively* from zero for every rational number."[185]

With these notions in mind, we will see how Griss constructs an intuitionistic mathematics on the basis of conceptions that are negationless. This presents a challenge even from the beginning, because were we to stick with Brouwer's procedures, we would employ some negational concepts. For Brouwer, at the outset of our intuitive construction of mathematical notions—following after the "first moment" of time-consciousness—in what he calls the "second moment" when we begin to discern species, we already here understand difference negationally in terms of absurdity: "Two mathematical entities will be called different if their equality proves to be absurd."[186] And also, two terms are equal if their inequality is absurd.[187] Now, the natural numbers will admit of equality and difference, and, in fact, each successive number will need to be defined as being different from the others; for otherwise, it would not be an additional number but rather one that has already been given. This means that Griss has the difficult challenge of defining difference without negation, that is, without simply saying that different numerical values are ones whose equality is absurd:

> To construct negationless mathematics one must begin with the elements and a positive definition of difference must be given instead of a negative one. *But even from a general intuitionistic point of view a positive construction of the theory of natural numbers must be given*: one cannot define 2 is not equal to 1 (i.e. it is impossible that 2 and 1 are equal), for from this one could never conclude that 2 and 1 differ positively.[188]

An important philosophical point to emphasize here is that Griss is arguing that you cannot draw a positive conception from a negative one, namely, you cannot infer that 1 and 2 differ positively by first acknowledging that it is impossible for them to be equal. Here we see a strong intuitionist and constructivist philosophy. Negational thinking constructs nothing, conceptually speaking. It only does so if you hold the Principle of Excluded Middle. Griss thinks that you cannot build knowledge simply by destroying or negating other knowledge. It really needs to be fashioned creatively and constructively for an intuitionist, and this is one reason why Deleuze, who believes that philosophical thinking is a creative act, takes particular interest in intuitionist philosophy.[189]

The way that Griss constructs the natural numbers without negation is somewhat tricky, because it involves us implementing mathematical structures that by design are exclusive to one another and would thus seem to involve a negational conceptualization of some sort. But as we will see, its use of excluded middle reasoning operates only after constructively creating all the available items, rather than inferring any of them simply on the basis of the negation of the others. To see how this works, we should first recall how for Brouwer, the notion of a species (similar to a subset) being included in another set was understood as going hand in hand with the impossibility of its exclusion from that set. And we saw this with our illustration of 4 not being odd and with Socrates not being immortal. Now, if it is absurd for any of the evens to be in the set of odds,

Complementary Sets are Mutually Exclusive

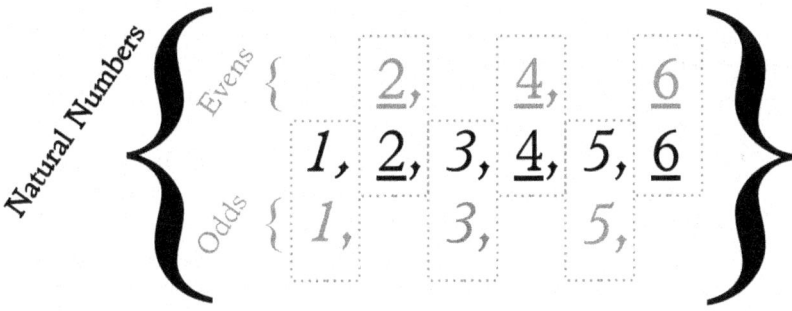

Figure 6.13 Illustration of complementary sets.

and if it is absurd for any of the odds to be in the set of evens, then even and odd are "complementary" sets, meaning that they exhaustively divide the larger set that they jointly compose, such that anything excluded from one subset is necessarily included in the other. Brouwer describes such a complete complementary of sets in the following way: "*If* a, b *and* c *are species of mathematical entities, if further* a *and* b *form part of* c, *and if* b *consists of the elements of* c *which cannot belong to* a, *then* a *consists of the elements of* c *which cannot belong to* b."[190] To illustrate this, consider a set of numbers, 1, 2, 3, 4, 5, 6. This would be like *species c* in Brouwer's formulation. And let us divide this setup into a set of evens and a set of odds (Figure 6.13).

The odds would be like *species a* and the evens like *species b*. Note that on account of their complementarity, whatever does not belong to *a* belongs to *b*, and whatever does not belong to *b* belongs to *a*. As we will see, Griss will define the natural numbers in terms of their differences from one another, with that difference being understood positively as their belonging to a complementary set, rather than their not being equal, and this will also yield a positive notion of disjunction.

In defining the natural numbers, Griss first has us take distinguishability and identity as equally fundamental notions,[191] and on their basis we derive the mathematical relations of equality and difference (inequality).[192] They are not further defined in these texts, so it is not absolutely clear and obvious how distinguishability in particular is conceived without any negative elements to that conception. But let us return to this issue after seeing how Griss constructs the natural numbers.

To construct the natural numbers, Griss has us begin by imagining a selfsame object: "Imagine an object, e.g. 1. It remains the same, 1 is the same as 1, in formula 1 = 1."[193] Next we imagine another object that is distinguishable from the first one. We call it "2": "Imagine another object, remaining the same, and distinguishable from 1. e.g. 2; 2 = 2; 1 and 2 are distinguishable (from one another), in formula $1 \neq 2, 2 \neq 1$."[194] These numbers 1 and 2 form the set {1, 2}. So if some unspecified number belongs to this set, either it is 1, or otherwise, it is 2. And since they each belong in complementary subsets, if one member of the set "is distinguishable from 1, it is 2; if it is distinguishable from

2, it is 1."[195] This holds also as we add the next number 3, making a set that can also be divided into complementary subsets in such a way that 3 is determined uniquely: "If an element belongs to {1, 2, 3}, it belongs to 1, 2 or it is 3. If it is distinguishable from each element of {1, 2}, it is 3; if it is distinguishable from 3, it is an element of {1, 2}."[196] We can keep adding members, going up to some number n: {1, 2, ..., n}. And we can always imagine an additional n' to make any such set one more larger:

> If, in this way, we have proceeded to {1, 2, ..., n}, we can, again, imagine an element n', *remaining the same, $n' = n'$, and distinguishable from each element* p *of* {1, 2, ..., n}, *in formula $n' \neq p$, $p \neq n'$*. They form the set {1, 2, ..., n'}. If an element belongs to {1, 2, ..., n'}, it belongs to {1, 2, ..., n} or it is n'. If it is distinguishable from each element of {1, 2, ..., n}, it is n'; if it is distinguishable from n', it is an element of {1, 2, ..., n}.[197]

Now that we have taken a look at the construction of the natural numbers, we can return to our discussion of how to understand distinguishability in a non-negational way. Griss first has us keep in mind the difference between a negative proposition and negative reasoning. A negative proposition is one where you negate a predicate. We saw that already with the two definitions of parallel lines. Negative reasoning is the sort that uses excluded middle, as with *reductio* arguments, which we have also seen. Negationless mathematics does not use either sort of negation, even though it is based on distinguishability. He says that in the construction of the natural numbers, we do indeed pose a distinguishable new number 2, which is not 1; and when a number in the set {1, 2} is not 1, then it must be 2. But instead of "not" here, Griss uses "other than" (*autre que*).[198] And the way that this otherthanness is understood positively here is crucial. Recall that for the constructivist/intuitionist, "3" does not preexist its construction. And "3" is constructed by placing it outside the set {1, 2}. What this means is that, for Griss, *the otherthanness that constitutes the distinguishability of 3 is the means by which it was constructed in the first place.*[199] It is not that 3 was already there, and then next we observe its property of not being 1 or 2. Rather, we constructed 1, then we constructed 2, and by means of positing an otherness to 1 and 2, we constructed 3. In other words, 3 is *constituted constructively* by its otherthanness and distinguishability to 1 and 2, and any number beyond 1 whatsoever will be likewise constituted, constructively, by its otherthanness to all the prior numbers. Put another way, we have constructed the set {1, 2}. In order to get the next number, we create an "outside space" to that set in an act which thereby fashions a larger set with another member that is unique, meaning that it occupies that singular "outside space." We should not then think of 3 primarily as being not 1 or 2. We should instead think of 3 as being what positively occupies the "space," so to speak, that is constructed beyond or outside 1 or 2. So we have one thing, 1, and we *add* to it a positive difference or otherthanness, by means of which we construct 2, and so on. In terms of our many-valued non-classical notions of negation, the otherthanness here would seem in some sense to be "non-exhaustive." For, an otherness between complementary things (like 2 being other to 1) does not exhaust all possible othernesses, because there could always be a new otherthan (namely 3) that is later constructed outside the bounds of the first two. So while we may have been concerned at first that Griss is painting a picture of what Deleuze calls an "order of God" where the entirety of the world is already divided up completely into exclusive parts that are mutually determinable using exclusive disjunctive syllogism, we see now that instead the whole can never become permanently complete for Griss.

With all this in mind, let us see how Griss defines the equality of natural numbers without negation or absurdity. He has us recall Brouwer's formulation: "If it is impossible, that a is not the same as b, then a is the same as b."[200] Griss then reformulates this negational definition for equality in the following negationless way: "*If for two elements* a *and* b *of* $\{1, 2 ..., m\}$ *holds:* $a \neq c$ *for each* $c \neq b$, *then* $a = b$"; and also more compactly as "$a \neq c$ for each $c \neq b \rightarrow a = b$."[201]

To see how this definition works, suppose we have the following problem to solve. We begin with two unspecified natural numbers in a constructed set, and we want to know whether or not they are equal. Griss's negationless formulation says that if they are both distinguishable (unequal) from precisely every other same number in the set, then they are equal to one another. In other words, two numbers are equal if they share all the same differences or distinguishability relations to the other members. This means that they stand outside the set of all other numbers except their own, and thus they share the same uniqueness property. If we think of a simplistic case where we have three numbers, with 1 and 3 included, then a and b would be equal if they are each different from those other terms (in this case, a and b both stand for 2) (Figure 6.14).

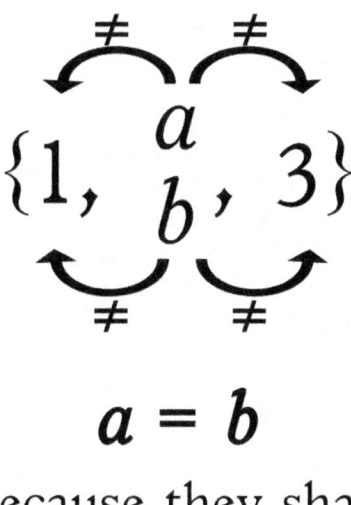

Figure 6.14 An illustration of Griss's equality of natural numbers on the basis of shared differences.

Thus we have so far seen the "affirmative definition of inequality ($\neq$) for two natural numbers" (which is their constructed distinguishability) that Deleuze mentioned in the above-quoted passages from *Difference and Repetition*, and we furthermore have just seen how it can be used to give a positive definition of equality (as two terms sharing the same distinguishabilities).[202]

So to recapitulate and reemphasize, Griss has shown how in a negationless intuitionistic mathematics, natural numbers can be constructed member by member in a positive way on the basis of their distinguishability from all the other natural numbers already in the set. And, this is not a matter of negatively *not being in* the set of all the other numbers, but rather of positively *being in* the new additional and unique set, which, when combined with the first set of already given numbers, constitutes the whole set.[203] Furthermore, properties like equality can be defined without the notion of an impossibility of things being otherwise but rather as an affirmation of numbers' shared differences or distinguishabilities to other numbers.

But Deleuze is even more interested in Griss's notion of the real numbers being defined negationlessly in terms of a positive notion of distance, because this will help him characterize his notion of difference understood not as the negation or opposite of identity but rather positively as an intensive depth. Briefly recall the following: the *natural numbers* are 1, 2, 3, etc., the *rational numbers* are ones that can be expressed as the ratio of an integer over an integer, and the *irrational numbers* are ones that cannot be expressed by such a ratio. The *real numbers*, which include both the rationals and the irrationals, are more difficult to define. It will be useful for us to consider here decimal expansions for distinguishing these kinds of numbers. Natural numbers do not need any decimals to distinguish them (for instance, 1 can be written as 1.00, but those zeros are superfluous). And, a rational number can have a series of decimals, even one that goes on without terminating, but such an endless series would be repeating in that case. So for instance one-third would be 0.333 …. But irrational numbers, included among the reals, have non-terminating, non-repeating decimal expansions. Consider for instance π. As such, irrational numbers cannot be precisely determined by providing a decimal-expansion representation of their value. However, we can mathematically determine how such expansions are tending toward a precise value.[204] And that "movement" or progression, so to speak, toward this precise value can be conceived as a narrowing more and more upon it in an infinite series of smaller and smaller "approximating intervals" that ultimately homes in on (or "converges upon") the precise value.

To conceptualize such approximating intervals in real numbers, let us begin with a simpler and more intuitive conception, which comes from Edna Kramer's *The Nature and Growth of Modern Mathematics*.[205] Suppose we have a number with a non-repeating, non-terminating decimal expansion like 3.47628 …. In our normal understanding of such a number, we can already obtain an intuition of approximating intervals for it, as each new decimal determines a more precise interval. For instance, because some decimal comes after the "4" in 3.4 …, that means the more precise value lies in the interval between 3.4 and 3.5, which here is 7, giving us now 3.47 … (Figure 6.15, left). And again, since another decimal comes after the 7, that gives us a more precise approximating interval for the number's value, placing it between 3.47 and 3.48. And so on, infinitely, meaning that it converges ultimately on the precise value of that number, despite the fact that we may not be able to actually write out every decimal in its expansion in some cases. (In others, we can, as for instance 0.999 repeating converges upon 1.)[206]

Griss uses a similar sort of conception for determining real numbers, and it lends itself to spatial intuitions, which we will employ here to keep matters simple, even if a little imprecise. He has us think of intervals between two values, with the value between them being called their "length."[207] Next we consider an infinite series of such intervals, each one narrower than the previous one. This means that the approximating intervals will ultimately converge upon a determinate value, which is the real number value for that sequence (Figure 6.15, right). Griss defines equal real numbers as ones for which the corresponding intervals everywhere overlap at least a little, no matter how far you go down the chain. This means that they will nowhere diverge and thus they ultimately converge upon the same value. If real numbers a and b are equal in this way, we write $a = b$. But, if for the corresponding intervals for a and b there comes a point in the sequence after which they begin to lie apart from one another and thus no longer overlap, sharing no space in common, then a and b are said to be "apart" from one another, symbolized as $a \# b$ (Figure 6.16).[208]

Now, recall from the above *Difference and Repetition* quotation that Deleuze says that this apartness relation is "a positive definition of distance ($\neq \neq$) which brings into play three terms in an infinite series of affirmative relations." Here, to be more typographically accurate, it should probably read ($\# \#$) and not ($\neq \neq$). But what is this double apartness relation, and what is the infinite series of affirmative relations that are involved in it?

Having defined the difference between real numbers, Griss's next challenge is defining their equality non-negationally. As Heyting notes, "One of the main properties

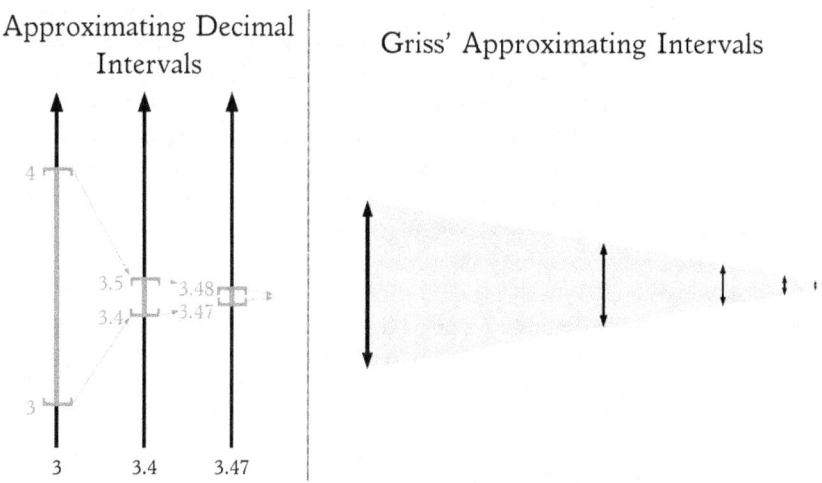

Figure 6.15 Approximating intervals.

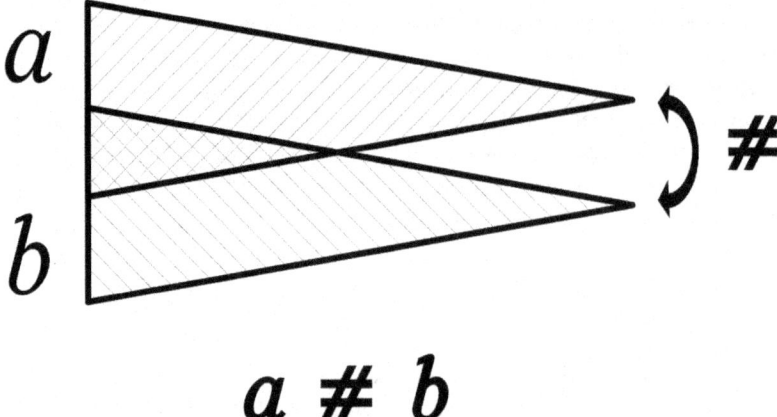

Figure 6.16 Griss's non-negational definition for *different* real numbers on the basis of their distance.

of the apartness relation is: if it is impossible that $a \# b$, then $a = b$. This contains again the negation and hence must be replaced by a positive property."[209] Note that in the previous conception of identity, real values were said to be equal if their approximating intervals do *not* diverge anywhere. Griss needs a definition of equality where this lack of divergence is instead construed solely with positive notions. Heyting formulates Griss's solution in the following way, which is similar to the one Griss gave for the equality of natural numbers,[210] only now we are employing a notion of apartness: "If every real number c that is apart from a is also apart from b, then $a = b$."[211] In other words, two real numbers are equal if they are both distant to all the same, infinitely many other real numbers (Figure 6.17).[212] This would seem to be, then, what Deleuze was referring to with regard to the "infinite series of affirmative relations."

But Deleuze's interest with this is not in the extensive distances between the real number values along the continuum. For, he continues, "The distance referred to here is by no means an extensive magnitude, but must be related to its intensive origin."[213] Before some value, like 1, can have an extensive unit distance to 2, it must already have an intensive "distance" in some sense. In certain important respects, this sounds similar to what we saw with natural numbers when constructed otherthanness was a precondition for any specific value to be placed into a relation of difference with another one. So in other words, the extensive distance between two number values is

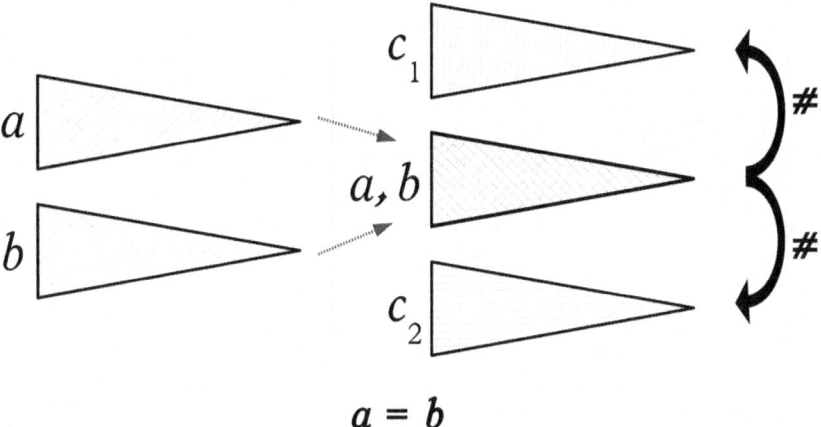

$a = b$

because they share the same distances to all other numbers

Figure 6.17 Griss's non-negational definition of the equality of real numbers, based on shared distances.

not already there from the beginning. It comes about only by means of the construction of the second value. And for that construction to be made, first there needs to be a self-othering that happens in the original value (or set). This internal otherness or difference, by means of the constructive operation, comes to expand the value (or set) outward, and it creates a new complementary place for the next value in a larger set. In that way, the intensive difference in the first value's *self-othering without yet another* is the more primal origin for the extensive distance that is constructed on its basis.[214] Yet, this notion of intensity, especially in a mathematical context, is something we will analyze to a much greater extent in the next volume.

So as we can see, this particular aspect of intuitionism that interests Deleuze is not a matter of undecidable propositions, and it is also not so obvious how we might discern a "logic" to it. It could be that it involves paracomplete, analetheic reasoning, in the sense that the world of facts is not entirely given or givable at the beginning, as new numbers and other mathematical constructions can be continually added. But this paracompleteness is not entirely obvious because, according to Griss, we can only form such new conceptions once they are positively constructed in our minds. And so it is not as if we can say the world of facts has propositions that are neither true nor false, because any such propositions cannot be under consideration in the first place. For instance, suppose we want to say that when we just have the set $\{1, 2\}$, that means 3 is outside the set, and so we have a sort of paracomplete, analetheic situation (for, we might reason, propositions about 3 will be neither true nor false, as they have a non-existent referent.) However, we only could have had such a 3 that is mentioned in these propositions if we had already constructed it, thereby entering it into the set of existing values. So again it is not certain that Deleuze's conception here is analetheic. Another important aspect of the non-negational intuitionistic mathematics is that real number values are said to be different on the basis of an affirmation of the distance between them, and they are said to be equal by affirming the distances they share to all other values. As such, it is not entirely foreign to the dialetheic sorts of conceptions we have been considering where something and its non-exclusive other are mutually affirmed, thereby affirming the difference or "distance" between them. Or, to put it another way, the distance between the values is itself an affirmation of the conjunction of two non-exclusive otherthans.

Taking everything regarding intuitionism into consideration that we have discussed here, we see that particular aspects of it fit quite well within certain of Deleuze's ideas. For instance, Deleuze, like the intuitionists, prefers to think of propositions initially as undecided problems, and more generally he sees philosophy as something that problematizes issues and concepts rather than fixes them with definitive conceptions. Also, Deleuze often speaks of the undecidability or indiscernibility of certain alternate things (the virtual and actual, real and imaginary, etc.), which we analyze more in the remaining chapters. Yet, in many ways, intuitionistic logic is not a great fit for what Deleuze has in mind for these notions. What he likes about such undecidable matters is how they escape judgment and the regulative confines of rigid, axiomatic systems. But, in intuitionism, such undecidable propositions may not be asserted or affirmed in the first place; and, if they ever are asserted, their truth-value is fixed as true forever after. However, the rebel, undecidable propositions that Deleuze is interested in are affirmative in some sense, and moreover, they seem to be even more affirmative than propositions whose truth-values are definitively decided from within an axiomatic system. Surely Deleuze does not then think that undecidable propositions should *not* be asserted or affirmed in any way. Rather, it would seem they should be affirmed for the purpose of defying and problematizing the systems they spring from.

When you combine that fact with how, under closer analysis, Deleuze's supposedly intuitionistic notions of difference as distance and of included middle lend themselves more to a dialetheic interpretation, we can see that intuitionistic logic is in the least not a perfect fit for helping us understand Deleuze's logic, and it is also seemingly a less viable one than dialetheic logic. Let us turn now to something that will better clarify the affirmative nature of the rebelliousness of rebel flows, namely, the *deviance* of "false motion."

Part Three

Falsity

7

False Movements

Introduction

The notion of falsity and its creative powers occupies an important place in Gilles Deleuze's logic. We will examine first false motion, which, generally speaking, is the unpredictability of becoming, understood as involving deviating movement. Afterward, we consider Deleuze's definitions for truth and falsity, and lastly we examine the role that "having done with judgment" plays in this conception.

The Being of Falsity

We turn now to Deleuze's philosophy of truth in the context of his notion of the falsifier's power of the false. There is some variety in the array of conceptions and definitions Deleuze employs here for truth, falsity, and the falsifier, so some initial cataloging will be in order before we tie the ideas together. Yet, before moving on to the more pertinent cinematic context for these notions, let us briefly note a conception of falsity that Deleuze offers in a lecture on Spinoza from shortly before his work on cinema. Here Deleuze first notes a conventional notion of truth and falsity as belonging to judgments that are either adequate or inadequate to an extra-linguistic reality; for instance, we hold a real piece of gold and say "it is gold," and thus the statement is true; or we hold a piece of fool's gold, make the same assertion, and here the statement is false. But Deleuze proposes a different notion of falsity that he claims has nothing to do with judgment. We take the piece of fool's gold and put it to a test by placing it into interaction with other bodies to determine its powers of affection, namely, we touch it, bite it, and apply acid to it. Of course, it fails the test for gold. Yet, before we even evaluate the test results and pronounce that judgment, its actively failing the test is the *being false* of the fool's gold itself.[1] Deleuze's account here is still not entirely straightforward, because the fool's gold is affirmatively iron pyrite and passes the tests for that mineral. It is only false insofar as it holds out the appearance of being something it is not, as having the potential to confuse us about its identity. While this definition of falsity is not exactly congruous with the ones bound up with the powers of the false that we turn to now, it is still useful for showing us how for Deleuze, truth and falsity can be "*manners of being*" and not simply truth-values for assertions.[2]

Errant Motion

In Deleuze's cinema courses and writings, the first notion of falsity that appears is "false movement." Initially it is used with Bergson's pejorative sense for motions whose temporal parts are understood as spatially related and immobile.[3] However, from the preface to the English edition of *Cinema 1* and from lectures coming after the original publication of that book, we see that Deleuze will use the term "false movements" (*faux mouvements*) for the "aberrant movements" (*mouvements aberrants*) that occur in transitions with a "false continuity" (*faux raccord*) and that are the creative movements in the world's constant changing.[4] To grasp these notions, we should briefly review their Bergsonian context and cinematic illustrations. In *Creative Evolution*, Bergson claims that science tries to isolate systems to restrict its study to just their inner workings. But "the isolation is never complete"; for, any "so-called isolated system remains subject to certain external influences."[5] Each system is in fact bound up into a larger one that mutually affects its workings, and "these influences are so many threads which bind up the system to another more extensive, and to this a third which includes both, and so on," thereby transmitting "the duration immanent to the whole of the universe"—that is, of the "Whole" itself—all the way "down to the smallest particle of the world in which we live."[6] Deleuze locates this sort of inner-outer exchange between Whole and smallest part in the way directors relate what is shown in the visual frame with what is implied to be outside it, using as one example D. W. Griffith's *The Massacre* (1912).[7]

Here the thread connecting the nested systems begins from a child's terror, given in a close-up of her face (Figure 7.1, right), then continues through the fierce and desperate fighting of the besieged settlers who are protecting that child, shown at a mid-shot (middle panel), and finally extends out to the attacking natives encircling them on horseback, seen at an extreme long shot (left panel). For Bergson, even though the Whole is an entire sum, that does not mean it is fully complete. For, it is durational, meaning that time "bites" into it, and so it is always in a process of generating the new and unforeseeable.[8] As Deleuze notes, it is *open* to the fourth dimension, time.[9] The Whole is thus "the Open," because the entirety of the given does not complete the world: at every moment it is already changing to something else not determinable by what is present.[10] And because there are "threads" running from the smallest parts to

Figure 7.1 Shots at different scales showing nested systems of interactivity, from D. W. Griffith's *The Massacre* (© Biograph 1912. All rights reserved).[11]

the whole, that means were someone to intervene into the changes on the local level, this could affect the overall movements of variation in the whole. (Later we will see that this is what the "falsifier" accomplishes.)

This part–whole relation in cinema is also found on the level of editing or montage, which has bearing more generally on our conception of the discontinuity of the Whole's development. D. W. Griffith was an early innovator of cinematic editing techniques, especially continuity editing that makes the visual transitions as seamless and coherent as possible. Yet, many of Griffith's more notable editing innovations involve some sort of a visual discontinuity, although they ultimately create a sense of the continuity and unity of events and places in the story world.[12] Deleuze calls this "organic" montage, meaning that the edits may show contrasts; yet together, they form a coherent whole: "Griffith conceived of the composition of movement-images as an organization, an organism, a great organic unity," which "is firstly, unity in diversity, that is, a set of differentiated parts; there are men and women, rich and poor," etc.[13] The whole that is constructed often has a rigid social structure that maintains itself throughout the development of the story, which can span across human history. Thus in *Intolerance* (1916), Griffith cuts between four different epochs, but one thing that never changes throughout the times is the class hierarchies.[14] As Eisenstein notes, they are like the strips of fat and meat in bacon, one always above the other.[15] So while Griffith's organic montage does suggest a whole, it is not an open one where the developments can change the basic organization of the world.

In Deleuze's analysis, it is *falsity* which ensures an openness of the Whole, specifically the false movements of *false continuity* whereby the Whole suddenly diverges or "forks" down an unexpected path, imposing "a new 'meander', a new break in causality, which itself forks from the previous one, in a collection of non-linear relations."[16] (We saw this in Chapter 5 with bifurcational or "forking" time.) In cinematic terminology, false continuity transitions, also called "jump-cuts," are ones where there is an edit causing a noticeable change that abruptly breaks continuities in motion, time, space, or other visual features of the sequence.[17] Eisenstein does not level an aesthetic critique at Griffith's montage but rather a political one: the discontinuities in Griffith's organic montage only serve to reinforce "the structure of bourgeois society" rather than raise them to the level of social revolution.[18] In Eisenstein's *The General Line* or *The Old and the New* (1929), for instance, the film begins by showing peasant farmers toiling in the fields under a capitalist system that materially divides people, even siblings, thereby impoverishing them (Figure 7.2, panel 1).

They decide to organize a dairy collective, and they pool their resources to purchase a cream separator (panel 2). What follows is a dazzling montage sequence. As the farmers wait skeptically to see if the new machine will work, Eisenstein cuts back and forth from concerned faces to the spinning mechanisms of the creamer (panels 3–4). Finally it works, to their great relief and joy (panels 5–6).[19]

Here there is a critical instantaneous transition when the cream first starts flowing, and this small local change becomes indicative of the larger changes in their village, in Soviet society more broadly, and ultimately in the whole of nature and history.[20] Eisenstein calls the effect this has on the viewer "pathos," meaning that we undergo the "constant transition to a different quality" as we "move to a new state": "Sitting—he

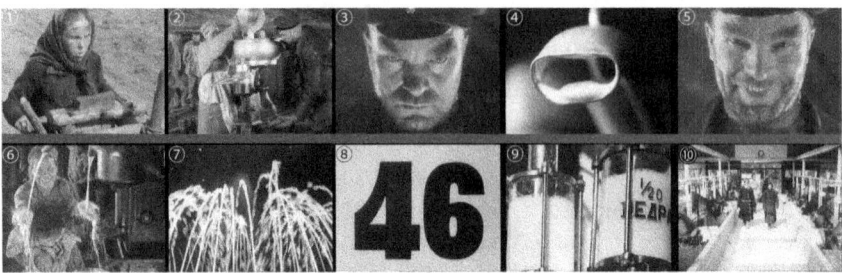

Figure 7.2 Shots from Eisenstein's *The General Line* (*The Old and the New*) (© Sovkino 1929. All rights reserved).[21]

stood up. Standing—he jumped. Motionless—he moved."[22] But following the joyful faces in that sequence, Eisenstein creates even more drastic jumps. The imagery goes from the realism of this scene to the metaphoricity of water fountain jets suggesting a great flow of cream, then to images of numbers indicating a membership increase (Figure 7.2, panels 7 and 8), and in lost footage, there are even changes from black and white to color.[23] After that sequence, we see there has been a movement or change in the larger world: in stark contrast to the opening scenes of rural poverty, we are then shown a modern, successful collective farm (panels 9 and 10).

Now, although this sequence shows a drastic shift in the movement of the world, it is not false movement in the strongest sense. For, it has a dialectical structure that in the end preserves organicism. One reason for this is that what is to come is already built into what is now happening, on account of it following a repetitive, and somewhat predictable, dialectical movement of opposites. Thus, although there are brief intervals between contrasting shots when change takes place, the outcome is not entirely undetermined. And for Eisenstein, the local dialectical and revolutionary changes still form a higher "organic unity" of history that is like a spiral pattern of revolutionary turns, which, although being open at both ends, maintains its same structure as it expands.[24] For Deleuze, falsity would not simply be a discontinuous change to an opposite state; rather, it is an aberration in the movement of the Whole, a veering away that is not initially directed by a logic of oppositions, even though they often result:[25] "False continuity is neither a connection of continuity, nor a rupture or a discontinuity in the connection. False continuity is in its own right a dimension of the Open, which escapes sets and their parts. [...] Far from breaking up the whole, false continuities are the act of the whole [...]."[26] For this slightly stronger sense of falsity in the movement and duration of the Whole, we turn now to Deleuze's work on the powers of the false.

Erroneous Falsity

Deleuze begins his 1983–4 cinema courses, which he entitles in the first session "Truth and Time: The Falsifier," with two main definitions for truth and falsity, on the basis of which he characterizes the power of the false and gives four definitions for the "falsifier," the wielder of that power.[27] By means of these conceptual innovations, Deleuze challenges the conventional notion of truth by placing a greater emphasis upon a different sense for what can constitute the true, namely, the New, which is created by means of the power of the false.

The first definition for truth and falsity concerns a set of pairings, the most prevalent of which is the real and the imaginary, but it includes as well: essence and appearance, actual and virtual, objective and subjective, physical and mental, and world and I.[28] Deleuze emphasizes that here the true is not simply the real (or essence, etc.), and the false is not just the imaginary (or appearance, etc.). Rather, the true is somehow the *distinction* between the real and the imaginary, and the false is the *confusion* of the two. When we effectuate such a confusion, we fall into error.[29] Here again, Deleuze uses the notion of the "organic" by calling this "truthful" or veridical distinction between the real and imaginary the "organic form of the true."[30] The organicism here has partly to do with the way this conception of truth is built upon a self-consistent and self-continuous world, as errors or falsities would introduce inconsistencies into the world, making it double over upon itself with combinations of facts that cannot both be true. Deleuze illustrates this with Worringer's distinction between organic lines in classical ornamentation and Northern lines in Gothic ornamentation.[31]

In organic, classical ornamentation, the lines, although varying, do so in a way that follows a certain regularity and consistency, thereby forming a coherent whole (Figure 7.3, left). In Northern lines, however, the direction of the movement is perpetually ruptured as it twists and turns unexpectedly like a labyrinth,[32] in a continuous "movement of decomposition"[33] that is "whirling [...] in a formlessness," as Deleuze describes it (right panel).[34]

To grasp the distinction between the real and the imaginary in the organic form of the true, we should note that in his course lectures, Deleuze gives two sets of definitions for them: one regards a notion of modification and representation, and the other is built from Bergson's *Matter and Memory*. The first is not completely developed in his lectures and does not enter entirely into his *Cinema 2* book afterward. However, it will prove useful for drawing needed distinctions later, so let us render it into a formulation convenient for that purpose. The real and the imaginary are here understood as two functional poles of the image.[35] The imaginary corresponds to the

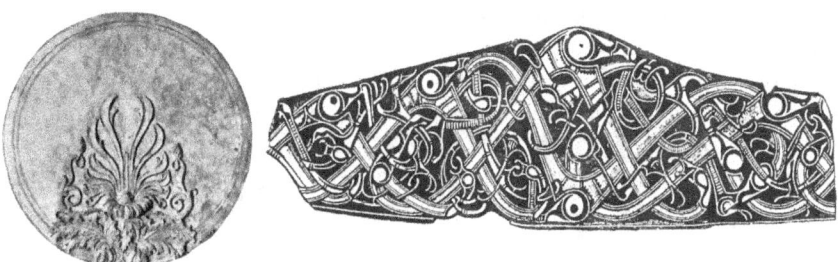

Figure 7.3 Worringer's ornamentation types. **Left:** Organic lines in classical ornamentation. **Right:** Inorganic, Northern lines in Gothic ornamentation.[36]

way the image modifies our body and mind, and the real corresponds to how the image represents some idea. To illustrate, we might consider an example Deleuze uses for a similar but not equivalent purpose, namely, his description of false recognition, as when we say, "'Good morning Theodorus' when it is Theaetetus who passes by."[37] If we depend primarily on our reasoning and take into account all the relevant facts of the situation, as for instance our knowing that Theodorus is in another town today, that under the given lighting, Theaetetus would look like Theodorus, and so forth, we would be able to conclude that the idea represented by the image is the idea for Theaetetus, and we would not let the modification on our body and mind serve as the indicator for who is there. But when we take this modificatory element itself as instead representing the idea of Theodorus, thereby confusing the modification the image has on us (the "imaginary") with the idea it properly represents (the "real"), then we will mistakenly misrecognize the image, thinking that the representational component is contained sufficiently in the modification.[38] As Deleuze says, for classical philosophers, the truth must be drawn apart from the false; otherwise, we become locked in a world of illusions.[39]

This lesser elaborated definition of falsity will aid us in two main ways, which will become more apparent as we proceed into the next chapter. The first is that it will allow us to distinguish unethical deception from artistic falsification; for, to deceive someone is to confuse them such that they take the imaginary for the real in ways like we illustrated above. It also allows us to distinguish the veridical person from higher sorts of falsifiers, because veridical people insist on not committing the error of confusing appearances with realities, even though, as we will see, this is an ultimately fruitless and counter-productive hope.

The second conception Deleuze gives in this context for the real and the imaginary is from the third chapter of Bergson's *Matter and Memory*. Bergson notes that on the one hand we commonly believe that perceived objects exist outside our perception.[40] So "beyond the walls of your room, which you perceive at this moment, there are the adjoining rooms, then the rest of the house, finally the street and the town in which you live."[41] However, we do not likewise extend that conception to the realm of our psychic life, because we do not normally think that mental states extend outside our present consciousness. They seem to exist exactly when they happen, but not before or after. In this context, Deleuze regards the mental as the imaginary, and the perceivable, physical things as the real.[42] What characterizes the real is that it obeys certain laws that order its arrangement on the basis of continuous connectivities between neighboring spatial objects, along with logical, causal relations that link them through actions; for instance, because we are in the room, we must have entered it from the hallway, which had to have a starting place, and so on.[43] But since we often recall any random past mental state erratically or at whim (like suddenly having a memory of our childhood for three seconds and then returning to what we are doing in the present, seemingly jumping over all those other moments in between), the imaginary operates instead by caprice and discontinuity.[44]

And like in the previous definition, Deleuze says that the "organic" form of the true is the *distinction* between these zones of the real and the imaginary, and the false is effectuated in the error that *confuses* them.[45] Deleuze then offers a challenging interpretation regarding this schema. He first notes how for Bergson mental acts do in fact extend outside of present consciousness, on its "fringe," because they exist in the future and past in connection to the present one. And he next claims that this fringe of the imaginary and the fringe of the real (what is out of view) somehow overlap in a shared "fringe of indistinction."[46] While the details of this conception are unclear at this point, we will see in the next chapter that the falsifier as a clairvoyant seer senses in this fringe how the present movements of the world might diverge in new directions.

Formless Falsity

Deleuze's other main definition for truth and falsity is that the true is what has a form and the false is whatever lacks form.[47] Having a form means there are certain definitional judgments about it that are in principle (*de droit*) universal and necessary; however, if they can vary per person or over time, then it is formless and thus false. While it may seem odd to say that an entity is false rather than non-existent, we might recall that for Deleuze, truth and falsity can be modes of being for entities in some sense, and this is one of them. Deleuze clarifies with some illustrations. The first is the triangle, which is true, because it has a form, as evinced by the fact that any time you think a triangle, you cannot deny, for instance, that it has three angles equaling two right angles. The second example is that a human is a rational animal, because this applies necessarily and universally to all humans that ever were or that ever may come to be.[48] But the third example is of something formless and false, namely, the chimera. Here Deleuze playfully narrates his own rendition of a Platonic sort of dialogue.[49] In it, Socrates asks one person, "What is the form of a chimera?" They reply, "A chimera has wings, hooves, and big teeth." But then he asks the same question to a second person, and they instead say, "A chimera is toothless and has fins rather than wings." Socrates, here in Deleuze's fabulation, then adds that he himself saw a chimera with altogether different features than the ones given in these two descriptions. Since its form is endlessly variable, it cannot really qualify as a form, which needs to be universal and necessary, and hence chimeras are formless and false. We will return to this notion of formless variability in the next chapter when discussing how such variations can instead create *new* forms.

Truth Undone

As these judgments hold whenever they are made, no matter when, they implicitly endow forms with an eternal or "infinite" in temporality. In "To Have Done with Judgment," Deleuze claims that this sort of placing of verdicts into an infinite future is in fact one of the conditions for any judgment in the first place.[50] In a moral or juridical context, to judge someone guilty means that in all moments for the rest of time, no one can change the fact that this person is guilty of that crime they had once

Figure 7.4 The hero of Welles's *The Lady from Shanghai* escaping his guilty verdict by creating mayhem (© Mercury and Columbia 1947. All rights reserved).[51]

committed. It is to make a determination about someone that becomes eternally a part of their essence or form. Here Deleuze employs the figure of God as being the one we sin against and within Whom our eternal guilt remains an infinite debt.[52] But one of the requisites for falsity to have its unique creative power is that we must be done with leveling judgments and instead let matters settle themselves more on the level of immediate, physical interactivity.[53]

Deleuze gives a cinematic illustration. The hero of Orson Welles's *The Lady from Shanghai* (1947) is on trial, being framed for murder. But before his guilty verdict can be handed to him, he swallows a bottle of pills (Figure 7.4, left), causing a ruckus in the courtroom. He is then taken to the judge's office where he creates more chaos by ransacking it and beating those holding him there (middle panel), finally sneaking out undetected (right panel). What is important here is that the hero does not reverse his judgment to the "true" one but rather changes the physics of the situation to make it impossible to level any judgment upon him in the first place, redirecting the unlawful forces acting upon him back into the courtroom. Thus "Welles constantly creates characters who are unjudicable and who have not to be judged, who evade any possible judgement," and hence "the ideal of truth crumbles."[54] Similarly, we might think of the chimera example. If we do not make judgments about it that are thought to hold universally and necessarily regarding what the chimera should always have to be, then its variability in form is simply a matter of it undergoing metamorphosis. A chimera might have wings. And indeed, a chimera might also not have wings but rather fins. How? When it is transforming. If we do away with the judgments that might fix its form, it can be itself and yet at variance with itself in a simultaneous movement of becoming.

> Judgment prevents the emergence of any new mode of existence. For the latter creates itself through its own forces, that is, through the forces it is able to harness, and is valid in and of itself inasmuch as it brings the new combination into existence. Herein, perhaps, lies the secret: to bring into existence and not to judge. If it is so disgusting to judge, it is not because everything is of equal value, but on the contrary because what has value can be made or distinguished only by defying judgment. What expert judgment, in art, could ever bear on the work to come?[55]

Deleuze calls this requisite and status of the New "the innocence of becoming," with reference to Nietzsche's commentaries on Anaximander and Heraclitus.[56] The Anaximander fragment, Nietzsche says, leads us to "view [...] all coming-to-be as though it were an illegitimate emancipation from eternal being, a wrong for which destruction is the only penance."[57] However, for Heraclitus, there can be no such "sphere of guilt, of penance, of judgment" in this world where there is "nothing other than becoming" and where "everything forever has its opposite along with it."[58] For, as Heraclitus would say, "not the punishment of what has come-to-be did I see, but the justification of that which is coming-into-being."[59] When there is no eternity of forms, what comes to be in immediate duration cannot be judged as a degradation of something perfect and timeless. It is simply that new thing that it happens to be for that brief time that it exists and nothing less or more than that.

Moreover, this Heraclitean coming-into-being is a matter of non-judgmental, creative *play*, like that of a child or artist:

> In this world only play, play as artists and children engage in it, exhibits coming-to-be and passing away, structuring and destroying, without any moral additive, in forever equal innocence. And as children and artists play, so plays the ever-living fire. It constructs and destroys, all in innocence. Such is the game that the aeon plays with itself. Transforming itself into water and earth, it builds towers of sand like a child at the seashore, piles them up and tramples them down. From time to time it starts the game anew. An instant of satiety—and again it is seized by its need, as the artist is seized by his need to create. Not hybris but the ever self-renewing impulse to play calls new worlds into being. The child throws its toys away from time to time—and starts again, in innocent caprice.[60]

So how should we understand the "logic" involved in these conceptions of deviant movement? What is important here is that no matter what is given, it is always open to new variations or deformations. And thus, the world never forms a completed Whole. Moreover, it is judgment that fixes things through time, and so by doing away with judgment, that in a sense can be seen as helping things to undergo variation. This strongly suggests analetheic conceptions. For instance, Deleuze might be thinking that the statement, "the chimera has wings," when it is not judged true or false, can then be open to "the chimera does not have wings" being asserted, when it is seen to have fins instead. So, this is some of the strongest material for suggesting that Deleuze's logic is analetheist.

But it is not certainly so. For one thing, suppose we are taking the analetheist view. According to Beall's and Ripley's definition, analetheism is "the thesis that some sentences lack truth-value, *coupled with the willingness to assert such sentences*."[61] That suggests these sentences are asserted and also *judged* to have the logical truth-value of neither true nor false. Or suppose otherwise that it is something more like the intuitionist sort of analetheism. Here the position would be that such unproven sentences should not be asserted (if even they can be conceived in the first place). But, even under Deleuze's assumption that things are always changing, and that for instance the chimera changes from having wings to having fins, it would still seem that something or other needs to be affirmed in order for it be said that the transition is from wings to fins and not rather from legs to tentacles, for example.

And yet, it is also not so obvious that this is a dialetheic conception either. It might be so, however, if we are to conceive the moment of transition when the winged chimera becomes the finned chimera as involving it both being winged and not winged at the same time. (It is winged insofar as it is changing away from something with wings in that moment of becoming, and it is not-winged insofar as it is also in that act transforming into something with fins instead of wings.) And what about doing away with judgment? Can this notion in Deleuze's philosophy be seen as a dialetheic conception? Perhaps it could, if we think of doing away with judgment as being a "problematizing" of the truth of statements, by saying that they are at least true and thus are assertable, but also that they are at least false, and so their negation is equally assertable. In other words, Deleuze's notion of doing away with judgment would need to be understood more precisely as doing away with monoletheic judgment, but not with dialetheic judgment. So far it is not at all clear that this is what Deleuze has in mind. However, these notions regarding deviant motion and doing away with judgment are directly tied into his discussion of the falsifier's power of the false, which, as we will see, is more apparently a dialetheic rather than an analetheic conception. So let us examine those ideas now.

8

False Creations

Introduction

To more fully grasp the creative power of the false, we lastly examine Gilles Deleuze's notion of the "falsifier." To do so, we begin with his concept of the simulacrum in terms of perspectival deformations. After that, we work through the main types of falsifiers, including the fabulist and seer, culminating in the self- and world-creative artist. Alongside that discussion, we examine the role of time and incompossibility in this account, noticing a strong dialetheic component to Deleuze's conception, especially with regard to his use of Gottfried Leibniz's "ambiguous signs."

Deformation's Creations

In order to clarify how falsification has the power of transformation, we will need to first address Deleuze's notion of the simulacrum and the reversal of Platonism, which he develops in *The Logic of Sense* and *Difference and Repetition*. Deleuze notes that one of Plato's motivations was "to distinguish essence from appearance, intelligible from sensible, Idea from image, original from copy, and model from simulacrum,"[1] in other words, to ground the organic form of the true. We find such an exercise in Plato's *Statesman* for example, where first the method of division defines a statesman as a "herdsman" of people, and second there is an evaluation of potential candidates who could fulfill this definition, which includes not just kings but also merchants, farmers, bakers, gymnastics teachers, and doctors.[2] Deleuze calls the candidates "claimants" or "pretenders" (*prétendants*), and he likens them to the rival suitors for a bride.[3] The task then is to "distinguish the true pretender from the false one,"[4] which is the "simulacrum" (*phantasma*/φάντασμα),[5] by placing the rivals along a scale of trueness to the form; in the case of the statesman, they would range from "the true statesman or the well-found aspirer, then relatives, auxiliaries, and slaves, down to simulacra and counterfeits. Malediction weighs heavily on these last—they incarnate the evil power of the false pretender."[6]

Deleuze's aim is to show that the "demonic character"[7] of the simulacrum in Plato's philosophy presents a subversive tendency to overturn and reverse this ordering, that is, to put simulacra on the side of the original and at the top of the hierarchy. In the

Sophist, Plato distinguishes two sorts of images. The first kind is the good copy (*eikōn*/ εἰκών), which is a likeness of its Idea, and the more general model for its resemblance is the Idea of the Same.[8] It could be a statue for instance that "conforms to the proportions of the original in all three dimensions."[9] Yet, Plato notes, were a giant sculpture to have the correct proportions, "the upper parts would look too small, and the lower too large, because we see the one at a distance, the other close at hand."[10]

Thus, to make the figure appear with the right proportions to the viewer on the ground, the upper parts need to be stretched out (Figure 8.1, A). Or suppose the Parthenon were formed exactly to the desired proportions (Figure 8.1, B). Given its enormous size, were we standing in front at the middle, our perspective would distort those perfect proportions (Figure 8.1, C). Thus, to compensate for this, the actual structure itself needs to be deformed (Figure 8.1, D), such that it appears with the right proportions (again, Figure 8.1, B). And as Vitruvius noted, the sides of large columns were made to bulge out so that they appear with straight lines (Figure 8.1, E).[11] Hence an icon, the "good" copy, only shows its "true" proportions from God's point of view, infinitely far away where parallel lines will always appear as parallel.[12]

However the simulacrum, the second kind of image, like the intentionally distorted sculpture, only has the effect of resembling the Idea, which it does "underhandedly, under cover of an aggression, an insinuation, a subversion, 'against the father', and without passing through the Idea," as Deleuze puts it.[13] Simulacra, then, "are precisely demonic images, stripped of resemblance."[14] And because the simulacrum is *not* constituted by its resemblance to the form, its defining characteristic is its "dissemblance" to it, taking the Other rather than the Same as its model.[15] Now, if the simulacrum is defined by this difference to forms, then it must have something absolutely unique about it; and thus the simulacrum is itself constituted by its originality among all other models and copies.[16] Moreover, in its act of creation, this original component of the simulacrum has no respective form or prior model against which it can be judged and evaluated in terms of resemblances, and so it is not a "degraded copy"; and furthermore, in its raw newness, it has not yet been copied, so it is not initially a model. But after its creation, it has "a positive power," namely, "the highest power of the false," to become a model and original that expresses new

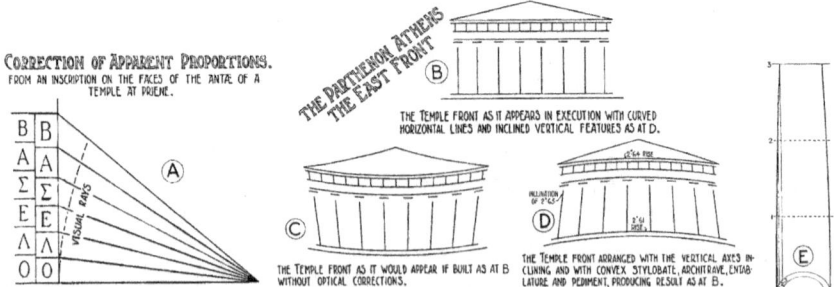

Figure 8.1 Deformations of the actual proportions in Greek architecture to correct for perspectival distortions.[17]

forms. If instead we simply exercise judgment, which requires a preexisting form and "previous similitude or identity" to determine what something is modeled after, then we limit or neglect anything original or new that might arise.[18] Reversing Platonism, however, means doing away with judgment and thereby granting simulacra not only a place among copies and models,[19] but also the premier position; for, it is the "triumph of the false pretender"[20] and "glorifying the reign of simulacra and reflections," because "simulacra are the superior forms."[21]

In other words, the Sophist as sorcerer and artisan of simulacra does not keep all the known forms intact, while at the same time deceptively making certain appearances only seem to resemble the forms when in fact they do not. Rather, they falsify the given forms themselves by fashioning non-resemblances to them that have their own originating power in the movement of becoming: "The different, the dissimilar, the unequal—in short, becoming—may well be [...] models themselves, terrifying models of the *pseudos* in which unfolds the power of the false."[22]

And so it is especially in Deleuze's notion of the simulacrum that we can find an account for how the deviance of becoming may be prior to any forms. Here he also calls it the "becoming-mad" or "becoming-unlimited" of the simulacrum, again with reference to Plato's *Philebus*.[23] We addressed this notion already in Chapter 1. Recall that the idea is that if something is becoming hotter, then because it is still in an act of becoming, it is not of some determinate temperature but is rather already going above some temperature. Or put another way, it is not simply "hot," nor is it just "hotter" than something else. Rather, it is somehow hotter than it itself is, while it is in the act of rising in temperature.[24] In the context here of the simulacrum, something's becoming is "mad" in the sense that its changing means it has no definitive form, and also, what it is changing into is not predetermined when it begins altering.

In sum, this becoming-mad and becoming-unlimited can involve perspectival deformations that slip "between"[25] forms and thus, while the becoming is still in effect, will counteract any judgment to what is universal and necessary about them:

> The simulacrum includes the differential point of view; and the observer becomes a part of the simulacrum itself, which is transformed and deformed by his point of view. In short, there is in the simulacrum a becoming-mad, or a becoming unlimited, as in the *Philebus* where "more and less are always going a point further," *a becoming always other*, *a becoming subversive* of the depths, able to evade the equal, the limit, the Same, or the Similar: always more and less at once, but never equal.[26]

One final point is that this deformation involves the unity of divergent, incompossible worlds.[27] Although something that is getting hotter has no determinate temperature, insofar as we can say something about how hot it is, we could propose that it is both the temperature that it just now has been and, in the same stroke, the temperature that it is now becoming.[28] But if the world were unitary and perfectly self-consistent, such a pairing of normally exclusive states would be impossible. Hence, in order to preserve and explain the inherent paradoxes of becoming, Deleuze here introduces his modified form of Leibniz's incompossible worlds. We saw a little of this conception in

Chapter 5 when we discussed temporal bifurcation. Recall that in Leibniz's account, before creating the world, God considered every possible series of events, with each sequence being a distinct possible world.[29] In one possible world, Adam does not sin; he remains happy, does not work, and has many wise children. In another, our world in fact, Adam eats the fruit, he toils, and his children murder one another.[30] God chooses the best possible world, which is the one with greatest amount of essence, variety, and perfection.[31] This means, however, that with the way God assigns predicates to things at the very beginning of time, that despite us being unable to predict the future, all forthcoming events are built into the initial state.

Yet, as Bergson and Deleuze note, a world where all the future is built into the present has no need of any duration or events.[32] Bergson himself notes this specifically for Leibniz's conception of time. Here Bergson's point is that a mechanistic interpretation of the world where every future event is determined by past ones strips time out of the picture just as much as does a Leibnizian conception where God has already chosen a world whose course of events is known from the beginning:

> The doctrine of teleology, in its extreme form, as we find it in Leibniz for example, implies that things and beings merely realise a programme previously arranged. But *if there is nothing unforeseen, no invention or creation in the universe, time is useless again*. As in the mechanistic hypothesis, here again it is supposed that *all is given*. [...] succession remains [...] a mere appearance, as indeed does movement itself. In the doctrine of Leibniz, time is reduced to a confused perception, relative to the human standpoint, a perception which would vanish, like a rising mist, for a mind seated at the centre of things.[33]

In other words, supposing there to be such a Leibnizian God, the movement of the world becomes superfluous. What additionally is there to gain for such a God to watch the future unfold? It is already completely given and perfectly known in all its detail at the beginning. Bergson sees a similar sort of stripping of duration out of time in how astronomical predictions are made, such that all future stellar events are "instantaneously unfurled like a fan"[34] simply in a present mathematical calculation. The durational movement of the world cannot know where it is going if it is to have any real temporal character to it. Thus, Deleuze proposes that we keep Leibniz's theory of incompossibles with one exception: we subtract the God who decides the world's path of unfolding at the beginning and introduce a Devil who will make the world's movements twist and fork a wicked path at every instant, causing divergent incompossible worlds to consolidate in Dupréelian fashion and be undecidable for that moment.[35] Thus, at that event when Adam is being tempted and feels pulled very strongly in two directions of action, he is both sinner and not-sinner in the same stroke of becoming. And two incompossible worlds—the one where he ends up sinning and the one where he never does (along with all the infinity of their ramifications)—coalesce in that moment despite being fundamentally at odds. We will return to the dialetheic nature of this conception of incompossible temporality in Chapter 8, after we first learn a little more about the falsifier's role in it.

The Falsifier

The Scale of Falsification

We are now sufficiently prepared to see how the falsifier employs the power of the false to create the New, which is a more profound sort of the "true."[36] As we will later see, Deleuze differentiates various roles for the falsifier, but first we should note distinctions that can be made regarding their levels of power. The least powerful falsifier is the truth-seeker or veridical person (*l'homme véridique*). They aim to avoid deceiving others and being deceived themselves by trying to keep the real and the imaginary distinct and thereby also never giving the false the form of the true, that is to say, never mistakenly attributing universal and necessary features to something that lacks them.[37] Nonetheless, as Nietzsche notes, if there is no world other than the one before us that we can sense and that is always in a process of becoming, then the veridical person is only lying to him or herself, and they may even end up deceiving others inadvertently.[38] Furthermore, the value of seeking such truths is called into question when it raises unfortunate costs, which Deleuze illustrates with Welles's *Touch of Evil* (1958).

Here a law officer, Vargas, catches the police captain, Quinlan, planting evidence to frame a suspect (Figure 8.2, left). Vargas becomes determined to uncover Quinlan's long past of committing such crimes (middle panel). But in his obsession to do so, he neglects his wife who is kidnapped, drugged, and framed for murder by Quinlan and his associates (right panel). Vargas is a veridical person, and his judgment of life in accordance with the organic form of the true is a result of a deeper sickness, a rejection of the possibilities of life. Quinlan, a "higher person" who judges without laws and truths, exercises more power, but it too is a sickly kind. What ultimately groups veridical people and higher people together is that the forces they implement are only applied to others and to themselves "in a single, uniform and invariable way."[39] In Welles's *Mr. Arkadin*, the title character tells the tale of the frog and the scorpion. The scorpion wants to cross a river and asks a frog for a ride. The frog does not trust the scorpion, who finally convinces the frog by noting that if it stings her on the way over, both will die. Nonetheless, the scorpion stings in the middle of the river, explaining that "I can't help it; it's my character," which she was powerless to change.[40] Vargas only knows how to obey and enforce the law; Quinlan only knows how to fix evidence.[41] Thus

Figure 8.2 Crimes and investigations in Welles's *Touch of Evil* (© Universal 1958. All rights reserved).[42]

even this higher power does not know how to transform itself, and will to dominate is therefore ultimately a weakness rather than a manifestation of will to power. The highest power is instead the power of the false, which "knows how to transform itself, to metamorphose itself according to the forces it encounters, [...] always opening new 'possibilities.'"[43]

Truth and Time: The Falsification

At this point, we will need to address some of Deleuze's comments on logic that have bearing on his philosophy of time. We will be dealing here with some old and difficult philosophical problems, namely, future contingents and the Master Argument. Given our purposes, we will not get into the complexities and textual sourcing of these problems too much, and specifically we will not evaluate the accuracy of Deleuze's textual interpretations on these matters. Doing so would prove to be a very complicated task, and it would not further our primary aims anyway, which are to assess Deleuze's *own* logical thinking. So we will see what sort of logical ideas he expresses in his commentaries, and we will follow his account closely, which we take from a couple of his course lectures on cinema and truth. Here we will find some of his direct criticisms of many-valued logics. But as we will see, we will need to translate what he says into the sort of modern logical terminology that we are using here, and in the end we will find that not only is he not expressly criticizing a dialetheist view, he may also in fact be favoring one.

Deleuze's main philosophical point in these commentaries, similar to what we saw in his discussion of the principles of logic in Chapter 5, is that classical logic works just fine when we are dealing with eternal essences, but we run into problems when we apply a classical notion of truth to certain matters involving time. And one of his purposes for using this illustration is to introduce his notions of the falsifier making the past be not necessarily true and also making the impossible follow from the possible.

The problem of future contingents gives us good reason to think that there are truth-value gaps. Future contingent statements are ones that can be uttered now but for which there presently are no facts that make them either true or false. Priest offers this as an example: "The first pope in the twenty-second century will be Chinese."[44] It is impossible to say with certainty whether that statement is true or false. Another example, which is a classic one, is whether a sea battle will happen tomorrow.[45] Here we again see how logic and metaphysics mutually constrain one another. For, there is a view that if future contingent statements must be either true or false, just like every other statement, then that involves a fatalistic stance, because it means all future events are determined well in advance and cannot be changed. So if we believe that the Principle of Excluded Middle must be valid no matter what, this can constrain our metaphysics to a fatalistic kind.[46] Those who want to avoid this fatalism may want to take the analetheic position and say that future contingents are neither true nor false.

The Master Argument, like the problem of future contingents, is about time and fatalism. But before we continue, we should note Deleuze's logical assumptions here. He says that the argument is called the "Master" argument, because it is concerned with the question of whether the future is "Mastered" (or "Dominated") by the Principle of Non-Contradiction and by necessity.⁴⁷ Here is one place we will need to translate his terminology. In this context, Deleuze defines the Principle of Non-Contradiction as the requirement that of a pair of contradictory statements (including such future contingent pairings as "the sea battle will take place" and "the sea battle will not take place") *one and only one must be true*.⁴⁸ Now, that *only one* of the two can be true is in fact what the Principle of Non-Contradiction directly requires. But that *at least* one must be true is the direct requirement of the Principle of Excluded-Middle.⁴⁹ So when Deleuze speaks of the Principle of Non-Contradiction in this discussion, we will need to determine whether he is concerned just with that principle, or just with the Principle of Excluded Middle, or with both at the same time. This will allow us later to see that his objections to many-valued logics apply to analetheic ones with truth-value gaps and not necessarily to dialetheic ones that have truth-value gluts, despite his claim that this is all an issue of the Principle of Non-Contradiction.

The Master Argument is notoriously difficult to navigate, given the sparse original sourcing on it and the difficulties of reconstructing it in a straightforward way.⁵⁰ As such, it would be best if we only consider the elements that are required for our purposes here. The argument is structured with three propositions about truth, time, and possibility, but it is said that all three cannot be true, as any two will disallow the third (so if you affirm any two, you thereby infer the negation of the third one). As Epictetus lays them out, the three are:

{1} that everything that has happened is necessarily true;
{2} that the impossible cannot be a consequence of the possible; and
{3} that something is a possibility which neither is nor ever will be true.⁵¹

The first one, that everything that has happened is necessarily true, is thought to be based on our intuition that we cannot change the past. The second one, that the impossible cannot be a consequence of the possible, is vague and it is not obvious whether it refers to a logical or a causal consequence.⁵² For our purposes, our concern with it is whether or not a future contingent can begin as a statement of a possibility and later become a statement of an impossibility, after the event expressed by its negation is what instead transpires. In other words, suppose tomorrow is the 1st of the month. When tomorrow ends and the sea battle never takes place, then the statement "a sea battle happens on the 1st" will go from being a statement of something that is possible to a statement of something that is impossible. For, now that the day has passed and is out of our reach, it can never be the case that a battle will happen on that day. And the third proposition of the Master Argument, that something is a possibility which neither is nor ever will be true, says that some things can be possible now, even if in fact they never will take place in the future.

According to Epictetus, Diodorus selects the first two options and denies the third. So Diodorus claims that all past events are necessarily true and that possibilities cannot become impossibilities, and this means that the only things that are possible are what in fact will happen. And thus, whatever does happen could not have been otherwise, and similarly, whatever will happen cannot now be altered. This is a strict fatalistic view. In the course lecture, Deleuze does not mention Diodorus's solution. But we can be mostly sure Deleuze would not find much resonance between his own philosophy and Diodorus's, given Deleuze's indeterministic metaphysics.

The first solution Deleuze does give is not one of the three that Epictetus speaks of. It comes rather from Aristotle.[53] It says that of the two contradictory future contingent statements, we cannot say that either one in particular is necessarily true, but we can still claim that their disjunction is necessarily true. Aristotle explains this in the following way:

> Everything necessarily is or is not, and will be or will not be; but one cannot divide and say that one or the other is necessary. I mean, for example: it is necessary for there to be or not to be a sea-battle tomorrow; but it is not necessary for a sea-battle to take place tomorrow, nor for one not to take place—though it is necessary for one to take place or not to take place.[54]

In Deleuze's assessment, we are using in this case a three-valued logic. He says that the truth-values here are true, false, and "possible," with this third option being understood as neither true nor false.[55] (The disjunction is just true, but neither disjunct is true or false. Rather, they each have the truth-value *possible*, for Deleuze.) When thinking about our non-classical logic systems, Deleuze's characterization here is a little confusing. Normally in these "gappy" three-valued logics, there is a third value, something like "indeterminate," symbolized by *i*, for instance. A separate matter would be the modal operators, necessary and possible. There are gappy modal logics where you can have a proposition taking the possibility operator, while also that same proposition may be assigned any of the three values: true, false, or neither.[56] So we need to translate what Deleuze is saying here, because it is not obvious how we should conceive of "possible" as a third logical value. Now, his objection to this third truth-value option is that he thinks it makes things too complicated, and he also says it is problematic because it violates the Principle of Non-Contradiction.[57] From this we will draw a couple of things. We will assume that when he speaks of the third value as being "possible," we can translate that into the gappy "indeterminate" value, as what he seems to be saying is that when a future contingent is not necessarily true, that means the event it expresses is not predetermined, and so we would assign it some kind of a gappy value. (He is not for instance simply saying that it is true that it is possible, as that does not involve a third truth-value, at least using the systems we are considering here.) The second thing we draw from this is that while he claims it violates the Principle of Non-Contradiction, it would seem to be more straightforwardly a violation of the Principle of Excluded Middle, as neither the proposition nor its negation is said to be true. Taking all of this into account, we can see that Deleuze's criticisms are more likely directed at an analetheic, gappy logic than to a dialetheic, glutty one.

The second solution Deleuze mentions is the one Chrysippus's takes, according to Epictetus. Of the three Master Argument propositions, Chrysippus is said to have affirmed that the past is necessarily true and also that things can be possible even if they never do come to pass, but that the impossible can in fact be a consequence of the possible. This violates the Principle of Non-Contradiction, Deleuze says.[58] To see why, consider again our example statement, "a sea battle happens on the 1st," where tomorrow is the first. It begins as possible. And we again suppose that tomorrow ends, and the battle does not take place. We cannot change what happened that day after it closes, so the same future contingent statement expresses now something that is not possible on account of the necessity of the present and past. So here, one might object that one same proposition cannot be both possible and not-possible.[59] At any rate, Deleuze is not concerned primarily with how well this solves the problem, but rather with the idea of making the impossible follow from the possible, which is something the falsifier is able to do. We will see what he means by this later, but we should note the following. Deleuze will build from this notion of the impossible following from the possible, which he says violates the Principle of Non-Contradiction.[60] Thus the new concept he constructs might violate this principle as well, and hence it may have dialetheic features.

The third solution is said to come from Cleanthes. He claims that the impossible cannot follow from the possible and that there can be possibilities that never obtain, but Cleanthes also holds that everything that has happened is not necessarily true. This one has presented a special challenge throughout the ages for forming an interpretation of it, because it goes against our strong intuition that the past cannot now become otherwise. Deleuze's explanation has to do with the Stoic distinction of the corporeals and incorporeals that we saw in Chapter 5 (and note that there will be some incompatibilities between these two accounts, as we previously were attributing certain related notions to Chrysippus and not Cleanthes, in accordance with our source texts). Deleuze says that Cleanthes distinguishes the fated from the necessary, and on that basis, Cleanthes would claim that the past is fated, but it is not necessary. According to Deleuze, the interactions of bodies are matters of physical necessity for Cleanthes. And so in the sea-battle, when the oarsman acts upon the oar, pulling it in a certain manner, the oar by physical necessity would be impelled to move in a corresponding way. The event of the battle itself would then be the incorporeal effect resulting from the sum total of all the particular ways that the bodies are interacting, including whether or not, for instance, the boats were maneuvered in place, the weather permitted the battle, the generals decided to engage, and so on. What is necessary is that each physical influence has an immediate effect. But one of the points here about fate and necessity is that no one single influence is sufficient for bringing about the resulting event. Deleuze says that we must also take into account the issue of cofatality.[61] There is an illustration that Cicero and Gellius attribute to Chrysippus and not to Cleanthes, but it will be useful for us here.

> [Chrysippus] uses an illustration [...]. [...] he says, 'if you push a stone cylinder on steeply sloping ground, you have produced the cause and beginning of its forward motion, but soon it rolls forward not because you are still making it do so, but because such are its form and smooth-rolling shape.[62]

Working with Deleuze's interpretation, we would say that, were it co-fated instead that the drum be lying on a dented side or that right in front of it stands a wall, it would not be *fated* for the drum to roll, even though it is *necessitated* for the drum to be impelled forward when we push it. This example is used in the context of Chrysippus's notion of assent. To use the sea-battle illustration, we would say that it is a matter of necessity, for instance, for all the pressures and circumstances of the battle situation to compel the generals to engage their navies, but what determines if they make that decision is a matter of a cofatality, namely, whether they assent to those impulses, or, by means of their reasoning, act on alternative ones.[63]

Regardless, in all this discussion of Stoic physics and metaphysics here, Deleuze never clarifies what it means for the past to be not necessarily true. Is he saying that for Cleanthes, the past is fated but not necessitated? It seems also that this illustration can be seen as showing that the past is necessitated but not fated. Or is he making a different point? Deleuze does not specify what he has in mind here for how this solves the problem. But making that determination was not his main purpose anyway. He is using this illustration as a starting point for formulating his own conception for how the past can be made not necessarily true. We will examine that notion in the following sections, but the basic idea is that the falsifier can do things in the present which call into question what really was happening in the past and perhaps even assign different causal origins than were previously known to be there. This is a matter of exercising the power of the false, so let us turn now to this concept.

Falsifier as Fabulist

> "The evokers of the devil must before all things belong to a religion which admits a devil, creator and rival of God. To invoke a power, we must believe in it. Given this firm faith in the religion of the devil, we must proceed as follows to enter into correspondence with this pseudo-Deity:
>
> MAGICAL AXIOM.
> In the circle of its action, every word creates that which it affirms.
>
> DIRECT CONSEQUENCE.
> He who affirms the devil, creates or makes the devil."
> Éliphas Lévi[64]

Deleuze defines the power of the false as the indiscernibility or undecidability of the real and the imaginary (and essence and appearance, actual and virtual, etc.), which happens when they coalesce or consolidate in the Dupréelian sense where they remain distinct yet fused into what Deleuze calls a "crystalline formation" rather than an organic form.[65] One way Deleuze illustrates how a falsifier can bring about this indiscernibility and undecidability is with New Novel (*Nouveau roman*) narrative and description, which can bring about disorienting shifts from the real to the imaginary by cycling them one after the other so rapidly that it becomes impossible to tell which is which. Deleuze has us consider a velodrome bicycle race where the cyclists have been circling around very fast for so long that we lose count of their laps, meaning that even if one racer is right behind another, we still cannot know which of the two is the leader, as the one behind could actually be almost a lap or more ahead in the count.[66] A cinematic example Deleuze uses for this is the fun-house mirror scene at the end of Welles's *The Lady from Shanghai*.

The reflections of the real people bounce around a series of mirrors making the real and the imaginary figures indiscernible. Yet, they remain distinct; for, otherwise the characters would not keep shooting the images in hopes of eventually killing the real one (Figure 8.3).[67]

Deleuze elaborates how this indiscernibility works by employing Jean Ricardou's notions of "capture" and "liberation" from his theoretical study of New Novel narration.[68] Capture occurs when something in the story is first shown to be real and then in the exact same scene it is also shown to be imaginary. For instance, in Alain Robbe-Grillet's novel *Project for a Revolution in New York*, an elaborate scene is described involving characters committing various actions, so it cannot be a still picture, and yet we are next told it was the image on the cover of a book. This captures the real scene into the imaginary one in the picture.[69] Liberation is the inverse of this: what begins as something imaginary is then shown to be real. For instance, again in *Project for a Revolution in New York*, a man looks into the decorative wavy lines on a door and imagines in them a bound woman, but immediately after we learn it is also something that is actually happening behind the door, thereby liberating this fantasy image into reality.[70] To see how capture and liberation transitions can cycle so as to become undecidable or indiscernible, consider the opening sequences to Robbe-Grillet's film *Trans-Europ-Express* (1966).

Figure 8.3 Real and imaginary images cycling too quickly to discern which is which, in Welles's *The Lady from Shanghai* (© Mercury and Columbia 1947. All rights reserved).[71]

Figure 8.4 Capture and liberation of images in Robbe-Grillet's *Trans-Europ-Express* (© Como 1966. All rights reserved).[72]

It begins with Robbe-Grillet himself noticing a suspicious looking man at a train station (Figure 8.4, top left). Next, he joins his wife and a companion in a passenger car, and they decide to compose, by dictation, a screenplay about a drug smuggler (top middle). So far, everything is presented as real. As they then verbally narrate the story, we are shown at the same time a ridiculously disguised man making a drug deal with the suspicious man from before, which captures the previously real man into this fantasy (top right). After the title credits we see now another man, who serves throughout the film as the main character of their subsequent narrations. At first we see him seemingly make a drug deal with the suspicious man (bottom left), which suggests the hero is the imaginary criminal of the fictional story they are composing. But then the hero enters the train that Robbe-Grillet is on and sits with them in their car (bottom middle, with Robbe-Grillet pictured in the mirror). This dually captures the "real" Robbe-Grillet into the fiction of the criminal all while liberating this "imaginary" criminal into the real world of Robbe-Grillet. Or is it that the criminal is currently real and only after the encounter he becomes captured into the imaginary story to follow? And do not forget that even Robbe-Grillet himself is playing a fictional role for the film; it is not a documentary, although we also see him shooting these very sequences (bottom right). Furthermore, at the end of the film, one of the events in the narrated story is displayed in a "real" newspaper that Robbe-Grillet is holding, which puts into question the statuses of the two worlds. All these rapid shifts and complex relations between the images make it ultimately impossible to discern the real from the imaginary; and the narrator, in this case the real/imaginary Robbe-Grillet, is a falsifier wielding that power of the false. Deleuze calls this the "story-telling function" (*fonction de fabulation*): it is a fabulating and "falsifying narration" that is different than mere fiction on account of that power.[73]

So we thereby lose the ability to judge what is real and what is imaginary, and this is also one of the main features of New Novel *description*. Prior to it, in what Deleuze calls "organic description," the thing being described is treated like something independent of the description, just waiting somewhere to be described. Yet, with the crystalline description of the New Novel, there are "falsifications" of what is being said, which prevent there being an independent standard or model that could be described either accurately or not, and as such, the description becomes the object itself.[74] For instance, at the beginning of *Project for a Revolution in New York*, the mouth of the bound woman we mentioned before is "open in a long cry of suffering or terror," but also her "mouth, which has been wide open too long, must be distended by some kind of gag."[75] If her mouth is gagged, then it was never wide open as if crying out. Were there to be some woman regarded as outside the description, her mouth would be in one or another state, but not both. Yet, since New Novel description makes this determination impossible, there is only the woman in the description with her bifurcating, incompossible states. Or consider the hero in Robbe-Grillet's film *The Man Who Lies* (1968).

He is seemingly fighting an army at the beginning (Figure 8.5, left) and later enters an inn, which he falsely claims is empty, by the way (middle panel). And yet we learn from the dialogue that all this is happening some years after that first battle. As Deleuze notes, this man "should not have the same suit and tie several years later" (right panel), and this is a "detail which falsifies the image."[76] Here falsity is no longer

Figure 8.5 Narrative falsification in Robbe-Grillet's *The Man Who Lies* (© Como 1968. All rights reserved).⁷⁷

an incorrect description but is rather a description that transforms and bifurcates the story world, which it does by forcing into one narrative flow a set of incompossible worlds, none of which are discernibly the "real" one.⁷⁸ And "contrary to what Leibniz believed, all these worlds belong to the same universe and constitute modifications of the same story."⁷⁹ Somehow this Liar, while sitting in the inn, is both in a world where he just came from the battle and jointly in another world where there has been some years since, with both of these worlds coinciding indiscernibly and undecidedly in one same image or event.

These forking falsifications, by mutating the story world and deviating its movement into alternate routes, make the path that the world is now heading down no longer be the one that will necessarily prevail. Thus falsifying, crystalline narration generates "contingent futures," like the classic example we saw before of the naval battle that either will or will not take place tomorrow, depending on how things proceed before then.⁸⁰ Likewise, these contradictions in the present call the past into question, like the Liar in *The Man Who Lies* who constantly tells contradictory things about his past, and we never can judge what had actually happened. Thus, remarkably, such narration creates *contingent pasts* as well, despite our intuition telling us that the past cannot be changed and is thus necessary.⁸¹ All this happens by making the present itself be contingent, that is, by making it such that the way things are now proceeding need not necessarily be how they currently continue. For, as we noted, if we do away with judgment and create the New rather than seek the organic true, movements can open into unforeseen directions. In sum, then, the movement of the world that "forks and keeps on forking" into incompossible futures also passes "through *incompossible presents*, returning to *not-necessarily true pasts*."⁸² It is in this way that "the powers of the false which weave a narration [...] take effect in 'false movements.'"⁸³

The Past That Never Was

Deleuze further elaborates on this notion of contingent pasts with Maurice Leblanc's novella, *La vie extravagante de Balthazar*. He mentions it in his Leibniz book, *The Fold*, and he even summarizes the whole story at great length in one of his courses.⁸⁴ He also works through the entire plot of a film, *Subterfuge* (*Faux-fuyants*), for similar purposes. Let us just consider them briefly, along with a contemporary illustration of a contingent past, as it will help us better grasp Deleuze's notion of the past being not necessarily true.

Leblanc's story is of Balthazar, who teaches the philosophy of everyday living at a school for young women. He was orphaned at a young age, and he does not know or remember his early life, so he cannot say who his parents are. One day, he begins getting mysterious information about his true father, and after a series of improbable adventures, a total of five unrelated men have claimed Balthazar as their son, each with equally verifiable proof. At the end, the fifth one, a local drunkard, Vaillant du Four, who is also Balthazar's drinking buddy at the time, tells the following story, which explains how this all came to be. Vaillant du Four claims that he fathered Balthazar off in the countryside. He and his wife Gertrude were living at an inn on the banks of the river Saône in a place called Val Rouge. Their business was doing poorly, so Gertrude had the idea of making the nursery be a place where illegitimate children could be cared for at a remote location so that their parents could keep them and their own love affairs secret. They looked after four such children, along with Balthazar, who was the same age as the other boys. One day a flash flood swept away the mother and four of the children. But instead of notifying the parents, Vaillant du Four ran off with Balthazar, still keeping the other parents thinking their children were alive and growing up, so that he could continue receiving their payments, although now by fraud. At one point he lost Balthazar in a crowd, and the boy went on to live and work as an orphan without ever knowing his origins. Vaillant du Four had given to all of the fathers Balthazar's fingerprints and a description of a unique tattoo he had, to make the fathers think that one day they could reclaim "their" child. This explains why Balthazar, as an adult, was legally verified to be the son of four different men. So throughout much of this story, Balthazar has multiple contingent pasts, one for each father. That of course changes when Vaillant du Four explains how all this mess came to be in the first place. Yet, the mystery is not really solved conclusively. Vaillant du Four says that he was drinking so much back during the nursery days that he in fact is not sure if Balthazar is really his son or if instead he is the father of one of the other four boys they were taking care of and who died in the flood.[85]

It is in this way that Balthazar's past was contingent upon facts that presented themselves only as the present time advanced. And given Vaillant du Four's uncertainty about being Balthazar's father, the past contingent statement "Vaillant du Four fathered Balthazar" has an undecidable truth-value. Of course, this is not a strong case of the indeterminacy or non-necessity of the past, as it must have been determinately one case or the other, without that past fact ever actually changing. However, Deleuze emphasizes at least the role of Vaillant du Four's *falsification* in creating these uncertainties about the past. And note also that since Balthazar could only have one father, when he was *legally* identified as having a second father, that means there was a dialetheic situation at least for that time, namely, that he was both legally the son of the first father and not legally his son (insofar as the second legalization delegitimizes the first and the first delegitimizes the second).[86]

Deleuze's other example of contingent pasts will illustrate another way that falsification can put posited origins into question, namely, Bergala's and Limosin's *Subterfuge* (*Faux-fuyants*, 1983). It starts with a narrative deviation, a literal hit-and-run accident where the hero runs over a man with his car, killing him, and inexplicably begins an odd relationship with the victim's daughter. The rest of the story is likewise composed of such sudden and erratic false flights from the way things are going. And near the end, the hero puts into question the very origin of the story by accusing another man of having done his own hit-and-run, namely, pushing the original victim under the car in the first place. But the hero is a falsifier, and we cannot know if this is true or a lie. In other words, falsification in the present takes priority over any supposed prior origins, because it can make any such origin become undecidable.[87]

Yet still, in these cases, the past contingent statements can be said to relate to past events in the story that either did or did not transpire. In a recent article, "The Puzzle of the Changing Past," Luca Barlassina and Fabio Del Prete give the following example of how the past can change in the real world we live in. It is based on the true story of Lance Armstrong. He was officially declared the winner of the Tour de France on July 23, 2000. Next, we fast-forward two years to December 25, 2002. And we will call this new temporal context "Context A." On this day, two years after Armstrong's victory, we suppose that a man named Frank utters the following proposition (named as "(2)"):

(2) Lance Armstrong won the Tour de France in 2000.

At that point, we would think that he uttered a true statement. But, some time goes by, and it is discovered that Armstrong violated the rules by using banned substances to enhance his athletic performance. Then, on October 22, 2012, he is officially stripped of his Tour de France wins, including the one we mentioned. Fast-forward again a couple of months to December 25, 2012, which we will call temporal "Context B." In this context, Frank again utters the same statement, "Lance Armstrong won the Tour de France in 2000," but now it would seem to be false, even though, supposedly, the past is unchangeable.

> What's the moral of this story? (2) is a temporally specific sentence that is about a past time in both Context A and Context B. Moreover, [...] it expresses the same proposition at both Context A and Context B, namely, [...] *that Lance Armstrong won the Tour de France in 2000*. Since (2) is *true* in Context A, it follows [...] that, relative to the past of Context A, the year 2000 has the property of being a time in which Armstrong won the Tour de France. And since (2) is *false* in Context B, it follows [...] that, relative to the past of Context B, the year 2000 does not have the property of being a time in which Armstrong won the Tour de France. However, Context A and Context B are located in the same world, that is, the actual world. This means that, in moving from Context A to Context B, *the past (of the actual world) has changed*: the year 2000 had a certain property on Christmas 2002, but did not have that property on Christmas 2012 any longer.[88]

There is also another sense in which the facts of the past can be seen as changing, and it will be relevant to what we say next about the falsifier. Suppose you are following an exchange rate of your own currency. On day 1, its value goes up. But after thirty more days of going up and down, it ends the month with a much lower value. So you can look back to that first day and think that while it seemed as if its value was trending upward, that little uptick was just a small part of a larger downward movement. So it was really in a downward movement back then, even though it appeared with an increase for that particular day. But then, suppose for that year, after its monthly ups and downs, it ultimately has gone way up. So now we see that in fact, on that first day, we were right to think that it was trending upward, and we were wrong after a month to think it was instead heading downwards. The reason I mention this sort of example is that with Deleuze we are dealing generally with notions like events and movements rather than with static states of affairs. The value of the currency may have been some determinate amount at a given time. But even its former movements, now in the past, have certain tendencies of variation that can change retroactively depending on how events unfold as time goes forward. In this limited sense, we can change the past— not its concrete, temporally fixed states of affairs—but the directions it was moving. Deleuze, when asked if he is a pessimist, says, "No, I'm not at all pessimistic since I don't believe in the irreversibility of situations. Take the current catastrophic state of literature and thought. To me, that doesn't seem grave for the future."[89] We might also think of problems like our current ecological decline. We cannot change the destruction we have done in the past, but moving forward we can set things on a path that ultimately improves ecological conditions better than even before the twentieth century started, thereby making the past declines of that century be expressions of broader movements of improvement.

Falsifier as Clairvoyant Sorcerer-Seer

To produce the bifurcating falsifications like the ones we have been examining above, the falsifier would first need to somehow have a guiding sense that things can be otherwise. Deleuze here uses a notion of clairvoyant seeing (*voyance*). It is distinct from normal vision (*vision*), in that the alternatives the falsifier "sees" (metaphorically speaking) may not be visibly clear. It is something like a sorceress looking into a murky crystal ball or caldron.[90] As we noted before with Bergson in Chapter 7, there is a "fringe" of present consciousness in which past and future mental events are situated, and these other moments are evoked capriciously and discontinuously. There is also the fringe of physical things outside the ones that we are directly seeing, and they instead are connected to one another by logical, law-governed relations. We now will see how these distinct regions can overlap. The falsifier uses clairvoyant seeing to make the physically real take on a logic of caprice, endowing a playful non-necessity and logical discontinuity to what is physically before us, and the imaginary future will in turn take on logical connections to the present such that it can follow from what is happening now, like how the hallway follows logically from the door that we are presently observing. This playing with the real and concretizing the imaginary in their shared "fringe of indetermination" allows the world to move in actuality down deviant paths of becoming that are not determinately built into their given physical dynamics.[91] And the clairvoyant "seeing" here is the ability to look at how things are and have an indeterminate "fifth sense" for the ways that things can be happening otherwise.[92] This is hence another reason why the sorcerer is such an important figure in Deleuze's philosophy. As Éliphas Lévi explains, the magician "realises beforehand the Possible, and invents even the Impossible";[93] and, by using "the soul's eye, [...] forms are outlined and preserved; thereby we behold the reflections of the invisible world." By means of this clairvoyance, the magician can change the course of events in this world and even "modify the seasons" or "drive death away from the living."[94] Thus, sorcerers are not mere confidence artists selling you a false dream or tricking you to believe that the imaginary is the real.[95] They are rather "metaphysical scamps," using a term Deleuze borrows from Melville's *The Confidence Man*:[96] they make the world move falsely by combining, on the one hand, the capricious power of the imagination with, on the other hand, the law-governance of the physical world that necessitates that actual outcomes will result from what is happening now.

Nevertheless, this does not mean that there is no confidence artistry involved in the falsifier's craft. For Deleuze, metaphysical scamps believe not in another world, but in the otherness of this world, that is, in its power to "incompossibilize" itself, so to speak, by introducing deviant alternatives into its movements. They affirm "a world in *process*," and "attempt to transform the world, to think a new world or a new man insofar as they *create themselves*." Simply believing in this new world would make it too imaginary and unobtainable. Rather, the confidence artist as a metaphysical scamp has more precisely "confidence" in the newness of this world, which means having a trust in the ways it may transform through deviation.[97] For instance, as Deleuze suggests to us, the metaphysical scamp with the highest power of the false in Melville's *The Confidence-Man*, namely, the colorfully dressed Cosmopolitan, convinces his companion to believe that his stool doubles as a life-preserver and to have trust in its alternativeness, and hence more broadly, to recognize that what our vision can perceive is little compared to what our clairvoyant seeing can envisage in the world's givens.[98]

Thus, the sorcerer as clairvoyant seer must not only indeterminately "see" that things can be otherwise, but the deviations they sense must be "persuasive" in order to earn our confidence in them.[99] And note that falsification is not for Deleuze a sort of moral or political degradation. In fact, the falsifier with the highest power is endowed with a "goodness" and "generosity" from the "beneficent" power of the false.[100] For, the forces of deviance that the falsifier lets loose express the cry of the people to come. In these matters of minoritarian peoples, Deleuze often cites African-American cultures.[101] To propose an illustration for persuasive clairvoyant seeing that creates confidence in the beneficent deviance of this world, consider when the American civil rights leader Martin Luther King, Jr. boldly and eloquently proclaimed his dream of a racially non-segregated South. Such a people did not yet exist. It was a falsification. But they cried out in his voice, and his clairvoyant vision of an incompossible South was so deeply persuasive that the long arc of history began bending toward that justice.

Falsifier as Self- and World-Creative Artist

We will now examine the falsifier with the highest power of the false, the self- and world-creative artist, whom Deleuze contrasts with the art forger. Part of this conception builds upon what we said regarding the simulacrum and its perspectival distortions. Suppose you are looking at a circle, directly down at it from above. It will appear perfectly circular, of course. Now, as your angle of vision is moving down to its side, it will appear as a gradually narrowing ellipse. In projective geometry, even open figures like parabolas can take on the closed form of ellipses. Deleuze, following Michel Serres's commentaries on Leibniz, notes that these and other figures are metamorphoses of the circle, all generated by changing perspectives.[102]

Yet, since these metamorphoses suppose there being something outside the point of perspective, and thus, only its *appearance* is anamorphically altered but not necessarily its form, I suggest a modification to Deleuze's account that builds from his notion of the simulacrum. Suppose we have a conic section that is a circular slice. And consider like before that we take a perspective above that circle such that it appears perfectly circular. Not only does this keep the circle's appearance the same, it also has done nothing to change the conic form we began with (Figure 8.6, left conic section).

This would be like the remarkable feat of painting a replication of a great work of art that remains uncannily faithful to it. For instance, John Myatt makes such incredible paintings, like his rendition Vermeer's *Girl with a Pearl Earring* (Figure 8.6, bottom left detail; original, top left). This would be seeing the artistic work and style from the same perspective as the original artist, analogous to viewing the circle from above.

Now, if an art forger were to create and sell such a replication, their fraudulence would of course be discovered right away, supposing that the original is still somewhere in existence. So art forgers, like Elmyr de Hory, who is featured in Welles's *F for Fake* (1973), painted works in the exact style of great painters, but he creates his own contents in keeping with the artist's preferences. The paintings were so good that they fooled museum curators into mistaking these imaginaries for reals and misjudging them as true works, because the paintings fulfilled the criteria for the essence of that painter's form and style. For these sorts of forgeries, Deleuze also cites "Van Meegeren's false Vermeers."[103] We might consider then for example one of van Meegeren's forgeries of Vermeer, entitled *The Supper at Emmaus* as creating a

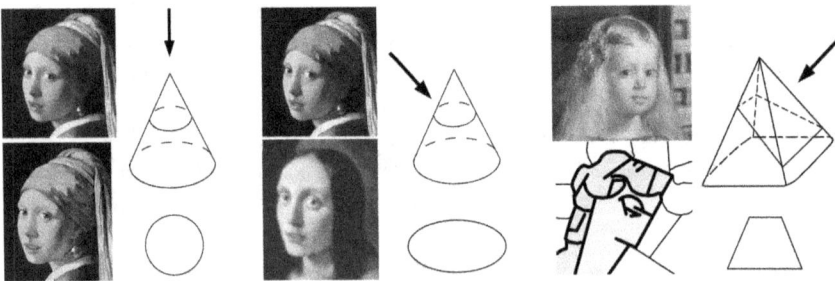

Figure 8.6 Changing perspectives as transformation. **Left:** Detail from Vermeer's *Girl with a Pearl Earring*, above a detail from John Myatt's recreation, *Girl with a Pearl Earring (in the style of Johan Vermeer)* (© John Myatt, 2012, used with permission). **Middle:** Same detail from Vermeer's *Girl with a Pearl Earring*, above a detail from van Meegeren's forgery of Vermeer's style in *The Supper at Emmaus*. **Right:** Detail from Velázquez's *Las Meninas*, above a diagrammatic representation of a detail from Picasso's *Girl with a Mandolin* (used in place of his *Las Meninas* variations to depict something of their stylistic deformations).[104]

novel perspective on Vermeer's style that provides a new and original appearance of it (Figure 8.6, bottom middle detail). It was so good that at the time a leading Dutch scholar announced that "we have here—I am inclined to say—the masterpiece of Johannes Vermeer of Delft."[105] This would be like changing our perspective of the circular conic section, giving us an anamorphosis of it, but doing nothing to change the conic form itself (middle panel).

Yet, Deleuze then asks, "where does the 'bad' relation of Elmyr the forger of Picasso end and the 'good' relation of Picasso and Velázquez begin?"[106] Deleuze never specifies what this relation is between Picasso and Velázquez, but given the context, he may perhaps be referring to Picasso's *Las Meninas* series (1957), which are all derivations of Velázquez's painting by that very name (Figure 8.6, top-right detail), but at the same time, they are remarkable in their stylistically uniqueness and deviation not only from the original but also from each other. Picasso here not only gives a series of new "takes" on Velázquez's painting, he in the process of varying it creates new forms and styles that others might adopt or mutate in their own way (see substitute illustration, bottom right detail). It is something like a change of perspective that morphs not only the appearance but also the form or model itself. This would be analogous to a changing perspective on the circle that in the process alters the conic form in significant ways (right panel). This self-variance of the artist him or herself is expressed in a Picasso anecdote that Welles recounts in *F for Fake*:

> A friend [...] once showed a Picasso to Picasso, who said, "no, it was a fake." The same friend brought him, from yet another source another would-be Picasso, and Picasso said "that, too, was a fake." Then yet another from another source. "Also fake," said Picasso. "But, Pablo," said his friend, "I watched you paint that with my own eyes." "Ha-ha," said Picasso, "I can paint false Picassos as well as anybody."[107]

While falsifying the world, the self- and world-creative artist must also falsify him or herself, in the sense of self-metamorphosis.[108] Yet here I would suggest an alteration to Welles's terminology. After transforming himself as a painter through his stylistic variations, were Picasso to paint like he had once before, he would be making *fake* Picasso forgeries, because they would not express his current becoming.[109] But insofar as he reinvents himself, he falsifies who he is by "pretending" or "claiming" to already be the painter he might become; thereby, he would be acting as an imposter of a yet-to-be Picasso, and the paintings he would be making in that process would be *false* Picasso variations rather than fake Picasso forgeries. As Deleuze explains:

> The difference between the forger, the expert and Vermeer is that the first two barely know how to change. Only the creative artist takes the power of the false to a degree which is realized, not in form, but in transformation. [...] There is a point of view which belongs so much to the thing that the thing is constantly being transformed in a becoming identical to point of view. Metamorphosis of the true. What the artist is, is *creator of truth*, because truth is not to be achieved, formed, or reproduced; it has to be created. There is no other truth than the creation of the New.[110]

We can now grasp the four characterizations Deleuze gives for the falsifier.[111] {1} Falsifiers fabricate the "crystalline image" in which the real and the imaginary become indiscernible, like we saw with New Novel crystalline narration and description. {2} They are the ones who pass through the facets of the crystal, as with Robbe-Grillet entering the crystalline images of *Trans-Europ-Express*, meaning above all that falsifiers themselves are transformed through their falsifying acts of creation.[112] {3} Falsifiers make the impossible follow from the possible.[113] Deleuze later modifies the wording to say that falsifiers make the *incompossible* follow from the possible.[114] But given all that we have learned so far, we might be surprised that Deleuze did not further say that the falsifiers make the incompossible follow from the *compossible*. For, as we have seen, falsifiers take a self-consistent world and add incompossible deviations into it, thereby making the incompossible come out of the compossible. And lastly, {4} falsifiers make the past not necessarily true, meaning that while it may seem that we are moving on a path that was determined by the movements of the world leading up to now, instead, by bending the current movements, we find that we were never in fact going in the directions of those past movements anyway.[115] In other words, we change our past origins or orientations by shifting where we are now headed, as we saw with past contingency.

The Garden of Ambiguous Adams: Crystalline Time

We should finish this chapter by assessing how Deleuze's philosophy of falsity and incompossibility fit within our discussion of logic. To do this, we will first expand on some Leibniz-related notions that we mentioned before, namely, vague Adams and the convergence of incompossible worlds, and we will add another one: ambiguous signs. This will allow us to assess whether or not Deleuze's conception of coalescent incompossible worlds involves a many-valued sort of logic, and if so, if it is dialetheic or analetheic.

Recall again that for Leibniz, everything in our world is entirely determined from the beginning, because God calculated all possible worlds and chose ours as the best one. That means, for any predicate you can possibly assign to a being in our world, either it is certainly true for that being or its negation is true, and thus there are no "vague" beings, like "vague Adams," whose missing predicates mean that they could be the Adam in more than one world. For instance, the Adam in any world, whether ours or some other possible one, either will certainly sin or will certainly not sin by eating the forbidden fruit. But this also means that by thinking of the Adam in our own world in a vague way by subtracting some of his predicates, like removing "sinner," we can thereby have in mind his counterparts in other possible worlds where he did not sin (along with all the ones where he does sin too). Deleuze, as we have noted, is subtracting God from this Leibnizian picture, and thus incompossible worlds can somehow coexist. We saw how this might work in cases of self- and world-creative falsification. When inventing a new style and identity for himself, Picasso is both himself and not himself at the same time; he is the self that he is and he is the self he is becoming, which he brought about through creative falsification. These Picassos reside in incompossible worlds, as the new world of the new Picasso is divergent from the world Picasso was in up until then. Yet, in the act of creation, those worlds cross through each other.

We will now look at another way that Deleuze elaborates on this notion of incompossible worlds that coalesce and thereby crystalize. Our normal, linear, chronological stream of time, Deleuze says, is built upon a more fundamental, non-chronological depth of time, which is the full multiplicity of all incompossible timelines, all crisscrossing one another.[116] So recall Nolt's diagram, "A Picture of Time" (Figure 5.2), that was shaped like a tree branch, where the past is a straight line (because there was only one past), but the future is an infinite set of branches upon branches. But as we have seen, for Deleuze and his notion of contingent pasts, those branches should be understood as extending both forward into the future and backward into the past. Now consider that under this new, symmetrical structure (where the past and future both bifurcate), if you go down any one of the future branches, it will have a past that not only leads back to our present, but it too will branch off backward in infinitely many ways at each juncture. So the result is a great intertwined jumble of incompossible timelines intersecting everywhere along them and leading every which way. And time moves not by staying on one line where the future is compossible with the past, but rather, under Deleuze's Bergsonian conception, time can *only* move forward if events take the world down directions that are inconsistent with what came before.

Here it would be useful to examine some of Deleuze's illustrations to see how we are to understand the multiple and diverging times as "crystalizing" into a Dupréelian conglomerate. The first one is Deleuze's commentary of Leibniz's Sextus story in the *Theodicy*.[117] In Leibniz's telling, Sextus Tarquinius goes to the Oracle of Apollo for a prediction. Apollo says that Sextus will die poor and in exile, because, although he is pious now, he will later be proud, adulterous, and a traitor to his country. For, Jupiter gave Sextus a wicked soul that will lead him to commit these crimes. Sextus next goes to Jupiter and asks him why he condemned him to be wicked and unhappy. Jupiter says that Sextus can instead be wise and happy if he does not go to Rome and thus renounces his kingship. Sextus is unable to give that up, so he accepts his doomed fate and goes to Rome.[118]

A philosophical problem that Leibniz is trying to solve here is that, from Sextus's perspective, his lot is unfortunate but chosen by God; so how could God be considered just and wise, if he knowingly makes some people wicked and thus destined for a life of agony? We have heard the answer already. The world in which Sextus is wicked is the best of all possible worlds. For instance, Sextus's crimes will lead to the creation of the Roman Republic. And even Adam's sinning is bound up ultimately with Christ and redemption. To convey this message, Leibniz adds a new character to the story, Theodorus. He is high priest who goes to Jupiter's daughter Pallas to learn why Jupiter made Sextus evil. Pallas watches and wards over the palace of fates. It is shaped like an infinite pyramid of chambers, each one telling the story of one complete possible world in its own "book of fate," all of which taken together show every possible variation in Sextus's life: "You will find in one world a very happy and noble Sextus, in another a Sextus content with a mediocre state, a Sextus, indeed, of every kind and endless diversity of forms."[119]

In one world, Sextus does not go to Rome where he will be wicked, but instead goes off in another direction to a place like Corinth, where he cultivates a garden, finds treasure, is loved by the city, and dies old. In another room there is a Sextus who also obeys Jupiter, but this time he goes instead to Thrace where he marries the king's daughter, succeeds the king, and is adored by the subjects. Theodorus and Pallas go to a number of rooms, each time with another possible world and life for Sextus. And as they ascend the pyramid, the worlds, overall, become better, even though for Sextus they become less favorable. The one at the apex is the best possible world that Jupiter/God therefore chose as the existing one. But even though there is a certain apex world, the pyramid has no bottom, because the worlds degrade infinitely going down. In the best possible world, Sextus is displayed as he actually is: he goes to Rome, creates confusion, and violates his friend's wife and is then driven out of Rome, beaten and unhappy. But even though choosing a different world could have made Sextus be a happy, prosperous person, God could not have chosen otherwise than he had, because then God would be renouncing God's divine wisdom (which calls for God to choose the best of all possible worlds, despite the costs to certain particular beings in it.) For, "The crime of Sextus serves for great things: it renders Rome free; thence will arise a great empire, which will show noble examples to mankind."[120]

Deleuze conceives this pyramid of fates as being a giant, multifaceted *crystal*.[121] Each incompossible world in this structure is fused and crystallized with the others. But each "facet" or chamber is like a distorted reflection of the other chambers, as if the sum of the pyramid were a jumble of images bouncing around from facet to facet, modifying a little with each refraction or reflection.

Deleuze, in one of his course lectures, further characterizes this sort of crystallization of images with a Victor Hugo poem that impressed him deeply, but which he could not easily locate again, and without knowing it, he misremembered it a little bit. (In fact, in *Difference and Repetition*, he also misquotes it there too and does not cite the source.)[122] But this only reinforces the main point here, because the poem itself has thus refracted and deviated in his memory. At any rate, Deleuze remembers it as something like:

An emerald in its facets
Hides a nymph with eyes that shine;
The Viscountess of Cette
Had Aegean colored eyes.[123]

Deleuze notes that when we look into the emerald, we see the Viscountess of Cette, whom we also regard as a bright-eyed water-nymph. And he says that the crystal shows us a series of modifications and thus *metamorphosis in a perpetual state*.[124] It is not entirely clear what he is describing, but it would seem to be the following. How did the Viscountess's image get into the emerald in the first place? Perhaps she was looking into it, casting her own image there, and that is how she had such greenish eyes in her reflection. But, there is a series of modifications, which would seem to be her image bouncing continually around the facets, multiplying and further varying its appearance, like the many incompossible Sextuses all in the same pyramidic crystal palace, "crystallizing" or coalescing together in that one same structure. In *Difference and Repetition*, Deleuze makes similar comments regarding this Hugo poem: "Every phenomenon is of the 'bright-eyed water-sprite' type, made possible by an emerald. Every phenomenon is composite."[125] Returning to the lecture course, Deleuze says that the falsifier is the one who (using clairvoyant seeing) looks into the crystal, sees the alternate incompossibilities of the given, and then "passes into" the crystal, thereby opening the given world to being able to deviate into alternate paths.[126]

With respect to time understood in terms of lines, Deleuze illustrates their coalescence using Borges's "Death and the Compass."[127] It is a somewhat vague illustration, but it highlights the dialetheism in this conception of time. It is the story of a detective named Erik Lönnrot who goes to the crime scenes of four murders, which on the map are spaced apart in a diamond shape, with the points at North, South, East, and West. The final one in fact is his own murder, and it takes place in a villa with a very odd labyrinthine structure that seems endlessly self-replicative and with opposing mirrors in which "he was multiplied infinitely."[128] After wandering through it, he finally meets the assassin, Red Scharlach, who says that he compelled Lönnrot to go from one direction to the next in the diamond pattern to weave a labyrinth around him. Lönnrot replies that, in fact, there are three lines too many in this diamond-shaped labyrinth. His last wish is that "in some other incarnation" Red Scharlach would hunt him down in a single-lined labyrinth, in which he first must move far to the East, then double back to the West until reaching the halfway point, then West yet again until reaching the first quarter-way point. One basic notion here is that of different directions of movement that otherwise would diverge into opposing directions, but which instead somehow coalescence along one path, like the diamond shape collapsing down to a single line but still involving alternate directionalities of movement.[129] Not all of this conception is useful for us, but the main idea it illustrates is that we can think of incompossible time-lines—which, under Leibnizian assumptions, together form a labyrinth of sorts of divergent, separate times and worlds—instead, under Deleuze's conception, coalesce together and coincide in some way, despite their incompatibilities and inconsistencies.

That this is a dialetheic conception of time becomes clearer with Deleuze's characterization of vague Adams in terms of ambiguous signs. Leibniz uses this notion on certain occasions in mathematical contexts.[130] We will examine one of the simplest such accounts he gives, which comes from his "On the Method of Universality." Here Leibniz aims to show in geometry "the reduction of several different cases to a single formula, rule, equation, or construction."[131] To do this, he employs *ambiguous characters*, of which there are two kinds.[132] The first are *ambiguous letters*, and they are similar to the variable letter-symbols in algebraic sorts of equations (like x and y). What makes them "ambiguous" is that they stand for any number of values rather than being limited only to some specific one. The other sort of ambiguous characters are *ambiguous signs*. Instead of representing a variety of numerical values, they rather stand for more than one mathematical operation. Leibniz gives the following simplistic illustration. Suppose we will want one formula to express two lines of different sizes (the two lines AC in Figure 8.7, top). (Notice already that "C" is an ambiguous sign for two distinct points.) To make one formula that expresses both lines, we can find the point B that lies right between the two endpoints C. That means the distance of C to

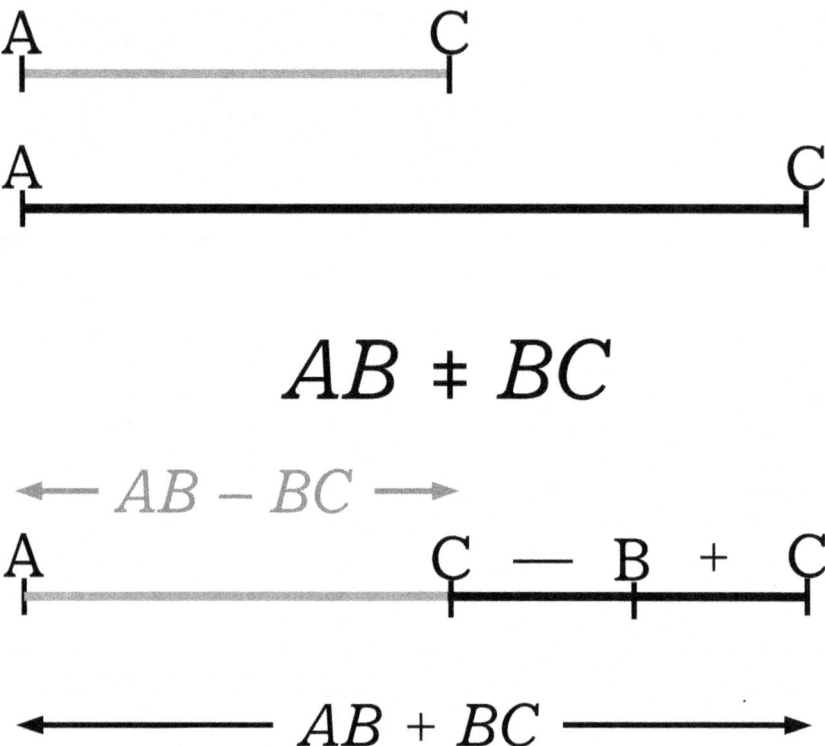

Figure 8.7 Leibniz's ambiguous signs. In $AB \mp BC$, the $\mp$ is an ambiguous sign for addition and subtraction, and the formula represents two distinct lines at the same time, line $AB + BC$ and line $AB - BC$.

B is the same in both cases, regardless of which C we are using. So if we subtract BC from AB, then we get the smaller line, and if we add BC to AB, then we get the larger line (Figure 8.7, bottom). Leibniz then fashions the ambiguous sign "$\mp$" to mean both addition and subtraction, and gives the following single formula to represent both lines: $AB \mp BC$, which means *both* lines $AB + BC$ and $AB - BC$. Leibniz later gives a more complicated example that is far harder to intuit and illustrate. In brief, he writes out an "ambiguous formula"[133] using ambiguous signs and letters that expresses all the conic sections. Depending on how you specify the ambiguous characters, the formula will express a hyperbola, or a parabola, etc.[134]

Deleuze employs this notion of ambiguous signs to characterize the way that incompossibility generates new realities rather than excludes them. And he does this in part by reconceiving Leibniz's notion of vague Adams as involving ambiguous signs. After describing the ambiguous formula for the conic sections that we mentioned above, Deleuze says that the ambiguity of the signs is what divides the one same "Event" of this ambiguous formula into the diverse events of each conic section that may be obtained from it. In other words, ambiguous signs allow for a sort of virtual multiplicity that can be actualized, in some particular event, one or another way.[135] One of the notions here is that there are "aleatory points," which Deleuze characterizes in terms of the bifurcation points that we studied in Chapter 5.[136] At these points of bifurcation, there are two or more virtual paths of development, and the present situation is tending along all of them, with the chosen path being decided largely by chance. This means that such ambiguous signs, by acting as bifurcation points, generate series of incompossible worlds that coalesce in the present.[137] Deleuze writes:

> We must therefore understand that incompossible worlds, despite their incompossibility, have something in common [...] which represents the ambiguous sign of the genetic element in relation to which several worlds appear as instances of solution for one and the same problem (every throw, the result of a single cast). Within these worlds, there is, for example, an objectively indeterminate Adam, that is, an Adam positively defined *solely* through a few singularities which can be combined and can complement each other in a very different fashion in different worlds (to be the first man, to live in a garden, to give birth to a woman from himself, etc.) [...] indeed, as Borges says, "[...] In Ts'ui Pen's work ['The Garden of Forking Paths'], all possible solutions occur, each one being the point of departure for other bifurcations."[138]

So for Deleuze, what makes Adam vague is not simply that he lacks some certain pair of contradictory predicates, as Leibniz sees it (for instance, that he is neither sinner nor non-sinner, and thus this vague Adam can correspond generically to the Adams on all possible worlds), but moreover, that we can think of there being an "ambiguous" sign that can then become filled-in with one or another specific predicate. For Leibniz, this additional point about ambiguous signs does not factor in for him, because he thinks there are no vague Adams anyway. God fully conceived every Adam, and in particular, the one that lived in our chosen best world was never missing any predicates (God knew in advance that he would sin). However, for Deleuze's conception of incompossibility—where we remove God and thus also we have things whose predicates will only be decided in the future by contingent factors—such ambiguous signs are like the placeholders for both predicates, of which one will be actualized later on.

Now, in contrast to a dialetheic interpretation, there is an analetheic one that we should evaluate as well, as it very strongly suggests itself here. And, to better determine which of the two conceptions is a better fit, we need to be more precise about the alethic properties of the predicates involved in ambiguous signs. So recall that the dialetheic way for Adam to be in incompossible worlds would be for him to have contradictory predicates *at the moment of temptation*. Before and after the event he might be lacking in them, but what most concerns us in this context is the *event* insofar as it is still *in effect*. The analetheic conception would say that at the moment of temptation, we can neither affirm that Adam is a sinner nor that he is a non-sinner. Yet, the passages we examined above lend themselves to both interpretations, so consider what he writes next: "We are now faced with the aleatory point of singular points, with the ambiguous sign of singularities [...] which *holds good for many of these worlds*, or [...] for all worlds, despite their divergences and the individuals which inhabit them."[139] Note that it is the ambiguity of the sign that allows it to *hold good* for various, divergent worlds. This suggests the predicates are being affirmed; for, how could a world hold good if the predicate proper to it does not? Deleuze also writes that these predicates "open different worlds and individualities to them as so many variables or possibilities."[140] Yet, if the predicate is not being affirmed (i.e., if it does not hold good), how can it be said to be opening up the path it belongs to (where it does hold good)? Although an analetheic conception still remains possible here, the dialetheic one lends itself quite readily: the one predicate is affirmed and holds good for the paths it opens out, while its contradictory counterpart is also affirmed, holding for the other paths that it lays forth as alternate possibilities. As the negation is dialetheic here, the incompossible paths can all hold good without the affirmation of the one entailing the denial of the other. But it must be stressed that this account applies only to the undecidable event while it is still in effect and the bifurcation is underway.

What Deleuze says next reinforces this interpretation. He writes, "Instead of each world being the analytic predicate of individuals described in a series," that is to say, unlike Leibniz's notion that each thing has a complete predication that determines everything about it and the rest of the world it resides in, "it is rather the incompossible worlds which are the synthetic predicates of persons defined in relation to disjunctive syntheses."[141] In other words, on account of disjunctive synthesis, which brings incompossibilities together, one individual, especially at moments of bifurcation, resides in multiple, incompossible worlds that have coalesced, meaning that the individual also possess the incompossible predicates proper to those coalescent incompossible worlds. It would seem, then, that Deleuze is characterizing Adam's situation as being one where "Adam is in the world where he sins" and "Adam is in the world where he never sins" are both true, and thus that "Adam is a sinner" and "Adam is a non-sinner" are likewise both true, at least during the moment of temptation. Moreover, if we look at the wording here, Deleuze characterizes the predicates as "synthetic." As such, they do not belong necessarily to the subject, and so it will be left up to the way things are decided to determine which predicates/worlds will ultimately prevail.

For Deleuze, then, the world is much larger than it may seem to be, because it contains multiple, coalescing incompossible worlds at any one moment. He expresses this with the following terminological distinction: "The *Umwelt* [...] organizes the singularities in circles of convergence [...]. Then a second, very different field (*complexe*) appears, built upon the first: the *Welt* common to several or to all worlds; the persons who define this 'something in common.'"[142] By being pulled bifurcationally in two directions of action at the same time, an ambiguous Adam, standing before the serpent and deliberating on whether or not to eat the fruit, is himself the nexus for these coalescing incompossible worlds. There is thus the "unfurling of divergent series in the same world, [...] the irruption of incompossibilities on the same stage, where Sextus will rape *and* not rape Lucretia, where Caesar crosses *and* does not cross the Rubicon, where Fang kills, is killed, and neither kills nor is killed."[143] With this in mind, it becomes difficult to doubt that Deleuze's notions of incompossibility and disjunctive synthesis in many important respects involve dialetheic thinking.

Conclusion

Introduction

To conclude, we summarize our findings, make a case for Gilles Deleuze's dialetheism, and preview the topics in the remaining volumes.

What Has Followed Here?

Let us conclude by first summarizing our findings:

{1} There are a number of concepts in Deleuze's philosophy that are fruitfully elaborated by placing them into the context of modern logics. We considered ones that enabled us to examine Deleuze's logical thinking in terms of basic principles that it may or may not employ. In particular, we were concerned with ideas in his philosophies of truth and thinking and in his metaphysics, namely: heterogeneous composition and becoming; loss of identity and proper name; affirmative synthetic disjunction and coalescent incompossibility; and the creative power of falsity. We left out one of his most fundamental concepts, difference, which presents some challenges when trying to explicate its logic.[1] Deleuze characterizes it in terms of intensity, which is a topic we address in the next volume, and on that occasion we will be better able to discuss difference in logical terms. For now, we might already see hints of how it could be explicated, supposing that its logic were to be similar to affirmative synthetic disjunction.[2] Putting that matter aside for the moment, we can say that in all, we have reason to believe that Deleuze's philosophy may in fact have a logic to it that, while perhaps it is not *fully* explicatable using modern, formal logics, it in the very least can be understood to a greater extent by means of them, which is something we accomplished here.

{2} Deleuze's logic is almost certainly non-classical. This assessment is problematic, however, because, as we saw with his usage of the terms "negation" and "contradiction," he normally employs such logical expressions with their classical meanings. Yet, in his critiques of these logical notions, he also seemed to be instead affirming non-classical counterpart conceptions (for instance, dialetheic negation), although without stating them by name. It appears that he tried to articulate his non-classical conceptions by contorting classical notions, like assigning to inclusive disjunction, in some unspecified way, both conjunctive and disjunctive logical properties. Non-classical notions, however, proved more capable at capturing what Deleuze seems to have in mind in these cases.

{3} There are three particularly attractive options for characterizing Deleuze's logic, namely, fuzzy logic, intuitionistic logic, and many-valued logics. These are the only three that he ever mentions. Also, each of them applies to some degree of success to one or another logically relevant notion in Deleuze's philosophy. Fuzzy logics can come into play when articulating his notion of heterogeneous composition. Intuitionistic logic might be at work in Deleuze's conception of undecidability. And many-valued logics, especially analetheic and dialetheic ones, prove handy when trying to understand Deleuze's philosophy of truth.

{4} Of these three non-classical options, the many-valued logics were ultimately the best fit for all of Deleuze's logical conceptions that we evaluated here. Fuzzy was the least useful for characterizing Deleuze's logic, because he never expresses a notion of truth as admitting of degrees; and also, fuzzy logic at its basis operates by means of precise values in a manner that Deleuze and Guattari think is not conducive to concept creation. Intuitionism is more promising. But it is questionable whether Deleuze implements the notion of undecidability with the same logical sense that it has in intuitionism. It would seem that for him the undecidabilities that he has in mind when discussing intuitionism are to be asserted or affirmed for subversive or other purposes. But in intuitionism they are not assertable or affirmable, at least not until they are proven, in which case they are no longer undecidable. Many-valued logics, however, were applicable to a greater or lesser extent to all the concepts we examined.

{5} Of the many-valued logics we considered, dialetheic logic was the best overall fit. The other option, analetheism, still stands as a strong contender, because Deleuze's notions of doing away with judgment and undecidability seem much more like analetheic conceptions than dialetheic ones. Throughout this book, we found that dialetheic logic applies more or less successfully in all other cases than these two, but that analetheism seems not to work very well in many instances. The main problem with it is that the analetheic situations, whose propositional formulations would be neither true nor false, are lacking an affirmative character that many of Deleuze's conceptions call for. That is not so certain, because as we saw, according to Beall and Ripley, analetheism includes the willingness to assert formulations that are neither true nor false.[3] But still, by doing so, we do not thereby affirm either of the disjuncts in these cases. If neither disjunct is affirmed, then how affirmative could the difference between them be, which is the issue that concerns Deleuze? Put another way, if you affirm the difference between two disjuncts, how are we to understand that additionally neither of the disjuncts is affirmed? You might say that it is a difference without terms, a pure differential relation. But then it is not an analetheic formulation, which does in fact have terms. If you rather say that we are only concerned with the logical operations holding between the terms, and not with the terms themselves, then we can do the same with the dialetheic formulation, which we saw was better in that respect anyway.

So neither analetheism nor dialetheism alone is an obvious fit, but dialetheism still covers more ground in Deleuze's philosophy. And, it could handle all the notions we considered, if having done with judgment and undecidability could be convincingly construed as dialetheic conceptions. Let us consider the case of the undecidability of the real and the imaginary, which coalesce in the crystal image. Would Deleuze say that the claim, "the crystal image is real," is neither true nor false simply because it is undecidable which part of it is real and which is imaginary? The way he characterizes this situation is that the real and imaginary are both components, but they are cycling so fast that we lose the basis for determining which is which. So it seems that he would say both "the crystal image is real" and "the crystal image is imaginary" are true. That is not an analetheic conception. But it is not yet a dialetheic one either. It would only be so if he understood being real and being imaginary as logical "otherthans" to one another. We know they cannot be classical otherthans (understood logically in terms of classical negation), where the one would exclude the other. But they could be dialetheic otherthans (understood in terms of paraconsistent negation). That captures both the sense that the real and the imaginary have a difference or distance to one another, without the affirmation of the one involving the elimination of the other, or the affirmation of both entailing total trivialization. In other words, supposing that Deleuze conceives the imaginary as a paraconsistent otherthan to the real, then he would be able to say that "the crystal image is real" is both true and false: it is true insofar as the real is cycling within it, and it is false insofar the imaginary, its non-exclusive otherthan, is also cycling within it.

And what about having done with judgment? In the first place, its analetheic conceptualization is not without its problems. Recall the example of the chimera. According to Deleuze, if we do away with judging it, it can go from having wings to not having wings but fins instead. The idea here was that if we affirm that it has wings, then in some sense, we are fixing its essence for eternity, meaning that it cannot ever lose its wings (or put another way, something without wings could not then qualify as a chimera). Now, the analetheic conception would say that "the chimera has wings" is neither true nor false. Similarly, it would say that "the chimera does not have wings but fins instead" is neither true nor false. But how can we say that the chimera goes from having wings to fins if neither one of those things is true? The dialetheic conception holds up better here. It would say that its having wings is both true and false (true insofar as it still has wings, false insofar as it is now gaining fins instead of wings).

Nonetheless, given the strengths of each option, why not just combine the two, and say that Deleuze's logic is both dialetheic and analetheic? And there are logics corresponding to such a composite view, including First Degree Entailment and four-valued logics that are equivalent to it (so a proposition could then be either: {1} just true, {2} just false, {3} neither true nor false, or {4} both true and false).[4] This would solve the problem. Let's all go home now.

But wait. There is a real debate to be had here about what is really going on in Deleuze's philosophical thinking. There has been much recent interest in Culp's characterization of Deleuzian philosophy as *not* being affirmative. He wants to release its negational tendencies by leaving aside the affirmational ones. This is not precisely my battle, but it gets to the basic question of how we should understand the fundamentals of Deleuze's philosophy. Using Culp's dichotomy, we might ask: is Deleuze a philosopher of peace, harmony, and integration, given its positivity; or, is he a philosopher of destruction and negativity on account of difference and disjunction being what is most fundamental? The reason I do not favor the analetheic interpretation is because it strips out both the affirmativity and the differential tension from certain important conceptions. When Adam is confronted by the serpent, is he neither sinner nor non-sinner? Or is he both in the same stroke of temptation and deliberation? Deleuze always emphasizes the *difference* holding between such options. If neither one is affirmed, then how can the difference between them have any force or effect? So put in very generic terms, if you favor the Nietzschean trend in Deleuze's thinking, especially with the notions of plays of forces, conflict, power differentials, and so on, but you also insist on keeping the Spinozist and Bergsonist affirmative and creative elements too, then dialetheism would seem to be your most attractive option. It is for this reason that I rest with my conclusion that Deleuze's logic is dialetheic.

Yet, I welcome a debate if you have drawn different conclusions. Nonetheless, it is important for the forthcoming works that we let ourselves acknowledge a strong, viable option, because that will make the foregoing analyses much less complicated. Of course we will at times come back to these other logical options and even consider additional ones. Nothing is entirely decided yet.

And What's to Follow

There are many related topics that we excluded from our analyses, because they are more fitting for the forthcoming volumes. Let us preview them quickly, so that there is not a sense that something is being left out. The next volume on experience will examine dialetheism in Deleuze's notions of coupled, incompatible sensations, the discord of the faculties in the new image of thought, time-consciousness, continuously varying bodily intensities and decompositions (Body without Organs), becoming-animal, the experience of the Other, machinics, rhythm, analog and digital communication, and differential selfhood (including "I is another"). The third volume on meaning will examine paradoxes (including semantic paradoxes of self-reference), polysemy, non-sense, minor literature, prelinguistic signaletic material, continuously varying utterance, cut-up and pick-up composition, the conjunctive "AND" of stuttering, and meaning disruption, also under the lens of dialetheism.

Notes

Introduction

1. Cressole, *Deleuze*, 103. See Stivale, *Two-Fold Thought*, 6.
2. Deleuze and Guattari, *Thousand Plateaus*, 262–78 [291–308]; Deleuze, *Course 1983.11.22,2* (00:17:30–00:25:10).
3. Deleuze and Guattari, *Thousand Plateaus*, 262–72 [291–302].
4. Priest and Eckert, Interview with Eckert (00:22:10–00:22:30).
5. Lapoujade, *Aberrant Movements*, 27 [13].
6. Ibid., 26 [11].
7. Ibid., 27 [13].
8. For a similar discussion, see Bell, "Dialetheism."
9. Deleuze, *Difference and Repetition*, 56, 69, 155, 264 [79, 95, 201, 339]. See Somers-Hall, *Deleuze's* Difference and Repetition, 82, 124–5, 159–61.
10. Deleuze, *Difference and Repetition*, 226 [292]. See Smith, *Essays on Deleuze*, 82.
11. Jeffrey Bell notes in particular the problems with giving Deleuze's notion of difference a dialetheic formalization. Bell, "Dialetheism."
12. Priest, "Classical Logic: Aufgehoben," 135–45.
13. Priest, *Doubt Truth*, 125–9 (section 7.4, "The Rationality of Inconsistency"). Here Priest argues that it is more rational to accept a paraconsistent logic when dealing with the liar paradox, because its ability to handle contradiction makes it more adequate to the given data of the problem, it gives a simpler sufficient solution, it has greater explanatory power with regard to the underlying phenomena, and it provides a more complete account.
14. Priest, "Classical Logic: Aufgehoben," 135–41.
15. Voisset-Veysseyre, "Toward a Post-Identity Philosophy," 2.
16. Smith, "Logic and Existence," 375.
17. Olkowski, *Postmodern Philosophy*, 68–85; 181–2.
18. Olkowski, "Using Our Intuition," 12–16.
19. Bell, "The Nondenumerable." The related post from 2010 is Bell, "Dialetheism."
20. See for instance: Villani, *Logique de Deleuze*, 61–87; 103–7.
21. See, especially, Livingston, *Politics of Logic*, 95–112.
22. Lapoujade, *Aberrant Movements*, 27 [13].
23. Priest, *Introduction to Non-Classical Logic*, 3, emphasis mine.
24. Lapoujade, *Aberrant Movements*, 26–7 [12–13].
25. Priest, "Logic: A Short Introduction 2" (00:03:20–00:07:20). More precisely, Priest says that logic constrains metaphysics. In a conversation I had with him on August 25, 2018, he added that metaphysics similarly constrains logic.
26. Olkowski, *Postmodern Philosophy*, 71.
27. Priest, *Introduction to Non-Classical Logic*, 5.
28. Ibid., 124.
29. Ibid., 4.
30. Ibid., 3.
31. Ibid.

32 Historically speaking, Deleuze seems to place what he calls "classical logic" (*logique classique*) as spanning from Ancient through Medieval times, with the (modern) logic coming after it beginning in the seventeenth century, primarily with Descartes and Leibniz. However, like with the usage of "classical logic" that we apply here, Deleuze also associates classical logic with the classic three principles, including the Principle of Non-Contradiction. See Deleuze, *Course 1978.03.28* (no audio); Deleuze, *Course 1980.02.05,1* (00:07:30–00:09:50); Deleuze, *Course 1980.04.29,1* (00:45:00–00:46:30); Deleuze, *Course 1980.05.06,2* (00:07:10–00:07:50); Deleuze, *Course 1983.05.03,2* (00:12:40–00:13:50). Note that there is another case of his use of the term, and here Deleuze speaks of seventeenth-century philosophers as using a "classical logic," but in this instance Deleuze is working with Foucault's designation for this so-called "classical age" and speaking of the logic at that time. Deleuze, *Course 1986.03.04,2* (00:12:40–00:14:10). See Foucault, *Order of Things*, xxiv [13].
33 Priest, *Doubt Truth*, 7–11.
34 Priest, "Classical Logic: Aufgehoben," 132; Priest, "Paraconsistency and Dialetheism," 135.
35 Priest, "Classical Logic: Aufgehoben," 138–9.
36 Priest and Routley, "First Historical Introduction," 30–1.
37 Priest, "Classical Logic: Aufgehoben," 137–42.
38 Ibid., 138.
39 Fuzzy logics are especially applicable in matters regarding Deleuze's notion of flexible and indeterminate composition. Intuitionistic logics are relevant when considering whether or not Deleuze rejects the Principle of Excluded Middle and also when examining his notion of difference without negation. And many-valued logics are especially useful when analyzing Deleuze's philosophy of truth. Explaining the inadequacy of the other options, however, is another matter. In Priest's *Introduction to Non-Classical Logic*, we encounter a number of other non-classical logics. Conditional logics are modal logics with "a multiplicity of accessibility relations of a certain kind." Priest, *Introduction to Non-Classical Logic*, 82. They are useful for handing certain problematic inferences involving the conditional, but these are not obviously the sorts of inferences that Deleuze is concerned with (see ibid., 82–4). Relevant logics are closely related to some other logics we address (in fact, the Routley and Routley material that we deal with in Chapter 4 is largely about relevant logic), and their differences are primarily technical with regard to our concerns here (ibid., 188). (Also note that Deleuze does not complain about irrelevant inferences.) So with what we uncover in the following, we might be inclined to say Deleuze is using a relevant logic like what Routley and Routley describe, but then we might also in that case instead say it is a many-valued sort of logic that is similar to First Degree Entailment. So for simplicity, we will just deal with many-valued logics rather than relevant logics. The remaining non-classical logics mentioned in Priest's *Introduction to Non-Classical Logic*, like free logics and non-normal modal logics, are not so obviously related to the philosophical ideas we consider here, but they may be interesting to consider in more limited contexts. So in this and the following volumes, we will mention them in the notes when they become relevant. One notable non-classical logic not covered in Priest's book *Introduction to Non-Classical Logic* is quantum logic, but it would be more of a concern for us in the next volume.
40 Nolt, *Logics*, 427–8.
41 Ibid., 428, boldface changed to italics.
42 Woleński, "Abstract Approach," 3–4.

43 "It should be noted, though, that even fuzzy logic is not entirely unproblematic. For if truth comes by degrees, there must be some point in a sorites transition where the truth value changes from *completely true* to *less than completely true*. The existence of such a point would itself seem to be intuitively problematic." Priest, *Introduction to Non-Classical Logic*, 224.
44 Ibid., 130–1.
45 Deleuze, *Course 1982.12.07,1* (00:37:10–00:40:10); Deleuze, *Course 1982.12.07,2* (00:38:30–00:41:10).
46 Deleuze, *Course 1983.11.29,1* (00:43:10–00:45:20, 00:56:20–00:57:20).
47 Deleuze, *Course 1985.08.01,2* (00:02:10–00:03:00).
48 Deleuze and Guattari, *Thousand Plateaus*, 275–6 [306].
49 Deleuze, *Logic of Sense*, 196, 203 [200, 208].
50 Deleuze and Guattari, *Thousand Plateaus*, emphasis mine.
51 Deleuze and Guattari, *What Is Philosophy?*, 135–8 [128–31].
52 Jeffrey Bell credits Priest for having problematized established functions and representations, but he says this was not enough to create concepts, because it only served to enhance our representational powers. Bell, "Dialetheism." This factor of course should be acknowledged for such an evaluation, and Bell is right that we must be attentive to these issues when working jointly with Priest's and Deleuze's philosophies. Yet, a further question we can ask is if the conceptualization of a dialetheia in any way involves the implementation of intuitions that are not directly representable. For example, when we conceive the sense of the liar's paradox, could there not be something in our mental grasp that escapes our powers of symbolic representation?

Chapter 1

1   Many parts of these discussions on Bergson and Russell take their inspiration from: Ansell-Pearson, *Philosophy and the Adventure*, 24–8.
2   Russell, *Our Knowledge*, 3–6.
3   Ibid., 7–8.
4   Ibid., 11.
5   Ibid., 12–14. Russell levels two main critiques of this evolutionist trend, which we will mention only in summary: {1} No philosophical consequences follow from the fact of biological evolution; for instance, just because there seems to be progress in evolution does not mean that our present ethical notions are also progressing. And {2}, evolutionist philosophy wants to be grounded in scientific knowledge, but it does not want to take the "disinterested intellectual curiosity which characterizes the genuine man of science"; and moreover, philosophy deals with different kinds of questions than any science can address, anyway. Ibid., 16–17.
6   Russell, *Our Knowledge*, 4.
7   Ibid., 17.
8   Ibid., 18.
9   Bergson, *Creative Mind*, 9 [1].
10 Ibid., 9 [1–2].
11 Ibid., 10 [2].
12 Ibid., 35 [26–7].

13 Ibid., 35–6 [27].
14 Bergson, *Creative Evolution*, 1–2 [1–2].
15 Bergson, *Creative Mind*, 35 [27].
16 Bergson, *Matter and Memory*, 239 [203].
17 Bergson, *Creative Mind*, 168 [158]. "I have spoken of movement; but I could say the same for any change whatever. All real change is an indivisible change." Ibid., 172 [162].
18 Bergson, *Creative Mind*, 168 [158].
19 Bergson, *Creative Evolution*, 309–10 [309]. See the similar description in Bergson, *Matter and Memory*, 246–8 [209–11].
20 Bergson, *Creative Mind*, 168–9 [158–9].
21 Ibid., 14 [6].
22 Ibid., 175–6 [165–6].
23 Bergson, *Matter and Memory*, 253 [215].
24 "In reality the body is changing form at every moment; or rather, there is no form, since form is immobile and the reality is movement. What is real is the continual *change of* form: *form is only a snapshot view of a transition.*" Bergson, *Creative Evolution*, 302 [302].
25 "*There are changes, but there are underneath the change no things which change: change has no need of a support. There are movements, but there is no inert or invariable object which moves: movement does not imply a mobile.*" Bergson, *Creative Mind*, 173 [163]. "Reality is mobility itself. [...] there is change, but [...] there are not things which change." Ibid., 177 [167].
26 Bergson, *Creative Mind*, 177 [167].
27 Bergson, *Creative Evolution*, 308 [307]. See Deleuze, *Cinema 1*, 2 [10].
28 Bergson, *Creative Evolution*, 305 [304].
29 Ibid., 305–6 [305].
30 Ibid., 306 [305].
31 Ibid., 307–8 [307].
32 Ibid., 312 [311].
33 Ibid., 313 [312].
34 Ibid.
35 Arist. *Ph*. VI, 8–9, 239b5–239b33 (*Physics*, 120 [330]).
36 Bergson, *Creative Evolution*, 308 [308].
37 Ibid., 314 [313–14].
38 Ibid., 310–11 [309–10].
39 Ibid., 308–9 [308].
40 Ibid., 313–14 [313].
41 It should be noted that, as Koray Akçagüner has shown, even our "mathematical intuitions," which we would expect to remain unchangeable, in fact, are also prone to development. See Akçagüner, "Poincaré's Philosophy."
42 Russell, *Our Knowledge*, 130.
43 Ibid.
44 Ibid., 137–8.
45 Ibid., 138.
46 Ibid., 141–5.
47 "When any nerve is stimulated, so as to cause a sensation, the sensation does not cease instantaneously with the cessation of the stimulus, but dies away in a short finite time. A flash of lightning, brief as it is to our sight, is briefer still as a physical

phenomenon: we continue to see it for a few moments after the light-waves have ceased to strike the eye. Thus in the case of a physical motion, if it is sufficiently swift, we shall actually at one instant see the moving body throughout a finite portion of its course, and not only at the exact spot where it is at that instant. Sensations, however, as they die away, grow gradually fainter; thus the sensation due to a stimulus which is recently past is not exactly like the sensation due to a present stimulus. It follows from this that, when we see a rapid motion, we shall not only see a number of positions of the moving body simultaneously, but we shall see them with different degrees of intensity—the present position most vividly, and the others with diminishing vividness, until sensation fades away into immediate memory. This state of things accounts fully for the perception of motion. A motion is *perceived*, not merely *inferred*, when it is sufficiently swift for many positions to be sensible at one time; and the earlier and later parts of one perceived motion are distinguished by the less and greater vividness of the sensations." Ibid., 139–40.

48 Ibid., 145, emphasis mine.
49 Ibid., 137.
50 "It is now time to consider what mathematics has to say concerning infinity. Only when this has been accomplished, shall we be in a position adequately to discuss the closely allied philosophical problems of infinity and continuity." Russell, *Principles of Mathematics*, 303. "Hence many of the topics which used to be placed among the great mysteries—for example, the natures of infinity, of continuity, of space, time and motion—are now no longer in any degree open to doubt or discussion. Those who wish to know the nature of these things need only read the works of such men as Peano or Georg Cantor; they will there find exact and indubitable expositions of all these quondam mysteries." Russell, "Mathematics and Metaphysicians," 80. "The argument against continuity, in so far as it rests upon the supposed difficulties of infinite numbers, has been disposed of by the positive theory of the infinite [...]. [...] It is, I believe, the absence of this kind of intimacy which makes many philosophers regard the mathematical doctrine of continuity as an inadequate explanation of the continuity which we experience in the world of sense." Russell, *Our Knowledge*, 130. "Philosophers, mostly in ignorance of the mathematician's analysis, have adopted other and more heroic methods of dealing with the *prima facie* difficulties of continuous motion. A typical and recent example of philosophic theories of motion is afforded by Bergson." Ibid., 137.
51 Russell, *Our Knowledge*, 132.
52 Russell, "Mathematics and Metaphysicians," 80–3. See Russell, *Our Knowledge*, 135.
53 Russell, "Mathematics and Metaphysicians," 83.
54 Russell, *Our Knowledge*, 133–4.
55 Russell, "Mathematics and Metaphysicians," 80–3; Russell, *Our Knowledge*, 135; Russell, *Principles of Mathematics*, 325–54. "There is no such thing as an infinitesimal stretch; [...] infinitesimals as explaining continuity must be regarded as unnecessary, erroneous and self-contradictory. [...] Cantor's continuum is free from contradictions. [...] the continuity to be discussed does not involve the admission of actual infinitesimals." Ibid., 345, 347.
56 Russell, *Our Knowledge*, 129.
57 Ibid., 130.
58 Russell, "Mathematics and Metaphysicians," 84. "The arrow is where it is at one moment, but at another moment it is somewhere else, and this is just what constitutes motion." Russell, "Philosophy of Bergson," 339. "A motion [...] expresses

the fact that a thing may be in different places at different times, and that the places may still be different however near together the times may be." Ibid., 341.

59 Russell, *Our Knowledge*, 136. See his explanation with a diagram for an even more precise account: Ibid., 136-7.
60 Russell, *Principles of Mathematics*, 473.
61 Bergson, *Creative Mind*, 35 [27].
62 Russell, "Philosophy of Bergson," 341.
63 Russell, "Mathematics and Metaphysicians," 80-1, emphasis mine.
64 Ibid., 83-4, emphasis mine.
65 Russell, *Principles of Mathematics*, 473.
66 Bergson, *Creative Evolution*, 9 [9]. See ibid., 338-40 [338-40].
67 Russell, "Philosophy of Bergson," 339.
68 Ibid., 338.
69 Bergson, *Creative Evolution*, 308-9 [308].
70 Russell, "Philosophy of Bergson," 340.
71 Russell, *Principles of Mathematics*, 469, emphasis mine.
72 Ibid., 352.
73 Ibid., 467.
74 Ibid., 472.
75 Ibid., 347, quoting and translating Poincaré, "Continu mathématique," 26-7. Russell also writes: "Suppose we halve a given distance, and then halve the half, and so on, we can continue the process as long as we please, and the longer we continue it, the smaller the resulting distance becomes. [...] The continued bisection of our distance, though it gives us continually smaller distances, gives us always *finite* distances. If our original distance was an inch, we reach successively half an inch, a quarter of an inch, an eighth, a sixteenth, and so on; but every one of this infinite series of diminishing distances is finite. 'But,' it may be said, '*in the end* the distance will grow infinitesimal.' No, because there is no end. The process of bisection is one which can, theoretically, be carried on for ever, without any last term being attained. Thus infinite divisibility of distances, which must be admitted, does not imply that there are distances so small that any finite distance would be larger." Russell, *Our Knowledge*, 135.
76 Russell, "Mathematics and Metaphysicians," 83.
77 "Where there is change, there must be a succession of states. There cannot be change—and motion is only a particular case of change—unless there is something different at one time from what there is at some other time. Change, therefore, must involve relations and complexity, and must demand analysis. So long as our analysis has only gone as far as other smaller changes, it is not complete; if it is to be complete, it must end with terms that are not changes, but are related by a relation of earlier and later. In the case of changes which appear continuous, such as motions, it seems to be impossible to find anything other than change so long as we deal with finite periods of time, however short. We are thus driven back, by the logical necessities of the case, to the conception of instants without duration, or at any rate without any duration which even the most delicate instruments can reveal." Russell, *Our Knowledge*, 151.
78 Russell, "Theory of Knowledge," 197.
79 Priest, *One*, xviii.
80 Priest, *In Contradiction*, 160.
81 Ibid.
82 Ibid.

83 Ibid., 161.
84 Beall and Ripley, "Analetheism and Dialetheism," 30.
85 See Priest, *In Contradiction*, 64–6, 161.
86 Kabay, "Defense of Trivialism," 142.
87 Otherwise we need to invent a new term, but let us leave it for the logicians to do that in the most appropriate way.
88 Hegel, *Science of Logic*, 439 [75]. See Priest, *In Contradiction*, 170.
89 Another option would be to give the extra truth-value situations their own symbol, for instance, *i,* and then specify the *designated value(s)* for a valid inference in that system, which would mean that for the inference to be valid, it would have to be that none of the evaluations make the premises all be a designated value but the conclusion a non-designated one. See for instance Priest, *Introduction to Non-Classical Logic*, 120–5. That approach is more efficient, but the way we will do it here involves a little less technicality, and it makes matters a bit more visual.
90 See Priest, *Introduction to Non-Classical Logic*, 124.
91 See for instance Haack, *Deviant Logic*, 61; Priest, *Introduction to Non-Classical Logic*, 122, 146–7.
92 Priest, *Introduction to Non-Classical Logic*, 124.
93 Priest, "Logic of Paradox," 226; Priest, *Introduction to Non-Classical Logic*, 124, 146–7.
94 For a similar kind of setup with gaps and gluts, see Nolt, *Logics*, 442–4.
95 "In textbooks on classical logic, $\neg(A \wedge \neg A)$ is normally regarded as the LNC, negating any contradiction of the form $A \wedge \neg A$." Brady, "On the Formalization," 41, notation modified; see Priest, *Doubt Truth*, 79.
96 Priest, *Doubt Truth*, 79.
97 Priest gives a more detailed account that makes the truth evaluation more explicit. "Now, consider a body, *b*, in motion [...] moving along a one dimensional continuum, also represented by the real line. Let us write Bx for '*b* is at point *x*'. Let us also suppose that each real, *r*, has a name, $\underline{r}$. [...] Let the motion of *b* be represented by the equation $x = f(t)$. Then the evaluation, *v*, which corresponds to this motion according to the Russellean account, is just that given by the conditions: (1a) $1 \in v_t(B\underline{r})$ iff $r = f(t)$; (1b) $0 \in v_t(B\underline{r})$ iff $r \neq f(t)$." Priest, *In Contradiction*, 177. Here is something like the diagram Priest gives for this.

v_t : $\neg B\underline{r}$ $B\underline{r}$ $\neg B\underline{r}$

←----------)(----------→

r : $f(t)$

Based on: ibid., 178. See Priest, "Inconsistencies in Motion," 342–3.
98 Priest, *In Contradiction*, 180.
99 Ibid., 175.
100 Hegel, *Science of Logic*, 440 [76].
101 Priest, *In Contradiction*, 176.
102 Ibid.
103 Ibid., 177.
104 Ibid., 178. Priest here gives a more specific formulation: "In accordance with the [spread] hypothesis, there is an interval containing t, θ_t [...] such that, in some

sense, if $t' \in \theta_t$, b's occupation of its location at t' is reproduced at t. I suggest that a plausible formal interpretation of this is that the state description of b at t is just the 'superposition' of all the Russellean state descriptions, $v_{t'}$, where $t' \in \theta_t$. More precisely, it is the evaluation, v, given by the conditions: (2a) $1 \in v_t(B\underline{r})$ iff, for some $t' \in \theta_t, r = f(t')$; (2b) $0 \in v_t(B\underline{r})$ iff, for some $t' \in \theta_t, r \neq f(t')$. [...] we write Σ_t for the *spread* of all the points occupied at t [...]. [...] then at t a number of contradictions are realized. For all $r \in \Sigma_t$, $1 \in v_t(B\underline{r} \wedge \neg B\underline{r})$." Ibid., bracketed insertion is mine. And here is something like his diagram for that:

$$
\begin{array}{c}
B\underline{r} \\
v_t: \quad \neg B\underline{r} \quad (\text{-------}) \quad \neg B\underline{r} \\
\leftarrow \text{----------})(\text{-----------} \rightarrow \\
\hline
r: \quad\quad\quad\quad f(t) \\
(\text{--------}) \\
\Sigma_t
\end{array}
$$

Based on: ibid., 178. See Priest, "Inconsistencies in Motion," 343.
105 Priest, *In Contradiction*, 178.
106 Priest, "Motion," 410.
107 Ibid. See Priest, "Inconsistencies in Motion," 344.
108 Priest, *In Contradiction*, 181.
109 Carroll, *Alice's Adventures in Wonderland*, 18–29.
110 Ibid., 28.
111 Ibid., 29.
112 Ibid.
113 Ibid., 30.
114 Ibid., 43–6.
115 Deleuze, quoted and translated in Blake, "On the Incipit," 1, emphasis mine. See Deleuze, *Logic of Sense*, 3 [9].
116 Ibid.
117 Ibid.
118 Public domain images are from Archive.org: Carroll and Tenniel, *Alice's Adventures*, 15, 26, 45.
119 Deleuze, quoted and translated in Blake, "On the Incipit," 1. See Deleuze, *Logic of Sense*, 3 [9].
120 Deleuze, *Course 1983.04.12,3* (00:00:20–00:02:40). Rough translation is mine.
121 Deleuze, *Logic of Sense*, 3–4 [9–11].
122 Pl. *Phlb.* 24d (*Philebus*, 412 [246]).
123 Deleuze, *Logic of Sense*, 296 [298].

Chapter 2

1 Deleuze, *Logic of Sense*, 201 [206].
2 Ibid., 197, 200, 322–3, 332–4 [201, 206, 326–7, 338–42]; Deleuze, *Course 1972.02.15* (no audio); Deleuze, *Course 1983.11.08,2* (00:34:00–00:25:10); Deleuze, *Course*

1983.11.22,2 (00:34:00–00:25:10); Deleuze, *Course 1983.11.29,2* (00:10:00–00:10:30); Deleuze, *Course 1983.11.29,3* (00:03:30–00:06:50).

3   Deleuze, *Logic of Sense*, 303–4 [307–9].
4   Deleuze and Guattari, *Thousand Plateaus*, 268–74 [297–304].
5   Waite, *Book of Black Magic*, 225 [Venitiana del Rabina, *Grand grimoire*, 67]; Beta and Crowley, *Goetia (Crowley)*, 71–2; Hall, *Secret Teaching*, 101–4; Lévi, *Transcendental Magic*, 301–3 [*Dogme et rituel 2*, 230–3].
6   Public domain images are from Archive.org. (Top left) Waite, *Book of Black Magic*, 2. https://archive.org/details/A.EWaiteTheBookOfBlackMagicAndOfPacts1910 Complete. (Top middle) Lévi, *Transcendental Magic*, 299 [*Dogme et rituel 2*, 208]. https://archive.org/details/transcendentalma00leviuoft. (Top right) de Laurence, *Goetia (de Laurence)*. https://archive.org/details/lesserkeyofsolom00dela. (Bottom left) Lévi, *Transcendental Magic*, 174 [*Dogme et rituel 2*, frontispiece] (quotations from: *Transcendental Magic*, 288, 297 [*Dogme et rituel 2*, 208, 224–5]). (Bottom middle) Collin de Plancy, *Dictionnaire infernal: planches*. https://archive.org/details/bub_gb_1YbyOXeMzIsC. (Bottom right) Frank Adams's illustration in Dumas, *Wolf-Leader*, frontispiece. https://archive.org/details/wolfleader00dumauoft.
7   Hall, *Secret Teaching*, 103.
8   Deleuze and Guattari, *Thousand Plateaus*, 276 [306].
9   Dumas, *Wolf-Leader*, 32 [83].
10 Ibid., 109 [295].
11 Deleuze and Guattari, *Thousand Plateaus*, 276 [306].
12 Ibid., 37–8 [46–7]; Deleuze, *Course 1973.02.12* (no audio).
13 Canetti, *Crowds and Power*, 29–30 [30–2].
14 Deleuze and Guattari, *Thousand Plateaus*, 266–7, 271–2 [295–6, 301].
15 Canetti, *Crowds and Power*, 93–7 [109–14].
16 Deleuze and Guattari, *Thousand Plateaus*, 275 [305].
17 Ibid., 262 [291].
18 Deleuze and Parnet, *Dialogues II*, 2 [8].
19 Deleuze and Guattari, *Thousand Plateaus*, 262 [291].
20 Deleuze and Parnet, *Dialogues II*, 2 [8].
21 Deleuze and Guattari, *Thousand Plateaus*, 262 [291].
22 Deleuze, "Literature and Life," 1 [11].
23 Deleuze and Guattari, *Mille plateaux*; Deleuze and Guattari, *Thousand Plateaus*, 263 [292]. See Deleuze, "Literature and Life," 2 [12].
24 Bergson, *Creative Mind*, 107 [99].
25 Ibid., 120–1 [112–13].
26 Ibid., 118 [110].
27 Deleuze, *Difference and Repetition*, 222 [286].
28 Deleuze, *Course 1982.11.02,2* (00:14:00–00:15:00).
29 Deleuze and Guattari, *Thousand Plateaus*, 361–3, 611 [403–6]; Deleuze, *Course 1983.11.08,2* (00:22:40–00:28:00). Coalescence (*coalescence*) and concretion (*concrétion*) are Deleuze's own terminological contributions, in keeping with Dupréel's thinking.
30 Dupréel, *Consistance et la probabilité*, 7–8.
31 Ibid., 9–10.
32 Ibid., 11.
33 Ibid., 12–14.
34 Ibid., 13–14.
35 Dupréel, "Théorie de la consolidation," 158–9.

36 Ibid., 158; Dupréel, *Esquisse d'une philosophie*, 129–30.
37 Dupréel, "Théorie de la consolidation," 161.
38 See http://ehgc.org.uk/hertfordshire-puddingstone/puddingstone-use. This photo by Jane Tubb is of Hertfordshire puddingstone. She explains that it is found in southeast England, with similar stones in northern France. But from Dupréel's description of the puddingstone's composition, she says that it may instead be ferricrete, which has an even more heterogeneous composition of pebble types that are less rounded.
39 Dupréel, *Esquisse d'une philosophie*, 150–1; Dupréel, "Théorie de la consolidation," 162.
40 Dupréel, *Esquisse d'une philosophie*, 151.
41 Ibid., 153; Dupréel, "Théorie de la consolidation," 165.
42 Left and middle panels are my re-imaginings of Dupréel's figures 1 and 2 (Ibid., 159–60).
43 Dupréel, *Esquisse d'une philosophie*, 125–6, 136.
44 Ibid., 147–9. See Lapoujade, *Aberrant Movements*, 204 [186].
45 Dupréel, *Esquisse d'une philosophie*, 130–1; Dupréel, "Théorie de la consolidation," 160–1.
46 Dupréel, "Théorie de la consolidation," 161. See Dupréel, *Esquisse d'une philosophie*, 131.
47 Dupréel, *Esquisse d'une philosophie*, 89–92; Deleuze and Guattari, *Thousand Plateaus*, 611 [405].
48 Dupréel, *Esquisse d'une philosophie*, 37–8; Dupréel, "Cause et l'intervalle," 200–1.
49 Dupréel, *Esquisse d'une philosophie*, 130–1; Dupréel, "Théorie de la consolidation," 164–5; Dupréel, "Cause et l'intervalle," 201.
50 Dupréel, "Cause et l'intervalle," 204.
51 Dupréel, *Esquisse d'une philosophie*, 39–41.
52 Ibid., 38; Dupréel, "Cause et l'intervalle," 204.
53 Dupréel, "Cause et l'intervalle," 200.
54 Dupréel, *Esquisse d'une philosophie*, 131–2.
55 Ibid., 151–2.
56 See Lapoujade, *Aberrant Movements*, 204 [186].
57 Deleuze and Guattari, *Thousand Plateaus*, 357 [398].
58 Ibid., 362 [405].
59 Thorpe, *Animal Nature*, 158.
60 Thorpe, *Learning and Instinct*, 372.
61 Ibid., 370; Deleuze and Guattari, *Thousand Plateaus*, 363 [406].
62 Deleuze and Guattari, *Thousand Plateaus*, 364 [407], emphasis mine.
63 Ibid., 362 [405].
64 "il n'y a de *croissance* que par intercalation." Dupréel, "Théorie de la consolidation," 177. Translation is Brian Massumi's. Deleuze and Guattari, *Thousand Plateaus*, 362. It is also translated as "there is only growth through intercalation" in Mary McAllester Jones's translation of Bachelard's *La dialectique de la durée*. Bachelard, *Dialectic of Duration*, 95 [83].
65 "At first, they constitute no more than a fuzzy set [...] that later takes on consistency." Deleuze and Guattari, *Thousand Plateaus*, 357 [398]. "The philosopher Eugene Dupréel proposed a theory of *consolidation*; he demonstrated that life went from a [...] fuzzy aggregate to its consolidation." Ibid., 362 [405]. Dupréel discusses the substitutions that can occur for intercalated elements: Dupréel, "Théorie de la consolidation," 173–5.
66 Deleuze and Guattari, *Thousand Plateaus*, 363 [406].

67 "Consistency concretely ties together heterogeneous, disparate elements as such: it assures the consolidation of fuzzy aggregates, in other words, multiplicities of the rhizome type." Ibid., 558 [632].
68 Ibid., 365 [408].
69 Thorpe includes a picture of a stagemaker's stage: Thorpe, *Learning and Instinct*, 322–3.
70 Deleuze and Guattari, *Thousand Plateaus*, 365 [408].
71 Marshall, *Bower-Birds*, 159.
72 Deleuze and Guattari, *Thousand Plateaus*, 379 [424].
73 Deleuze and Guattari, *What Is Philosophy?*, 228 [134].
74 Nolt, *Logics*, 426, emphasis mine.
75 Zadeh, "Préface (to Kaufmann's *Introduction*)," vi.
76 Kaufmann, *Introduction to the Theory*, xi [x].
77 Ibid.
78 "More technically, a fuzzy set is defined by a function that assigns to each entity in its domain a value between 0 and 1 inclusive, representing the entity's degree of membership in the set." Bergmann, *Introduction to Many-Valued and Fuzzy Logic*, 177.
79 "We may now use fuzzy sets assigned to predicates to determine truth-values. Our truth-values will be values between 0 and 1 inclusive, and in the case of simple sentences will correspond directly to degrees of membership. If Anne's height […] is tall to degree .2, then we will assign the value .2 to the sentence *Anne is tall*, and so on. We call these values *degrees of truth*. […] When the bases for assigning the degrees of truth are fuzzy sets, we call the system a *fuzzy logic*." Ibid., 178.
80 For more on how fuzzy logics are set up, see for instance Deleuze's cited sources: Kaufmann, *Introduction to the Theory*, 4–7 [4–7]; Sinaceur, "Logique et mathématique du flou," 514–24; Engel, *Norme du vrai*, 265–8. Otherwise see for instance Nolt, *Logics*, 421–6; Priest, *Introduction to Non-Classical Logic*, 224–6.
81 Dumas, *Wolf-Leader*, 114–15 [310–11].
82 Deleuze and Guattari, *What Is Philosophy?*, 141, 228 [134]. One of their sources writes: "It is necessary to say *fuzzy subset* and not *fuzzy set*—the reference set will not be fuzzy." Kaufmann, *Introduction to the Theory*, 1 [1].
83 Deleuze and Guattari, *What Is Philosophy?*, 143 [136–7]. Deleuze and Guattari also write, "Between true and false (1 and 0), degrees of truth are introduced that are not probabilities but produce a kind of fractalization of the peaks of truth and the troughs of falsity, so that the fuzzy sets become numerical again, but through a fractional number between 0 and 1. However, this is on condition that the fuzzy set is the subset of a normal set, referring to a regular function." Ibid., 228 [134]. Kaufmann writes: "The reference set will always be an ordinary set, that is, such as one defined intuitively in modern mathematics, that is again, a collection of well-specified and distinct objects. It is the subsets that will be fuzzy." Kaufmann, *Introduction to the Theory*, xiv [xii]. As Nolt explains: "In fuzzy-set theory, membership is assigned strict numerical values from 0 to 1, like the truth values in infinite-valued semantics. But in defining truth values, Zadeh compounds the fuzziness. He might, for example, define a truth value AT (almost true), which is a fuzzy set of numerical values in which, say, numbers no greater than 0.5 have membership 0, 0.6 has membership 0.3, 0.7 has membership 0.5, 0.9 has membership 0.8, and 0.99 has membership 0.95. Such a fuzzy set of numerical values is for Zadeh a truth value. A logic whose semantics is based on such fuzzy truth values is called a fuzzy logic." Nolt, *Logics*, 426.

84 Deleuze and Guattari, *Thousand Plateaus*, 613 [425], emphasis mine.
85 Ibid., 363 [406].
86 Ibid., 288 [319].
87 Bergson, *Creative Evolution*, 313 [312].
88 Ibid., 9.
89 Ibid., 8–9.
90 Priest explains it more precisely, with reference to the "Bradley Regress": "Here, then, is our problem of unity. Let me lay it out in abstract terms. Take any thing, object, entity, with parts, $p_1, \ldots, p_n$. (Suppose that there is a finite number of these; nothing hangs on this.) A thing is not merely a plurality of parts: it is a unity. There must, therefore, be something which constitutes them as a single thing, a unity. Let us call it, neutrally (and with a nod in the direction of particle physics), the *gluon* of the object, g. Now what of this gluon? Ask whether it itself is a thing, object, entity? It both is and is not. It is, since we have just talked about it, referred to it, thought about it. But it is not, since, if it is, $p_1, \ldots, p_n, g$, would appear to form a congeries, a plurality, just as much as the original one. If its behaviour is to provide an explanation of unity, it cannot simply be an object." Ibid., 9. "We can state the regress problem generally in terms of gluons. Suppose that we have a unity comprising the parts, a, b, c, d, for example. There must be something which, metaphysically speaking, binds them together. This is the object's gluon, g. But then there must be something which binds g and a, b, c, d together, a hyper-gluon, g'. There must, then, be something which binds g', g, and a, b, c, d together, a hyper-hyper-gluon, g''. Obviously we are off on an infinite regress. Moreover, it is a vicious one." Ibid., 11.
91 Priest, *One*, 15.
92 Ibid., 11.
93 Ibid., 12.
94 Ibid., 467; Suppes, *Introduction to Logic*, 213–19.
95 Priest, *One*, 16. In another instance, Priest uses g to symbolize the gluon in such a diagram. Priest, "Contradiction and the Structure."
96 Priest, *One*, 16–17.
97 Based on ibid., 17.
98 Ibid.
99 Based on ibid., 18.
100 Ibid., 19. Priest uses a different symbol for the quantifier: $a = b$ if and only if $X(Xa \equiv Xb)$. See ibid., xxii.
101 The sort of notation here is along the lines of Agler, *Symbolic Logic*, 248–50; Priest, *Introduction to Non-Classical Logic*, 263–4.
102 See Nolt, *Logics*, 382–3.
103 This gluonic factor will be made much more apparent in the next volume when we see how this logic can be understood as operating in Deleuze's and Guattari's notions of the Body without Organs and machinic assemblages.
104 Deleuze and Guattari, *Thousand Plateaus*, 613 [425], emphasis mine.
105 Fitzgerald, *Crack-up with Other Pieces*, 39.
106 This notion of a temporal gluon is not in Priest's texts, but he discussed it with me in a conversation we had on August 25, 2018.
107 Dorothea Olkowski's analysis should be noted here, although she is not construing the matter in terms of dialetheism: "In this notion of becoming, two meanings are affirmed at once so that identity is evaded, an identity which, as Irigaray attests, is fixed by language insofar as language limits and measures, and so fixes qualities such

that small is 'the small' and large is 'the large' because they each receive the action of the Idea." Olkowski, "Body, Knowledge and Becoming-Woman," 102.
108 Priest clarified this to me in a discussion on August 25, 2018, over a discussion of his argument regarding non-classical identity at: Priest, *Introduction to Non-Classical Logic*, 468–9.
109 Deleuze, *Logic of Sense*, 5 [11–12].

Chapter 3

1 Hawking, "Unified Theory."
2 Hawking and Mlodinow, *Grand Design*, 5.
3 Dawkins and Tyson, "Poetry of Science."
4 "The philosopher believes they are actually asking deep questions about nature," but the scientist is compelled to ask the philosopher, "what are you doing? Why are you wasting your time? Why are you concerning yourself with the meaning of meaning?" Tyson, *Neil deGrasse Tyson Returns*.
5 "I am still even worried about a healthy balance [between science and philosophy]. If you are distracted by your questions so that you cannot move forward, you are not being a productive contributor to our understanding of the natural world. [...] When you [...] derail yourself on questions that you think are important, because philosophy class tells you this [...], the scientist says, 'look, I've got all this world of unknown out there. I'm moving on. I'm leaving you behind.' And you cannot even cross the street, because you are distracted by what you are sure are deep questions you've asked of yourself. [...] I don't have time for that." Ibid.
6 Dawkins and Tyson, "Poetry of Science."
7 Tyson says: "I am disappointed because there is a lot of brain power there [in philosophy] that might otherwise could be contributed mightily [in theoretical physics], but today simply does not." Ibid.
8 Tyson, "Closing Talk."
9 Ibid.
10 Deleuze and Guattari, *What Is Philosophy?*, 5 [10].
11 Deleuze, "What Is the Creative Act?," 312–14 [291–3].
12 Ibid., 314 [293].
13 Ibid., 313–14 [292–3].
14 See Collet, "Concept and History," 73.
15 Deleuze, "Brain Is the Screen," 284 [265], emphasis mine.
16 Deleuze, "How Philosophy Is Useful," 166 [152].
17 Ibid., 166–7 [153].
18 Ibid., 167 [153], with my emphasis added and Deleuze's removed.
19 As Knox Peden explains, "Among the major thinkers of twentieth-century French philosophy, few had as wide a field of interest as Gilles Deleuze [...]—from the writings of Leopold von Sacher-Masoch to the paintings of Francis Bacon [...]. [...] his major philosophical statement *Difference and Repetition* takes us from the occultism of Józef Maria Hoene-Wronski's post-Kantian consideration of differential calculus to the biophysical gnosticism of one of Deleuze's contemporaries, Raymond Ruyer. These figures are joined by a cast of characters that is alternately ancient, medieval, and modern." Peden, *Spinoza Contra Phenomenology*, 191.

20 Deleuze, Parnet, and Boutang, *A to Z*, "N Is for Neurology and the Brain [N comme neurologie]."
21 Ibid.
22 Deleuze, *Cinema 1*, 46 [67].
23 Deleuze, *Cinema 1*, 50, 53–5 [73–4, 77–81]; Deleuze, *Course 1983.03.22,2* (01:06:10–01:09:30); Deleuze, "Brain Is the Screen," 286 [266].
24 Deleuze, "Brain Is the Screen," 287 [267].
25 Deleuze, *Course 1982.11.30,1* (00:00:40–00:01:50). See Deleuze, *Cinema 1*, 60–3 [86–90].
26 Deleuze, Parnet, and Boutang, *A to Z*, "N Is for Neurology and the Brain [N comme neurologie]."
27 Ibid., "C Is for Culture [C comme culture]."
28 Delaunay, *Portuguese Woman*. Public domain image is from Wikimedia Commons: https://commons.wikimedia.org/wiki/File:Delaunay_Portuguese_Woman.jpg.
29 Michelson and Morley, "On the Relative Motion," 335. Public domain image is from Wiki Source: https://en.wikisource.org/wiki/On_the_Relative_Motion_of_the_Earth_and_the_Luminiferous_Ether.
30 *The Lighthouse Keepers (Gardiens de Phare)* directed by Jean Grémillon © Films du Grand Guignol 1929. All rights reserved.
31 Ibid.
32 Ibid.
33 Ibid., "F Is for Fidelity [F comme fidélité]." See Deleuze and Guattari, *What Is Philosophy?*, 3–4 [9–10].
34 Deleuze, Parnet, and Boutang, *A to Z*, "F Is for Fidelity [F comme fidélité]."
35 Ibid.
36 Deleuze and Guattari, *What Is Philosophy?*, 3 [8].
37 Ibid., 4 [9].
38 Ibid.
39 Ibid., 4 [9–10].
40 Deleuze, Parnet, and Boutang, *A to Z*, "N Is for Neurology and the Brain [N comme neurologie]."
41 Ibid.
42 Ibid.
43 Deleuze, "On *The Time-Image*," 60 [85–6].
44 Deleuze, Parnet, and Boutang, *A to Z*, "N Is for Neurology and the Brain [N comme neurologie]."
45 See for instance: Burns, *Uncertain Nervous System*, 82.
46 Deleuze, Parnet, and Boutang, *A to Z*, "N Is for Neurology and the Brain [N comme neurologie]," Montparnasse, 2004; Semiotext(e) and MIT, 2012.
47 Ibid.
48 Ibid.; Deleuze, *Course 1984.12.18,1* (00:16:10–00:19:40).
49 Deleuze, *Cinema 2*, 204 [275].
50 Rose, *Conscious Brain*, 90, emphasis mine.
51 Ibid.
52 Deleuze, *Cinema 2*, 204 [275].
53 Deleuze and Guattari, *Thousand Plateaus*, 17 [24].
54 Burns, *Uncertain Nervous System*, 58–65.
55 Deleuze and Guattari, *Thousand Plateaus*, 17, 24 [24, 32–3].

56 Deleuze, Parnet, and Boutang, *A to Z*, "N Is for Neurology and the Brain [N comme neurologie]." See Deleuze, *Cinema 2*, 115 [156].
57 Prigogine and Stengers, *Order out of Chaos*, 269 [245–6].
58 Deleuze, Parnet, and Boutang, *A to Z*, "N Is for Neurology and the Brain [N comme neurologie]."
59 Deleuze, "Brain Is the Screen," 285 [266].
60 Deleuze, "On *The Time-Image*," 60 [86].
61 Ibid., 269 [246].
62 But a concept cannot have all possible parts. "There are no simple concepts. Every concept has components and is defined by them. It therefore has a combination [*chiffre*]. […] There is no concept with only one component. […] Neither is there a concept possessing every component, since this would be chaos pure and simple." Ibid., 15 [21].
63 Ibid., 18 [23].
64 Ibid., 16 [21].
65 Ibid., 18 [23].
66 Ibid., 19 [25].
67 Ibid.
68 Ibid., 19–20 [25].
69 Ibid., 20 [25].
70 Ibid., 20 [25–6].
71 Ibid., 20–1 [26].
72 "Diverse movements of the infinite are so mixed in with each other that, far from breaking up the One-All of the plane of immanence, they constitute its variable curvature […]. Every movement passes through the whole of the plane by immediately turning back on and folding itself and also by folding other movements or allowing itself to be folded by them, giving rise to retroactions, connections, and proliferations in the fractalization of this infinitely folded up infinity (variable curvature of the plane)." Ibid., 38–9 [41].
73 Ibid., 21 [26].
74 Ibid., 20 [25]. See ibid., 90 [87].
75 Deleuze and Guattari, *What Is Philosophy?*, 24 [29].
76 Ibid., 25 [29].
77 Based on: ibid., 25 [30].
78 "The concept is not discursive, and philosophy is not a discursive formation, because it does not link propositions together." Ibid., 22 [27].
79 Ibid., 25–6 [30].

Chapter 4

1 Culp, *Dark Deleuze*, 1–2.
2 Ibid., 20.
3 See for example Culp's discussion of Deleuze's claim from the second *Cinema* book that "*we need reasons to believe in this world.*" Deleuze, *Cinema 2*, 166 [223]. Culp says, "Although his suggestion is not wrong, *it is incomplete*. In his haste, Deleuze forgets to pose the problem with the ambivalence found in all his other accounts of power—how affects are ruled by tyrants, molecular revolutions made fascist, and nomad war machines enrolled to fight for the state. Without it, he becomes

Nietzsche's braying ass, which says yes only because it is incapable of saying no (NP, 178–86). *We must then make up for Deleuze's error* and seek the dark underside of belief." Culp, *Dark Deleuze*, 8, italics mine, with Culp citing the Columbia University English translation edition (1983) of Gilles Deleuze, *Nietzsche and Philosophy*. Culp's claim seems to be that in such cases, Deleuze normally would at least open movements down the dark road, but here, as an exception, he refrained. Nonetheless, this still involves an admission that Deleuze refrains here, and Culp's judgment is that Deleuze has erred by making this exception and that we instead should take this line of thinking down the darker path Deleuze chose not to take. As we can see, there is an ambivalence in Culp's treatment of Deleuze: on the one hand he seems to want to say that the dark reading is consistent with what Deleuze writes, while on the other hand he shows how the dark reading at times requires detours from Deleuze's texts. My suggestion here instead is that Deleuze is using a non-classical sort of reasoning that would explain what might seem to be a conceptual ambivalence in his texts, namely, I am proposing that the negational elements in Deleuze's philosophy can have a logically affirmative character and thus do not need not be given an exclusionary sense.

4   Culp, *Dark Deleuze*, 2, emphasis on "negativity" and bracketed insertion are mine, all else is in the original.
5   Ibid., 32.
6   Deleuze, *Logic of Sense*, 199 [204], emphasis mine; Culp, *Dark Deleuze*, 32. Culp speaks of exclusive disjunctive synthesis as "our own" version of the concept, so I assume he is acknowledging this is not a Deleuzian notion; for, as his cited Deleuze passages show, it cannot suffice as one.
7   Routley and Routley, "Negation and Contradiction," 201.
8   Culp, *Dark Deleuze*, 1.
9   Deleuze, "Letter to a Harsh Critic," 6 [14–15].
10 See Duffy, *Logic of Expression*, especially for instance pp. 113–17. Despite the fact that Spinoza does not use the term "intensity" very much, Deleuze and Guattari say it factors in prominently in his thinking: "Spinoza was the philosopher who knew full well that immanence was only immanent to itself and therefore that it was a plane traversed by movements of the infinite, filled with intensive ordinates." Deleuze and Guattari, *What Is Philosophy?*, 48 [49].
11 I will be referring to these authors by the names they took during the publication of this article. They now go by Val Plumwood and Richard Sylvan.
12 Routley and Routley, "Negation and Contradiction," 205.
13 Ibid; Priest, *Doubt Truth*, 31–2.
14 Routley and Routley, "Negation and Contradiction," 206, 212; Priest, *Doubt Truth*, 31.
15 Priest, *Doubt Truth*, 31.
16 Routley and Routley, "Negation and Contradiction," 206, definition modified in accordance with Mares, *Relevant Logic*, 92.
17 Priest, *Doubt Truth*, 31.
18 Routley and Routley, "Negation and Contradiction," 217.
19 Based on: ibid., 207.
20 Ibid., 214–15.
21 Priest, "Paraconsistency and Dialetheism," 135.
22 Routley and Routley, "Negation and Contradiction," 208.
23 Ibid., 220.

24 That is, "for worlds where A and $\neg A$ (strictly $A \wedge \neg A$) hold but B does not," and "for worlds where C holds but neither D nor $\neg D$ do." Ibid., 209, notation modified.
25 Ibid., 209, 212.
26 Ibid., 209; Priest, *Doubt Truth*, 31.
27 Routley and Routley, "Negation and Contradiction," 217, 220.
28 Ibid., 212.
29 Ibid., 201.
30 Ibid., 209, notation modified.
31 Ibid., 217.
32 Ibid., 208, notation modified and original italics removed with my own inserted, to highlight the passage's relevance in our Leibnizian context.
33 Based on: ibid., 216.
34 Routley and Routley, "Negation and Contradiction," 206, 212.
35 Priest, *Logic: Very Short Introduction*, 7–8.
36 Carnielli and Rodrigues, "On the Philosophy," 62.
37 Ibid.
38 See for instance Deleuze, *Difference and Repetition*, xix, 63 [2, 74].
39 Mares, *Relevant Logic*, 93.
40 Priest himself does not use the term "affirmation," because he does not give it any special meaning; however, he says that were he ever to have used it, he would have meant it the same as "assert." His clarification was given to me by email on January 26, 2015. Also, Edwin Mares, who likewise says that denial is a speech act, considers *rejection* to be "the propositional attitude that is expressed by denial." Mares, *Relevant Logic*, 93. As such, it seems appropriate that *affirmation* be considered the propositional attitude that is expressed by assertion.
41 Priest and Aroutiounian, "Interview with Noted Logician."
42 Priest, "Paraconsistency and Dialetheism," 194.
43 Mares, *Relevant Logic*, 93, notation modified.
44 Deleuze, *Difference and Repetition*, 53 [75]. Additional text where affirmation and negation are contrasted can be found in Deleuze, *Nietzsche and Philosophy*, 50–3, 62–3 [60–5, 76–7].
45 "Pour poser sa propre identité, il faut que la chose s'oppose à ce qui la nie, deux négations. Pour poser sa propre identité, il faut que la chose s'oppose à ce qui la nie, A n'est pas non-A. A n'est pas [s'oppose] non-A [à ce qui la nie]." Deleuze, *Course 1986.04.08,2* (00:37:10–00:38:00), bracketed insertions are in the transcript.
46 His criticism probably also applies to the first kind of negation, which yields even more exclusion.
47 Hegel, *Lectures on the History 2*, 57–8 [80].
48 Smith, *Essays on Deleuze*, pp. 72–80.
49 Deleuze, *Course 1983.05.03,2* (00:45:40–00:49:30).
50 Deleuze, *Course 1983.05.17,1* (00:02:50–00:03:30).
51 Here we are using Daniel Smith's example rather than Deleuze's "chimera," for consistency with another of Deleuze's use of this illustration, discussed in Chapter 7. Smith, *Essays on Deleuze*, 73.
52 Deleuze, *Course 1983.05.17,1* (00:06:00–00:09:40).
53 Ibid. (00:09:30–00:12:00).
54 Ibid. (00:11:40–00:12:30).
55 Ibid. (00:12:30–00:15:40).
56 Ibid. (00:15:40–00:16:40).

57 For more explanation, see for instance: Jones, *New Law of Thought*, 1–2; Jones, *Elements of Logic*, 46–52. Deleuze explicitly works with the subject–predicate formulations for the principles of logic in: Deleuze, *Course 1978.03.14* (no audio).
58 On this matter, especially in the context of Hegel, see for instance: Siemens, "Hegel and the Law," 105–6; Russell, *Our Knowledge*, 39–40 (especially footnote 1).
59 For some discussion on the problems with these formulations that Deleuze is employing, see for instance: Jones, *Elements of Logic*, 51; 175–7; Jones, *New Law of Thought*, 1–11.
60 "For Deleuze, thought must think something that is contrary to the principles of thought, it must think difference, it must think that which is absolutely different from thought but which none the less gives itself to thought, and wrests thought from its natural stupor. This is no longer thought attempting to think existence, but existence forcing itself on thought, forcing itself to be thought, albeit in the form of an intelligible problem or Idea." Smith, *Essays on Deleuze*, 85.
61 Deleuze, *Course 1983.05.17,1* (00:18:50–00:32:40).
62 Ibid. (00:32:40–00:34:15).
63 Ibid. (00:34:10–00:40:42); Deleuze, *Course 1983.05.17,2* (00:00:00–00:03:10).
64 Leibniz, *Monadology*, 272 [612].
65 Deleuze, *Course 1983.05.17,2* (00:03:10–00:19:40). As Leibniz explains, "One particular substance never acts on another particular substance any more than it is acted on by it. For consider: what happens to each one is only a consequence of its idea or complete notion and nothing else, because that idea already involves all predicates or events, and expresses the whole universe." Leibniz, *Discourse on Metaphysics*, 67 [1551]. "The predicate or consequent therefore always inheres in the subject or antecedent. [...] In identities this connection and the inclusion of the predicate in the subject are explicit; in all other propositions they are implied and must be revealed through the analysis of the concepts, which constitutes a demonstration a priori." Leibniz, "First Truths," 267–8 [518–19]. "All these contingent propositions have reasons why they are so rather than otherwise—or alternatively (and this is the same thing), that they have a priori proofs of their truth which make them certain, and which show that the connection of the subject with the predicate in these propositions has its foundation in the nature of each." Leibniz, *Discourse on Metaphysics*, 65 [1549].
66 Kant writes: "Either the predicate *B* belongs to the subject *A* as something that is (covertly) contained in this concept *A*; or *B* lies entirely outside the concept *A*, though to be sure it stands in connection with it. In the first case I call the judgment analytic, in the second synthetic." Kant, *Critique of Pure Reason*, A6–7/B10 (130 [52]).
67 Deleuze, *Course 1983.05.17,2* (00:24:10–00:33:00).
68 Ibid. (00:32:50–00:35:00). Although Deleuze does not here specify it, the element that is over and beyond thought and Self which Kant employs in his synthetic identity might be sensible intuitions of the self. As Daniela Voss explains, "The Kantian subject is premised on the synthesis of two opposed faculties: the active faculty of thought and the merely passive faculty of receptivity. While the faculty of thought presupposes the transcendental form of the 'I think' and the a priori categories of the understanding, the faculty of receptivity provides sensible intuition given in the forms of space and time. In drawing this firm distinction, Kant made the human subject and its claim to knowledge and truth dependent on 'the touchstone of experience' (*CPR* A viii). The human subject has become a finite subject by virtue

of its dependence on the receptivity of intuition." Voss, *Conditions of Thought*, 211. For more detail, see Shores, "Self-Shock," 171-3. For the notion that the German Idealists were dissatisfied with Kant's synthetic identity, see for instance Fichte, "Second Introduction," 44-51 [346-56]; "According to Kant, all consciousness is merely conditioned by self-consciousness, that is, its content can be founded upon something outside self-consciousness; now the results of this foundation are simply not supposed to *contradict* the conditions of self-consciousness; simply not to eliminate the possibility thereof; but they are not required actually to *emerge* from it. According to the Science of Knowledge, all consciousness is determined by self-consciousness, that is, everything that occurs in consciousness is founded, given and introduced by the conditions of self-consciousness." Ibid., 50 [356].
69 Bertman, "Basic Particulars," 1-4.
70 Kant says that the predicates in synthetic judgments "amplify" them: "The first case I call the judgment analytic, in the second synthetic. [...] One could also call the former judgments of clarification and the latter judgments of amplification." Kant, *Critique of Pure Reason*, A6-7/B10-11 (130 [52]).
71 Deleuze, *Course 1983.05.17,2* (00:34:40-00:38:20). See for instance Fichte's *Science of Knowledge*. "The self's own positing of itself is thus its own pure activity. The *self posits itself*, and by virtue of this mere self-assertion it *exists*." Fichte, *Science of Knowledge*, 97 [16]. "*The self posits itself as limited by the non-self.*" Ibid., 122 [47]. "The self posits itself as *determined by the not-self.*" Ibid., 123 [48]. "The self, as at present conceived, is simply the counterpart of the not-self, and nothing more; and the not-self simply the counterpart of the self and nothing more. No Thou, no I: no I, no Thou." Ibid., 172-3 [108-9]. "The self posits itself absolutely, and is thereby complete in itself and closed to any impression from without. But if it is to be a self, it must also posit itself as self-posited; and by this new positing, relative to an original positing, it opens itself, if I may so put it, to external influences; simply by this reiteration of positing, it concedes the possibility that there might also be something within it that is not actually posited by itself. Both types of positing are conditions for an operation of the not-self." Ibid., 243 [193-4]. "According to the Science of Knowledge, then, the ultimate ground of all reality for the self is an original interaction between the self and some other thing outside it, of which nothing more can be said, save that it must be utterly opposed to the self. In the course of this interaction, nothing is brought into the self, nothing alien is imported; everything that develops therein, even out to infinity, develops solely from itself, in accordance with its own laws; the self is merely set in motion by this opponent, in order that it may act; without such an external prime mover it would never have acted, and since its existence consists solely in acting, it would never have existed either. But this mover has no other attribute than that of being a mover, an opposing force, and is in fact only felt to be such." Ibid., 246 [196].
72 Deleuze, *Course 1983.05.03,2* (00:54:50-01:01:40); Deleuze, *Course 1983.05.17,2* (00:38:10-00:46:48); Deleuze, *Course 1983.05.17,3* (00:33:00-00:33:15). See for instance: Hegel, *Jena System*, 132-41; 165-9.
73 Deleuze, *Course 1983.05.03,2* (00:49:25-00:53:35); Deleuze, *Course 1983.05.17,1* (00:02:50-00:05:00).
74 Deleuze, *Course 1983.05.03,2* (01:02:00-01:04:20); Deleuze, *Difference and Repetition*, 49 [70].
75 Deleuze, *Course 1983.05.17,3* (00:00:00-00:04:10).

76 Also see Ficara, "Hegel's Glutty Negation"; Ficara, "Dialectic and Dialetheism"; Priest, "Dialectic and Dialetheic"; Priest and Routley, "Outline of the History"; Ueberweg, *System of Logic*, 242 [196].

77 Hegel, *Science of Logic*, 439 [74]. See Deleuze, *Difference and Repetition*, 310 (ft. 10) [64 (ft. 1)]; Deleuze, *Logic of Sense*, 202 (ft. 3) [202 (ft. 4)]. During one class, in a playful, joking manner, Deleuze uses even stronger terms for those who would argue that Hegel affirms contradiction, with language that seems to go explicitly against these Hegel quotations: "Il faut être un imbécile pour croire que, [...] Que Hegel renverse le principe de contradiction et croit que les choses se contredisent. Il faut être vraiment un débile, quoi. Il faut être débile. Car, qu'est-ce qu'il fait, Hegel? Voyez, supposons un enfant pas doué qui aurait mal compris Hegel, il dirait: Hegel, c'est un monsieur, c'est un philosophe, un drôle de philosophe qui dit A est non-A. Euh, on peut toujours dire n'importe quoi, mais ce serait une drôle d'idée de dire 'A est non-A'. L'intérêt serait très petit d'abord, ensuite ce serait idiot, ce serait vraiment idiot." Deleuze, *Course 1986.04.08,2* (00:33:40–00:35:00).

78 Hegel, *Science of Logic*, 440 [76].

79 Hegel, *Lectures on Logic*, 4.

80 Priest and Routley, "First Historical Introduction," 5–7.

81 Sigwart, *Logic 1*, 139 [188].

82 Ibid.

83 Kant, *Critique of Pure Reason*, A151/B190 (279 [196]).

84 Sigwart, *Logic 1*, 144–5 [195–6].

85 Hegel, *Lectures on Logic*, 5; Redding, *Analytic Philosophy*, 200; de Boer, *On Hegel*, 364.

86 Łukasiewicz, "On the Principle," 493–4.

87 Deleuze, *Difference and Repetition*, 310 (ft. 10) [64 (ft. 1)].

88 Hegel, *Encyclopaedia Logic*, 180 [237].

89 Hegel, *Science of Logic*, 413 [41].

90 Ibid., 417 [47].

91 Ibid., 417 [46–7]. As Henry Somers-Hall explains: "What Hegel is pointing to here is that we cannot see difference as the difference between two terms, as such a difference would rely on a prior identity; that is, they would differ in respect to something that was an identical determination [...]. Difference rather simply differs from itself; it is not a relation between two beings, but a relation purely to itself. Through this self-relation, however, difference turns out to be identity, as in differing from itself, difference differs from difference, and what differs from difference is identity." Somers-Hall, *Hegel, Deleuze ... Critique*, 147.

92 Hegel, *Science of Logic*, 415–16 [43–4].

93 Ibid., 416 [45]. "The *propositional form* itself already contradicts it, since a proposition promises a distinction between subject and predicate as well as identity; and the identity-proposition does not furnish what its form demands." Hegel, *Encyclopaedia Logic*, 180 [237]. "Equality is only an identity of [terms] that are *not the same*, not identical with one another." Ibid., 183 [242], brackets in the original. John Hibben clarifies the synthetic nature of the Principle of Identity by distinguishing the two A's in the formulation: "The formula which expresses the law of identity is not $A = A$. It should be $A = A'$, that is, A differs from A', and yet in spite of the difference is one with it. The former equation, $A = A$, expresses merely an absolute identity which is wholly stripped of all differences, and as such is without significance and value. Hegel defines identity, therefore, as an identity which reflects

its own self in every changing variety of manifestation, and in such a manner that the reflection of self is different from it, and yet so intimately connected with it as to be the same." Hibben, *Hegel's Logic*, 150-1.
94 Hegel, *Encyclopaedia Logic*, 181 [239]. See Hegel, *Science of Logic*, 414, 418 [42, 47].
95 Ibid., 422 [52]. See Hegel, *Encyclopaedia Logic*, 182 [240].
96 See Hegel, *Science of Logic*, 422-4 [53-5].
97 Ibid., 422 [53].
98 Hegel, *Lectures on Logic*, 136, brackets in the original.
99 Hyppolite, *Logic and Existence*, 119 [154].
100 See Hegel, *Science of Logic*, 423 [54].
101 Hegel, *Lectures on Logic*, 137, brackets in the original.
102 Ibid., 138.
103 Ibid.
104 Hegel, *Science of Logic*, 424-6 [55-8].
105 Ibid., 428-9 [61-2]; Hegel, *Encyclopaedia Logic*, 186 [245].
106 Hegel, *Lectures on Logic*, 139, italics are mine. We might still find it odd to think of the air as the opposite of the human body. Hyppolite speaks of the opposition being more between one thing and all that it is not in an exclusive, contradictory (rather than contrary) manner: "Not-A signifies all of what is not A." Hyppolite, *Logic and Existence*, 113 [145]; "Opposition is inevitable not because there is only a multiplicity of things, of finite modes, or of monads, but because each is in relation with the others, or rather with all the others, so that its distinction is its distinction from *all the rest*. The complete distinction of a thing reconnects it to the whole Universe." Ibid., 115 [148].
107 "*Contradiction resolves itself*. In the self-excluding reflection we have just considered, positive and negative, each in its self-subsistence, sublates itself; each is simply the transition or rather the self-transposition of itself into its opposite." Hegel, *Science of Logic*, 433 [67]. "Ordinary thinking […] holds these two determinations over against one another and has in mind *only them*, but not their *transition*, which is the essential point and which contains the contradiction. *Intelligent* reflection, to mention this here, consists, on the contrary, in grasping and asserting contradiction." Ibid., 441 [77-8].
108 Hegel, *Science of Logic*, 427 [59]. "It is thus the contradiction that, in positing identity with itself by *excluding* the negative, it makes itself into the *negative* of what it excludes from itself, that is, makes itself into its opposite. This, as excluded, is posited as free from that which excludes it, and therefore as reflected into itself and as itself exclusive. The exclusive reflection is thus a positing of the positive as excluding its opposite, so that this positing is immediately the positing of its opposite which it excludes. This is the absolute contradiction of the positive, but it is immediately the absolute contradiction of the negative." Ibid., 432 [65-6]. See Deleuze, *Logic of Sense*, 197 [202].
109 Deleuze, *Logic of Sense*, 202 (ft. 4) [202 (ft. 4)].
110 Deleuze, *Difference and Repetition*, 45 [64].
111 See Somers-Hall, *Hegel, Deleuze … Critique*, 149.
112 Hegel, *Science of Logic*, 442 [78].
113 Deleuze, *Difference and Repetition*, 53 [76].
114 Robert Brandom, who also emphasizes the logical exclusivity in Hegel's negation, makes a claim that is similar to Deleuze's: "Far from rejecting the law of

noncontradiction, I want to claim that Hegel radicalizes it, and places it at the very center of his thought." Brandom, *Tales of the Mighty*, 179.

115 Ralph Palm notes in a similar way how Hegel reconceives non-contradiction as double negation in terms of a contradiction of a contradiction: "In effect, what Hegel is after in each transition of his logic is [...] a double negation. If one thinks of contradiction as the strongest possible sort of negation, then a contradiction of a contradiction would be a type of double negation [...]. [...] There is an important difference between *non-contradiction* and the *contradiction of contradiction*; the first is a mere absence of contradiction, while the second is a determinate negation (or sublation) of contradiction." Palm, "Hegel's Contradictions," 139.

116 Deleuze, *Difference and Repetition*, 49 [70].

117 As Karen de Boer notes, "Hegel equally treats [the classical principle of non-contradiction] under the heading of the concept of identity." de Boer, "Hegel's Account of Contradiction," 358, bracketed insertion is mine. See Deleuze, *Course 1983.05.03,2* (00:03:50–00:07:40). Nathan Widder, when discussing the distinction between Hegelian contradiction and Deleuzian difference and heterogeneity, notes, "Dialectics does maintain a disjunction among differences, but Deleuze holds that in treating differences as opposites, it allows them to communicate only to the degree they mirror one another, thereby submitting them to the principles of identity." Widder, "Negation, Disjunction ... Forces," 28.

118 McGill and Parry, "Unity of Opposites," 421 (ft. 7), italics are mine.

119 Deleuze, *Course 1983.05.17,3* (00:58:40–01:00:10). As Ueberweg explains: "*Heraclitus* thought that anything is and is not, at the same time, and that all fleets. [...] *Plato* seeks to overcome this opposition by his distinction between the invariable world of Being or Ideas, whose every essence is always like to itself [...] and the changeable world of Becoming or of sensible things." Ueberweg, *System of Logic*, 232 [188–9].

120 Deleuze, *Course 1983.05.17,1* (00:15:40–00:16:40): "qui serait à la fois ce qu'elle est et ce qu'elle n'est pas (elle contredirait au tiers exclu)."

121 See Deleuze, *Course 1983.05.03,2* (00:54:10–00:55:20); Deleuze, *Course 1986.04.08,2* (00:33:50–00:35:00).

122 See Smith, *Essays on Deleuze*, 79–80.

123 Deleuze, *Course 1983.05.17,3* (00:28:10–00:35:00).

124 *The Cabinet of Dr. Caligari (Das Cabinet des Dr. Caligari)* directed by Robert Wiene © Decla-Bioscop 1920. All rights reserved. *Metropolis* directed by Fritz Lang © Universum Film 1927. All rights reserved. *Diary of a Country Priest (Journal d'un curé de campagne)* directed by Robert Bresson © Union générale cinématographique 1951. All rights reserved.

125 Deleuze, *Course 1983.05.17,3* (00:35:10–00:39:00); Deleuze, *Cinema 1*, 45–6 [66–7].

126 Deleuze, *Cinema 1*, 46 [67].

127 Deleuze, *Course 1983.05.03,2* (01:05:20–01:08:20).

128 Ibid. (01:08:20–01:12:30).

129 Pascal, *Pensées*, 27 [269].

130 Deleuze, *Course 1983.05.24,1* (00:23:30–00:27:00).

131 Ibid. (00:28:20–00:36:50). See Serres, *Système de Leibniz 2*, 666.

132 See Teo Grünberg's excellent account of the logical operators or connectives, including the disjunctions: Grünberg, *Modern Logic*, 8–15.

133 See for instance: Priest, *Introduction to Non-Classical Logic*, 154.

134 Kant, *Jäsche Logic*, 560 [53].

135 Ibid., 560, 600 [53, 104].

136 Ibid., 600 [104].
137 Ibid., 602–3 [106].
138 Ibid., 603 [107].
139 Ibid.
140 Ibid., 604 [108]. Public domain images are from Archive.org (the German edition): https://archive.org/details/kantsgesammeltes09imma.
141 Ibid., 603 [107].
142 Ibid., 117 [611].
143 Ibid., 623 [130]. For the more formal formulation of disjunctive syllogism, see ibid., 624 [130].
144 Kant, *Critique of Pure Reason*, A304/B360–61 (390 [315]).
145 Rohlf, "Ideas of Pure Reason," 195–7.
146 Kant, *Critique of Pure Reason*, A331/B387–88 (404 [333–4]).
147 Ibid., A322/B378 (400 [327]).
148 Ibid., A322/B378 (399–400 [327]), non-elliptical, bracketed insertion is in the original.
149 Ibid., A323/B379–80, A331/B387 (400, 404 [328, 333]).
150 Rohlf, "Ideas of Pure Reason," 195.
151 Ibid.
152 Ibid., 196, quoting Kant, *Critique of Pure Reason*, A viii (99 [11]).
153 Kant, *Critique of Pure Reason*, A323/B379 (400 [328]).
154 Ibid., A335/B392 (406 [337]).
155 Ibid., A323/B379–80 (400 [328]).
156 Ibid., A335/B392 (406 [337]).
157 Ibid., A334/B391 (406 [336]).
158 Ibid., A334–35/B392 (406 [336]).
159 Deleuze, *Logic of Sense*, 335 [343].
160 Ibid.
161 Ibid.
162 Ibid., 336 [344].
163 Ibid., 336 [343].
164 Ibid., 295–6, 324, 340–1 [297–8, 329, 348–50].
165 Ponce, "Introduction (*Baphomet*)," xv.
166 Lévi, *Transcendental Magic*, 288, 297 [*Dogme et rituel 2*, 208, 224–5].
167 Klossowski, *The Baphomet*, 5–8, 81–2 [7–11, 112–13].
168 Ibid., 7 [10].
169 Ibid., 31–7 [43–52].
170 Ibid., 39–40 [53–5].
171 Deleuze, *Logic of Sense*, 332–3 [339].
172 Klossowski, *The Baphomet*, 62 [87].
173 Deleuze, *Logic of Sense*, 333 [340].
174 Klossowski, *The Baphomet*, 40 [54].
175 Ibid., 40 [55].
176 Ibid., 41 [56].
177 Ibid., 58 [80], bracketed insertion is mine.
178 Ibid., 63–4 [88–9].
179 Ibid., 64 [89–90].
180 Ibid., 65–6 [91–2].
181 Ibid., 41 [55].

182 "The saint underwent the ultimate test she had assigned herself, bound to the law that modifies the breaths among themselves, she herself being modified in Ogier, [...] If indeed she could confuse her own movements with those of the juvenile body she had usurped ... " Ibid., 144 [200]. In another scene, the Theresa/Ogier figure is first referred to as female, but after her/his male genitals are exposed, the character is said to be "a young boy." Ibid., 105-6 [146-7].
183 Klossowski, *The Baphomet*, 90, 136, 150 [123, 189-90, 210].
184 Ibid., 93 [130].
185 And note that this androgyny is at times brought out by Klossowski's alternating between the male and female pronouns when describing Theresa's/Ogier's actions: "Now he [*lui*]- chin steady in his girlish palm—was defying me with everything which in past times she [*elle*] would only let me glimpse in passing [...]." Ibid., 150 [210].
186 Ibid., 91-6 [127-34].
187 Ibid., 133 [185].
188 Ibid., 97 [135-6].
189 Ibid., 99 [138].
190 Ibid., 133-4 [185-7].
191 Ibid., 90, 104-6 [124, 144-8].
192 Ibid., 102 [141-2].
193 Ibid., 102-3 [142-3].
194 Ibid., 110-11 [154].
195 Deleuze, *Logic of Sense*, 334 [341], enumerations are my additions, for comparison with the previous enumerated list of the order of God.
196 Ibid., 339 [348].
197 Ibid.
198 Deleuze and Guattari, *Anti-Oedipus*, 76 [90].
199 Deleuze, *Logic of Sense*, 199 [203].
200 Deleuze and Guattari, *Anti-Oedipus*, 76 [90-1].
201 Ibid., 76 [90], emphasis mine.
202 Ibid., 76 [91].
203 Ibid., 76-7 [91].
204 In the text, just before speaking of the schizophrenic not reducing "two contraries to an identity of the same" (*Il n'identifie pas deux contraires au même*), they say that the schizophrenic "does not abolish disjunction by identifying the contradictory elements" (*il ne supprime pas la disjonction en identifiant les contradictoires*). Ibid.
205 Ibid., 77 [92].

Chapter 5

1 For, then they would be identical anyway, according to Leibniz' law of identity. Leibniz, *Discourse on Metaphysics*, 60 [1541].
2 Ibid., 59-60 [1540]. On these and related matters concerning Leibniz's notion of individual substance, see Woolhouse, "On the Nature." Note that in the following I have selected the passages in Leibniz that more or less suit the sort of interpretation Deleuze gives to Leibniz's incompossibility. The task of giving a completely accurate and consistent account of Leibniz's theories of possible worlds and of compossibility

is far more complex than this, and there are a variety of theories on how to do so. On these matters, see especially Brown and Chiek, *Leibniz on Compossibility*, 7–14. Similarly, the next section on the Stoics is meant to present their ideas in a way that corresponds to Deleuze's interpretation and is not meant to stand on its own as a reliable representation of their philosophy. For accurate studies of the Stoics in comparison to Deleuze's interpretations, see for instance Sellars, "Six Theses"; Sellars, "Ethics of the Event"; Sellars, "Aiôn and Chronos."
3. Leibniz, "First Truths," 268 [520]; Leibniz, *Correspondence between Leibniz and Arnauld*, 78–9, 121–2, 233 [19–20, 49, 126]; Leibniz, *Discourse on Metaphysics*, 63–4 [1546–7].
4. Leibniz, *Correspondence between Leibniz and Arnauld*, 128 [54].
5. Deleuze, *The Fold*, 59 [79].
6. Leibniz, *Theodicy*, 128 [107]; Leibniz, *Monadology*, 275 [616]; Leibniz, *Discourse on Metaphysics*, 60 [1541]; Leibniz, *Correspondence between Leibniz and Arnauld*, 79, 89–90, 109–10, 133, 233 [19, 27, 40–1, 57, 126].
7. Leibniz, *Correspondence between Leibniz and Arnauld*, 131 [55].
8. Priest and Routley, "Outline of the History," 24–5.
9. Leibniz, *Theodicy*, 128 [107].
10. Leibniz, *Monadology*, 275 [615–16]; Leibniz, *Correspondence between Leibniz and Arnauld*, 134 [58].
11. Leibniz, "On Contingency," 29 [1651].
12. See Leibniz, "On First Truths," 29–30 [1442–3]; Brown and Chiek, "Introduction," 4–5.
13. Leibniz, *Theodicy*, 128 [107]; Leibniz, *Correspondence between Leibniz and Arnauld*, 80, 123 [20, 50].
14. Leibniz, *Monadology*, 275 [615–16]; Leibniz, "First Truths," 268–9 [520]; Leibniz, *Correspondence between Leibniz and Arnauld*, 78, 120 [18–19, 48].
15. Leibniz, *Correspondence between Leibniz and Arnauld*, 108 [40].
16. Deleuze, *The Fold*, 59 [79].
17. Leibniz, "Letters to Louis Bourguet," 661 [572–3].
18. Canguilhem, *On the Normal*, 81 [119].
19. "[…] le *grisonner* n'est pas moins positif que le *noircir*." Deleuze, *Logic of Sense*, 195 [200], emphasis in the original. In a later section we see why the adjectives were converted to verbs in this passage.
20. Deleuze, *Logic of Sense*, 196 [200–1]. While the real world incompatibility of the predicates is "alogical," I still think that their affirmative synthetic disjunction is another matter that can be understood using non-classical logic.
21. Leibniz, *Correspondence between Leibniz and Arnauld*, 120, 131 [48, 55–6].
22. "Letter to Coste," 193 [400]; Leibniz, *Theodicy*, 267–8 [252]; Leibniz, *Monadology*, 275 [615–16].
23. Leibniz, "On the Secrets," 21–3 [472].
24. Leibniz, *Monadology*, 275 [616], emphasis mine. Deleuze defines compossibility along similar lines: "the condition of a maximum of continuity for a maximum of difference." Deleuze, *Logic of Sense*, 332 [339].
25. Leibniz, *Correspondence between Leibniz and Arnauld*, 127–8 [53], emphasis mine.
26. Ibid., 111–12, 128, 132 [42–3, 53, 56].
27. Nolt, *Logics*, 310.
28. Based on: ibid., 366. Nolt's diagram has more branches, and its caption reads: "The thick line represents the actual world. The thinner lines represent temporal portions

of merely possible worlds that share the actual world's past. Specific times are represented by points on any of the lines."

29 Leibniz, *Correspondence between Leibniz and Arnauld*, 78, 128-9 [18-19, 54].
30 As "plusieurs Adams disjunctivement possibles." Leibniz, *Correspondence with Arnauld*, 110 [54], emphasis mine.
31 Leibniz, *Discourse on Metaphysics*, 58 [1537].
32 Ibid., 64 [1546-47]; Leibniz, *Correspondence between Leibniz and Arnauld*, 125-6 [52].
33 Deleuze, *Logic of Sense*, 197 [201].
34 Ibid.
35 Ibid.
36 Ibid., 197 [201-2].
37 Nolt, *Logics*, 385.
38 Deleuze, *Cinema 2*, 47, 280 [69].
39 Maxwell, "Last Essays," 443, quoted in Prigogine and Stengers, *Order out of Chaos*, 73 [85].
40 Prigogine and Stengers, *Order out of Chaos*, 161-2 (see *Nouvelle alliance*, 161-9).
41 Deleuze, *Cinema 2*, 47 [69].
42 Prigogine and Stengers, *Order out of Chaos*, 169-70 (see *Nouvelle alliance*, 167-8).
43 This diagram is a modification, drawing from the one at: Prigogine and Stengers, *Order out of Chaos*, 161.
44 Based on the diagram at: Prigogine and Stengers, *Order out of Chaos*, 170 [168].
45 Borges, "Garden of Forking Paths," 24-8 [109-15]; Deleuze, *Course 1980.04.22,1* (00:39:00-00:46:22); Deleuze, *Course 1983.11.29,3* (00:09:30-00:14:10); Deleuze, *Course 1984.01.10,3* (00:11:30-00:11:50); Deleuze, *Cinema 2*, 47 [68]; Deleuze, *The Fold*, 62 [83-4].
46 Borges, "Garden of Forking Paths," 24 [109].
47 Ibid., 26 [111-12].
48 Ibid., 26 [112].
49 Ibid., 28 [114-15].
50 Otherwise see the excellent presentations of Stoic philosophy in relation to Deleuze's in Bowden, *Priority of Events*; Bowden, "Deleuze et les Stoïciens"; Williams, *Gilles Deleuze's Logic*; Williams, *Gilles Deleuze's Philosophy*, and also in Sellars, "Aiôn and Chronos"; Sellars, "Ethics of the Event"; Sellars, "Six Theses."
51 Bréhier, quoted and translated in Long, *Hellenistic Philosophy*, 120 [*Histoire de la Philosophie*, 299]. See Deleuze, *Logic of Sense*, 162 [167]; and Diog. Laert. *Vit. phil.* 7.39-40 (*Lives 2*, 149-51 [148-50]).
52 As Anneli Luhtala observes, the Stoics, with one known exception (Posidonius), advocated starting a philosophical education with the study of logic. Luhtala, *On the Origin*, 58. So like the Stoics, we here begin our "course with Logic, go on to Physics, and finish with Ethics." Diog. Laert. *Vit. phil.* 7.40 (*Lives 2*, 151 [150]).
53 Luhtala, *On the Origin*, 58-9; Long, *Hellenistic Philosophy*, 120.
54 Sanford, *If P Then Q*, 14-15. Sanford quotes a passage by Aristotle where the constituents of the conditional are given as sentences, but he remarks that Aristotle nonetheless developed a logic of terms while the Stoics instead created a logic of sentences or propositions.
55 Diog. Laert. *Vit. phil.* 7.74-75 (*Lives 2*, 183 [182]).
56 Cic. *Fat.* 6.11-19.45 (*De oratore 3*, 205-43 [204-42]).
57 Goldschmidt, *Système stoïcien*, 82-3.

58 Diog. Laert. *Vit. phil.* 7.65–66 (*Lives 2*, 175 [174]).
59 Diog. Laert. *Vit. phil.* 7.63–64 (*Lives 2*, 173 [172]); Clem. *Stom.* 8.9.26.3–4 (*Eighth Stromateus*, 117 [96-7]); Bréhier, *Théorie des incorporels*, 14–20; Graeser, "Stoic Theory of Meaning," 94.
60 Bréhier, *Théorie des incorporels*, 14–15; Sext. Emp. *Adv. math.* 8.11–12 (*L&S 1*, 195–6 [*Opera 2.5*, 106]).
61 Priest, "Speaking of the Ineffable," 15, italics at the end and bracketed insertions are mine.
62 Bréhier, *Théorie des incorporels*, 1.
63 Ibid., 2; Sen. *Ep.* 58.13–15 (*In Ten Volumes 4.1*, 393–7 [392–6]); Alex. *In Ar. Top.* 301,19–25 (*L&S 1*, 162 [*Commentaria in Aristotelem 2.2*, 301]).
64 Sext. Emp. *Adv. math.* 10.218 (*L&S 1*, 162 [*Opera 2.5*, 349]).
65 Gal. *Meth. med.* 10.155,1–8 (*L&S 1*, 163 [*Medicorum Graecorum 10*, 155]); Stob. *Ecl.* 1.106,5–23 (*L&S 1*, 304 [*Anthologium 1*, 106]).
66 Gold schmidt, *Système stoïcien*, 91–5.
67 Sext. Emp. *Pyr.* 3.14 (*In Three Volumes 1*, 335 [334]).
68 Goldschmidt, *Système stoïcien*, 95–6.
69 Euseb. *Praep. evang.* 15.14.1–2, 15.18.2 (*L&S 1*, 273, 276 [*Werke 8.2*, 378–9, 383]); Diog. Laert. *Vit. phil.* 7.141 (*Lives 2*, 245 [244]); Aet. *Plac.* 1.7.33 (*L&S 1*, 274–5 [*De placita philosophorum*, 305–6]).
70 Stob. *Ecl.* 1.25,3–27,4 (*L&S 1*, 326–7 [*Anthologium 1*, 25–7]); Plut. *Comm. not.* 1075E (*L&S 1*, 327 [*Moralia 6*, 331]).
71 Calc. *In Tim.* 144 (*L&S 1*, 331 [*Plato latinus 4*, 183]).
72 Euseb. *Praep. evang.* 15.14.1 (*L&S 1*, 273 [*Werke 8.2*, 378–9]); Aet. *Plac.* 1.7.33 (*L&S 1*, 274–5 [*De placita philosophorum*, 305–6]).
73 Diog. Laert. *Vit. phil.* 7.142 (*Lives 2*, 247 [246]).
74 Plut. *Comm. not.* 1085C–D (*L&S 1*, 282 [*Moralia 6*, 359]); Gal. *Plen.* 7.525,9–14 (*L&S 1*, 282 [*Medicorum Graecorum 7*, 525]). See Sambursky, *Physics of the Stoics*, 4.
75 Gal. *Plac.* 5.3.8 (*L&S 1*, 282 [*Medicorum Graecorum 7*, 525]); Alex. *Mixt.* 224,14–27 (*L&S 1*, 282 [*Supplementum Aristotelicum 2.2*, 224]).
76 Alex. *Mixt.* 218,2–6 (*L&S 1*, 291 [*Supplementum Aristotelicum 2.2*, 218]).
77 Cic. *Nat. D.* 1.39–41, 2.18–22, 2.87–90 (*In Twenty-Eight 19*, 41–3, 141–5, 207–11 [40–2, 140–4, 206–10]); Aet. *Plac.* 1.7.33 (*L&S 1*, 274–5 [*De placita philosophorum*, 305–6]).
78 Philo. *Quaes. Gen.* 2.4 (*L&S 1*, 285 [*Paralipomena Armena*, 77]); Diog. Laert. *Vit. phil.* 7.138–140 (*Lives 2*, 243–5 [242–4]); Gal. *Musc. mot.* 4.402,12–403,10 (*L&S 1*, 283 [*Medicorum Graecorum 4*, 402–3]); Alex. *Mixt.* 223,25–36 (*L&S 1*, 283 [*Supplementum Aristotelicum 2.2*, 223]); Clem. *Stom.* 5.47.6–48.3 (*Writings of Clement 2*, 249 [358]). See Sambursky, *Physics of the Stoics*, 5.
79 Alex. *Mixt.* 224,23–6 (*L&S 1*, 282 [*Supplementum Aristotelicum 2.2*, 224]); Nem. *Nat. hom.* 70,6–71,4 (*L&S 1*, 283 [*De natura hominis*, 70–1]); Philo. *Quaes. Gen.* 2.4 (*L&S 1*, 285 [*Paralipomena Armena*, 77]).
80 Alex. *Mixt.* 216,14–17 (*L&S 1*, 290 [*Supplementum Aristotelicum 2.2*, 216]). See Deleuze, *Logic of Sense*, 7 [13].
81 Gal. *Intr.* 14.726,7–11 (*L&S 1*, 284 [*Medicorum Graecorum 14*, 726]). See Sambursky, *Physics of the Stoics*, 7–8.
82 Nem. *Nat. hom.* 78,7–79,2 (*L&S 1*, 272 [*De natura hominis*, 78–9]).

83 Philo. *Leg. alleg.* 2.22-23 (*L&S 1*, 284 [*Opera quae supersunt 1*, 95]); Cic. *Off.* 1.132 (*De officiis*, 133-5 [132-4]); Gal. *Intr.* 14.726,7-11 (*L&S 1*, 284 [*Medicorum Graecorum 14*, 726]); Orig. *Princ.* 3.1.2-3 (*L&S 1*, 313 [*Werke 5*, 196-7]).

84 Gal. *Foet.* 4.698,2-9 (*L&S 1*, 314 [*Medicorum Graecorum 4*, 698]); Calc. *In Tim.* 220 (*L&S 1*, 315 [*Plato latinus 4*, 232-3]).

85 Aet. *Plac.* 4.21.1-4 (*L&S 1*, 315-16 [*De placita philosophorum*, 410]); Stob. *Ecl.* 1.368,12-20 (*L&S 1*, 316 [*Anthologium 1*, 368]); Luhtala, *On the Origin*, 67-8.

86 Euseb. *Praep. evang.* 15.14.1 (*L&S 1*, 273 [*Werke 8.2*, 378-9]); Cic. *Acad.* 1.39-40 (*In Twenty-Eight 19*, 449 [448]); Sext. Emp. *Adv. math.* 8.263 (*L&S 1*, 272 [*Opera 2.5*, 162]); Nem. *Nat. hom.* 78,7-79,2 (*L&S 1*, 272 [Nemesius, *De natura hominis*, 78-9]).

87 Plut. *St. rep.* 1053F-1054B (*L&S 1*, 284 [*Moralia 6*, 270]). See Sambursky, *Physics of the Stoics*, 7-8.

88 Alex. *Mixt.* 218,1-2 (*L&S 1*, 291 [*Supplementum Aristotelicum 2.2*, 218]).

89 A related example is given in Clem. *Stom.* 8.9.29.1 ("Eighth Stromateus," 121 [98]). But here the discussion is about the "suitability" of the wood to burn when mixing with fire.

90 For, under Stoic metaphysics where only bodies are real, we would not say that the iron is participating in some idea for hotness or that it falls under some incorporeal class that groups hot things. Nor would we say that it is one body enclosed in another body, because the hotness, although corporeal, is something physically inherent to the iron rather than being a body into which the iron is contained. See Bréhier, *Théorie des incorporels*, 20-1.

91 Ibid., 19.

92 "On ne doit pas dire, pensaient-ils « L'arbre est vert » mais « L'arbre verdoie »." Ibid., 20., using the English translation for certain terminology from Deleuze, *Logic of Sense*, 24 [33]. For a more detailed linguistic discussion of the relation between verbs and incorporeal predicates, see Luhtala, *On the Origin*, 84, 88-100.

93 Deleuze, *Logic of Sense*, 25 [33].

94 Luhtala, *On the Origin*, 62-3; Bréhier, *Théorie des incorporels*, 2.

95 Sellars, "Aiôn and Chronos."

96 Sext. Emp. *Adv. math.* 8.263, 9.211 (*L&S 1*, 272, 333 [*Opera 2.5*, 162, 258-9]); Clem. *Stom.* 8.9.26.3-4 ("Eighth Stromateus," 117 [96-7, 99]); Stob. *Ecl.* 1.138,14-139,4 (*L&S 1*, 333 [*Anthologium 1*, 138-9]); Cic. *Acad.* 1.39-40 (*In Twenty-Eight 19*, 449 [448]); Nem. *Nat. hom.* 78,7-79,2, 81,6-10 (*L&S 1*, 272 [*De natura hominis*, 78-9, 81]). See Deleuze, *Logic of Sense*, 7-8 [13-14].

97 Long and Sedley, *L&S 1*, 343, emphasis mine.

98 For, on the one hand there is a durationless cut dividing an eternal time that goes on forever in both directions, while on the other hand, the act of dividing any durational present always yields a smaller duration; and every expansion of a durational present always yields another finitely limited duration, too. Stob. *Ecl.* 1.105,8-16, 1.106,5-23 (*L&S 1*, 304-5 [*Anthologium 1*, 105-6]).

99 Goldschmidt, *Système stoïcien*, 38-40. See Marc. Aur. *Med.* 4.3,7, 5.24, 12.7, 12.32 (*Meditations*, 48, 66, 146, 151 [25, 43, 117, 121]). Also see Sellars's critique of Goldschmidt's implementation of this term. Sellars, "Aiôn and Chronos," 193-6.

100 Stob. *Ecl.* 1.105,8-16, 1.106,5-23 (*L&S 1*, 304-5 [*Anthologium 1*, 105-6]). See Chrysippus's notion of interminable corporeal division: Stob. *Ecl.* 1.142,2-6 (*L&S 1*, 297 [*Anthologium 1*, 142]); Diog. Laert. *Vit. phil.* 7.150 (*Lives 2*, 255 [254]); Plut. *Comm. not.* 1078E-1079C (*L&S 1*, 298 [*Moralia 6*, 340-2]).

101 Diog. Laert. *Vit. phil.* 7.141 (*Lives 2*, 245 [244]); Goldschmidt, *Système stoïcien*, 30–43. As with corporeals and incorporeals, only the present exists, the past and future subsist. Plut. *Comm. not.* 1081C–1082A (*L&S 1*, 304–5 [*Moralia 6*, 347–9]); Stob. *Ecl.* 1.106,5–23 (*L&S 1*, 304 [*Anthologium 1*, 106]).
102 Plut. *Comm. not.* 1081C–1082A (*L&S 1*, 304–5 [*Moralia 6*, 347–9]); Stob. *Ecl.* 1.105,8–16 (*L&S 1*, 305 [*Anthologium 1*, 105]).
103 "Par là, l'étendue temporelle qui « accompagne » l'acte, prend toute la réalité dont elle est capable, sans cependant cesser d'être un incorporel." Goldschmidt, *Système stoïcien*, 41.
104 Based on the diagrams at: Sellars, "Aiôn and Chronos," 183. See Deleuze, *Logic of Sense*, 186–92 [190–7]. For the now as durationless limit, see Plut. *Comm. not.* 1081C–1082A (*L&S 1*, 304–5 [*Moralia 6*, 347–9]) and Sellars, "Aiôn and Chronos," 188.
105 Cleom. *Mot. circul.* 202,11–23 (*Cleomedes' Lectures on Astronomy*, 149–50 [202]); Stob. *Ecl.* 1.106,5–23 (*L&S 1*, 304 [*Anthologium 1*, 106]); Stob. *Ecl.* 1.219,24–1.220,2 (Brunschwig, *Papers in Hellenistic Philosophy*, 142–3, especially ft.128 [*Anthologium 1*, 219–20]); Plut. *Comm. not.* 1084C-D (*L&S 1*, 306 [*Moralia 6*, 356–7]); Goldschmidt, *Système stoïcien*, 30–1, 40–1.
106 Goldschmidt, *Système stoïcien*, 79–83, 91–9.
107 See Cic. *Div.* 1.127 (*De senectute, amicitia, divinatione*, 363 [362]).
108 In our example, the activity that expresses *heating* all throughout its duration also expressing *forging*, binding it into a longer duration, but it also expresses *waring*, and we can go up and up through the temporal scales to the whole of human history and finally to the whole of cosmic history by considering the broader activities and ends that each is fatally and causally bound up with.
109 Goldschmidt, *Système stoïcien*, 81–8.
110 See Williams, *Gilles Deleuze's Philosophy*, 150.
111 Sen. *Ep.* 117.13 (*Ad Lucilium 3*, 345–7 [344–6]).
112 Diog. Laert. *Vit. phil.* 7.157–158 (*Lives 2*, 261 [260]).
113 Aet. *Plac.* 4.21.1–4 (*L&S 1*, 315–16 [*De placita philosophorum*, 410–11]).
114 Aet. *Plac.* 4.11.1–4 (*L&S 1*, 238 [ibid., 400]); Diog. Laert. *Vit. phil.* 7.49–52 (*Lives 2*, 159–61 [158–60]); Cic. *Acad.* 1.40 (*In Twenty-Eight 19*, 449 [448]). See Bréhier, *Théorie des incorporels*, 16.
115 Diog. Laert. *Vit. phil.* 7.49–52 (*Lives 2*, 159–61 [158–60]); Sext. Emp. *Adv. math.* 8.409–410 (*L&S 1*, 163 [*Opera 2.5*, 196]); Bréhier, *Théorie des incorporels*, 17; Goldschmidt, *Système stoïcien*, 81–3. Note that the sayable is never actually signified by a sentence. A significant utterance is a body that signifies its corresponding concept, which in turn expresses *but does not signify* the incorporeal sayable that organizes this corporeal rational impression as well as the external corporeal activity. In other words, the veridical correspondence between the external world and our propositional thoughts about it is built upon our thoughts and their respective external activities sharing the same incorporeal sayable, whose rational order is that of the external world and of thinking. Sext. Emp. *Adv. math.* 8.11–12 (*L&S 1*, 195–6 [*Opera 2.5*, 106–7]); Bréhier, *Théorie des incorporels*, 14–18.
116 Aet. *Plac.* 4.12.1–5 (*L&S 1*, 237 [*De placita philosophorum*, 401–2]); Diog. Laert. *Vit. phil.* 7.45–46 (*Lives 2*, 155 [154]); Sext. Emp. *Adv. math.* 7.247–252 (*L&S 1*, 243 [*Opera 2.5*, 58–9]).
117 Sext. Emp. *Adv. math.* 7.242–243 (*L&S 1*, 238 [*Opera 2.5*, 57]); Cic. *Acad.* 2.37–39 (*In Twenty-Eight 19*, 515–17 [514–16]).

118 Sext. Emp. *Adv. math.* 7.402–408 (*L&S 1*, 244 [*Opera 2.5*, 93]); Stob. *Ecl.* 2.88,2–6 (*L&S 1*, 197 [*Anthologium 2*, 88]); Orig. *Princ.* 3.1.2–3 (*L&S 1*, 313 [*Werke 5*, 196–97]); Cic. *Off.* 1.132 (*De officiis*, 133–5 [132–4]); Philo. *Leg. alleg.* 1.30 (317 [*Opera quae supersunt 1*, 68]); Stob. *Ecl.* 2.86,17–87,6 (*L&S 1*, 317 [*Anthologium 2*, 86–7]).
119 See Goldschmidt, *Système stoïcien*, 85–9, 100–1.
120 Cic. *Fat.* 41 (*L&S 1*, 387 [*De oratore 3*, 236]). Deleuze adds to this the notion of affirmation: "The Stoics went to astonishing lengths in order to escape necessity and to affirm the 'fated' without affirming the necessary." Deleuze, *Logic of Sense*, 40 [47].
121 Goldschmidt, *Système stoïcien*, 89, 99–100, 109, 231.
122 Hippol. *Haer.* 1.21 (*L&S 1*, 386 [*Refutatio Omnium Haeresium*, 83]).
123 Cic. *Fat.* 28–30 (*L&S 1*, 339 [*De oratore 3*, 224]).
124 Cic. *Fat.* 40 (ibid., 237 [236]).
125 Cic. *Fat.* 40–1 (ibid.); Aet. *Plac.* 1.28.4 (*L&S 1*, 336 [*De placita philosophorum*, 324]); Gell. *Noc. Att.* 6.2.3 (*L&S 1*, 336 [*Noctes Atticae 1*, 412]. Note: as 7.2 in *L&S* and *Stoicorum veterum fragmenta* 2.1000).
126 Stob. *Ecl.* 1.138,23–139,4 (*L&S 1*, 333 [*Anthologium 1*, 138–9]).
127 Stob. *Ecl.* 1.79,1–12 (*L&S 1*, 337 [*Anthologium 1*, 79]). And from Cicero: "By 'fate', I mean what the Greeks call heimarmenē—an ordering and sequence of causes, since it is the connexion of cause to cause which out of itself produces anything. It is everlasting truth, flowing from all eternity. Consequently nothing has happened which was not going to be, and likewise nothing is going to be of which nature does not contain causes working to bring that very thing about. This makes it intelligible that fate should be, not the 'fate' of superstition, but that of physics, an everlasting cause of things—why past things happened, why present things are now happening, and why future things will be." Cic. *Div.* 1.125–126 (*L&S 1*, 337 [*De senectute, amicitia, divinatione*, 360]).
128 See Epict. *Diss.* 2.19.1–5 (*Discourses*, 122–3 [189–91]) and Cic. *Fat.* 11–21 (*De oratore 3*, 205–17 [204–16].
129 Cic. *Fat.* 43–5 (*De oratore 3*, 241–3 [240–2]).
130 Gell. *Noc. Att.* 19.1.17 (*L&S 1*, 419 [*Attic Nights 3*, 352], the parentheses are brackets in Long and Sedley.
131 Clem. *Paid.* 1.8.63.1–2 (*L&S 1*, 371–2 [*Clemens Alexandrinus 1*, 127]).
132 Goldschmidt, *Système stoïcien*, 88.
133 Marc. Aur. *Med.* 5.8,12 (*Meditations*, 61 [37]), typography modified. "Love and desire that alone which happens to you, and is destined by providence for you." Marc. Aur. *Med.* 7.57 (*Meditations*, 91 [67]). See also Marc. Aur. *Med.* 2.3, 4.34, 4.44, 4.49, 5.27, 6.1, 6.41, 6.38, 7.18, 7.45, 8.17, 8.36, 8.50, 10.5, and 11.34.
134 Diog. Laert. *Vit. phil.* 7.86 (*L&S 1*, 346 [*Lives 2*, 194]).
135 Gell. *Noc. Att.* 19.1.17–18 (*L&S 1*, 419 [*Attic Nights 3*, 352]).
136 Epict. *Diss.* 2.18.15–18 (*Discourses*, 120–1 [186]).
137 Epict. *Diss.* 2.18.24–25 (*Discourses*, 121 [187–8]), emphasis mine. In this way, the force of the given impression "slides over [our minds] fairly smoothly and without obstruction." Gell. *Noc. Att.* 6.2 (*L&S 1*, 388 [*Attic Nights 3*, 413], see *L&S 2*, 384), bracketed insertion is mine. Note: as 7.2 in *L&S* and *Stoicorum veterum fragmenta* 2.1000. Here we do seem to have an exclusion when the better impulses succeed. Or maybe they continue but not to an effectual degree. Regardless, my claim is that before the exclusion would happen, there would need first to be a paraconsistent combination.

138 Deleuze, *Logic of Sense*, 166 [172]; Goldschmidt, *Système stoïcien*, 100-1, see especially ft.1 of p. 101; Epict. *Diss*. 1.12.8-9, 1.17.18-26, 1.22.9-11, 2.1.4-12, 2.10.1-13, 2.15, 2.23.1-20, Epict. *Ench*. 1 (*Discourses*, 33, 42-3, 51, 75-6, 95-6, 109-11, 137-9, 287 [51, 65, 78-9, 113-15, 145-7, 167-70, 212-16, 5*-6*]). For *prohairesis* applied to the handsome man of beautiful woman situation, see Epict. *Diss*. 3.3.14-15 (*Discourses*, 158 [244-5]).
139 Sen. *Ep*. 92.11-13 (*Ad Lucilium 2*, 453-5 [452-4]). And the Stoics think we should live our lives in accordance with nature. Stob. *Ecl*. 2.75,11-76,8 (*L&S 1*, 394 [*Anthologium 2*, 75-6]); Diog. Laert. *Vit. phil*. 7.86-87 (*Lives 2*, 195 [194]).
140 Stob. *Ecl*. 2.76,9-15 (*L&S 1*, 357 [*Anthologium 2*, 76]); Sext. Emp. *Adv. math*. 11.22-26 (*L&S 1*, 371 [*Opera 2.5*, 380-1]).
141 Alex. *Mantissa* 164,3-9 (*L&S 1*, 401 [*Supplementum Aristotelicum 2.1*, 164]).
142 Epict. *Diss*. 1.1.7-17, 2.19.32 (*Discourses*, 5-6, 125 [8-9, 195]); Goldschmidt, *Système stoïcien*, 110; Deleuze, *Logic of Sense*, 164-5 [169-71] (translated there as "usage of representations").
143 Deleuze writes: "To the extent that divergence is affirmed and disjunction becomes a positive synthesis, it seems that all events, even contraries, are compatible [...]. Incompatibility does not exist between two events, but between an event and the world or the individual which actualizes another event as divergent. At this point, there is something which does not allow itself to be reduced to a logical contradiction between predicates and which is nevertheless an incompatibility." Ibid., 203 [208].
144 Deleuze, *Logic of Sense*, 166 [172], bracketed insertion is mine.
145 Deleuze, *Cinema 2*, 142 [191-2].
146 Cic. *Fat*. 41-4 (*De oratore 3*, 237-41 [236-40]).
147 Cic. *Fat*. 30 (*De oratore 3*, 225-7 [224-6]; see *L&S 1*, 339-40); Euseb. *Praep. evang*. 6.8.25-9 (*L&S 1*, 389 [*Werke 8.1*, 325-6]); Deleuze, *Logic of Sense*, 14, 11, 196 [15, 18, 200].
148 See Cic. *Fat*. 36-45 (*De oratore 3*, 233-43 [232-42]). There is an important distinction between "perfect and principal causes," which necessitate one particular outcome and not others, and "auxiliary and proximate causes," which on their own are not sufficient to necessitate some certain effect. The impulses that we receive are given to us by perfect and principal causality, and our reaction will still be caused by these impressions that we have received; however, our response results from auxiliary and proximate causality. See Goldschmidt, *Système stoïcien*, 107-10.
149 See Williams, *Gilles Deleuze's Philosophy*, 151.

Chapter 6

1 Deleuze, *Course 1972.02.15* (no audio). See Deleuze and Guattari, *Anti-Oedipus*, 233 [277].
2 Deleuze, *Course 1972.03.07* (no audio).
3 For a thorough analysis of how Deleuze's and Guattari's sense of axiomatics and its related concepts are not entirely in line with their precise mathematical sense, see Roffe, "Axiomatic Set Theory." For our purposes here, we need not critique Deleuze's and Guattari's portrayal of these notions. We simply must come to an explicit articulation of how exactly they conceive them.

4   For those who seek a richer, more detailed, and faithful account, there are a number of excellent sources, including for instance: Buchanan, *Deleuze and Guattari's Anti-Oedipus*; Bogue, *Deleuze and Guattari*; Massumi, *User's Guide*.
5   Deleuze, *Course 1971.11.16* (no audio); *Course 1971.12.14* (no audio); Deleuze, *Course 1971.12.21* (no audio); Deleuze, *Course 1972.02.22* (no audio); Deleuze, *Course 1972.03.07* (no audio); Deleuze, *Course 1972.04.18* (no audio); Deleuze, *Course 1980.02.05,1* (00:40:30–00:42:10).
6   Deleuze, *Course 1971.11.16* (no audio).
7   Ibid.
8   See for instance: Deleuze and Guattari, *Anti-Oedipus*, 5–6, 8, 33, 36, 142, 149, 168, 176 [12, 14, 40, 43–4, 166, 175, 198, 208].
9   Deleuze, *Course 1972.02.15* (no audio).
10 Deleuze, *Course 1971.11.16* (no audio).
11 Deleuze and Guattari, *Thousand Plateaus*, 509–10 [577].
12 Ibid. See Deleuze and Guattari, *Anti-Oedipus*, 181 [214].
13 Deleuze and Guattari, *Thousand Plateaus*, 172 [192–3]. The masochistic element here is that one variety of masochist is the "horse masochist." Deleuze and Guattari's cited text describes how one such horse masochist had a saddle and other horse-riding equipment made special to fit his body so that his wife, wielding a whip, could ride him. See Dupouy, "Du masochisme," 395–9. Deleuze and Guattari claim that despite this resemblance to a horse in training, the horse masochist nonetheless is not simply imitating a horse; rather, he lets the horse's forces be transmitted to him in order to replace his own innate forces, thereby regulating them, but also enabling him to "become-animal" in the Deleuzian and Guattarian sense.
14 Deleuze and Guattari, *Thousand Plateaus*, 172 [193].
15 Ibid., 387 [434].
16 Deleuze, *Course 1971.12.21* (no audio); Deleuze, *Course 1972.02.15* (no audio); Deleuze, *Course 1972.02.22* (no audio); Deleuze and Guattari, *Anti-Oedipus*, 227–8, 234, 237–8 [270, 278, 282–3].
17 Deleuze, *Course 1972.03.07* (no audio).
18 *Anti-Oedipus*, 33, 140 [41, 164]; Deleuze and Guattari, *Thousand Plateaus*, 500 [565]; Deleuze, *Course 1971.12.21* (no audio); Deleuze, *Course 1972.02.15* (no audio); Deleuze, *Course 1972.02.22* (no audio). "Marx accurately constructs a concept of capitalism by determining the two principal components, naked labor and pure wealth, with their zone of indiscernibility when wealth buys labor." Deleuze and Guattari, *What Is Philosophy?*, 97 [93].
19 Deleuze, *Course 1972.02.15* (no audio); Deleuze, *Course 1972.03.07* (no audio).
20 Deleuze, *Course 1972.02.22* (no audio).
21 Deleuze, *Course 1980.01.29,2* (00:24:00–00:24:20); Deleuze, *Course 1980.03.25,1* (00:33:20–00:34:00); Deleuze, *Course 1980.04.22,1* (00:29:30–00:32:10). See also Deleuze, *Nietzsche and Philosophy*, 50–1 [57–8]. We will further elaborate on this notion of the derivative and tangent in the next volume.
22 Deleuze, *Course 1980.03.25,1* (00:32:00–00:32:50).
23 Deleuze, *Course 1971.11.16* (no audio).
24 Deleuze, *Course 1980.02.05,3* (00:14:40–00:15:30); Deleuze, *Course 1980.03.25,1* (00:41:30–00:43:40).
25 Deleuze, *Course 1971.12.21* (no audio); Deleuze, *Course 1972.02.22* (no audio).
26 Deleuze, *Course 1972.02.15* (no audio); Deleuze, *Course 1972.02.22* (no audio).
27 Deleuze, *Course 1971.11.16* (no audio).

28 Deleuze, *Course 1980.03.18,2* (00:06:30–00:13:50); Deleuze, *Course 1980.03.25,1* (00:37:30–00:38:10); Deleuze and Guattari, *Thousand Plateaus*, 518, 641 [585–6].
29 Deleuze, *Course 1972.03.07* (no audio).
30 Deleuze, *Course 1972.02.22* (no audio).
31 Ibid.
32 Ibid.
33 *Course 1980.02.26,2* (00:08:40–00:15:00); Deleuze and Guattari, *Thousand Plateaus*, 158–9 [179].
34 A more thorough treatment of this topic is found in Smith, *Essays on Deleuze*, 290–9.
35 Deleuze, *Course 1980.02.26,2* (00:22:30–00:30:40).
36 Ibid. (00:24:00–00:24:20).
37 Ibid. (00:27:20–00:27:40).
38 Euclid and Byrne, *First Six Books*, xix. See Euclid and Heath, *Thirteen Books 1*, 153.
39 Euclid and Byrne, *First Six Books*, 85. See Euclid and Heath, *Thirteen Books 2*, 21.
40 Euclid and Byrne, *First Six Books*, xix, 85. Public domain images are from Archive. org: https://archive.org/details/firstsixbooksofe00eucl.
41 Deleuze and Guattari, *Thousand Plateaus*, 399, 616 [448].
42 Proclus, *Commentary on Euclid*, 64 [78], emphasis mine.
43 Ibid., 64 [78].
44 Euclid and Heath, *Thirteen Books 1*, 153.
45 Proclus, *Commentary on Euclid*, 88 [109].
46 See Morrow's comments in ft.45: Ibid., 88, and Heath's note: Archimedes and Heath, *Works*, 3. Deleuze, in the context of Kant and Leibniz, says that we cannot draw from Euclid's definition that it is the shortest distance between two points. Deleuze, *Course 1980.05.06,2* (00:20:00–00:20:30).
47 Deleuze, *Course 1978.03.14*, (no audio); Deleuze, *Course 1978.04.04* (no audio).
48 "Of all lines which have the same extremities, the straight line is the least." Archimedes, *On the Sphere*, 3 [8–9].
49 Deleuze, *Course 1980.05.06,2* (00:22:50–00:23:50).
50 Hoüel, *Essai critique*, 76–7; Deleuze, *Difference and Repetition*, 174 [226].
51 Archimedes, *Quadrature of the Parabola*, 251–2 [348–53].
52 Hoüel, *Essai critique*, 77.
53 Deleuze, *Course 1980.02.26,2* (00:27:40–00:28:50).
54 Archimedes, *Quadrature of the Parabola*, 251 [346]. Modified public domain image is from Archive.org: https://archive.org/details/worksofarchimede00arch.
55 Deleuze and Guattari, *Thousand Plateaus*, 402 [451–2]; Deleuze, *Course 1980.02.26,2* (00:34:45–00:35:15). This title translation is Brian Massumi's (see the above citation for *A Thousand Plateaus*). The original title is "Brouillon project d'une atteinte aux événements des rencontres du cône avec un plan." One English translation of the book renders it as "Rough Draft for an Essay on the Results of Taking Plane Sections of a Cone." Desargues, "Rough Draft," 69 [103].
56 Public domain images are from Archive.org and Wikimedia Commons: (Left) Bosse and Desargues, *Pratique du trait*, 53. (Top right) https://commons.wikimedia.org/wiki/File:Conic_sections_small.png. (Top left) https://commons.wikimedia.org/wiki/File:Hyperbola_(PSF).svg.
57 Deleuze, *Course 1980.02.26,2* (00:34:15–00:34:50).
58 Ibid. (00:30:30–00:32:50).
59 Deleuze, *Course 1980.02.26,1* (00:20:00–00:20:30); Deleuze, *Course 1980.02.26,2* (00:17:10–00:20:30); Deleuze and Guattari, *Thousand Plateaus*, 640 [576]. Deleuze

relates his axiomatic/problematic distinction to Bouligand's distinction between global synthesis and problems. See Bouligand and Desgranges, *Déclin*, 18–28; Deleuze, *Cinema 2*, 179 [241].

60 See Bourbaki, "Architecture of Mathematics," 222 [36–7].
61 Ibid., 224 [38].
62 Deleuze, *Course 1980.02.05,3* (00:02:50–00:04:30); Bourbaki, "Architecture of Mathematics," 224 [39]. For simplicity, I have kept the formula as Deleuze reads it with a "plus," but the operator is more generic in Bourbaki's text: $e \, \tau \, x = x \, \tau \, e = x$. In other course sessions, Deleuze uses a relation symbol (R) for this more generic operator. Deleuze, *Course 1980.02.05,2* (00:39:00–00:39:40); Deleuze, *Course 1980.02.26,1* (00:06:30–00:07:00). For the above quotation, Deleuze specifies it is in the domain of arithmetic, but for convenience I have made the operator more specific, because "+" can also generically have the sense of a change in position and also because I skipped Deleuze's previous axiom for convenience, which would have explained this operator a little more.
63 Deleuze, *Course 1980.02.05,3* (00:04:20–00:05:10); Bourbaki, "Architecture of Mathematics," 224 [39]. Again, Bourbaki's rendition has the more generic operator: $x \, \tau \, x' = x' \, \tau \, x = e$, and Deleuze normally uses the more generic relation symbol (R).
64 Blanché, *Axiomatics*, 36 [38].
65 Deleuze, *Course 1979.11.20,3* (00:03:30–00:05:00); Deleuze, *Course 1980.02.05,3* (00:07:20–00:09:10); Deleuze, *Course 1980.03.18,2* (00:16:50–00:38:20); Deleuze, *Course 1980.03.18,3* (00:16:10–00:20:20); Deleuze and Guattari, *Thousand Plateaus*, 481–2 [543–4].
66 Deleuze and Guattari, *Thousand Plateaus*, 482 [544].
67 Deleuze, *Course 1980.02.05,3* (00:09:40–00:12:10).
68 Ibid. (00:12:00–00:15:20).
69 Deleuze and Guattari, *Anti-Oedipus*, 233–4 [277–8]; Deleuze and Guattari, *Thousand Plateaus*, 518–20 [586–8]; Deleuze, *Course 1980.02.05,3* (00:12:00–00:15:30). See Brunschvicg, *Étapes de philosophie mathématique*, 388–9; Blanché, *Axiomatique*, 80–1. (The Blanché material is not included in its English translation.)
70 Vergauwen, *Metalogical Theory of Reference*, 15.
71 Cantor, *Contributions to the Founding*, 86–7 [283].
72 Ibid., 86, 98 [285, 290]; Cantor, "Foundations of a General Theory," 884 [167]; Brunschvicg, *Étapes de philosophie mathématique*, 386; Vergauwen, *Metalogical Theory of Reference*, 16.
73 Vergauwen, *Metalogical Theory of Reference*, 15.
74 Ibid.
75 Deleuze, *Course 1980.02.05,3* (00:12:00–00:15:20); Deleuze, *Course 1980.03.25,1* (00:41:30–00:43:40); Deleuze and Guattari, *Thousand Plateaus*, 640 [576].
76 Vergauwen, *Metalogical Theory of Reference*, 17.
77 Based on: ibid.
78 Ibid., 16.
79 Blanché, *Axiomatics*, 31–2 [33].
80 Based on: Vergauwen, *Metalogical Theory of Reference*, 18.
81 See Brouwer, "Intuitionism and Formalism," 127–8, 133–4. Jeffrey Bell notes that "there's a clear similarity between the Deleuzo-Guattarian notion of a line of flight and the function of diagonalization." Bell, "The Nondenumerable." See also the comments there by Paul Livingston for a discussion on the issue of constructive procedures.

82 Cantor, "On an Elementary Question," 921.
83 See Vergauwen, *Metalogical Theory of Reference*, 19.
84 Deleuze, *Course 1980.02.26,2* (00:18:30–00:22:40); Deleuze and Guattari, *Thousand Plateaus*, 616–17, 509, 616 [448, 576].
85 Kolmogorov, "On the Interpretation," 328–9 [58–9].
86 Ibid., 329 [59–60]. Although Deleuze mentions Kolmogorov, he directly cites related works by Paulette Destouches-Février. Deleuze, *Difference and Repetition*, 158, 322 [205]; Deleuze, *Course 1980.02.26,2* (00:21:00–00:22:00); Destouches-Février, "Rapports entre le calcul."
87 van Stigt, "Brouwer's Intuitionist Programme," 5.
88 Brouwer, "Life, Art, and Mysticism," 391.
89 van Stigt, "Brouwer's Intuitionist Programme," 5.
90 Brouwer, "Life, Art, and Mysticism," 392–3, emphasis mine.
91 van Stigt, "Brouwer's Intuitionist Programme," 4.
92 Ibid.
93 Ibid., 4–5.
94 Ibid., 5.
95 Weyl, "On the New Foundational Crisis," 86 [39]; van Stigt, "Brouwer's Intuitionist Programme," 1.
96 Weyl, "On the New Foundational Crisis," 56 [99]; van Stigt, "Brouwer's Intuitionist Programme," 1.
97 van Stigt, "Brouwer's Intuitionist Programme," 2.
98 Brouwer, "On the Foundations," 97.
99 Brouwer, "Consciousness, Philosophy, Mathematics," 480.
100 van Stigt, "Brouwer's Intuitionist Programme," 5.
101 Brouwer, "Consciousness, Philosophy, Mathematics," 480; van Stigt, "Brouwer's Intuitionist Programme," 5.
102 Brouwer, "Consciousness, Philosophy, Mathematics," 480.
103 Ibid.
104 van Stigt, "Brouwer's Intuitionist Programme," 6.
105 Brouwer, "Consciousness, Philosophy, Mathematics," 480.
106 van Stigt, "Brouwer's Intuitionist Programme," 6.
107 Brouwer, "Life, Art, and Mysticism," 393.
108 Brouwer, "Historical Introduction," 4.
109 Brouwer, "On the Foundations," 97.
110 Brouwer, "Historical Introduction," 4–5.
111 Brouwer, "Will, Knowledge, Speech," 418.
112 Brouwer, "On the Foundations," 61, 70.
113 Brouwer, "Intuitionism and Formalism," 127–8. However, as D.A. Gillies notes, Brouwer later changes his approach to how we arrive upon the continuum. Gillies, "Brouwer's Philosophy of Mathematics," 112.
114 Brouwer, "Historical Introduction," 8; Brouwer, "Consciousness, Philosophy, Mathematics," 482; Brouwer, "Guidelines of Intuitionistic Mathematics," 477.
115 Brouwer, "On the Foundations," 97; Brouwer, "Historical Background," 511; Brouwer, "Essentially Negative Properties," 478.
116 Brouwer, "Guidelines of Intuitionistic Mathematics," 477.
117 van Stigt, "Brouwer's Intuitionist Programme," 7. See Olkowski, "Using Our Intuition," 13–14.

118 Brouwer, "Consciousness, Philosophy, Mathematics," 488. See van Stigt, "Brouwer's Intuitionist Programme," 8. As Dummett explains: "The platonistic picture is of a realm of mathematical reality, existing objectively and independently of our knowledge, which renders our statements true or false. On an intuitionistic view, on the other hand, the only thing which can make a mathematical statement true is a proof of the kind we can give: not, indeed, a proof in a formal system, but an intuitively acceptable proof, that is, a certain kind of *mental* construction. Thus, while, to a platonist, a mathematical theory relates to some external realm of abstract objects, to an intuitionist it relates to our own mental operations: mathematical objects themselves are mental constructions, that is, objects of thought not merely in the sense that they are thought about, but in the sense that, for them, *esse est concipi*. They exist only in virtue of our mathematical activity, which consists in mental operations, and have only those properties which they can be recognized by us as having." Dummett, *Elements of Intuitionism*, 5.
119 Brouwer, "Intuitionism and Formalism," 128. See Haack, *Deviant Logic*, 92.
120 Brouwer, "Intuitionism and Formalism," 133–4.
121 Read, *Thinking about Logic*, 215, bracketed insertion is mine.
122 Brouwer, "Consciousness, Philosophy, Mathematics," 483.
123 Ibid., 480.
124 Ibid.
125 van Stigt, "Brouwer's Intuitionist Programme," 6.
126 Brouwer, "Unreliability of the Logical Principles," 107.
127 Brouwer, "On the Foundations," 53.
128 Brouwer, "Consciousness, Philosophy, Mathematics," 481. See van Stigt, "Brouwer's Intuitionist Programme," 6.
129 Brouwer, "On the Foundations," 53.
130 Brouwer, "Will, Knowledge, Speech," 419.
131 Brouwer, "On the Foundations," 53.
132 Brouwer, "Intuitionism and Formalism," 123–4.
133 Brouwer, "Life, Art, and Mysticism," 395.
134 Brouwer, "Consciousness, Philosophy, Mathematics," 482.
135 Brouwer, "Will, Knowledge, Speech," 419.
136 Brouwer, "Volition, Knowledge, Language," 443. (Alternate translation: Brouwer, "Will, Knowledge, Speech," 417.)
137 Brouwer, "Intuitionism and Formalism," 128; Haack, *Deviant Logic*, 91–2.
138 van Stigt, "Brouwer's Intuitionist Programme," 9.
139 Brouwer, "Volition, Knowledge, Language," 443.
140 Brouwer, "Life, Art, and Mysticism," 401. See van Stigt, "Brouwer's Intuitionist Programme," 6.
141 Brouwer, "Will, Knowledge, Speech," 422.
142 van Stigt, "Brouwer's Intuitionist Programme," 9.
143 Brouwer, "On the Foundations," 53–4, 74–5; Brouwer, "Will, Knowledge, Speech," 427.
144 Brouwer, "Historical Background," 508; Brouwer, "Historical Introduction," 2.
145 Brouwer, "Effect of Intuitionism," 551; Brouwer, "Statements," 101.
146 Brouwer, "Disengagement of Mathematics," 441. See Brouwer, "Historical Introduction," 1.
147 Brouwer, "Unreliability of the Logical Principles," 107.
148 Brouwer, "Intuitionism and Formalism," 125.

149 Heyting, quoted in van Stigt, *Brouwer's Intuitionism*, 290. See Brouwer, "On the Foundations," 72–5, 92, 97; Brouwer, "Effect of Intuitionism," 551–2; Haack, *Deviant Logic*, 91.
150 Brouwer, "Historical Introduction," 1.
151 Brouwer, "On the Foundations," 74–5; van Stigt, "Brouwer's Intuitionist Programme," 9.
152 For more on the intuitionistic construction of the natural numbers and their arithmetic, see Heyting, *Intuitionism: An Introduction*, 13–14, and for even numbers, see particularly ibid., 14.
153 Brouwer, "On the Foundations," 74–5.
154 Brouwer, "Unreliability of the Logical Principles," 109.
155 Brouwer, "On the Foundations," 74.
156 Brouwer, "Unreliability of the Logical Principles," 109.
157 Brouwer, "On the Foundations," 74.
158 Brouwer, "Historical Introduction," 6. For a similar π example and discussion, see Dummett, "Wittgenstein's Philosophy," 326.
159 Brouwer, "Historical Introduction," 6.
160 Brouwer, "Unreliability of the Logical Principles," 110, bracketed insertion is mine. And, "A conscientious rational reflection leads to the result that this may be expected for the principles of identity, of contradiction and of the syllogism, but for the principium tertii exclusi only in so far as it is restricted to affirmations about parts of a definite, *finite* mathematical system, given once and for all whilst a more extensive use of this principle would not occur, because in general its application to purely mathematical affirmations would produce word complexes devoid of mathematical sense and hence devoid of any sense whatever." Brouwer, "Volition, Knowledge, Language," 443.
161 Michael Dummett writes regarding this: "The law of excluded middle will, strictly speaking, be true only for statements that have already been decided." Dummett, *Elements of Intuitionism*, 12.
162 Brouwer, "Effect of Intuitionism," 552, paragraph spacing is mine.
163 Dummett, "Philosophical Basis," 121. See Dummett, "Wittgenstein's Philosophy," 341.
164 Heyting, *Intuitionism: An Introduction*, 18–19.
165 Ibid.
166 Ibid.
167 Read explains this in greater detail: "'Even', 'greater than 2' and 'prime' are decidable predicates: we may assert of any number that either it is even or odd, that it is greater than 2 or not, or that either it is prime or not, for there are algorithms for determining them (division by 2, subtraction of 2 and Eratosthenes' sieve, respectively). But the general claim, commonly known as Goldbach's Conjecture, that every even number greater than 2 is the sum of two primes, is not decidable. That is, we have a predicate $A(x)$ which is decidable ('x is even, greater than 2, and there are y and z which are prime such that $x = y + z$'), for we can work systematically through all pairs y, z less than x, testing whether they are prime. But 'for every x, $A(x)$' is not decidable. We have no method which is guaranteed to establish or refute this universal claim for every number x. Thus, while we may assert '$A(x)$ or not-$A(x)$' for every number x, we may not assert 'for every x, $A(x)$ or not for every x, $A(x)$', that is, we may not assert that either Goldbach's Conjecture is true or it is not. For no one has yet shown which, and we possess no algorithm for determining it. If it is false, one day someone may hit on a number which refutes it; if it is true, someone may

provide a general proof that for every x, $A(x)$. But until that time, the constructivist refrains from asserting their disjunction." Read, *Thinking about Logic*, 220–1.
168 Brouwer, "Effect of Intuitionism," 552. See Dummett, *Elements of Intuitionism*, 12.
169 Priest, *Introduction to Non-Classical Logic*, 106.
170 Olkowski, "Using Our Intuition," 14. van Stigt echoes this temporalization: "Brouwer […] speaks of 'unproven hypotheses', 'the case that α has neither been proved to be true nor to be absurd'. Negation in this case expresses the simple absence of proof, which in *the world of mathematics as construction in time* may well be reversed: Unsolved problems may one day become proven truth or absurdity. Moreover, 'a mathematical entity is not necessarily predeterminate, and may, in its state of free growth, at some time acquire a property it did not possess before' (BMS59, p. 1), leading to further distinctions, in particular, between 'cannot now' and 'cannot now and ever', the latter term frequently used by Brouwer in his later work as an alternative description of 'absurdity'." van Stigt, "Brouwer's Intuitionist Programme," 15, emphasis mine. (The "BMS59, p. 1" citation is equivalent to: Brouwer, "Changes in the Relation," 452. See also Brouwer, "Effect of Intuitionism," 552.)
171 Haack, *Deviant Logic*, 94–6. One of Deleuze's own sources even suggests such a third truth-value for intuitionistic logic: Destouches-Février, "Manifestations et sens," 384–5.
172 Dummett, *Elements of Intuitionism*, 11; Mancosu and van Stigt, "Intuitionistic Logic," 280. See Nolt, *Logics*, 429–31; Priest, *Introduction to Non-Classical Logic*, 105.
173 Dummett, *Elements of Intuitionism*, 9.
174 Read, *Thinking about Logic*, 219–20, emphasis mine.
175 Deleuze, *Course 1980.03.25,2* (00:23:10–00:25:30); Deleuze and Guattari, *Thousand Plateaus*, 516 [584].
176 Deleuze and Guattari, *Thousand Plateaus*, 517–18 [585].
177 Deleuze, *Difference and Repetition*, 234 [301–2].
178 Griss, "Negationless Intuitionistic Mathematics, I," 1130. See Haack, *Deviant Logic*, 99–100.
179 Griss, "Negationless Intuitionistic Mathematics, I," 1127.
180 Heyting, "Griss and Negationless Mathematics," 93.
181 Griss, "Negationless Intuitionistic Mathematics, I," 1128.
182 Ibid., 1127.
183 Ibid., 1128.
184 Ibid., 1127.
185 Ibid., 1128.
186 Brouwer, "Historical Introduction," 8.
187 Heyting, *Intuitionism: An Introduction*, 17; Brouwer, "Intuitionist Splitting," 278 [254].
188 Griss, "Negationless Intuitionistic Mathematics, I," 1130.
189 Deleuze and Guattari, *What Is Philosophy?*, 7, 35–6 [12, 36]; Deleuze, *Course 1980.02.26,3* (00:00:40–00:02:00).
190 Brouwer, "Consciousness, Philosophy, Mathematics," 490. Note that here Brouwer is formulating it as a "principle," namely, the "principle of reciprocity of complementarity," which he is against, because in intuitionism, which rejects excluded middle, it does not hold necessarily. See van Stigt, *Brouwer's Intuitionism*, 352–4. But of course complementarity does hold for subsets that exhaustively and exclusively divide the larger set.
191 Griss, "Logic of Negationless Mathematics," 44–5.

192 Griss, "Negationless Intuitionistic Mathematics, I," 1131.
193 Ibid.
194 Ibid.
195 Ibid.
196 Ibid.
197 Ibid.
198 Griss, "Sur la négation," 73.
199 Ibid., 72–3.
200 Griss, "Negationless Intuitionistic Mathematics, I," 1132. Note that Heyting gives a similar sort of Brouwerian definition for difference and inequality: "'a est différent de b', ($a \neq b$), signifie, dans la terminologie de BROUWER, que $a = b$ est impossible." Heyting, *Fondements des mathématiques*, 24. See Heyting, *Intuitionism: An Introduction*, 17.
201 Griss, "Negationless Intuitionistic Mathematics, I," 1132.
202 Deleuze, *Difference and Repetition*, 234 [302].
203 Heyting, "Griss and Negationless Mathematics," 93.
204 Kramer, *Nature and Growth*, 31–3.
205 Ibid., 32–4.
206 See ibid., 33.
207 Griss, "Negationless Intuitionistic Mathematics, III," 195.
208 Ibid., 195–6. Heyting, whose texts Deleuze is primarily implementing here, recasts Griss's formulations with a little more mathematical specificity. He writes: "A real number is defined by a convergent, contracting sequence of rational intervals; for the sake of brevity I shall call such a sequence a number-generator." Heyting, *Intuitionism: An Introduction*, 16. And a real number-generator is defined as a Cauchy sequence: "A Cauchy sequence of rational numbers is a *real number-generator*. Where no confusion is possible, we shall speak briefly of a number-generator." Ibid. He formulates such a Cauchy sequence as: "A sequence $\{a_n\}$ of rational numbers is called a Cauchy sequence, if for every natural number k we can find a natural number $n = n(k)$, such that $|a_{n+p} - a_n| < 1/k$ for every natural number p." This more or less defines a sequence of what, following Griss, we are calling "approximating intervals," where each following one is nested within the prior, larger one, going to infinity and thus converging upon a determinate value. See Read, *Thinking about Logic*, 221. Heyting then on this basis, in a manner very similar to Griss, defines the "coinciding" and "apartness" relations for real numbers. "The number-generators $a \equiv \{a_n\}$ and $b \equiv \{b_n\}$ *coincide*, if for every k we can find $n = n(k)$ such that $|a_{n+p} - b_{n+p}| < 1/k$ for every p. This relation is denoted by $a = b$," and "two number-generators $a = \{a_n\}$ and $b = \{b_n\}$ coincide, if a_n and b_n overlap for every n. Coinciding number-generators define the same real number." Heyting, *Intuitionism: An Introduction*, 16; Heyting, "Griss and Negationless Mathematics," 93. In other words, two real numbers are equal when their approximating intervals are always narrowing in toward the same value. And the apartness relation: "For real number-generators a and b, a *lies apart from* b, $a \# b$, means that n and k can be found such that $|a_{n+p} - b_{n+p}| > 1/k$ for every p," and "two real numbers, defined by the number-generators $a = \{a_n\}$ and $b = \{b_n\}$ are apart from each other ($a \# b$) if for some n, a_n and b_n are separated intervals." Heyting, *Intuitionism: An Introduction*, 19; Heyting, "Griss and Negationless Mathematics," 94. In other words, two real number sequences are apart if after some point in the series, there is always thereafter a gap between the intervals.

209 Heyting, "Griss and Negationless Mathematics," 94.
210 Griss, "Negationless Intuitionistic Mathematics, I," 1132.
211 Heyting, "Griss and Negationless Mathematics," 94. See Griss, "Negationless Intuitionistic Mathematics, III," 198. There Griss is discussing real numbers as parts of the continuum, and he formulates this as: "$A \# C$ for each $C \# B \rightarrow A \not\equiv B$." Here, $\#$ is apartness for continuum values, equivalent to the $\neq$ apartness relation for real number values. The $\not\equiv$ means distinguishability. See Griss, "Negationless Intuitionistic Mathematics, II," 463.
212 Heyting summarizes all this in the following way: "Dans la théorie des nombres réels la relation $\neq$, étant négative, n'intervient pas. Il n'y a que la relation $a = b$ et la relation de distance $a \# b$ [...]. Le théorème 'si $a \neq b$ est impossible, on a $a = b$' est remplacé par le suivant: 'si a est distant de tout nombre c qui est distant de b, on a $a = b$.' [...] 'a est différent de b,' ($a \neq b$), signifie, dans la terminologie de BROUWER, que $a = b$ est impossible. Pour le continu, on a en outre la relation 'a est positivement différent de b' ou 'a est écarté de b' ($a \# b$). Celle-ci est remplie quand, dans les suites d'intervalles qui définissent a et b, on connaît deux intervalles extérieurs l'un à l'autre." Heyting, *Fondements des mathématiques*, 14, 24–5.
213 Deleuze, *Difference and Repetition*, 234 [302].
214 So for instance, before 1 can first enter into an extensive relation with 2 as being one unit of "distance" away from it, 1 must have an internal, intensive "distance" or "depth," which does not yet have an extensive value (it is just a greater or lesser degree of tension of sorts), which provides the "potency" to "drive" the value to something greater, so to speak. So in a way, we might think of this intensive "depth" as somehow becoming converted into an extensive "space," when its tendency to expand is given actualized expression. (To make this more visual, we might imagine the 1 value undergoing a sort of disruptive, internal tension that can result in the value breaking out of its limits and expanding outward.)

Chapter 7

1   Deleuze, *Cours 1980.12.02,2* (00:52:40–01:02:10). Note that Deleuze may not be referencing iron pyrite specifically but rather some unspecified sort of gold-like material. Yet still, if it were not this sort of false gold, it would affirmatively pass the test for some other.
2   Ibid. (00:52:20–00:58:00).
3   Deleuze, *Cinema 1*, 2 [10]; Deleuze, *Course 1982.01.12,2* (01:03:50–01:04:30).
4   Deleuze, *Cinema 1*, 29 [44–5]; Deleuze, *Course 1984.06.12,3* (00:19:20–00:23:20); Deleuze, "Preface to the American Edition," 270 [252].
5   Bergson, *Creative Evolution*, 10 [10].
6   Ibid., 10–11 [10–11].
7   Deleuze, *Cinema 1*, 31 [48].
8   Bergson, *Creative Evolution*, 6–8 [6–8].
9   Deleuze, *Cinema 1*, 19 [31].
10 Ibid., 9–10 [19–20], quoting Bergson, *Creative Evolution*, 16 [16].
11 *The Massacre* directed by D. W. Griffith © Biograph 1912. All rights reserved.
12 Gunning, "D. W. Griffith," 145–8.
13 Deleuze, *Cinema 1*, 31 [47].

14 Ibid., 32–4 [49–51].
15 Eisenstein, *Film Form*, 234.
16 Deleuze, *Cinema 2*, 47 [69].
17 Roy, *Dictionnaire général du cinéma*, 169.
18 Eisenstein, *Film Form*, 234.
19 Eisenstein, *Nonindifferent Nature*, 40–4.
20 Ibid., 10–19; Deleuze, *Cinema 1*, 34–9 [51–7].
21 *The General Line/The Old and the New (Staroye i Novoye)* directed by Sergei Eisenstein © Sovkino 1929. All rights reserved.
22 Eisenstein, *Nonindifferent Nature*, 27.
23 Ibid., 51–5. See Christie, "Rediscovering Eisenstein," 6.
24 Eisenstein, *Nonindifferent Nature*, 10–12; Deleuze, *Cinema 1*, 38–9 [56–7].
25 Deleuze, *Course 1984.06.12,3* (00:26:20–00:27:40).
26 Deleuze, *Cinema 1*, 29 [45].
27 "Vérité et temps: Le faussaire," later revised to "Le vrai et temps: Le faussaire." Deleuze, *Course 1983.11.08,1* (00:03:50–00:04:40, 00:42:10–00:42:30). I am following Daniel Smith's translation of *le faussaire* as "the falsifier" (Smith, *Essays on Deleuze*, 139). However, later I keep Hugh Tomlinson's and Robert Galeta's translation, "the forger," when it is suitable in the more limited context of art production (Deleuze, *Cinema 2*, 141 [191]).
28 Deleuze, *Cinema 2*, 15, 100 [26, 136].
29 Deleuze, *Course 1983.11.08,1* (00:44:00–00:44:50); Deleuze, *Course 1983.11.22,1* (00:01:40–00:02:40).
30 Deleuze, *Course 1983.11.08,1* (01:05:10–01:09:30); Deleuze, *Course 1983.11.08,2* (00:29:40–00:32:00); Deleuze, *Course 1983.11.22,1* (00:13:10–00:16:00).
31 Deleuze, *Course 1983.11.08,1* (01:05:10–01:07:00); Deleuze, *Course 1983.11.22,1* (00:13:50–00:15:20).
32 Ibid., 47–51 [31–5].
33 Deleuze, *Course 1981.11.24,2* (00:16:50–00:21:10).
34 Deleuze, *Cinema 1*, 52 [76].
35 Further elaboration could be given for how those entities that we might normally consider as physical things are here instead conceived as images themselves. Deleuze is often working with certain Bergsonian notions from *Matter and Memory* and *Duration and Simultaneity* that he summarizes as "image = movement = matter = light." Deleuze, *Course 1982.11.30,1* (00:00:40–00:01:50). See Deleuze, *Cinema 1*, 60–3 [86–90]. The basic idea is that the physical world is fundamentally made up of figures of light movements that require no perceiving consciousnesses in order to be images in their own right.
36 Public domain images are from Archive.org: (Left [right]) Worringer, *Form Problems*, 38½ [4½].
37 Deleuze, *Difference and Repetition*, 149 [193]. Here the confusion is between something we see with something we conceive or remember. See Pl. *Tht.* 191b–194a (*Theaetetus*, 212–15 [326–30]).
38 For this notion of confusing modification and representation, Deleuze here specifically references seventeenth-century philosophers from Descartes to Malebranche. Deleuze, *Course 1983.11.08,1* (00:45:20–00:50:00); Deleuze, *Course 1983.11.08,2* (00:01:10–00:01:30). However, I have loosely based my interpretation above on the glossary entries for "Consciousness" and "Idea" in Deleuze's *Spinoza: Practical Philosophy*, on account of their terminological and conceptual similarities

with this cited course material and with the idea below of falsity lacking a form. Deleuze, *Spinoza: Practical Philosophy*, 58-61, 73-6 [82-4, 105-9].
39 Deleuze, *Course 1983.11.08,1* (01:00:60-01:04:00).
40 Bergson, *Matter and Memory*, 181-3 [156-8]; Deleuze, *Course 1983.11.22,1* (00:16:20-00:21:20).
41 Bergson, *Matter and Memory*, 183 [158].
42 Deleuze, *Course 1983.11.22,1* (00:16:20-00:32:40).
43 Ibid. (00:21:20-00:25.30:40).
44 Bergson, *Matter and Memory*, 188 [162]; Deleuze, *Cinema 2*, 123 [166]; Deleuze, *Course 1983.11.22,1* (00:21:20-00:25.30:40).
45 Deleuze, *Course 1983.11.22,1* (00:25:30-00:27:00).
46 Ibid. (00:26:50-00:32:40).
47 Deleuze, *Course 1983.11.08,1* (00:51:10-00:54:10); Deleuze, *Course 1983.11.08,2* (00:00:00-00:05:20).
48 Deleuze, *Course 1983.11.08,1* (00:54:00-01:01:00).
49 Deleuze, *Course 1983.11.08,2* (00:00:00-00:05:20).
50 Deleuze, "To Have Done," 127 [159].
51 *The Lady from Shanghai* directed by Orson Welles © Mercury and Columbia 1947. All rights reserved.
52 Ibid., 126-8 [158-61].
53 Ibid., 130-2 [163-5].
54 Deleuze, *Cinema 2*, 134-5 [182].
55 Deleuze, "To Have Done," 135 [168-9].
56 Deleuze, *Nietzsche and Philosophy*, 22-3 [25-6]; Deleuze, *Cinema 2*, 137 [185].
57 Nietzsche, *Philosophy in the Tragic Age*, 46 [819].
58 Ibid., 51-2 [822-3].
59 Ibid., 51 [822].
60 Ibid., 62 [830-1].
61 Beall and Ripley, "Analetheism and Dialetheism," 30.

Chapter 8

1 Deleuze, *Logic of Sense*, 294 [295].
2 Pl. *Plt.* 267a-268a (*Statesman*, 1032-3 [459-60]).
3 Deleuze and Parnet, *A to Z*, "F is for Fidelity [F comme fidélité]," "H is History of Philosophy [H comme histoire de la philosophie]"; Deleuze and Guattari, *What Is Philosophy?*, 4 [9]; Deleuze, *Logic of Sense*, 292 [293].
4 Deleuze, *Logic of Sense*, 292 [293].
5 Note that although they are not transliteral, *simulacre* is one French translation of φάντασμα (*phantasma*). See Audouard, "Simulacre," 58.
6 Deleuze, *Logic of Sense*, 293 [295].
7 Ibid., 295 [297].
8 Ibid.
9 Pl. *Soph.* 235d (*Sophist*, 978 [387]).
10 Pl. *Soph.* 235e-236a (Ibid., 978 [388]).
11 Vitruvius, *Ten Books on Architecture*, 84-6 [74-5].
12 Serres, *Système de Leibniz 1*, 153-4.

13 Deleuze, *Logic of Sense*, 295 [296].
14 Deleuze, *Difference and Repetition*, 127 [167].
15 Deleuze, *Logic of Sense*, 295 [297]; Deleuze, *Difference and Repetition*, 128 [167].
16 See Audouard, "Simulacre," 64–5.
17 Fletcher, *History of Architecture*, 174. Public domain image is from Archive.org: https://archive.org/details/historyofarchite00flet.
18 Deleuze, *Logic of Sense*, 299–300 [302–3].
19 Ibid., 299 [302].
20 Ibid., 300 [303].
21 Deleuze, *Difference and Repetition*, 66–7 [92–3].
22 Ibid., 128 [167].
23 Ibid., 236 [304]; Deleuze, *Logic of Sense*, 3–4, 90–1, 187–8, 298 [9–10, 91–8, 192–3, 296].
24 Pl. *Phlb.* 24d (*Philebus*, 412 [246]).
25 Deleuze, "Literature and Life," 1–2 [11–12].
26 Deleuze, *Logic of Sense*, 296 [298], emphasis mine.
27 Ibid., 297–9 [299–302].
28 Ibid., 3–5 [9–11].
29 Leibniz, *Monadology*, 275 [615–16]; Leibniz, "First Truths," 268–9 [520]; Leibniz, *Correspondence with Arnauld*, 78, 120 [18–19, 48].
30 Deleuze, *Course 1983.11.29,2* (00:27:20–00:28:00).
31 Leibniz, "Letter to Coste," 193 [400]; Leibniz, *Theodicy*, 267–8 [252]; Leibniz, *Monadology*, 275 [616]; Leibniz, "On the Secrets," 21–3 [472].
32 Bergson, *Time and Free Will*, 115–17, 192–8 [86–7, 144–9]; Deleuze, *Course 1983.11.29,3* (00:07:40–00:09:40); Deleuze, *Logic of Sense*, 197 [201].
33 Bergson, *Creative Evolution*, 39–40 [39–40], emphasis in the second sentence is mine.
34 Ibid., 9 [9].
35 Deleuze, *Logic of Sense*, 197 [201]; Deleuze, *Course 1983.11.29,2* (00:53:20–00:53:50); Deleuze, *Course 1983.11.29,3* (00:13:40–00:17:10).
36 Deleuze, *Course 1983.11.22,2* (00:39:50–00:44:40).
37 Deleuze, *Course 1983.11.08,1* (00:50:00–01:05:10); Deleuze, *Course 1983.11.08,2* (00:46:00–00:47:10); Deleuze, *Course 1983.11.22,2* (00:39:50–00:40:30); Deleuze, *Course 1983.11.22,3* (00:24:10–00:25:00); Deleuze, *Course 1983.11.29,2* (00:08:10–00:09:10); Deleuze, *Cinema 2*, 135–6 [183–4].
38 Nietzsche, *Twilight of the Idols*, 16–19 [74–9]; Nietzsche, *Gay Science*, 280–3 [574–7].
39 Deleuze, *Cinema 2*, 135 [183].
40 Welles, *Mr. Arkadin*.
41 Deleuze, *Cinema 2*, 135 [183].
42 *Touch of Evil* directed by Orson Welles © Universal 1958. All rights reserved.
43 Ibid., 137 [185].
44 Priest, *Introduction to Non-Classical Logic*, 132.
45 See ibid., 253.
46 Ibid., 251.
47 Deleuze, *Course 1983.11.29,1* (00:54:50–00:55:40).
48 Ibid. (00:42:30–00:43:10, 00:43:20–00:44:50).
49 While under classical assumptions, the formulations for the Principle of Non-Contradiction and the Principle of Excluded Middle can be shown by means of De Morgan's laws to be logically equivalent, we should still here be careful to distinguish

them, as we are not in these cases using the classical assumptions of strict bivalence. See McGill, "Concerning the Laws," 203.
50 There is even a long, rich history of attempts at such a reconstruction, including efforts by Aristotle, Ockham, and Leibniz. See for instance Deleuze's own sources: Schuhl, *Dominateur et les possibles*; Vuillemin, *Necessity or Contingency*.
51 Epict. *Diss.* 2.19.1–5 (Epictetus, *Discourses*, 122 [189–90]), bracketed enumerations are mine.
52 Schuhl, *Dominateur et les possibles*, 74–5; Vuillemin, *Necessity or Contingency*, 5 [17].
53 Schuhl, *Dominateur et les possibles*, 17–18.
54 Arist. *Int.* 19a27–21 (*De Interpretatione*, 53 [30]).
55 Deleuze, *Course 1983.11.29,1* (00:43:10–00:45:20, 00:56:20–00:57:20).
56 Priest, *Introduction to Non-Classical Logic*, 244–6.
57 Deleuze, *Course 1983.11.29,1* (00:43:10–00:45:20, 00:56:20–00:57:20).
58 Ibid. (00:45:10–00:55:00, 00:57:10–00:58:00).
59 One might instead say that it is never possible and impossible at the same time. But it seems those who object here consider propositions as having a timeless status, and so it was either always possible or always impossible.
60 Deleuze, *Course 1983.11.29,1* (00:51:10–00:52:10).
61 Ibid. (00:57:50–00:59:30); Deleuze, *Course 1983.11.29,2* (00:00:00–00:06:10).
62 Gell. *Noc. Att.* 6.2 (*L&S 1*, 388 [*Attic Nights 3*, 413]), bracketed insertion is mine.
63 Cic. *Fat.* 18.41–19.45 (*De oratore 3*, 237–43 [236–42]).
64 Lévi, *Transcendental Magic*, 297 [*Dogme et rituel 2*, 225].
65 Deleuze, *Course 1983.11.08,2* (00:05:00–00:59:20); Deleuze, *Course 1983.11.22,1* (00:00:00–00:16:30).
66 Deleuze, *Course 1983.11.08,2* (00:24:10–00:27:10).
67 Ibid. (00:27:00–00:29:20); Deleuze, *Course 1983.11.22,3* (00:27:00–00:29:20); Deleuze, *Cinema 2*, 68 [95].
68 Deleuze, *Cinema 2*, 67, 282 [93]; Deleuze, *Course 1983.11.22,2* (00:00:00–00:10:20).
69 Robbe-Grillet, *Project for a Revolution*, 70–2 [87–90]; Ricardou, *Nouveau roman*, 112–13.
70 Ricardou, *Nouveau roman*, 112, 118–19; Robbe-Grillet, *Project for a Revolution*, 1–2 [7–9].
71 *The Lady from Shanghai* directed by Orson Welles © Mercury and Columbia 1947. All rights reserved.
72 *Trans-Europ-Express* directed by Alain Robbe-Grillet © Como 1966. All rights reserved.
73 Deleuze, *Cinema 2*, 127, 145 [171, 196]; Deleuze, "Literature and Life," 3 [13].
74 Robbe-Grillet, *Towards a New Novel*, 143–6 [124–8]; Deleuze, *Course 1983.11.22,2* (00:10:20–00:14:10); Deleuze, *Course 1983.11.29,1* (00:00:00–00:11:10); Deleuze, *Cinema 2*, 122 [165].
75 Robbe-Grillet, *Project for a Revolution*, 2 [8–9].
76 Deleuze, *Cinema 2*, 127 [172]. See Deleuze, *Cinema 1*, 250 [288]; Robbe-Grillet, *Towards a New Novel*, 145, 150–1, 157 [127, 132–3, 139–40].
77 *The Man Who Lies* (*L'homme qui ment*) directed by Alain Robbe-Grillet © Como 1968. All rights reserved.
78 Deleuze, *Cinema 2*, 98 [133].
79 Ibid., 128 [172].
80 Ibid., 126 [170–1]; Deleuze, *Course 1983.11.29,1* (00:35:20–00:59:30); Deleuze, *Course 1983.11.29,2* (00:00:00–00:06:10).

81 Deleuze, *Course 1983.11.29,1* (00:57:50–00:59:30); Deleuze, *Course 1983.11.29,2* (00:00:00–00:11:00); Deleuze, *Course 1983.11.29,3* (00:17:00–00:38:20).
82 Deleuze, *Cinema 2*, 127 [171].
83 Ibid., 132 [178].
84 Deleuze, *The Fold*, 62 [83–4]; Deleuze, *Course 1983.11.29,3* (00:17:10–00:38:10).
85 Leblanc, *Vie extravagante*, 133–40.
86 See Priest's discussion of dialetheic legal contradictions: Priest, *Introduction to Non-Classical Logic*, 127–8.
87 Deleuze, *Cinema 2*, 131 [177]; Deleuze, *Course 1983.11.29,1* (00:13:40–00:23:50); Bergala and Limosin, *Subterfuge*.
88 Barlassina and Del Prete, "The Puzzle of the Changing Past," 61, emphasis in the final sentence is mine.
89 Deleuze and Villani, "Responses to a Series," 42 [130].
90 Deleuze, *Course 1983.11.22,2* (00:14:10–00:24:30).
91 Deleuze, *Course 1983.11.22,1* (00:16:20–00:37:10); Deleuze, *Cinema 2*, 129 [174].
92 Deleuze, *Course 1983.11.22,2* (00:14:10–00:36:50).
93 Lévi, *Theosophical Miscellanies 2*, 50–1.
94 Lévi, *Transcendental Magic*, 34 [*Dogme et rituel 1*, 117].
95 Deleuze, *Course 1983.11.08,2* (00:05:10–00:22:50).
96 Melville, *Confidence-Man*, 212; Deleuze, *Course 1983.11.08,2* (00:49:30–00:50:00); Deleuze, *Course 1983.11.22,3* (00:13:40–00:14:10); Deleuze, *Cinema 2*, 130 [175]; Deleuze, "Bartleby, or the Formula," 86 [110].
97 Deleuze, "Bartleby, or the Formula," 86–7 [110–11].
98 Deleuze, *Course 1983.11.22,3* (00:13:30–00:15:50); Melville, *Confidence-Man*, 393–4.
99 Deleuze, *Course 1983.11.22,2* (00:25:00–00:26:50); Deleuze, *Cinema 2*, 119, 292 [161]; Robbe-Grillet, *Last Year*, 10 [12].
100 Deleuze, *Course 1983.11.22,3* (00:29:10–00:30:50); Deleuze, *Cinema 2*, 137 [185–6]; Welles, Cobos, and Rubio, "Welles on Falstaff," 7.
101 Deleuze and Guattari, *Kafka: Minor Literature*, 17 [30]; Deleuze and Guattari, *Thousand Plateaus*, 112–14 [128–30]; Deleuze and Parnet, *Dialogues II*, 58–9, 118 [141, 72–3]; Deleuze, *Foucault*, 5 [15].
102 Serres, *Système de Leibniz 1*, 157–60; Deleuze, *Cinema 2*, 138–9 [187–8].
103 Deleuze, *Cinema 2*, 141 [190]. Roland Breeur's *Lies–Imposture–Stupidity*, which conducts a comprehensive and probing study of such impostures as these, draws a distinction that can help clarify these notions: "Although the class of impostors contains a diversity that is as rich as it is variegated, I would like to focus on the one that distinguishes mythomaniacal impostors, or 'real fakes', and counterfeiters of normality, or 'fake reals'. Real fakes invent an extraordinary life for themselves whereas fake reals try to pass as normal. Fake reals seek above all else to be accepted by or to be able to fit in with everyday social norms and constraints. They are known for their oft-clumsy gait and overzealousness: They are too polite, too friendly, too educated, too well-behaved, etc. The real fakes, on the other hand, want to surprise: They see themselves as, and seek to convince the world around them that they are, exceptional, uncommon, extraordinary, etc." Breeur, *Lies—Imposture—Stupidity*, 56. Although these passages deal with a different matter altogether (social self-presentation), they bring to light an important factor in Deleuze's thinking, namely, the falsifiers' attitude toward reality: is it something to simply conform to in a way that misleads others, or is it something to be played with creatively? While a

real fake might not, in Deleuze's account, have the highest power of the false, they nonetheless are high enough to realize that falsification should produce the unique and extraordinary rather than fall squarely within pre-established forms.

104 Public domain images are from Wikimedia Commons: (Top left) Vermeer, *Girl with a Pearl Earring*. https://commons.wikimedia.org/wiki/File:Johannes_Vermeer_(1632–1675)_-_The_Girl_With_The_Pearl_Earring_(1665).jpg. (Bottom middle) van Meegeren, *Supper at Emmaus*. https://commons.wikimedia.org/wiki/File:
EmmausgangersVanMeegeren1937.jpg. (Top Right) Velázquez, *Las Meninas*. https://en.wikipedia.org/wiki/File:Las_Meninas_01.jpg.
105 Koning, *World of Vermeer*, 178.
106 Deleuze, *Cinema 2*, 141 [191].
107 Welles, *F for Fake* (Janus; Les Films de l'Astrophore; SACI, 1973). See Deleuze, *Course 1983.11.08,2* (00:51:20–00:52:40).
108 Deleuze, *Course 1983.11.22,2* (00:30:50–00:44:40).
109 See Deleuze, *Course 1983.11.08,2* (00:51:50–00:53:00); Deleuze, *Course 1983.11.22,2* (00:41:50–00:44:30).
110 Deleuze, *Cinema 2*, 141-2 [191].
111 Deleuze, *Course 1983.11.22,2* (00:43:00–00:44:40); Deleuze, *Course 1983.11.29,2* (00:06:00–00:11:00).
112 Deleuze, *Course 1983.11.22,2* (00:28:10–00:36:50); Deleuze, *Cinema 2*, 130 [175].
113 Deleuze, *Course 1983.11.29,1* (00:50:20–00:52:10); Deleuze, *Course 1983.11.29,2* (00:10:30–00:10:50).
114 Deleuze, *Course 1983.11.29,2* (01:00:00–01:01:10).
115 Deleuze, *Cinema 2*, 129 [174].
116 Deleuze, *Course 1983.12.06,1* (00:41:40–00:46:00).
117 Deleuze, *Course 1983.11.29,2* (00:15:00–00:43:40). See Deleuze, *The Fold*, 61-2 [82-3].
118 Leibniz, *Theodicy*, 367-70 [359-62].
119 Ibid., 371 [363].
120 Ibid., 373 [364].
121 Deleuze, *Course 1983.11.29,2* (00:21:00–00:21:40).
122 Deleuze, *Difference and Repetition*, 222 [286].
123 This is my rough translation. Deleuze recites it as "L'émeraude en ses facettes/Cache une ondine aux yeux clairs;/La Vicomtesse de Cette/Avait les yeux couleur de pers." Deleuze, *Course 1983.11.08,2* (00:38:40–00:40:10). There he describes the eye color in the context of Homer and Ancient Greek mythology. In Hugo's original, it reads, "L'émeraude en sa facette/Cache une ondine au front clair;/La vicomtesse de Cette/Avait les yeux verts de mer." Hugo, "Ce que Gemma pense," 171-2. An English translation renders this: "Under the emerald's smooth lid/A bright-browed water-nymph lies hid./—A lady's eyes I saw at Cette/Were like the sea, but greener yet." Hugo, "Jeweller's Shop," 892.
124 Deleuze, *Course 1983.11.08,2* (00:43:00–00:43:40).
125 Deleuze, *Difference and Repetition*, 222 [286].
126 Deleuze, *Course 1983.11.08,2* (00:45:00–00:59:10).
127 Deleuze, *Course 1983.11.29,3* (00:14:00–00:17:10).
128 Borges, "Death and the Compass," 84 [158].
129 See Deleuze, "On Four Poetic Formulas," 28 [41].

130 See for instance: Leibniz, "New Method of Finding," 2–3 [220–2]; Leibniz, "Monitum de characteribus," 156–9; Leibniz, *De quadratura arithmetica*, 618–21.
131 Leibniz, "On the Method," 3 [98].
132 Ibid., [99].
133 Ibid., [118].
134 Ibid., [115–16].
135 *Logic of Sense*, 130 [138].
136 Ibid., 130–1 [138–9].
137 Ibid.
138 Ibid., insertions in brackets are mine.
139 Ibid., 131 [139], italics are mine: "Nous nous trouvons maintenant devant le point aléatoire des points singuliers, devant le signe ambigu des singularités, ou plutôt devant ce qui représente ce signe, et *qui vaut pour plusieurs de ces mondes*, et à la limite pour tous, au-delà de leurs divergences et des individus qui les peuplent." Ibid., italics are mine.
140 Ibid.
141 Ibid., 131 [140].
142 Ibid., 132 [140–1].
143 Deleuze, *The Fold*, 82 [112].

Conclusion

1 See Bell, "Dialetheism."
2 On this matter, much work has already been done and will need to be evaluated when we turn to this question in the forthcoming volume. Daniel Smith argues that in Deleuze's philosophy of difference, to think difference means to "think something that is contrary to the principles of thought." Smith, *Essays on Deleuze*, 85. Nathan Widder discusses how Deleuze's difference is deeper than Hegelian contradiction and calls for a rethinking of otherness, sense, and nonsense. Widder, "Thought after Dialectics"; Widder, "Negation, Disjunction … Forces." And most relevantly, Jeffrey Bell characterizes difference as being deeper than contraction, *including dialetheic contradiction*, because it is "the transcendental condition for such contradictions." Bell, "Dialetheism."
3 Beall and Ripley, "Analetheism and Dialetheism," 30.
4 See Priest, *Introduction to Non-Classical Logic*, 142–54.

References

Aetius. *De placita philosophorum*. In *Doxographi Graeci*, edited by Hermann Diels, 267–444. Berlin: Reimer, 1879.

Agler, David W. *Symbolic Logic: Syntax, Semantics, and Proof*. Lanham, MD: Rowman & Littlefield, 2013.

Akçagüner, Koray. "Poincaré's Philosophy of Mathematics and the Impossibility of Building a New Arithmetic." Thesis. Middle East Technical University. Ankara, Turkey, 2019.

Alexander of Aphrodisias. *Commentaria in Aristotelem Graeca*, Vol. 2.2: *In Aristotelis topicorum libros octo commentaria*. Edited by Maximilian Wallies. Berlin: Reimer, 1891.

Alexander of Aphrodisias. *Supplementum Aristotelicum*, Vol. 2.2: *Praeter commentaria scripta minora: Quaestiones, De fato, De mixtione*. Edited by Ivo Bruns. Berlin: Reimer, 1892.

Alexander of Aphrodisias. *Supplementum Aristotelicum*, Vol. 2.1: *De anima liber cum mantissa*. Edited by Ivo Bruns. Berlin: Reimer, 1887.

Ansell-Pearson, Keith. *Philosophy and the Adventure of the Virtual: Bergson and the Time of Life*. London: Routledge, 2002.

Archimedes. *Quadrature of the Parabola*. In *Works*, edited by Thomas Heath, 233–52. Cambridge: Cambridge University, 1897. [*Quadratura parabolae*. In *Opera omnia*, Vol. 2, edited by Johan Heiberg, 293–53. Leipzig: Teubner, 1881.]

Archimedes. *On the Sphere and Cylinder, Book 1*. In *Works*, edited by Thomas Heath, 1–55. Cambridge: Cambridge University, 1897. [[*De placita philosophorum*. In *Doxographi Graeci*, edited by Hermann Diels, 267–444. Berlin: Reimer, 1879.]

Archimedes and Thomas Heath. *Works*. Edited by Thomas Heath. Cambridge: Cambridge University, 1897.

Aristotle. *De interpretatione*. In *Categories and De Interpretatione*, translated by J. L. Ackrill, 43–68. Oxford: Oxford University, 1962. [*De interpretatione*. In *Opera omnia, Graece et Latine*, Vol. 1, 24–38. Paris: Didot, 1862.]

Aristotle. *Physics*. Translated by C. D. C. Reeve. Indianapolis, IN: Hackett, 2018. [*Physica*. In *Opera Omnia, Graece et Latine*, Vol. 2: *Continens Ethica, Naturalem auscultationem, De caelo, De generatione et metaphysica*, 248–366. Paris: Didot, 1874.]

Audouard, Xavier. "Le simulacre." *Cahiers pour l'analyse* 3 (June 1966): 57–72.

Bachelard, Gaston. *The Dialectic of Duration*. Translated by Mary McAllester Jones. Manchester: Clinamen, 2000. [*La dialectique de la durée*. New edition. Paris: Presses universitaires de France, 1963.]

Barlassina, Luca, and Fabio Del Prete. "The Puzzle of the Changing Past." *Analysis* 75, no. 1 (2015): 59–67.

Beall, J. C., and David Ripley. "Analetheism and Dialetheism." *Analysis* 64, no. 1 (2004): 30–5.

Bell, Jeffrey. "Dialetheism." *Aberrant Monism*, December 14, 2010. https://schizosoph.wordpress.com/2010/12/14/dialetheism.

Bell, Jeffrey. "The Nondenumerable." *Aberrant Monism*, January 9, 2011. https://schizosoph.wordpress.com/2011/01/09/the-nondenumerable.

Bergala, Alain, and Jean-Pierre Limosin. *Subterfuge (Faux-fuyants)*. La Cecilia, 1983.
Bergmann, Merrie. *An Introduction to Many-Valued and Fuzzy Logic: Semantics, Algebras, and Derivation Systems*. Cambridge: Cambridge University, 2008.
Bergson, Henri. *Creative Evolution*. Translated by Arthur Mitchell. Mineola, NY: Dover, 1998. [*L'évolution créatrice*. 5th ed. Paris: Quadrige/Presses universitaires de France, 1991.]
Bergson, Henri. *The Creative Mind*. Translated by Mabelle Andison. Westport, CT: Greenwood, 1946. [*La pensée et le mouvant: essais et conférences*. 3rd ed. Paris: Quadrige/Presses universitaires de France, 1990.]
Bergson, Henri. *Matter and Memory*. Translated by Nancy Paul and W. Scott Palmer. Mineola, NY: Dover, 2004. [*Matière et mémoire: essai sur la relation du corps à l'esprit*. 7th ed. Paris: Quadrige/Presses universitaires de France, 2004.]
Bergson, Henri. *Time and Free Will: An Essay on the Immediate Data of Consciousness*. Translated by F. L. Pogson. Mineola, NY: Dover, 2001. [*Essai sur les données immédiates de la conscience*. 4th ed. Paris: Quadrige/Presses universitaires de France, 1991.]
Bertman, Martin. "Basic Particulars and the Identity Thesis." *Journal for General Philosophy of Science* [*Zeitschrift Für Allgemeine Wissenschaftstheorie*] 3, no. 1 (1972): 1–8.
Beta, Hymenaeus, and Aleister Crowley, eds. *The Goetia. The Lesser Key of Solomon the King. Lemegeton, Book 1. Clavicula Salomonis Regis*. Translated by Samuel Liddell and MacGregor Mathers. Boston: Weiser, 1995.
Blake, Terence. "On the Incipit to *Deleuze's Logic of Sense*." *Agent Swarm*, February 28, 2018. https://terenceblake.wordpress.com/2018/02/28/on-the-incipit-to-deleuzes-logic-of-sense. [Page citations are based on the PDF published at: https://www.academia.edu/36462605/ON_THE_INCIPIT_TO_DELEUZES_LOGIC_OF_SENSE.]
Blanché, Robert. *Axiomatics*. Translated by G. B. Keene. London: Routledge & Kegan Paul, 1962. [*L'axiomatique*. Paris: Presses universitaires de France, 1955.]
Bogue, Ronald. *Deleuze and Guattari*. London/New York: Routledge, 1989.
Borges, Jorge. "Death and the Compass." In *Labyrinths: Selected Stories and Other Writings*, edited by Donald Yates and James Irby and translated by Donald Yates, 76–87. New York: New Directions, 1964. ["La muerte y la brújul." In *Ficciones*, 147–63. Madrid: Alianza, 1971.]
Borges, Jorge. "The Garden of Forking Paths." In *Labyrinths: Selected Stories and Other Writings*, edited by Donald Yates and James Irby and translated by Donald Yates, 19–29. New York: New Directions, 1964. ["El jardín de senderos que se bifurcan." In *Ficciones*, 101–16. Madrid: Alianza, 1971.]
Bosse, Abraham, and Girard Desargues. *La pratique du trait à preuves, de Mr Desargues Lyonnois, pour la coupe des pierres en l'architecture*. Paris: Des-Hayes, 1643.
Bouligand, Georges, and Jean Desgranges. *Le déclin des absolus mathématico-logiques*. Paris: Société d'édition d'enseignement supérieur, 1949.
Bourbaki, Nicolas. "The Architecture of Mathematics." Translated by Arnold Dresden. *The American Mathematical Monthly* 57, no. 4 (1950): 221–32. ["L'architecture des mathématiques." In *Les grands courants de la pensée mathématique*, edited by François Le Lionnais, 35–47. Marseilles: Cahiers du Sud, 1948.]
Bowden, Sean. "Deleuze et les Stoïciens: une logique de l'événement." *Bulletin de la société américaine de philosophie de langue française* 15, no. 1 (2005): 72–97.
Bowden, Sean. *The Priority of Events: Deleuze's Logic of Sense*. Edinburgh: Edinburgh University, 2011.
Brady, Ross. "On the Formalization of the Law of Non-Contradiction." In *The Law of Non-Contradiction: New Philosophical Essays*, edited by Graham Priest, J. C. Beall, and Bradley Armour-Garb, 41–8. Oxford: Oxford University, 2004.

Brandom, Robert. *Tales of the Mighty Dead: Historical Essays in the Metaphysics of Intentionality*. Cambridge, MA: Harvard University, 2002.
Breeur, Roland. *Lies—Imposture—Stupidity*. Vilnius: Jonas ir Jakubas, 2019.
Bréhier, Émile. *Histoire de la philosophie*, Vol. 1: *L'antiquité et le moyen âge*, Book 2: *Période hellénistique et romaine*. Paris: Alcan, 1927.
Bréhier, Émile. *La théorie des incorporels dans l'ancien stoïcisme*. 3rd ed. Paris: Vrin, 1962.
Bresson, Robert. *Diary of a Country Priest (Journal d'un curé de campagne)*. Union générale cinématographique, 1951.
Brouwer, L. E. J. "Changes in the Relation between Classical Logic and Mathematics (BMS 59)." In *Brouwer's Intuitionism*, by Walter van Stigt, 453-8. Amsterdam: Elsevier (North Holland), 1990.
Brouwer, L. E. J. "Consciousness, Philosophy, and Mathematics (1948C)." In *Collected Works*, Vol. 1: *Philosophy and Foundations of Mathematics*, edited by Arend Heyting, 480-94. Amsterdam: North-Holland, 1975.
Brouwer, L. E. J. "Disengagement of Mathematics from Logic (BMS 49)." In *Brouwer's Intuitionism*, by Walter van Stigt, 441-6. Amsterdam: Elsevier (North Holland), 1990.
Brouwer, L. E. J. "The Effect of Intuitionism on Classical Algebra of Logic (1955)." In *Collected Works*, Vol. 1: *Philosophy and Foundations of Mathematics*, edited by Arend Heyting, 551-4. Amsterdam: North-Holland, 1975.
Brouwer, L. E. J. "Essentially Negative Properties (1948A)." In *Collected Works*, Vol. 1: *Philosophy and Foundations of Mathematics*, edited by Arend Heyting, 478-9. Amsterdam: North-Holland, 1975.
Brouwer, L. E. J. "Guidelines of Intuitionistic Mathematics (1947)." In *Collected Works*, Vol. 1: *Philosophy and Foundations of Mathematics*, edited by Arend Heyting, 477. Amsterdam: North-Holland, 1975.
Brouwer, L. E. J. "Historical Background, Principles and Methods of Intuitionism (1952b)." In *Collected Works*, Vol. 1: *Philosophy and Foundations of Mathematics*, edited by Arend Heyting, 508-15. Amsterdam: North-Holland, 1975.
Brouwer, L. E. J. "Historical Introduction and Fundamental Notions (BMS 51)." In *Brouwer's Cambridge Lectures on Intuitionism*, edited by Dirk van Dalen, 1-20. Oxford: Oxford University, 1981.
Brouwer, L. E. J. "Intuitionism and Formalism (1912A)." In *Collected Works*, Vol. 1: *Philosophy and Foundations of Mathematics*, edited by Arend Heyting, 123-38. Amsterdam: North-Holland, 1975.
Brouwer, L. E. J. "Intuitionist Splitting of the Fundamental Notions of Mathematics (1923C)." In *From Brouwer to Hilbert: The Debate on the Foundations of Mathematics in the 1920's*, edited by Paolo Mancosu and translated by Walter van Stigt, 286-92. Oxford: Oxford University, 1998.
Brouwer, L. E. J. "Life, Art, and Mysticism (1905)." Translated by Walter van Stigt. *Notre Dame Journal of Formal Logic* 37, no. 3 (1996): 389-429.
Brouwer, L. E. J. "Statements." In *Collected Works*, Vol. 1: *Philosophy and Foundations of Mathematics*, edited by Arend Heyting, 98-101. Amsterdam: North-Holland, 1975.
Brouwer, L. E. J. "On the Foundations of Mathematics (1907)." In *Collected Works*, Vol. 1: *Philosophy and Foundations of Mathematics*, edited by Arend Heyting, 13-97. Amsterdam: North-Holland, 1975.
Brouwer, L. E. J. "The Unreliability of the Logical Principles (1908c)." In *Collected Works*, Vol. 1: *Philosophy and Foundations of Mathematics*, edited by Arend Heyting, 107-11. Amsterdam: North-Holland, 1975.

Brouwer, L. E. J. "Volition, Knowledge, Language (1933)." In *Collected Works*, Vol. 1: *Philosophy and Foundations of Mathematics*, edited by Arend Heyting, 443–6. Amsterdam: North-Holland, 1975.
Brouwer, L. E. J. "Will, Knowledge and Speech (1933)." In *Brouwer's Intuitionism*, by Walter van Stigt, 418–31. Amsterdam: Elsevier (North Holland), 1990.
Brown, Gregory, and Yual Chiek. "Introduction." In *Leibniz on Compossibility and Possible Worlds*, edited by Gregory Brown and Yual Chiek, 1–20. Cham, Switzerland: Springer, 2016.
Brunschvicg, Léon. *Les étapes de la philosophie mathématique*. Paris: Alcan, 1912.
Brunschwig, Jacques. *Papers in Hellenistic Philosophy*. Translated by Janet Lloyd. Cambridge: Cambridge University, 1994.
Buchanan, Ian. *Deleuze and Guattari's* Anti-Oedipus: *A Reader's Guide*. London/New York: Continuum, 2008.
Burns, Delisle. *The Uncertain Nervous System*. London: Edward Arnold, 1968.
Calcidius. *Plato latinus*, Vol. 4: Timaeus *a Calcidio translatus commentarioque instructus*. Edited by Raymond Klibansky. London: Warburg Institute, 1975.
Canetti, Elias. *Crowds and Power*. Translated by Carol Stewart. New York: Continuum, 1981. [*Masse und Macht*. Frankfurt: Fischer, 1980.]
Canguilhem, Georges. *On the Normal and the Pathological*. Translated by Carolyn Fawcett. Dordrecht: Reidel, 1978. [*Le normal et le pathologique*. 12th ed. Paris: Quadrige/Presses universitaires de France, 2013.]
Cantor, Georg. "On an Elementary Question in the Theory of Manifolds (1891)." In *From Kant to Hilbert: A Source Book in the Foundations of Mathematics*, Vol. 2, edited and translated by William Ewald, 920–2. Oxford: Oxford University, 1996. ["Über eine elementare Frage der Mannigfaltigkeitslehre." In *Gesammelte Abhandlungen mathematischen und philosophischen Inhalts*, edited by Ernst Zermelo, 279–81. Berlin: Springer, 1932.]
Cantor, Georg. *Contributions to the Founding of the Theory of Transfinite Numbers*. Translated by Philip Jourdain. New York: Dover, 1915. ["Beiträge zur Begründung der transfiniten Mengenlehre." In *Gesammelte Abhandlungen mathematischen und philosophischen Inhalts*, edited by Ernst Zermelo, 282–365. Berlin: Springer, 1932.]
Cantor, Georg. "Foundations of a General Theory of Manifolds: A Mathematico-Philosophical Investigation into the Theory of the Infinite (1883d)." In *From Kant to Hilbert: A Source Book in the Foundations of Mathematics*, Vol. 2, edited and translated by William Ewald, 878–920. Oxford: Oxford University, 1996. ["Über unendliche lineare Punktmannigfaltigkeiten (Nr. 5: Grundlagen einer allgemeinen Mannigfaltigkeitslehre)." In *Gesammelte Abhandlungen mathematischen und philosophischen Inhalts*, edited by Ernst Zermelo, 165–209. Berlin: Springer, 1932.]
Carnielli, Walter, and Abilio Rodrigues. "On the Philosophy and Mathematics of the Logics of Formal Inconsistency." In *New Directions in Paraconsistent Logic (5th WCP, Kolkata, India, February 2014)*, edited by Jean-Yves Beziau, Mihir Chakraborty, and Soma Dutta, 57–88. New Delhi: Springer, 2015.
Carroll, Lewis. *Alice's Adventures in Wonderland*. In *Complete Works*, 12–132. New York: Random House, 1976.
Carroll, Lewis, and John Tenniel. *Alice's Adventures in Wonderland and Through the Looking Glass (with Ninety-Two Illustrations by John Tenniel)*. New York: Macmillan, 1894.
Christie, Ian. "Rediscovering Eisenstein." In *Eisenstein Rediscovered*, edited by Ian Christie and Richard Taylor, 1–30. London: Routledge, 1993.

Cicero. *De officiis.* Translated by Walter Miller. London/New York: Heinemann/Macmillan, 1913. [Dual language edition].
Cicero. *De oratore*, Book 3: *De fato, Paradoxa stoicorum, De partitione oratoria*. Translated by H. Rackham. Cambridge, MA: Harvard University, 1942. [Dual language edition].
Cicero. *De senectute, De amicitia, De divinatione*. Translated by William Falconer. Cambridge, MA: Harvard University, 1923. [Dual language edition].
Cicero. *In Twenty-Eight Volumes*, Vol. 19: *De Natura Deorum, Academica*. Translated by H. Rackham. 1967 reprint. London/Cambridge, MA: Heinemann/Harvard University, 1933. [Dual language edition].
Clement of Alexandria. *Clemens Alexandrinus*, Vol. 1: *Protrepticus und paedagogus.* (*Die griechischen christlichen Schriftsteller der ersten Jahrhunderte*, Vol. 12). Edited by Otto Stählin. Leipzig: Hinrichs, 1905.
Clement of Alexandria. "The Eighth *Stromateus*." In *The So-Called Eighth* Stromateus *('Liber Logicus') by Clement of Alexandria: Early Christian Reception of Greek Scientific Methodology*, translated by Matyáš Havrda, 86–126. Leiden: Brill, 2016. [*Clemens Alexandrinus*, Vol. 3: Stromata Books 7–8, excerpta ex theodoto, eclogae propheticae, quis dives salvetur, fragmente. (*Die griechischen christlichen Schriftsteller der ersten Jahrhunderte*, Vol.17). Edited by Otto Stählin. Leipzig: Hinrichs 1909.]
Clement of Alexandria. *The Writings of Clement of Alexandria*, Vol. 2: *The Miscellanies*, Books 2–8 (*Ante-Nicene Christian Library. Translations of the Writings of the Fathers down to A.D. 325*, Vol. 12: *Clement of Alexandria*). Translated by William Wilson. Edinburgh: Clark, 1869. [*Clemens Alexandrinus*, Vol. 2: *Stromata*, Books 1–6. (*Die griechischen christlichen Schriftsteller der ersten Jahrhunderte*, Vol. 15). Edited by Otto Stählin. Leipzig: Hinrichs, 1906.]
Cleomedes. *Cleomedes' Lectures on Astronomy: A Translation of* The Heavens. Translated by Alan Bowen and Robert Todd. Berkeley: University of California, 2004. [θεωρίας μετεώρων, Book 2. Edited and translated by Hermann Ziegler. Leipzig: Teubner, 1891.]
Collet, Guillaume. "Concept and History: The (Trans)Disciplinarity of Deleuze and Guattari's Political Philosophy." *Stasis* 6, no. 2 (2018): 66–91.
Collin de Plancy, Jacques. *Dictionnaire infernal, ou bibliothèque universelle: planches*. Paris: Mongie, 1826.
Cressole, Michel. *Deleuze*. Paris: Universitaires, 1973.
Culp, Andrew. *Dark Deleuze*. Minneapolis, MN: University of Minnesota, 2016.
Dawkins, Richard, and Neil deGrasse Tyson. "The Poetry of Science: Richard Dawkins and Neil DeGrasse Tyson." Public lecture. Howard University. Cramton Auditorium, Washington, DC, September 28, 2010.
de Boer, Karen. "Hegel's Account of Contradiction in the Science of Logic Reconsidered." *Journal of the History of Philosophy* 48, no. 3 (2010): 345–74.
de Boer, Karen. *On Hegel: The Sway of the Negative*. London: Palgrave Macmillan, 2010.
Delaunay, Robert. *Portuguese Woman (Femme portugaise)*. Painting, 1915.
Deleuze, Gilles. "Bartleby, or the Formula." In *Essays Critical and Clinical*, translated by Daniel Smith and Michael Greco, 68–90. Minneapolis, MN: University of Minnesota, 1997. ["Bartleby, ou la formule." In *Critique et clinique*, 89–114. Paris: Minuit, 1993.]
Deleuze, Gilles. "The Brain Is the Screen." In *Two Regimes of Madness: Texts and Interviews 1975–1995*, edited by David Lapoujade and translated by Ames Hodges and Mike Taormina, 282–91. New York: Semiotext(e), 2006. ["Le cerveau, c'est l'écran." In *Deux régimes de fous: textes et entretiens, 1975–1995*, edited by David Lapoujade, 263–71. Paris: Minuit, 2003.]

Deleuze, Gilles. *Cinema 1: The Movement-Image*. Translated by Hugh Tomlinson and Barbara Habberjam. London: Continuum, 2005. [*Cinéma 1: L'image-mouvement*. Paris: Minuit, 1983.]

Deleuze, Gilles. *Cinema 2: The Time-Image*. Translated by Hugh Tomlinson and Robert Galeta. London: Continuum, 2005. [*Cinéma 2: L'image-temps*. Paris: Minuit, 1985.]

Deleuze, Gilles. **Courses**. **Formatted in the following way**. *BNF*: Whether recordings are available at Bibliothèque nationale de France/Gallica, and if so, the url address as coming after http://gallica.bnf.fr/ark:/12148. (For instance: http://gallica.bnf.fr/ark:/12148/bpt6k1282718). *Voix*: Whether recordings and transcripts are available at *La voix de Gilles Deleuze en ligne*, Université Paris 8, and if so, the transcribers and the url address as coming after http://www2.univ-paris8.fr/deleuze/article.php3?id_article. (For instance: http://www2.univ-paris8.fr/deleuze/article.php3?id_article=131). *Web Deleuze*: Whether recordings, transcripts, or translations are available at *Web Deleuze*, and if so, the transcribers and translators, and the url address as coming after https://www.webdeleuze.com/textes. (For instance: https://www.webdeleuze.com/textes/115).

Deleuze, Gilles. *Course 1971.11.16*. Paris. *BNF*: none. *Voix*: none. *Web Deleuze*: Transcript and English translation. Translation by Rojan Josh. …/115; …/116.

Deleuze, Gilles. *Course 1971.12.14*. Paris. *BNF*: none. *Voix*: none. *Web Deleuze*: Transcript and English translation. Translation by Rojan Josh. …/118; …/119.

Deleuze, Gilles. *Course 1971.12.21*. Paris. *BNF*: none. *Voix*: none. *Web Deleuze*: Transcript. …/121.

Deleuze, Gilles. *Course 1972.02.15*. Paris. *BNF*: none. *Voix*: none. *Web Deleuze*: Transcript. …/156.

Deleuze, Gilles. *Course 1972.02.22*. Paris. *BNF*: none. *Voix*: none. *Web Deleuze*: Transcript. …/158.

Deleuze, Gilles. *Course 1972.03.07*. Paris. *BNF*: none. *Voix*: none. *Web Deleuze*: Transcript. …/160.

Deleuze, Gilles. *Course 1972.04.18*. Paris. *BNF*: none. *Voix*: none. *Web Deleuze*: Transcript. …/162.

Deleuze, Gilles. *Course 1973.02.12*. Paris. *BNF*: none. *Voix*: none. *Web Deleuze*: Transcript. …/164.

Deleuze, Gilles. *Course 1978.03.14*. Paris. *BNF*: none. *Voix*: none. *Web Deleuze*: Transcript and English translation. Translation by Melissa McMahon …/58; …/66.

Deleuze, Gilles. *Course 1978.03.28*. Paris. *BNF*: none. *Voix*: none. *Web Deleuze*: Transcript and English translation. Translation by Melissa McMahon …/60; …/68.

Deleuze, Gilles. *Course 1978.04.04*. Paris. *BNF*: none. *Voix*: none. *Web Deleuze*: Transcript and English translation. Translation by Melissa McMahon …/57; …/65.

Deleuze, Gilles. *Course 1979.11.20, Part 3*. Paris. *BNF*: Recording. …/bpt6k1282718. *Voix*: none. *Web Deleuze*: none.

Deleuze, Gilles. *Course 1980.01.29, Part 2*. Paris. *BNF*: Recording. …/bpt6k1282765. *Voix*: none. *Web Deleuze*: none.

Deleuze, Gilles. *Course 1980.02.05, Part 1*. Paris. *BNF*: Recording. …/bpt6k128277j. *Voix*: none. *Web Deleuze*: none.

Deleuze, Gilles. *Course 1980.02.05, Part 2*. Paris. *BNF*: Recording. …/bpt6k128277j. *Voix*: none. *Web Deleuze*: none.

Deleuze, Gilles. *Course 1980.02.05, Part 3*. Paris. *BNF*: Recording. …/bpt6k128277j. *Voix*: none. *Web Deleuze*: none.

Deleuze, Gilles. *Course 1980.02.26, Part 1*. Paris. *BNF*: Recording. …/bpt6k128278x. *Voix*: none. *Web Deleuze*: none.

Deleuze, Gilles. *Course 1980.02.26, Part 2*. Paris. *BNF*: Recording. .../bpt6k128278x. *Voix*: none. *Web Deleuze*: none.
Deleuze, Gilles. *Course 1980.02.26, Part 3*. Paris. *BNF*: Recording. .../bpt6k128278x. *Voix*: none. *Web Deleuze*: none.
Deleuze, Gilles. *Course 1980.03.18, Part 2*. Paris. *BNF*: Recording. .../bpt6k128281m. *Voix*: none. *Web Deleuze*: none.
Deleuze, Gilles. *Course 1980.03.18, Part 3*. Paris. *BNF*: Recording. .../bpt6k128281m. *Voix*: none. *Web Deleuze*: none.
Deleuze, Gilles. *Course 1980.03.25, Part 1*. Paris. *BNF*: Recording. .../bpt6k1282820. *Voix*: none. *Web Deleuze*: none.
Deleuze, Gilles. *Course 1980.03.25, Part 2*. Paris. *BNF*: Recording. .../bpt6k1282820. *Voix*: none. *Web Deleuze*: none.
Deleuze, Gilles. *Course 1980.04.22, Part 1*. Paris. *BNF*: Recording. .../bpt6k128283c. *Voix*: none. *Web Deleuze*: Transcript and English translation. Translation by Charles Stivale. .../51; .../53.
Deleuze, Gilles. *Course 1980.04.29, Part 1*. Paris. *BNF*: Recording. .../bpt6k128284r. *Voix*: none. *Web Deleuze*: Transcript and English translation. Translation by Charles Stivale. .../54; .../55.
Deleuze, Gilles. *Course 1980.05.06, Part 2*. Paris. *BNF*: Recording. .../bpt6k1282854. *Voix*: none. *Web Deleuze*: Transcript and English translation. Translation by Charles Stivale. .../127; .../128.
Deleuze, Gilles. Deleuze, Gilles. *Course 1980.12.02, Part 2*. Paris. *BNF*: Recording. .../bpt6k128289n. *Voix*: Recording and transcript. Transcription by Christina Rosky. ...=131. *Web Deleuze*: none.
Deleuze, Gilles. *Course 1981.11.24, Part 2*. Paris. *BNF*: Recording. .../bpt6k128266t. *Voix*: Recording and transcript. Transcription by Claire Pano. ...=82. *Web Deleuze*: none.
Deleuze, Gilles. *Course 1982.01.12, Part 2*. Paris. *BNF*: Recording. .../bpt6k128263p. *Voix*: Recording and transcript. Transcription by Koné Assétou. ...=189. *Web Deleuze*: none.
Deleuze, Gilles. *Course 1982.11.02, Part 2*. Paris. *BNF*: Recording. .../bpt6k128323m. *Voix*: Recording and transcript. Transcription by Anna Mrozek. ...=159. *Web Deleuze*: none.
Deleuze, Gilles. *Course 1982.11.30, Part 1*. Paris. *BNF*: Recording. .../bpt6k128325c. *Voix*: Recording and transcript. Transcription by Lucie Lembrez. ...=184. *Web Deleuze*: Transcript (with different cut excisions than *Voix*'s, completing one another). .../76.
Deleuze, Gilles. *Course 1982.12.07, Part 1*. Paris. *BNF*: Recording. .../bpt6k128326r. *Voix*: Recording and transcript. Transcription by Binak Kalludra. ...=197. *Web Deleuze*: none.
Deleuze, Gilles. *Course 1982.12.07, Part 2*. Paris. *BNF*: Recording. .../bpt6k128326r. *Voix*: Recording and transcript. Transcription by Marie Hélène Tanné. ...=162. *Web Deleuze*: none.
Deleuze, Gilles. *Course 1983.03.22, Part 2*. Paris. *BNF*: Recording. .../bpt6k128337g. *Voix*: Recording and transcript. Transcription by Alice Haëck. ... =248. *Web Deleuze*: Partial transcript. ... /75. (The transcription for *Voix* part 1 of this date, by Elen Brandao Pimentel, is identical to the transcription at *Web Deleuze*. ...=234.)
Deleuze, Gilles. *Course 1983.04.12, Part 3*. Paris. *BNF*: Recording. ... /bpt6k128338v. *Voix*: None. (But *BNF*'s audio correlates with part of the transcript at *Voix*, part 1 for this date. ...=235.) *Web Deleuze*: Transcript. ... /72. (The *Web Deleuze* transcript is nearly identical to *Voix*, part 1 for this date. *Web Deleuze* is perhaps the original transcription source, but no transcriber is listed at either site. Proofing at *Voix* by Fabienne Kabou.)

Deleuze, Gilles. *Course 1983.05.03, Part 2*. Paris. *BNF*: Recording. .../bpt6k128341j. *Voix*: Recording and transcript. Transcription by Jean-Charles Jarrell. ...=243. *Web Deleuze*: none.

Deleuze, Gilles. *Course 1983.05.17, Part 1*. Paris. *BNF*: Recording. .../ bpt6k128342x. *Voix*: Recording and transcript. (No transcriber is named.) ...=236. *Web Deleuze*: Transcript. Transcription by François Zourabichvili. .../204. (The *Voix* transcript is identical to *Web Deleuze*, which is perhaps the original source, and thus the *Voix* one perhaps is also transcribed by Zourabichvili.)

Deleuze, Gilles. *Course 1983.05.17, Part 2*. Paris. *BNF*: Recording. .../ bpt6k128342x. *Voix*: Recording and transcript. (No transcriber is named.) ...=250. *Web Deleuze*: Transcript. Transcription by François Zourabichvili. .../204. (See transcription notes above for Part 1 of this date.)

Deleuze, Gilles. *Course 1983.05.17, Part 3*. Paris. *BNF*: Recording. .../ bpt6k128342x. *Voix*: Recording and transcript. (No transcriber is named.) ...=251. *Web Deleuze*: Transcript. Transcription by François Zourabichvili. .../204. (See transcription notes above for Part 1 of this date.)

Deleuze, Gilles. *Course 1983.05.24, Part 1*. Paris. *BNF*: Recording. .../bpt6k1283439. *Voix*: Recording and transcript. Transcription by Antonin Pochan. ...=244. *Web Deleuze*: none.

Deleuze, Gilles. *Course 1983.11.08, Part 1*. Paris. *BNF*: Recording. .../bpt6k128239x. *Voix*: Recording and transcript. Transcription by Farid Fafa. ...=260. *Web Deleuze*: none.

Deleuze, Gilles. *Course 1983.11.08, Part 2*. Paris. *BNF*: Recording. .../bpt6k128239x. *Voix*: Recording and transcript. Transcription by Nadia Ouis. ...=261. *Web Deleuze*: none.

Deleuze, Gilles. *Course 1983.11.22, Part 1* (of *BNF*; *Part 2* of *Voix*). Paris. *BNF*: Recording. .../bpt6k128240v. *Voix*: Recording and transcript. (*BNF*'s audio corresponds with *Voix*, part 2 of this date.) *Voix* Part 2 transcription by Hélène Burhy. ...=263. *Web Deleuze*: none.

Deleuze, Gilles. *Course 1983.11.22, Part 2*. Paris. *BNF*: Recording. .../bpt6k128240v. *Voix*: none. (The transcript at *Voix* for this part corresponds to *BNF*'s audio for part 1 of this date. No *Voix* transcript corresponds to this audio. See ...=263.) *Web Deleuze*: none.

Deleuze, Gilles. *Course 1983.11.22, Part 3*. Paris. *BNF*: Recording. .../bpt6k128240v. *Voix*: Recording and transcript. Transcription by Nadia Ouis. ...=264. *Web Deleuze*: none.

Deleuze, Gilles. *Course 1983.11.29, Part 1* (of *BNF*; *1983.11.22, Part 1* of *Voix*). Paris. *BNF*: Recording. .../bpt6k1282417. *Voix*: Recording and transcript. (*BNF*'s audio corresponds to *Voix 1983.11.22, Part 1*. ...=262.) *Web Deleuze*: none.

Deleuze, Gilles. *Course 1983.11.29, Part 2* (of *BNF*; *Parts 1* and *2* of *Voix*). Paris. *BNF*: Recording. .../bpt6k1282417. *Voix*: Recording and transcript. (The beginning of *Voix*, part 1 is repeated in *Voix*, part 2. The end of *Voix*, part 1 is repeated in *Voix*, part 3. Cut out of *Voix*, part 1 is material found in the middle of *BNF*, part 2. *Voix*, part 1 transcription by Alice Haëck. ...=265. And *Voix*, part 2 by Marina Llecha Llop. ...=266.) *Web Deleuze*: none.

Deleuze, Gilles. *Course 1983.11.29, Part 3* (of *BNF*; *Parts 1* and *3* of *Voix*). Paris. *BNF*: Recording. .../bpt6k1282417. *Voix*: Recording and transcript. (See transcription notes above for Part 2 of this date. *Voix*, part 1 transcription by Fofana Yaya and Alice Haëck. ...=265. And *Voix*, part 3 by Abigail Heathcote. ...=267.) *Web Deleuze*: none.

Deleuze, Gilles. *Course 1983.12.06, Part 1*. Paris. *BNF*: Recording. .../bpt6k128242m. *Voix*: Recording and transcript. Transcription by Fatemeh Malekahmadi. ...=268. *Web Deleuze*: none.

Deleuze, Gilles. *Course 1984.01.10, Part 3*. Paris. *BNF*: Recording. .../bpt6k128245r. *Voix*: Recording and transcript. Transcription by Agathe Vidal. ...=318. *Web Deleuze*: none.

Deleuze, Gilles. *Course 1984.06.12, Part 3*. Paris. *BNF*: Recording. .../bpt6k128260j. *Voix*: Recording and transcript. Transcription by Ian Parker. ...=364. *Web Deleuze*: none.

Deleuze, Gilles. *Course 1984.12.18, Part 1*. Paris. *BNF*: Recording. .../bpt6k1283528. *Voix*: Recording and transcript. Transcription by Ezequiel Romero Diaz. ...=285. *Web Deleuze*: none.

Deleuze, Gilles. *Course 1985.08.01, Part 2*. Paris. *BNF*: Recording. .../bpt6k128353n. *Voix*: Recording and transcript. Transcription by Charline Guilaume. ...=289. *Web Deleuze*: none.

Deleuze, Gilles. *Course 1986.03.04, Part 2*. Paris. *BNF*: Recording. .../bpt6k128385f. *Voix*: Recording and transcript. (Transcriber is unattributed.) ...=459. *Web Deleuze*: Transcription. .../277. (Transcriber is unattributed, and transcription is nearly identical to *Voix*.)

Deleuze, Gilles. *Course 1986.04.08, Part 2*. Paris. *BNF*: Recording. .../bpt6k128389z. *Voix*: Recording and transcript. (Transcriber is unattributed.) ...=476. *Web Deleuze*: Transcription. .../281. (Transcriber is unattributed, and transcription is nearly identical to *Voix*.)

Deleuze, Gilles. *Difference and Repetition*. Translated by Paul Patton. New York: Columbia University, 1994. [*Différence et répétition*. 11th ed. Paris: Presses universitaires de France, 2003.]

Deleuze, Gilles. *The Fold: Leibniz and the Baroque*. Translated by Tom Conley. Minneapolis, MN: University of Minnesota, 1993. [*Le pli: Leibniz et le baroque*. Paris: Minuit, 1988.]

Deleuze, Gilles. *Foucault*. Edited and translated by Seán Hand. Minneapolis, MN: University of Minnesota, 1988. [*Foucault*. Paris: Minuit, 2004.]

Deleuze, Gilles. "On Four Poetic Formulas That Might Summarize the Kantian Philosophy." In *Essays Critical and Clinical*, translated by Daniel Smith and Michael Greco, 27–35. Minneapolis, MN: University of Minnesota, 1997. ["Sur quatre formules poétiques qui pourraient résumer la philosophie kantienne." In *Critique et clinique*, 40–49. Paris: Minuit, 1993.]

Deleuze, Gilles. "To Have Done with Judgment." In *Essays Critical and Clinical*, translated by Daniel Smith and Michael Greco, 126–35. Minneapolis, MN: University of Minnesota, 1997. ["Pour en finir avec le jugement." In *Critique et clinique*, 158–69. Paris: Minuit, 1993.]

Deleuze, Gilles. "How Philosophy Is Useful to Mathematicians or Musicians." In *Two Regimes of Madness: Texts and Interviews 1975–1995*, edited by David Lapoujade and translated by Ames Hodges and Mike Taormina, 166–8. New York: Semiotext(e), 2006. ["En quoi la philosophie peut servir à des mathématiciens ou même à des musiciens—même et surtout quand elle ne parle pas de musique ou de mathématiques." In *Deux régimes de fous: textes et entretiens, 1975–1995*, edited by David Lapoujade, 152–54. Paris: Minuit, 2003.]

Deleuze, Gilles. "Letter to a Harsh Critic." In *Negotiations: 1972–1990*, translated by Martin Joughin, 3–12. New York: Columbia University, 1995. ["Lettre à un critique sévère." In *Pourparlers: 1972–1990*, 11–23. Paris: Minuit, 1990.]

Deleuze, Gilles. "Literature and Life." In *Essays Critical and Clinical*, translated by Daniel Smith and Michael Greco, 1–6. Minneapolis, MN: University of Minnesota, 1997. ["La littérature et la vie." In *Critique et clinique*, 11–17. Paris: Minuit, 1993.]

Deleuze, Gilles. *The Logic of Sense*. Translated by Mark Lester and Charles Stivale. London: Continuum, 2004. [*Logique du sens*. Paris: Minuit, 1969.]

Deleuze, Gilles. *Nietzsche and Philosophy*. Translated by Hugh Tomlinson. New York: Columbia University, 2006. [*Nietzsche et la philosophie*. 6th ed. Paris: Presses universitaires de France, 1983.]

Deleuze, Gilles. "Preface to the American Edition of *The Movement-Image*." In *Two Regimes of Madness: Texts and Interviews 1975–1995*, edited by David Lapoujade and translated by Ames Hodges and Mike Taormina. New York: Semiotext(e), 2006. ["Préface pour l'édition américaine de *L'image-mouvement*." In *Deux régimes de fous: textes et entretiens, 1975–1995*, edited by David Lapoujade. Paris: Minuit, 2003.]

Deleuze, Gilles. *Spinoza: Practical Philosophy*. Translated by Robert Hurley. San Francisco: City Lights, 1988. [*Spinoza: Philosophie pratique*. Revised and expanded edition. Paris: Minuit, 1981.]

Deleuze, Gilles. "On *The Time-Image*." In *Negotiations:1972–1990*, translated by Martin Joughin, 57–61. New York: Columbia University, 1995. ["Sur *L'image-temps*." In *Pourparlers: 1972–1990*, 82–87. Paris: Minuit, 1990.]

Deleuze, Gilles. "What Is the Creative Act?" In *Two Regimes of Madness: Texts and Interviews 1975–1995*, edited by David Lapoujade and translated by Ames Hodges and Mike Taormina, 312–24. New York: Semiotext(e), 2006. ["Qu'est-ce que l'acte de création?" In *Deux régimes de fous: textes et entretiens, 1975–1995*, edited by David Lapoujade, 291–302. Paris: Minuit, 2003.]

Deleuze, Gilles. *What Is Grounding?* Edited by Tony Yanick, Jason Adams, and Mohammad Salemy. Translated by Arjen Kleinherenbrink. Grand Rapids, MI: &&&, 2015. [*Qu'est-ce que fonder?* (Course 1955.11.30). *Web Deleuze*. Transcript by Pierre Lefebvre, 1955. https://www.webdeleuze.com/textes/218.]

Deleuze, Gilles, and Arnaud Villani. "Responses to a Series of Questions." In *Collapse*, edited and translated by Robin Mackay, Reissued edition. First published 2007, 3:39–43. Falmouth: Urbanomic, 2012. ["Réponses à une série de questions (Novembre 1981)." In *La guêpe et l'orchidée: essai sur Gilles Deleuze*, 129–31. Paris: Belin, 1999.]

Deleuze, Gilles, and Claire Parnet. *From A to Z*. DVD. Directed by Pierre-André Boutang. English subtitle translation by Charles Stivale. Los Angeles and Cambridge, MA: Semiotext(e) and MIT, 2012. [*L'abécédaire*. DVD. Paris: Montparnasse, 2004.]

Deleuze, Gilles, and Claire Parnet. *Dialogues II*. Translated by Hugh Tomlinson and Barbara Habberjam. Revised edition. New York: Columbia University, 2007. [*Dialogues*. Paris: Flammarion, 1996.]

Deleuze, Gilles, and Félix Guattari. *Anti-Oedipus: Capitalism and Schizophrenia, 1*. Translated by Robert Hurley, Mark Seem, and Helen Lane. Minneapolis, MN: University of Minnesota, 1983. [*L'anti-Œdipe: capitalisme et schizophrénie, 1*. Paris: Minuit, 1973.]

Deleuze, Gilles, and Félix Guattari. *Kafka: Toward a Minor Literature*. Translated by Dana Polan. Minneapolis, MN: University of Minnesota, 1986. [*Kafka: pour une littérature mineure*. Paris: Minuit, 1975.]

Deleuze, Gilles, and Félix Guattari. *A Thousand Plateaus: Capitalism and Schizophrenia, 2*. Translated by Brian Massumi. London: Continuum, 2004. [*Mille plateaux: Capitalisme et schizophrénie, 2*. Paris: Minuit, 1980.]

Deleuze, Gilles, and Félix Guattari. *What Is Philosophy?* Translated by Hugh Tomlinson and Graham Burchell. New York: Columbia University, 1994. [*Qu'est-ce que la philosophie?* Paris: Minuit, 1991.]

Desargues, Girard. "Rough Draft on Conics (1639)." In *The Geometrical Work of Girard Desargues*, edited and translated by Judith Field and Jeremy Gray, 69–143. New York: Springer, 1987. ["Brouillon project d'une atteinte aux événements des rencontres du cône avec un plan." In *Oeuvres*, Vol. 1, edited by Noël-Germinal Poudra, 103–302. Paris: Leiber, 1864.]

Destouches-Février, Paulette. "Manifestations et sens de la notion de complémentarité." *Dialectica* 2, no. 3/4 (1948): 383–412.

Destouches-Février, Paulette. "Rapports entre le calcul des problemes et le calcul des propositions." *Comptes rendus hebdomadaires des séances de l'Académie des sciences* 220 (1945): 484–6.

Diogenes Laertius. *Lives of Eminent Philosophers*, Vol. 2. Translated by R. Hicks. Revised and reprinted. Cambridge, MA: Harvard University, 1931. [Dual language edition].

Duffy, Simon. *The Logic of Expression: Quality, Quantity and Intensity in Spinoza, Hegel and Deleuze*. Aldershot: Ashgate, 2006.

Dumas, Alexandre. *The Wolf-Leader*. Translated by Alfred Allinson. London: Methuen, 1904. [*Le meneur de loups*. Paris: Lévy, 1868.]

Dummett, Michael. *Elements of Intuitionism*. 2nd ed. Oxford: Oxford University, 2000.

Dummett, Michael. "The Philosophical Basis of Intuitionistic Logic." In *Philosophy of Mathematics: Selected Readings*, edited by Paul Benacerraf and Hilary Putnam, 2nd ed., 97–129. Cambridge: Cambridge University, 1983.

Dummett, Michael. "Wittgenstein's Philosophy of Mathematics." *The Philosophical Review* 68, no. 3 (1959): 324–48.

Dupouy, Roger. "Du masochisme." *Annales médico-psychologiques* 12, no. 2 (1929): 393–405.

Dupréel, Eugène. "La cause et l'intervalle ou ordre et probabilité." In *Essais pluralistes*, 196–235. Paris: Presses universitaires de France, 1949.

Dupréel, Eugène. *La consistance et la probabilité constructive*. Brussels: Académie Royale de Belgique, 1961.

Dupréel, Eugène. *Esquisse d'une philosophie des valeurs*. Paris: Alcan, 1939.

Dupréel, Eugène. "Théorie de la consolidation: Esquisse d'une théorie de la vie d'inspiration sociologique." In *Essais pluralistes*, 150–95. Paris: Presses universitaires de France, 1949.

Eisenstein, Sergei. *Film Form: Essays in Film Theory*. Edited and translated by Jay Leyda. London: Dobson, 1951.

Eisenstein, Sergei. *The General Line/The Old and the New (Staroye i Novoye)*. Sovkino, 1929.

Eisenstein, Sergei. *Nonindifferent Nature*. Translated by Herbert Marshall. Cambridge: Cambridge University, 1987.

Engel, Pascal. *La norme du vrai*. Paris: Gallimard, 1989.

Epictetus. *The Discourses of Epictetus*. Edited by Christopher Gill. Translated by Robin Hard. Everyman edition. (Revised from Elizabeth Carter's English translation, Everyman, 1957). London/North Clarendon, VT: Dent/Tuttle, 1995. [*Dissertationes ab Arriano digestae*. Edited by Heinrich Schenkl. Leipzig: Teubner, 1916.]

Euclid, and Oliver Byrne. *The First Six Books of the Elements of Euclid, in Which Coloured Diagrams and Symbols Are Used Instead of Letters for the Greater Ease of Learners*. London: Pickering, 1847.

Euclid, and Thomas Heath. *The Thirteen Books of Euclid's Elements*, Vol. 1: *Introduction and Books I, II*. Cambridge: Cambridge University, 1908.

Euclid, and Thomas Heath. *The Thirteen Books of Euclid's Elements*, Vol. 2: *Books III–IX*. Cambridge: Cambridge University, 1908.

Eusebius. *Werke*, Vol. 8: *Die Praeparatio evangelica*, Part 1: *Einleitung, die Bücher I bis X*. (*Die griechischen christlichen Schriftsteller der ersten Jahrhunderte*, Vol. 43.1). Edited by Karl Mras. Berlin: Akademie, 1982.

Eusebius. *Werke*, Vol. 8: *Die Praeparatio evangelica*, Part 2: *Die Bücher XI bis XV, Register*. (*Die griechischen christlichen Schriftsteller der ersten Jahrhunderte*, Vol. 43.2). Edited by Karl Mras. Berlin: Akademie, 1956.

Ficara, Elena. "Dialectic and Dialetheism." *History and Philosophy of Logic* 34, no. 1 (2013): 35–52.

Ficara, Elena. "Hegel's Glutty Negation." *History and Philosophy of Logic* 36, no. 1 (2015): 29–38.

Fichte, Johann Gottlieb. *Science of Knowledge (Wissenschaftslehre) with the First and Second Introductions*. Edited and translated by Peter Heath and John Lachs. New York: Meredith, 1970. [*Grundlage der gesamten Wissenschaftslehre als Handschrift für seine Zuhörer (1794)*. Hamburg: Meiner, 1997.]

Fichte, Johann Gottlieb. "Second Introduction to the *Science of Knowledge*." In *Science of Knowledge (Wissenschaftslehre) with the First and Second Introductions*, edited and translated by Peter Heath and John Lachs, 29–85. New York: Meredith, 1970. ["Zweite Einleitung in die Wissenschaftslehre." *Philosophisches Journal* 5 (1797): 319–78.]

Fitzgerald, F. Scott. *The Crack-up with Other Pieces and Stories*. Harmondsworth: Penguin, 1965.

Fletcher, Banister. *A History of Architecture on the Comparative Method for the Student, Craftsman, and Amateur*. Revised and enlarged 5th edition. London: Batsford, 1905.

Foucault, Michel. *The Order of Things: An Archaeology of the Human Sciences*. Translated by Alan Sheridan. London/New York: Routledge, 1989. [*Les mots et les choses: Une archéologie des sciences humaines*. Paris: Gallimard, 1966.]

Galen. *Medicorum Graecorum opera quae exstant*, Vol. 4. Edited by Karl Kühn. Leipzig: Knobloch, 1822.

Galen. *Medicorum Graecorum opera quae exstant*, Vol. 7. Edited by Karl Kühn. Leipzig: Knobloch, 1824.

Galen. *Medicorum Graecorum opera quae exstant*, Vol. 10. Edited by Karl Kühn. Leipzig: Knobloch, 1825.

Galen. *Medicorum Graecorum opera quae exstant*, Vol. 14. Edited by Karl Kühn. Leipzig: Knobloch, 1827.

Gellius. *The Attic Nights*, Vol. 3. Translated by John Rolfe. London/New York: Heinemann/Putnam, 1928. [Dual language edition].

Gellius. *Noctes Atticae*, Vol. 1. Edited by Jakob Gronovius. London: Valpy, 1824.

Gillies, D. A. "Brouwer's Philosophy of Mathematics (Review of *Collected Works* by L. E. J. Brouwer, Edited by A. Heyting and H. Freudenthal)." *Erkenntnis* 15, no. 1 (1980): 105–26.

Goldschmidt, Victor. *Le système stoïcien et l'idée de temps*. Paris: Vrin, 1953.

Graeser, Andreas. "The Stoic Theory of Meaning." In *The Stoics*, edited by John Rist, 77–100. Berkeley and Los Angeles: University of California, 1978.

Grémillon, Jean. *The Lighthouse Keepers (Gardiens de Phare)*. Films du Grand Guignol, 1929.

Griffith, D. W. *The Massacre*. Biograph, 1912.

Griss, G. F. C. "Logic of Negationless Intuitionistic Mathematics." *Proceedings of the Koninklijke Nederlandse Akademie van Wetenschappen* 54 (1951): 41–9.

Griss, G. F. C. "Negationless Intuitionistic Mathematics, I." *Proceedings of the Koninklijke Nederlandse Akademie van Wetenschappen* 49, no. 10 (1946): 1127–33.

Griss, G. F. C. "Negationless Intuitionistic Mathematics, II." *Proceedings of the Koninklijke Nederlandse Akademie van Wetenschappen* 53, no. 4 (1950): 456–63.

Griss, G. F. C. "Negationless Intuitionistic Mathematics, III." *Indagationes Mathematicae (Proceedings)* 54 (1951): 193–9.

Griss, G. F. C. "Sur la négation (Dans les mathématiques et la logique)." *Synthese*, no. 1/2 (1949): 71–4.

Grünberg, Teo. *Modern Logic*. Ankara: Middle East Technical University, 2002.

Gunning, Tom. "D. W. Griffith and the Primal Scene." In *A Companion to D. W. Griffith*, edited by Charlie Keil, 137–49. Hoboken, NJ: Wiley, 2018.

Haack, Susan. *Deviant Logic, Fuzzy Logic: Beyond the Formalism*. 2nd ed. Chicago: University of Chicago, 1996.

Hall, Manly. *The Secret Teaching of All Ages: An Encyclopedic Outline of Masonic, Hermetic, Qabbalistic, and Rosicrucian Symbolical Philosophy*. Diamond Jubilee edition. Los Angeles: Philosophical Research Society, 1988.

Hawking, Stephen. "Unified Theory." Presented at the 6th European Zeitgeist conference, London, May 2011. https://www.zeitgeistminds.com/talk/60/unified-theory-professor-stephen-hawking.

Hawking, Stephen, and Leonard Mlodinow. *The Grand Design*. New York: Bantam, 2010.

Hegel, G. W. F. *The Encyclopaedia Logic (with the Zusätze): Part I of the* Encyclopedia of Philosophical Sciences *with the Zusätze*. Translated by T. F. Geraets, W. A. Suchting, and H. S. Harris. Indianapolis, IN: Hackett, 1991. [*Werke*, Vol. 8: *Enzyklopädie der philosophischen Wissenschaften im Grundrisse (1830)*, Part 1: *Die Wissenschaft der Logik. Mit den mündlichen Zusätzen*. Edited by Eva Moldenhauer and Karl Markus Michel. Frankfurt: Suhrkamp, 1986.]

Hegel, G. W. F. *The Jena System, 1804–5: Logic and Metaphysics*. Edited by John Burbidge and George di Giovanni. Translated by John Burbidge, Martin Donogho, George di Giovanni, Henry Harris, David Pfohl, and Kenneth Schmitz. Kingston and Montreal: McGill-Queen's University, 1986.

Hegel, G. W. F. *Lectures on Logic: Berlin, 1831*. Translated by Clark Butler. Transcribed by Karl Hegel. Bloomington, IN: Indiana University, 2008.

Hegel, G. W. F. *Lectures on the History of Philosophy*, Vol. 2. Translated by E. S. Haldane and Frances Simson. London: Kagen Paul, Trench, Trübner, 1894. [*Werke*, Vol. 19: *Vorlesungen über die Geschichte der Philosophie II*. Edited by Eva Moldenhauer and Karl Markus Michel. Frankfurt: Suhrkamp, 1986.]

Hegel, G. W. F. *Science of Logic*. Translated by A. V. Miller. Oxford/New York: Routledge, 2002. [*Werke*, Vol. 6: *Wissenschaft der Logik II*, Vol. 1: *Die objektive Logik*, Book 2: *Die Lehre vom Wesen*. Vol. 2: *Die subjektive Logik*. Edited by Eva Moldenhauer and Karl Markus Michel. Frankfurt: Suhrkamp, 1986.]

Heyting, Arend. *Les fondements des mathématiques. Intuitionnisme. Théorie de la démonstration*. Paris/Louven: Gauthier-Villars/E. Nauwelaerts, 1955.

Heyting, Arend. "G. F. C. Griss and His Negationless Intuitionistic Mathematics." *Synthese* 9, no. 2 (1953 1955): 91–6.

Heyting, Arend. *Intuitionism. An Introduction*. Amsterdam: North-Holland, 1956.

Hibben, John. *Hegel's Logic: An Essay in Interpretation*. New York: Scribner, 1902.

Hippolytus. *Refutatio Omnium Haeresium*. Edited by Miroslav Marcovich. Berlin: de Gruyter, 1986.

Hoüel, Jules. *Essai critique sur les principes fondamentaux de la géométrie élémentaire: ou commentaire sur les XXXII premières propositions des Éléments d'Euclide*. 2nd ed. Paris: Gauthier-Villars, 1883.

Hugo, Victor. "Ce que Gemma pense d'Emma." In *Toute la lyre*, Vol. 2, 171–4. Paris: Charpentier, 1889.

Hugo, Victor. "The Jeweller's Shop." In *Works*, Vol. 21: *Poems*, Vol. 3, translated by George Young, 892–4. Boston: Little, Brown, and Company, 1909.

Hyppolite, Jean. *Logic and Existence*. Translated by Leonard Lawlor and Amit Sen. Albany, NY: State University of New York, 1997. [*Logique et existence*. Paris: Presses universitaires de France, 1953.]

Jones, Emily. *A New Law of Thought and Its Logical Bearings*. Cambridge: Cambridge University, 1911.

Jones, Emily. *Elements of Logic as a Science of Propositions*. Edinburgh: Clark, 1890.

Kabay, Paul Douglas. "A Defense of Trivialism." Dissertation, University of Melbourne, 2008.

Kant, Immanuel. *Critique of Pure Reason*. Edited and translated by Paul Guyer and Allen W. Wood. Cambridge: Cambridge University, 1998. [*Kritik der reinen Vernunft*, Vol. 1. In *Werkausgabe*, Vol. 3, edited by Wilhelm Weischedel. Frankfurt: Suhrkamp, 1974.]

Kant, Immanuel. *The Jäsche Logic*. In *Lectures on Logic*, edited and translated by J. Michael Young, 517–640. Cambridge: Cambridge University, 1992. [*Logik. Ein Handbuch zu Vorlesungen*. In *Kant's gesammelte Schriften*, Vol. 9, edited by Königlich Preußischen Akademie der Wissenschaften, 1–150. Berlin/Leipzig: de Gruyter, 1923.]

Kaufmann, Arnold. *Introduction to the Theory of Fuzzy Subsets*. Vol. 1: *Fundamental Theoretical Elements*. Translated by D. L. Swanson. New York: Academic, 1975. [*Introduction à la théorie des sous-ensembles flous à l'usage des ingénieurs (Fuzzy sets theory)*, Vol. 1: *Eléments théoriques de base*. 2nd ed. Paris: Masson, 1977.]

Klossowski, Pierre. *The Baphomet*. Translated by Sophie Hawkes and Stephen Sartarelli. Hygiene, CO: Eridanos, 1988. [*Le Baphomet*. Paris: Mercure de France, 1965.]

Klossowski, Pierre. "Roberte Ce Soir." In *Roberte Ce Soir and the Revocation of the Edict of Nantes*, translated by Austryn Wainhouse, 7–92. Chicago: Dalkey Archive, 2002. [*Roberte ce soir*. Paris: Minuit, 1953.]

Kolmogorov, Andrei. "On the Interpretation of Intuitionistic Logic." In *From Brouwer to Hilbert: The Debate on the Foundations of Mathematics in the 1920's*, edited and translated by Paolo Mancosu, 328–34. Oxford: Oxford University, 1998. ["Zur Deutung der intuitionistischen Logik." *Mathematische Zeitschrift* 35, no. 1 (1932): 58–65.]

Koning, Hans. *The World of Vermeer, 1632–1675*. Alexandria, VA: Time-Life, 1967.

Kramer, Edna. *The Nature and Growth of Modern Mathematics*. Princeton: Princeton University, 1981.

Lang, Fritz. *Metropolis*. Universum Film, 1927.

Lapoujade, David. *Aberrant Movements: The Philosophy of Gilles Deleuze*. Translated by Joshua Jordan. South Pasadena, CA: Semiotext(e), 2017. [*Deleuze, les mouvements aberrants*. Paris: Minuit, 2014.]

Laurence, Lauron de, ed. *The Lesser Key of Solomon. Goetia: The Book of Evil Spirits*. Chicago: de Laurence, Scott, 1916.

Leblanc, Maurice. *La vie extravagante de Balthazar*. Paris: Le livre de poche, 1979.

Leibniz, Gottfried. "On Contingency." In *Philosophical Essays*, translated by Roger Ariew and Daniel Garber, 28–30. Indianapolis, IN: Hackett, 1989. ["De contingentia." In *Sämtliche Schriften und Briefe*, Series 6: *Philosophische Schriften*, Vol. 4, edited by Academy of Sciences of Berlin, 1649–52. Berlin: Akademie, 1999.]

Leibniz, Gottfried. *Correspondence between Leibniz and Arnauld*. In *Discourse on Metaphysics, Correspondence with Arnauld, and Monadology*, edited by Thomas McCormack and translated by George Montgomery, 65–248. Chicago: Open Court, 1908. [*Briefwechsel zwischen Leibniz, Landgraf Ernst von Hessen-Rheinfels und Antoine*

Arnauld (1686-1690). In *Die Philosophischen Schriften*, Vol. 2, edited by Carl Gerhardt, 1-138. Hildesheim: Olms, 1978.]

Leibniz, Gottfried. *Correspondence with Arnauld (1686-1690)*. In *Philosophical Texts*, edited and translated by Richard Francks and Roger Woolhouse, 94-138. Oxford: Oxford University, 1998. [*Briefwechsel zwischen Leibniz, Landgraf Ernst von Hessen-Rheinfels und Antoine Arnauld (1686-1690)*. In *Die Philosophischen Schriften*, Vol. 2, edited by Carl Gerhardt, 1-138. Hildesheim: Olms, 1978.]

Leibniz, Gottfried. "De quadratura arithmetica circuli ellipseos et hyperbolae." In *Sämtliche Schriften und Briefe*, Series 7: *Mathematische Schriften*, Vol. 6, edited by Academy of Sciences of Berlin, 520-676. Berlin: Akademie, 2012.

Leibniz, Gottfried. *Discourse on Metaphysics*. In *Philosophical Texts*, edited and translated by Richard Francks and Roger Woolhouse, 53-93. Oxford: Oxford University, 1998. [*Discours de métaphysique*. In *Sämtliche Schriften und Briefe*, Series 6: *Philosophische Schriften*, Vol. 4, edited by Academy of Sciences of Berlin, 1529-88. Berlin: Akademie, 1999.]

Leibniz, Gottfried. "First Truths." In *Philosophical Papers and Letters*, edited and translated by Leroy Loemker, 2nd ed., 267-71. Dordrecht: Kluwer, 1989. ["Primae veritates." In *Opuscules et fragments inédits de Leibniz. Extraits des manuscrits de la Bibliothèque Royale de Hanovre*, edited by Louis Couturat, 518-23. Paris: Alcan, 1903.]

Leibniz, Gottfried. "On First Truths." In *The Shorter Leibniz Texts: A Collection of New Translations*, edited and translated by Lloyd Strickland, 29-30. London: Continuum, 2006. ["De veritatibus primis." In *Sämtliche Schriften und Briefe*, Series 6: *Philosophische Schriften*, Vol. 4, edited by Academy of Sciences of Berlin, 1442-43. Berlin: Akademie, 1999.]

Leibniz, Gottfried. "Letter to Coste, on Human Freedom (19 December 1707)." In *Philosophical Essays*, edited and translated by Roger Ariew and Daniel Garber, 193-96. Indianapolis, IN: Hackett, 1989. ["Briefwechsel zwischen Leibniz und Coste (1706-1712)." In *Die Philosophischen Schriften*, Vol. 3, edited by Carl Gerhardt, 377-436. Hildesheim: Olms, 1978.]

Leibniz, Gottfried. "Letters to Louis Bourguet (1714-1715)." In *Philosophical Papers and Letters*, edited and translated by Leroy Loemker, 2nd ed., 661-5. Dordrecht: Kluwer, 1989. ["Briefwechsel zwischen Leibniz und Bourguet (1709-1716)." In *Die Philosophischen Schriften*, Vol. 3, edited by Carl Gerhardt, 537-96. Hildesheim: Olms, 1978.]

Leibniz, Gottfried. *Monadology*. In *Philosophical Texts*, edited and translated by Richard Francks and Roger Woolhouse, 267-81. Oxford: Oxford University, 1998. [*Monadologie*. In *Die Philosophischen Schriften*, Vol. 6, edited by Carl Gerhardt, 607-23. Berlin: Weidmann, 1885.]

Leibniz, Gottfried. "Monitum de characteribus algebraicis." In *Miscellanea Berolinensia ad incrementum scientarum ex scriptis Societati Regiae Scientarum exhibitis edita*, 155-60. Berlin: Papen, 1710.

Leibniz, Gottfried. "A New Method of Finding the Maxima and Minima, and Likewise for Tangents, and with a Single Kind of Calculation for These, Which Is Hindered Neither by Fractions Nor Irrational Quantities." Translated by Ian Bruce. Online translation at *Some Mathematical Works of the 17th & 18th Centuries, Including Newton's Principia, Euler's Mechanica, Introductio in Analysin, Etc., Translated Mainly from Latin into English*, 2012, 1-8. http://www.17centurymaths.com/contents/Leibniz/nova1.pdf. ["Nova methodus pro maximis et minimis, itemque tangentibus, quae nec fractas, nec irrationales quantitates moratur, et singulare pro illis calculi genus." In *Mathematische Schriften*, Vol. 5, edited by Carl Gerhardt, 220-6. Halle: Schmidt, 1858.]

Leibniz, Gottfried. "On the Method of Universality." In *Selections*, edited and translated by Philip P. Wiener, 3–4. New York: Scribner, 1951. ["De la méthode de l'universalité." In *Opuscules et fragments inédits de Leibniz. Extraits des manuscrits de la Bibliothèque Royale de Hanovre*, edited by Louis Couturat, 97–143. Paris: Alcan, 1903.]

Leibniz, Gottfried. "On the Secrets of the Sublime, or on the Supreme Being." In *De Summa Rerum: Metaphysical Papers, 1675–1676*, edited and translated by G. H. R. Parkinson, 20–33. New Haven, CT: Yale University, 1992. ["De arcanis sublimium vel de summa rerum." In *Sämtliche Schriften und Briefe*, Series 6: *Philosophische Schriften*, Vol. 3, edited by Academy of Sciences of Berlin, 472–7. Berlin: Akademie, 1980.]

Leibniz, Gottfried. *Theodicy: Essays on the Goodness of God, the Freedom of Man and the Origin of Evil*. Edited by Austin Farrer. Translated by E. M. Huggard. Eugene, OR: Wipf and Stock, 2001. [*Essais de Théodicée sur la bonté de Dieu, la liberté de l'homme et l'origine du mal*. In *Die Philosophischen Schriften*, Vol. 6, edited by Carl Gerhardt, 21–471. Berlin: Weidmann, 1885.]

Lévi, Éliphas. *Dogme et rituel de la haute magie*, Vol. 1: *Dogme*. Paris: Germer Baillière, 1861.

Lévi, Éliphas. *Dogme et rituel de la haute magie*, Vol. 2: *Rituel*. Paris: Germer Baillière, 1861.

Lévi, Éliphas. *Theosophical Miscellanies*, Vol. 2: *The Paradoxes of the Highest Science*. Translated by (unattributed). Calcutta: Calcutta Central Press, 1883.

Lévi, Éliphas. *Transcendental Magic: Its Doctrine and Ritual*. Translated by Arthur Waite. London: Redway, 1896.

Livingston, Paul. *The Politics of Logic: Badiou, Wittgenstein, and the Consequences of Formalism*. New York: Routledge, 2012.

Long, Anthony. *Hellenistic Philosophy*. New York: Scribner, 1974.

Long, Anthony, and David Sedley. *The Hellenistic Philosophers*, Vol. 1: *Translations of the Principle Sources with Philosophical Commentary*. Cambridge: Cambridge University, 1987.

Long, Anthony, and David Sedley. *The Hellenistic Philosophers*, Vol. 2: *Greek and Latin Texts with Notes and Bibliography*. Cambridge: Cambridge University, 1987.

Luhtala, Anneli. *On the Origin of Syntactical Description in Stoic Logic*. Münster: Nodus, 2000.

Łukasiewicz, Jan. "On the Principle of Contradiction in Aristotle." Translated by Vernon Wedin. *The Review of Metaphysics* 24, no. 3 (1971): 485–509.

Mancosu, Paolo, and Walter van Stigt. "Intuitionistic Logic." In *From Brouwer to Hilbert: The Debate on the Foundations of Mathematics in the 1920's*, edited by Paolo Mancosu, 275–85. Oxford: Oxford University, 1998.

Marcus Aurelius. *Meditations of the Emperor Marcus Aurelius Antoninus*. Edited by James Moore and Michael Silverthorne. Translated by Francis Hutcheson and James Moor. Indianapolis, IN: Liberty Fund, 2014. [*Ad se ipsum libri XII*. Edited by Joachim Dalfen. Leipzig: Teubner, 1979.]

Mares, Edwin. *Relevant Logic: A Philosophical Interpretation*. Cambridge: Cambridge University, 2004.

Marshall, A. J. *Bower-Birds: Their Displays and Breeding Cycles. A Preliminary Statement*. Oxford: Oxford University, 1954.

Massumi, Brian. *A User's Guide to Capitalism and Schizophrenia: Deviations from Deleuze and Guattari*. Cambridge, MA: MIT, 1992.

Maxwell, James Clerk. "Last Essays at Cambridge." In *The Life of James Clerk Maxwell*, edited by Lewis Campbell and William Garnett, 434–63. London: Macmillan, 1882.

McGill, V. J., and W. T. Parry. "The Unity of Opposites: A Dialectical Principle." *Science & Society* 12, no. 4 (1948): 418–44.
Meegeren, Han van. *The Supper at Emmaus (De Emmaüsgangers)*, 1937.
Melville, Herman. *The Confidence-Man: His Masquerade*. New York: Dix, Edwards, 1857.
Michelson, Albert, and Edward Morley. "On the Relative Motion of the Earth and the Luminiferous Ether." *American Journal of Science* 34, no. 203 (1887): 333–45.
Myatt, John. *Girl with a Pearl Earring (in the Style of Johan Vermeer)*, 2012.
Nemesius. *De natura hominis, Graece et Latine*. Halle: Gebauer, 1802.
Nietzsche, Friedrich. *The Gay Science*. Translated by Walter Kaufmann. New York: Random House, 1974. [*Die fröhliche Wissenschaft*. In *Sämtliche Werke. Kritische Studienausgabe*, Vol. 3, edited by Giorgio Colli and Mazzino Montinari, 343–651. Munich: Deutscher Taschenbuch, 1999.]
Nietzsche, Friedrich. *Philosophy in the Tragic Age of the Greeks*. Translated by Marianne Cowan. Washington, DC: Regnery, 1962. [*Die Philosophie im tragischen Zeitalter der Griechen*. In *Sämtliche Werke. Kritische Studienausgabe*, Vol. 1, edited by Giorgio Colli and Mazzino Montinari, 799–872. Munich: Deutscher Taschenbuch, 1988.]
Nietzsche, Friedrich. *Twilight of the Idols, or, How to Philosophize with a Hammer*. Translated by Duncan Large. Oxford: Oxford University, 1998. [*Götzen-Dämmerung*. In *Sämtliche Werke. Kritische Studienausgabe*, Vol. 6, edited by Giorgio Colli and Mazzino Montinari, 55–161. Munich: Deutscher Taschenbuch, 1999.]
Nolt, John. *Logics*. Belmont, CA: Wadsworth, 1997.
Olkowski, Dorothea. "Body, Knowledge and Becoming-Woman: Morpho-Logic in Deleuze and Irigaray." In *Deleuze and Feminist Theory*, edited by Ian Buchanan and Claire Colebrook, 86–109. Edinburgh: Edinburgh University, 2000.
Olkowski, Dorothea. *Postmodern Philosophy and the Scientific Turn*. Indiana University, 2012.
Olkowski, Dorothea. "Using Our Intuition: Creating the Future Phenomenological Plane of Thought." In *Feminist Phenomenology Futures*, edited by Helen Fielding and Dorothea Olkowski, 3–20. Bloomington, IN: Indiana University, 2017.
Origen. *Werke*, Vol. 5: *De principiis*. (*Die griechischen christlichen Schriftsteller der ersten Jahrhunderte*, Vol. 22). Edited by Paul Koetschau. Leipzig: Hinrichs, 1913.
Palm, Ralph. "Hegel's Contradictions." *Bulletin of the Hegel Society of Great Britain* 63 (2011): 134–58.
Pascal, Blaise. *Pensées*. Edited and translated by Roger Ariew. Indianapolis, IN: Hackett, 2004. [*Pensées*. In *Œuvres complètes*, Vol. 1, edited by Charles Lahure, 235–418. Paris: Hachette, 1858.]
Peden, Knox. *Spinoza Contra Phenomenology: French Rationalism from Cavaillès to Deleuze*. Stanford: Stanford University, 2014.
Philo of Alexandria. *Opera quae supersunt*, Vol. 1. Edited by Leopold Cohn and Paul Wendland. Berlin: Reimer, 1896.
Philo of Alexandria. *Paralipomena Armena*. Edited by John Baptist Aucher. Leipzig: Schwickert, 1826.
Picasso, Pablo. *Girl with a Mandolin (Jeune fille à la mandoline)*, 1910.
Plato. *Philebus*. In *Complete Works*, edited by John Cooper and translated by Dorothea Frede, 338–456. Indianapolis, IN: Hackett, 1997.[Φίληβος. In *In Twelve Volumes*, Vol. 8, translated by Harold Fowler, 202–399. Cambridge, MA: Harvard University, 1925.]
Plato. *Sophist*. In *The Collected Dialogues of Plato, Including the Letters*, edited by Edith Hamilton and Cairns Huntington and translated by Francis Cornford, 957–1017. Princeton:

Princeton University, 1989. [Σοφιστής. In *Opera*, Vol. 1: *Tetralogias I–II continens*, edited by John Burnet, 357–442. Oxford: Oxford University, 1900.]

Plato. *Statesman*. In *The Collected Dialogues of Plato, Including the Letters*, edited by Edith Hamilton and Cairns Huntington and translated by J. B. Skemp, 1018–85. Princeton: Princeton University, 1989. [Πολιτικός. In *Opera*, Vol. 1: *Tetralogias I–II continens*, edited by John Burnet, 443–525. Oxford: Oxford University, 1900.]

Plato. *Theaetetus*. In *Complete Works*, edited by John Cooper and translated by M. J. Levett and Myles Burnyeat, 157–234. Indianapolis, IN: Hackett, 1997. [Θεαίτητος. In *Opera*, Vol. 1: *Tetralogias I–II continens*, edited by John Burnet, 255–356. Oxford: Oxford University, 1900.]

Plutarch. *Moralia*, Vol. 6. Edited by Gregorios Bernardakis. Leipzig: Teubner, 1895.

Poincaré, Henri. "Le continu mathématique." *Revue de métaphysique et de morale* 1 (1893): 26–34.

Ponce, Juan García. "Introduction." In *The Baphomet*, edited by Pierre Klossowski and translated by Thomas Christensen and Juan García de Oteyza, ix–xviii. Hygiene, CO: Eridanos, 1988.

Priest, Graham. "Classical Logic *aufgehoben*." In *Paraconsistent Logic: Essays on the Inconsistent*, edited by Graham Priest, Richard Routley, and Jean Norman, 131–48. Munich: Philosophia, 1989.

Priest, Graham. "Contradiction and the Structure of Unity." In *Analytic Philosophy in China*, edited by Yi Jiang, 35–42. Hangzhou: Zhejiang University, 2010.

Priest, Graham. "Dialectic and Dialetheic." *Science & Society* 53, no. 4 (1990): 388–415.

Priest, Graham. *Doubt Truth to Be a Liar*. Oxford: Oxford University, 2006.

Priest, Graham. "Inconsistencies in Motion." *American Philosophical Quarterly* 22, no. 4 (1985): 339–46.

Priest, Graham. *In Contradiction: A Study of the Transconsistent*. 2nd ed. Oxford: Oxford University, 2006.

Priest, Graham. *An Introduction to Non-Classical Logic: From If to Is*. 2nd ed. Cambridge: Cambridge University, 2008.

Priest, Graham. "Logic: A Short Introduction, *Lecture 2*: Why Is Logic Important?" Online recorded lecture, Romanae Disputationes. Concorso nazionale di Filosofia. 10.01, February 20, 2017. http://romanaedisputationes.com/rd-world.

Priest, Graham. *Logic: A Very Short Introduction*. 1st ed. Oxford: Oxford University, 2000.

Priest, Graham. "The Logic of Paradox." *Journal of Philosophical Logic* 8, no. 1 (1979): 219–41.

Priest, Graham. "Motion." In *The Encyclopedia of Philosophy*, Vol. 6, edited by Donald Borchert, 408–11. New York: Macmillan, 2006.

Priest, Graham. *One: Being an Investigation into the Unity of Reality and of Its Parts, Including the Singular Object Which Is Nothingness*. Oxford: Oxford University, 2014.

Priest, Graham. "Paraconsistency and Dialetheism." In *Handbook of the History of Logic*, Vol. 8: *The Many Valued and Nonmonotonic Turn in Logic*, edited by Dov Gabbay and John Woods, 129–204. Amsterdam: Elsevier, 2007.

Priest, Graham. "Speaking of the Ineffable, East and West." *European Journal of Analytic Philosophy* 11, no. 2 (2015): 6–20.

Priest, Graham, and Edgar Aroutiounian. "An Interview with Noted Logician, Graham Priest." *Florida Student Philosophy Blog*, February 23, 2011. https://unfspb.wordpress.com/2011/03/02/part-ii-of-the-interview-with-graham-priest.

Priest, Graham, and Maureen Eckert. [Interview]. Video, 2011. http://www.philostv.com/maureen-eckert-and-graham-priest/.

Priest, Graham, and Richard Routley. "First Historical Introduction: A Preliminary History of Paraconsistent and Dialethic Approaches." In *Paraconsistent Logic: Essays on the Inconsistent*, edited by Graham Priest, Richard Routley, and Jean Norman, 3–75. Munich: Philosophia, 1989.

Priest, Graham, and Richard Routley. "An Outline of the History of (Logical) Dialectic." In *Paraconsistent Logic: Essays on the Inconsistent*, edited by Graham Priest, Richard Routley, and Jean Norman, 76–98. Munich: Philosophia, 1989.

Prigogine, Ilya, and Isabelle Stengers. *La nouvelle alliance: Métamorphose de la science*. Paris: Gallimard, 1979.

Prigogine, Ilya, and Isabelle Stengers. *Order Out of Chaos: Man's New Dialogue with Nature*. London: Fontana, 1985.

Proclus. *A Commentary on the First Book of Euclid's Elements*. Translated by Glenn Morrow. Princeton: Princeton University, 1992. [*In primum Euclidis Elementorum librum commentarii*. Edited by Gottfried Friedlein. Leipzig: Teubner, 1873.]

Read, Stephen. *Thinking about Logic: An Introduction to the Philosophy of Logic*. Oxford: Oxford University, 1995.

Redding, Paul. *Analytic Philosophy and the Return of Hegelian Thought*. Cambridge: Cambridge University, 2007.

Ricardou, Jean. *Le nouveau roman*. Paris: Seuil, 1973.

Robbe-Grillet, Alain. *Last Year in Marienbad*. Translated by Richard Howard. New York: Grove, 1962. [*L'année dernière à Marienbad*. Paris: Minuit, 1961.]

Robbe-Grillet, Alain. *Project for a Revolution in New York*. Translated by Richard Howard. London: Dalkey Archive, 2012. [*Projet pour une révolution à New York*. Paris: Minuit, 1970.]

Robbe-Grillet, Alain. "Towards a New Novel". In *Snapshots and Towards a New Novel*, translated by Barbara Wright, 41–161. London: Calder and Boyars, 1965. [*Pour un nouveau roman*. Paris: Minuit, 1961.]

Robbe-Grillet, Alain. *The Man Who Lies (L'homme qui ment)*. Como, 1968.

Robbe-Grillet, Alain. *Trans-Europ-Express*. Como, 1966.

Roffe, Jon. "Axiomatic Set Theory in the Work of Deleuze and Guattari: A Critique." *Parrhesia* 23 (2016): 129–54.

Rohlf, Michael. "The Ideas of Pure Reason." In *The Cambridge Companion to Kant's Critique of Pure Reason*, edited by Paul Guyer, 190–209. Cambridge: Cambridge University, 2010.

Rose, Steven. *The Conscious Brain*. Revised edition. Harmondsworth: Penguin, 1976.

Routley, Richard, and Val Routley. "Negation and Contradiction." *Revista Colombiana de Matematica* 19 (1985): 201–31.

Roy, André. *Dictionnaire général du cinéma: du cinématographe à internet*. Montreal: Fides, 2007.

Russell, Bertrand. "Mathematics and the Metaphysicians." In *Mysticism and Logic, and Other Essays*, 2nd ed., 74–96. London: Allen and Unwin, 1917.

Russell, Bertrand. *Our Knowledge of the External World as a Field for Scientific Method in Philosophy*. Chicago/London: Open Court, 1915.

Russell, Bertrand. "The Philosophy of Bergson." *The Monist* 22, no. 3 (1912): 321–47.

Russell, Bertrand. *The Principles of Mathematics*. 2nd ed. London: Allen and Unwin, 1937.

Russell, Bertrand. "Theory of Knowledge." In *Collected Papers*, Vol. 9: *Essays on Language, Mind and Matter, 1919–26*, edited by John Slater and Bernd Frohmann, 193–202. London: Unwin Hyman, 1988.

Sambursky, Samuel. *Physics of the Stoics*. Greenwood reprint. Westport, CT: Greenwood, 1973.

Sanford, David. *If P, Then Q: Conditionals and the Foundations of Reasoning*. London: Routledge, 1989.
Schuhl, Pierre-Maxime. *Le dominateur et les possibles*. Paris: Presses universitaires de France, 1960.
Sellars, John. "Aiôn and Chronos: Deleuze and the Stoic Theory of Time." In *Collapse*, edited by Robin Mackay, Reissued edition. First published 2007, 3: 177–205. Falmouth: Urbanomic, 2012.
Sellars, John. "An Ethics of the Event: Deleuze's Stoicism." *Angelaki: Journal of the Theoretical Humanities* 11, no. 3 (2006): 157–71.
Sellars, John. "Six Theses on Deleuze's Stoicism." Online recorded lecture. *A/V: Journal of Practical and Creative Philosophy* 4, 2006. www.actualvirtualjournal.com/2014/11/six-theses-on-deleuzes-stoicism.html.
Seneca. *Ad Lucilium epistulae morales*, Vol. 2. Translated by Richard Gummere. London/New York: Heinemann/Putnam, 1920. [Dual language edition].
Seneca. *Ad Lucilium epistulae morales*, Vol. 3. Translated by Richard Gummere. London/New York: Heinemann/Putnam, 1925. [Dual language edition].
Seneca. *In Ten Volumes*, Vol. 4: *Ad Lucilium Epistulae Morales*, Vol. 1. Translated by Richard Gummere. London/Cambridge, MA: Heinemann/Harvard, 1979. [Dual language edition].
Serres, Michel. *Le système de Leibniz et ses modèles mathématiques*, Vol. 1: *Étoiles*. Paris: Presses universitaires de France, 1968.
Serres, Michel. *Le système de Leibniz et ses modèles mathématiques*, Vol. 2: *Schémas—Point*. Paris: Presses universitaires de France, 1968.
Sextus Empiricus. *Opera*, Vol. 2: *Adversus dogmaticos*, Book 5: *Adversus mathematicos, VII–XI*. Edited by Hermann Mutschmann. Leipzig: Teubner, 1912.
Sextus Empiricus, *In Three Volumes*, Vol. 1: *Outlines of Pyrrhonism*. Translated by R. Bury. London/New York: Heinemann/Putnam, 1933.
Shores, Corry. "Affirmations of the False and Bifurcations of the True: Deleuze's Dialetheic and Stoic Fatalism." In *Deleuze and Guattari's Philosophy of Freedom: Freedom's Refrains*, edited by Dorothea Olkowski and Eftichis Pirovolakis, 178–223. New York: Routledge, 2019.
Shores, Corry. "Dialetheism in the Structure of Phenomenal Time." In *Logical Studies of Paraconsistent Reasoning in Science and Mathematics*, edited by Holger Andreas and Peter Verdée, 145–57. Cham, Switzerland: Springer, 2016.
Shores, Corry. "Self-Shock: The Phenomenon of Personal Non-Identity in Inorganic Subjectivity." In *The Yearbook on History and Interpretation of Phenomenology 2013*, edited by Anton Vydra, 157–83. Frankfurt: Peter Lang, 2013.
Shores, Corry. "In the Still of the Moment: Deleuze's Phenomena of Motionless Time." *Deleuze Studies* 8, no. 2 (2014): 199–229.
Shores, Corry. "The Primacy of Falsity: Deviant Origins in Deleuze." *Tijdschrift voor Filosofie* 81 (2019): 81–130.
Siemens, Reynold. "Hegel and the Law of Identity." *The Review of Metaphysics* 42, no. 1 (1988): 103–27.
Sigwart, Christoph. *Logic*, Vol. 1: *The Judgment, Concept, and Inference*. Translated by Helen Dendy. 2nd ed., revised and enlarged. London: Sonnenschein, 1895. [*Logik*, Vol. 1: *Die Lehre vom Urteil, vom Begriff und vom Schluss*. 3rd ed. Tübingen: Mohr Siebeck, 1904.]
Sinaceur, Hourya. "Logique et mathématique du flou." *Critique*, no. 372 (1978): 512–25.
Smith, Daniel. *Essays on Deleuze*. Edinburgh: Edinburgh University, 2012.

Smith, Daniel. "Logic and Existence: Deleuze on the 'Conditions of the Real.'" *Chiasmi International* 13 (2011): 361–77.
Somers-Hall, Henry. *Deleuze's Difference and Repetition: An Edinburgh Philosophical Guide*. Edinburgh: Edinburgh University, 2013.
Somers-Hall, Henry. *Hegel, Deleuze, and the Critique of Representation: Dialectics of Negation and Difference*. Albany, NY: State University of New York, 2012.
Stivale, Charles. *The Two-Fold Thought of Deleuze and Guattari: Intersections and Animations*. New York: Guilford, 1998.
Stobaeus. *Anthologium*, Vol. 1. Edited by Curt Wachsmuth and Otto Hense. Berlin: Weidmann, 1884.
Stobaeus. *Anthologium*, Vol. 2. Edited by Curt Wachsmuth and Otto Hense. Berlin: Weidmann, 1884.
Suppes, Patrick. *Introduction to Logic*. New York: Van Nostrand Reinhold, 1957.
Thorpe, W. H. *Animal Nature and Human Nature*. Garden City, NY: Anchor/Doubleday, 1974.
Thorpe, W. H. *Learning and Instinct in Animals*. London: Methuen, 1956.
Tyson, Neil deGrasse. "Closing Talk at the *Beyond Belief: Science, Religion, Reason and Survival* Event." Public lecture. Salk Institute for Biological Studies. La Jolla, California, November 7, 2006. http://thesciencenetwork.org/programs/beyond-belief-science-religion-reason-and-survival/session-10-2.
Tyson, Neil deGrasse. *Neil deGrasse Tyson Returns Again* (Interview, *The Nerdist*, 489). Podcast, 2014. http://www.nerdist.com/pepisode/nerdist-podcast-neil-degrasse-tyson-returns-again.
Ueberweg, Friedrich. *System of Logic and History of Logical Doctrines*. Translated by Thomas Lindsay. London: Longmans, Green, 1871. [*System der Logik und Geschichte der logischen Lehren*. 4th ed. Bonn: Marcus, 1874.]
van Stigt, Walter. *Brouwer's Intuitionism*. Amsterdam: Elsevier (North Holland), 1990.
van Stigt, Walter. "Brouwer's Intuitionist Programme." In *From Brouwer to Hilbert: The Debate on the Foundations of Mathematics in the 1920's*, edited by Paolo Mancosu, 1–22. Oxford: Oxford University, 1998.
Velázquez, Diego. *Las Meninas*, 1656–57.
Venitiana Del Rabina, Antonio. *Le grand grimoire*. Paris: Renault, 1845.
Vergauwen, Roger. *A Metalogical Theory of Reference: Realism and Essentialism in Semantics*. Lanham, MD: University Press of America, 1993.
Vermeer, Johannes. *Girl with a Pearl Earring (Meisje met de parel)*, 1665.
Villani, Arnaud. *Logique de Deleuze*. Paris: Hermann, 2013.
Vitruvius. *The Ten Books on Architecture*. Translated by Morris Morgan. Cambridge, MA: Harvard University, 1914. [*De architectura libri decem*. Edited by Valentin Rose and Hermann Müller-Strübing. Leipzig: Teubner, 1867.]
Voisset-Veysseyre, Cécile. "Toward a Post-Identity Philosophy: Along a Flight Line with Gilles Deleuze." *Trahir* 2, no. 7 (August 2011): 1–18.
Voss, Daniela. *Conditions of Thought: Deleuze and Transcendental Ideas*. Edinburgh: Edinburgh University, 2013.
Vuillemin, Jules. *Necessity or Contingency: The Master Argument*. Translated by Thomas Morran. Stanford: Center for the study of language and information, 1996. [*Nécessité ou contingence: l'aporie de Diodore et les systèmes philosophiques*. Paris: Minuit, 1984.]
Waite, Arthur. *The Book of Black Magic and of Pacts*. Chicago: de Laurence, 1910.
Welles, Orson. *F for Fake*. Janus; Les Films de l'Astrophore; SACI, 1973.
Welles, Orson. *The Lady from Shanghai*. Mercury; Columbia, 1947.

Welles, Orson. *Mr. Arkadin*. Filmorsa, 1955.
Welles, Orson. *Touch of Evil*. Universal, 1958.
Welles, Orson, Juan Cobos, and Miguel Rubio. "Welles on Falstaff." *Cahiers Du Cinema in English*, no. 11 (September 1967): 5–15.
Weyl, Hermann. "On the New Foundational Crisis of Mathematics." In *From Brouwer to Hilbert: The Debate on the Foundations of Mathematics in the 1920's*, edited by Paolo Mancosu and translated by Benito Müller, 86–118. Oxford: Oxford University, 1998. ["Über die neue Grundlagenkrise der Mathematik." *Mathematische Zeitschrift* 10 (1921): 39–79.]
Widder, Nathan. "Negation, Disjunction, and a New Theory of Forces: Deleuze's Critique of Hegel." In *Hegel and Deleuze: Together Again for the First Time*, edited by Karen Houle and Jim Vernon, 18–37. Evanston, IL: Northwestern University, 2013.
Widder, Nathan. "Thought after Dialectics: Deleuze's Ontology of Sense." *The Southern Journal of Philosophy* 41, no. 3 (2003): 451–76.
Wiene, Robert. *The Cabinet of Dr. Caligari (Das Cabinet des Dr. Caligari)*. Decla-Bioscop, 1920.
Williams, James. *Gilles Deleuze's* Logic of Sense: *A Critical Introduction and Guide*. Edinburgh: Edinburgh University, 2008.
Williams, James. *Gilles Deleuze's Philosophy of Time: A Critical Introduction and Guide*. Edinburgh: Edinburgh University, 2011.
Woleński, Jan. "An Abstract Approach to Bivalence." *Logic and Logical Philosophy* 23 (2014): 3–15.
Woolhouse, Roger. "On the Nature of an Individual Substance." In *Leibniz: Critical and Interpretive Essays*, edited by Michael Hooker, 45–64. Minneapolis, MN: University of Minnesota, 1982.
Worringer, Wilhelm. *Form Problems of the Gothic*. Translated by (unattributed). Authorized American edn. New York: Stechert, 1920. [*Formprobleme der Gotik*. 2nd ed. Munich: Piper, 1912.]
Zadeh, Lotfi A. "Préface." In *Introduction à la théorie des sous-ensembles flous à l'usage des ingénieurs (Fuzzy sets theory)*, Vol. 1: *Eléments théoriques de base*, by Arnold Kaufmann, v–viii, 2nd ed. Paris: Masson, 1977. [Dual language].

Index

affirmative synthetic disjunction. *See under* Deleuze, Gilles
aleatory point 211. *See also* bifurcation
ambiguous signs 209–11
Amin, Samir 163
analetheism, analetheic logic. *See under* logic
Archimedes 141–3
Aristotle 23, 152, 194
at-at account of motion 28–9, 33, 41–2, 46
axiomatics/problematics 137–50, 156, 160, 164, 174

Baker's Transformation 74
becoming 3, 9, 11, 22–3, 30, 47, 51–3, 60, 109–15, 143, 178–80, 184–92, 203–6, 208, 213
Beall, J. C. 185, 214
Bell, Jeffrey 3–4
Bergala, Alain 200–1
Bergson, Henri 17–26, 29–31, 34, 52–3, 60, 82, 152, 178–9, 181–2, 190, 202, 207, 216
bifurcation 121–3, 133–5, 179, 198–9, 207, 209, 211–12. *See also* incompossibility
birdsong 57–9
bivalence. *See under* principles of logic
Blake, Terence 45–6
Blanché, Robert 145–6, 148
Borges, Jorge Luis 123, 209, 211
Bourbaki, Nicolas 145
Breeur, Roland 261–2 n. 103
Bréhier, Émile 123, 126
Brouwer, L. E. J. 151–62, 164, 166–7, 169
Burns, Delisle 72–3

Canetti, Elias 51
Canguilhem, Georges 118
Cantor, Georg 147–9
Carroll, Lewis 44–6, 65–6

Chrysippus 124, 131, 134, 194–5
Cicero 124, 131, 134, 195
classical logic. *See under* logic
Cleanthes 195–6
concept creation 69–70, 75–7
conic sections 103, 144–5, 203–5, 210
consistency (logical) 85–9, 108
consistency (of composition), coalescence, conglomeration, consolidation. *See* heterogeneous composition
constructivism 150, 152, 154–73
contradiction 7, 11–12, 26, 34–6, 41–3, 82–90, 95–101, 113–15, 117–18, 198–9, 209, 211–13
creation 52–3, 185, 190, 192, 199, 203–6, 213, 216
crystal 54, 196–9, 202, 206–9, 215
Culp, Andrew 81–2, 216

de Boer, Karen 96
de Hory, Elmyr 204–5
Delaunay, Robert 70
Deleuze, Gilles
    affirmative synthetic disjunction 82–3, 112–16, 212–13
    logic 1–9, 11–13, 44–7, 55–8, 64–8, 81–3, 89–104, 108–23, 137–51, 163–4, 166–70, 173–4, 185–6, 192–6, 206–16, 218 n. 39
    neurobiology 72–4
    philosophy of thinking 67, 69–77, 91–2, 166, 213–14
    philosophy of truth and falsity 177–213
    sorcery 1–2, 49–53, 60, 109, 111, 187–90, 202–3, 209, 214
    transdisciplinarity 67–72
denial 89–90, 95
Desargues, Girard 144–5
Descartes, René 76–7, 92–3, 152

dialetheism, dialetheic logic. *See under* logic
Difference and Repetition 53, 89–90, 95–6, 164, 170–3, 187, 208–9
Diodorus Cronus 131, 193–4
disjunction 7, 104–9, 113–16, 92, 101–9, 112–16, 120–1, 167, 194, 212, 214, 216
disjunctive syllogism 104–9, 113–16
Dumas, Alexandre 51–2
Dummett, Michael 161–2
Dupréel, Eugène 53–6, 76–7, 190, 196, 207

Eisenstein, Sergei 179–80
Epictetus 132–4, 193–4
Euclid 141–3
explosion. *See under* principles of logic

falsity, falsification, falsifier 177–92, 195–206, 213
Frege, Gottlob 7, 152
future contingents 10–11, 192–6, 199, 211–12. *See also* past contingents
fuzzy logic. *See under* logic

gluon 61–6
Goldschmidt, Victor 124–8, 131
Grémillon, Jean 70, 102
Griffith, D. W. 178–9
Griss, G. F. C. 164–73
Guattari, Félix 2, 4, 8, 11–13, 51–3, 55–8, 64–5, 72–7, 113–15, 137–50, 163, 214

Hawking, Stephen 67–8, 72
Hegel, G. W. F. 42–3, 95–100
heterogeneous composition 8, 11–12, 51–60, 64–6, 74–7, 111, 196, 207, 209, 211, 213–14
Heyting, Arend 156, 161, 164, 171–2
Hoüel, Jules 143
Hugo, Victor 208–9
Hyppolite, Jean 97–8

identity. *See* personal identity; non-transitive identity; principles: principle of identity
incompossibility 3, 12, 117–23, 189–90, 198–9, 203, 206–13

indiscernibility 75, 77, 174, 196–201. *See also* undecidability
innocence of becoming 185
intuition 19–20, 24–6, 151–2
intuitionism 8–9, 141, 150–74. *See also* logic: intuitionistic

Kant, Immanuel 94, 96, 104–8, 112
Kaufmann, Arnold 58
Klossowski, Pierre 109–113, 115
Kolmogorov, Andrei 150
Kramer, Edna 170–1

Lapoujade, David 2, 4
Leblanc, Maurice 199–200
Leibniz, Gottfried 6, 93–4, 117–21, 189–90, 198, 204, 206–12. *See also* incompossibility
Lévi, Éliphas 109, 203
Limosin, Jean-Pierre 200–1
Livingston, Paul 4
logic
 analetheic 9–10, 35, 37–41, 85–9, 162–4, 173, 185–6, 192, 194, 211–12, 214–16
 classical 3–8, 25, 33, 37, 83–90, 108–9, 156, 160, 186, 213–14, 218 n. 32
 conditional 218 n. 39
 connexive 83
 dialetheic 3, 10–13, 23, 34, 37–41, 44, 77, 85–90, 95, 101, 104, 114–16, 132–5, 162–4, 174, 186, 190, 192, 194–5, 200, 209, 211–16
 free 218 n. 39
 fuzzy 8, 10, 57–60, 214
 intuitionistic 6–8, 83, 137, 150, 156–64, 173–4, 185, 214
 laws of 7. *See* principles of logic
 many-valued 3, 11, 214. *See also* logic: analetheic; logic: dialetheic
 modal 119, 161–2, 194
 monoletheic. *See* logic: classical
 non-classical 4, 7–8, 12–13, 82–5, 213, 218 n. 39. *See also* logic: fuzzy; logic: intuitionistic; logic: many-valued
 non-normal 218 n. 39
 paracomplete. *See* logic: analetheic
 paraconsistent. *See* logic: dialetheic

quantum 218 n. 39
relevant (and First Degree Entailment) 85, 215, 218 n. 39
Logic of Sense 2, 5, 13, 45–6, 95–6, 117, 187, 210–11
Long, Anthony 127
Łukasiewicz, Jan 96

many-valued logic. *See under* logic
Marcus Aurelius 128, 131
Mares, Edwin 90
Marshall, A. J. 58
Marxism 81, 146
Master Argument 131, 192–6
Melville, Herman 203
monoletheism. *See* logic: classical
Myatt, John 204

negation 81–91, 99–101, 103, 108–9, 164–73, 213, 215–16
negationless mathematics 164–73
neurobiology. *See under* Deleuze, Gilles
New Novel (*nouveau roman*) 196–8, 206
Nietzsche, Friedrich 185, 191, 216
Nolt, John 4, 8–9, 58, 119–20, 207
non-classical logics. *See under* logic
non-transitive identity 61–4
Northern line 181

Olkowski, Dorothea 3–4, 6, 162
otherness 82–5, 103, 105, 168, 171–3, 188, 203, 215

paracompleteness 85–9, 168–9, 173. *See also* logic: analetheic
paraconsistency 11, 85–9. *See also* logic: dialetheic
paradox 4
  of becoming 47, 189
  liar's paradox 3, 217 n. 13
  Russell's paradox 7
  sorites paradoxes 8, 58
  Zeno's paradoxes of motion 23–4, 29–31, 42
Pascal, Blaise 103
past contingents 195–6, 199–202, 206–7
Peirce, C. S. 11
personal identity 44–7, 65–6, 110–15, 205–6, 211

Picasso, Pablo 205–7
Plato 47, 100, 183, 187–9
powers of the false 133, 185–6, 188–92, 196–9, 203–6, 213. *See also* falsity, falsification, falsifier
Priest, Graham 1–5, 7, 10, 13, 33–44, 60–5, 83–5, 124, 161–2, 192
Prigogine, Ilya 74, 121–2
principles (laws) of logic 6–7, 37, 91–2, 157
  principle of bivalence 7, 9, 160, 163
  principle of contradiction 95–6, 98
  principle of double negation 7, 100
  principle of excluded middle 6–7, 9–10, 32, 37, 91–2, 101, 106, 145, 150, 152, 157, 160, 162–4, 166, 168, 192–4
  principle of explosion 7, 41, 86–7, 162
  principle of identity 6–7, 37–8, 91–4, 97, 100–1, 111, 121
  principle of included middle 162–4
  principle of non-contradiction 6–7, 9–10, 25–6, 32, 37, 91–2, 95–101, 106, 111, 158, 164, 193–5
  principle of sufficient reason 93–4
problematic. *See* axiomatics/problematics
Proclus 142–3

Read, Stephen 154, 161–3
Ricardou, Jean 197
Ripley, David 185, 214
Robbe-Grillet, Alain 197–9, 206
Rose, Steven 72–3
Routley, Richard, and Val Routley (Val Plumwood and Richard Sylvan) 83–5, 87, 90
Russell, Bertrand 5, 7, 17–18, 22, 24–34, 36, 41–3, 46–7, 152

Sedley, David 127
Sellars, John 126
Serres, Michel 204
Sigwart, Christoph 95–6
simulacra 187–9, 203–4
Smith, Daniel W. 3–4, 91–2, 101
sorcery. *See under* Deleuze, Gilles
Spinoza, Baruch 53, 70, 82, 177, 216
Stengers, Isabelle 74, 121–2
Stoicism 12, 123–35, 194–6

tautology (logical truth) 6, 37
time 19–20, 23–4, 27–35, 41–7, 65–6, 113–15, 119–23, 126–35, 152–4, 178–9, 183–4, 189–90, 192–6, 199–202, 206–9
Thorpe, W. H. 57
transdisciplinarity. *See under* Deleuze, Gilles
truth-value 6, 36–7, 157, 162, 174, 177, 194, 211, 227 n. 83
Tyson, Neil deGrasse 68–9

undecidability 75, 77, 137–8, 141, 150, 158–64, 173–4, 190, 196–201, 211–12, 214–15. *See also* indiscernibility

Velázquez, Diego 205
validity 5–6, 36–7, 77, 157
van Meegeren, Han 204–5
van Stigt, Walter 151
Vergauwen, Roger 147–9
Vermeer, Johannes 204–5
Voisset-Veysseyre, Cécile 3

Welles, Orson 184, 191, 196–7, 204–5
Weyl, Hermann 152
What Is Philosophy? 12, 71, 74
Wiene, Robert 101–2
Worringer, Wilhelm 181

Zadeh, L. A. 58

www.ingramcontent.com/pod-product-compliance
Lightning Source LLC
Chambersburg PA
CBHW072124290426
44111CB00012B/1765